Signed, Sealed, and Delivered

The Soulful Journey of Stevie Wonder

Mark Ribowsky

WILEY

John Wiley & Sons, Inc.

Published by John Wiley & Sons, Inc., Hoboken, New Jersey

Published simultaneously in Canada

The images on pages 148–158 are from the author's collection unless otherwise noted.

For general information about our other products and services, please contact our Customer Care Department within the United States at (800) 762-2974, outside the United States at (317) 572-3993 or fax (317) 572-4002.

Wiley also publishes its books in a variety of electronic formats. Some content that appears in print may not be available in electronic books. For more information about Wiley products, visit our web site at www.wiley.com.

Library of Congress Cataloging-in-Publication Data:

Ribowsky, Mark.
   Signed, sealed, and delivered: the soulful journey of Stevie Wonder / Mark Ribowsky.
      p. cm.
   Includes index.
   ISBN 978-0-470-48150-9 (cloth: alk. paper)
1. Wonder, Stevie. 2. Rhythm and blues musicians—United States—Biography.
3. Soul musicians—United States—Biography. I. Title.
   ML410.W836R53 2010
   782.421644092—dc22
[B]   2009037587

In memory of my mother, Frances Ribowsky, who never cared much for rock or soul music but noted one day, apropos of nothing, "You know, Smokey Robinson isn't too bad." Amen, Mom. Amen.

Contents

Photo gallery starts on page 148.

Acknowledgments

Deciphering and demystifying the life of Stevie Wonder—the mystery of which even extends to his real name—can be a tempestuous pursuit, and one that would have left the journey to actualize this book stranded on a lonely road had not a cadre of noble and generous souls agreed to keep moving it forward. Some of these fellow travelers helped to cover many miles at a time, some just a few critical paces, but as a whole they were all indispensable fellow travelers, without whom this work would have been left gasping for the nuance, balance, and previously untold, sometimes harsh truths essential to any major biography worth its salt.

Since the setting for much of these pages was Motown in its glorious prime, the ground filled in by those who were there sharing its glory is nothing less than historically profound. To my giddy delectation, their revelations replaced long-standing myths and fables with something rarely found in existing Motown literature—a sense of what really happened. For these blessed excavations, I am indebted to a wonderful cross-section of living, breathing Motown notables, who, for a Motown buff, are quite nearly Olympian in stature.

My eternal thanks to Kim Weston, who can still make one's knees weak breaking into "Take Me in Your Arms"; Bobby Rogers, the Miracles' venerable sideman, who helped provide Stevie's access route to Motown; Claudette Robinson, Smokey Robinson's early partner in the Miracles and his wife for twenty-seven years; Janie Bradford, who as a teenage assistant to Berry Gordy cowrote the immortal "Money (That's What I Want)"; the infectiously enthusiastic Mickey Stevenson, Gordy's right-hand man, who was pivotal in establishing the Stevie Wonder brand; Jimmy Ruffin, David Ruffin's brother, who scored one of Motown's biggest and best hits in "What Becomes of the Brokenhearted"; and last but hardly least, the wondrous Otis Williams, the only surviving member of the original Temptations, who is still out there ripping it up year after year and only getting younger.

Spending some time with Eddie "Chank" Willis was almost like a trip to Nirvana. A prideful man, with cause, Willis is one of the few surviving members of the Funk Brothers, the legendary Motown house band, which never got their due in their day. The Brothers' perfectly blended mix of soul and pop carried Stevie from boy to man and created the soundtrack of his—and our own—formative years, which will remain in the marrow of our souls forever. We cannot possibly pay them back for cruelly overlooking their contribution, but we sure can try.

For filling ground that stretches from pre-Motown to the present day, I am particularly grateful to John Glover, who performed with Stevie on the stoops and porches of poverty-scarred Detroit when they were both kids. A successful Motown songwriter himself in the 1960s, Glover was the perfect source to attest to where and how Stevie's genius germinated and reveal what drives Stevie Wonder even now, so many years later. He was also able to make profound sense out of the tangled and tainted family strains Stevie had to overcome.

For unlocking the doors and secrets to Stevie's life and art during the apogee of his creative genius in the 1970s—and parallel declination into a pawn for those who ran his affairs—I simply could not have found two better or kinder sources than Malcolm Cecil and Michael Sembello. An unsung musical genius himself, who is also regarded as the finest bass player ever to come out of England, Cecil, along with his partner Robert Margouleff—for little public attention or financial gain—channeled Stevie's genius as masters of the universe of synthesizers that gave life and bite to milestone masterworks like *Innervisions* and *Songs in the Key of Life*. Like that of the Funk Brothers, the contribution of Cecil and Margouleff to the evolution of modern music cannot be overstated, nor overlooked. Mike Sembello—who served as lead guitarist at many of those epochal sessions, as well as onstage in Stevie's backup band before going off to make his own chart history—not only played the music, he "got" it, and thus could think along with Stevie as he created it. To our joy, and his, he can also describe the music's raw power and seraphic nuances in the most vivid, trenchant, and sometimes metaphysical terms, as it deserves to be.

Not to be overlooked, either, is the incomparable Harry Weinger, producer of the sublime series of recent-day Motown time capsules for the ear, those essential and exhaustive box-set anthologies; the magnificent 1999 entry *Stevie Wonder: At the Close of a Century* is perhaps the best of the lot. Compiling these ultimate historical legacies requires culling meticulous and accurate details about a boatload of songs, both famous and not, so Weinger's expertise on the minutiae of Stevie Wonder's body of work may be without peer, which is all the more impressive given Motown's notorious neglect for archiving such data. *Century*, for legions of serious musical history scholars, restored the history that had been lost in the mist.

I would like to thank, too, a pair of fellow music and pop culture freaks who recognized the need for this book: my agent Michael Dorr of LitPub Ink, and Hana Lane, senior editor at John Wiley & Sons. Hana ushered the book into print with a sharp, uncompromising eye for a story told well, fully, entertainingly, and accurately, making it seem like a great victory when she was satisfied enough to wave the manuscript into print. That rigorous phase was only to my benefit, and in the end, to yours. And to history's.

Introduction

On May 13, 2010, a day when baby boomers officially get to feel like grumpy old men, Stevie Wonder begins drawing breath in his seventh decade. It's unlikely *he* will feel old, crotchety, or crusty, mind you. Or that he will be allowed to. He is, after all, the eternal man-child some of us fossils still remember as "Little Stevie," hardly little around the waist and maybe just a tad jowly but in many ways inherently the twelve-year-old who shot the frothing R&B revelation known as "Fingertips—Part 2" all the way up the pop chart. Little Stevie was never supposed to go the way of Bob Dylan, the Stones, and Bruce Springsteen across the divide of antiquity. *Can* a sixty-year-old man even be called "Stevie"?

But there he will be, surrounded by people making a big fuss over him, approaching each night as another opening, another concert, shakin' his way across the globe on another world tour, banking on the marketable concept of showing his longtime legion of fans he's still got it. He will come out in his giant wraparound shades and beaded hair extensions, harmonica strapped under his chin, and ethereally sit at his keyboard, head swiveling, smiling with those tusklike teeth from ear to ear, transporting everyone back in time to whenever.

It's not as if he ever stopped doing this, of course. It was and is his calling, even if he has conceded a wee bit to time. More than twenty years ago, he said, "In the past when I jumped up and down some people used to say, 'It looks like he's going through an epileptic fit.' I don't jump as much as I used to because I'm older [and] I thought I should cool it. But I wouldn't want to sit down all through my show. I would like to move, learn some choreography." He is no feebler now; he even learned some of those dance steps. He still shakes it down. On his 2007 tour, he did something he didn't when he was young(er) and spry(er), mounting his piano bench and standing atop it, leading a mass sing-along. As burly and, let's say, stocky as he is, he seems buff and robust enough these days to bench-press his Steinway.

But a man who sells over one hundred million records and has forty-nine Top 40 hits, thirty-four Top 10 hits, six No. 1 pop hits—*twenty-five* all told, pop, R&B, adult contemporary—twelve Top 10 albums, three No. 1 albums, and a record twenty-two Grammys in sixty-three Grammy nominations is entitled to kick back and coast a little.

As an elder, to be sure, certain things are no more. You can catalog them as a continuum of the lyrics of "I Just Called to Say I Love You": "No more April rain / No flowers bloom / No more dashikis and three-and-a-half-inch copper platform shoes." That was another April, another lifetime ago, the flowers those of a harvest of creativity when he shook all hell loose—or, as he once put it in distinctly nonlyrical, but very Stevie-like out-of-studio prose, "I want to get into as much weird shit as possible."

That was/is the Stevie who became more, much more, than a popular novelty; it was when he threw off the junior Ray Charles shtick and his blindness was finally declared a mere technicality. "Just because a man lacks the use of his eyes doesn't mean he lacks vision," he would remind us over and over through the years, most effectively in his music. If you were alive and sentient back then, his music *was* in the key of life. It could only have been made by eyes that "saw" more than ours did, so far did it come from an "inner vision" and so far did it carry into the universe.

Dripping with genius, it darted and dipped, forming from traditional soul and pop a new strain of fused terrestrial and extraterrestrial rhythm. Even now, early 1970s compositions like "Superwoman" and the towering "Superstition," from the flowering *Music of My Mind* and *Talking Book* albums, rumble and gum with undefinable boundaries, which is precisely how, as he insisted, music from a heavenly spout must be. Like us, God may groove on a good pop hook, but way out there, there's way too much space for three chords to fill. Stevie took it to the limit, and beyond. Light-years from now, we can be confident, they'll be hearing something new in songs like that and the more introspective, emotionally invested, sometimes morally irate ones that followed, from "Living for the City" to "Higher Ground" to his lacerating putdown of Richard Milhous Nixon, "You Haven't Done Nothin'."

None of these shining jewels have become artifacts; the relevance endures as does the man. In the chugging "Higher Ground," for example, Stevie turns shaman, unleashing the power of an inner god on the uniquely human heart of darkness, the reward being able to "try it again, 'cause the last time on earth I lived a whole world of sin." It was a living prophecy: what we didn't know was whether he could avoid the sins the second time around. Stevie himself was clearly ambivalent, as could be gleaned from the sometime misdirection in his own life. But he had tapped into something. *Innervisions* came out just before he was almost killed when a falling log crushed the automobile he was sitting in. The story is told that as he lay in a coma, the rhythm track of "Higher Ground" was played at his bedside. Soon, though he was still unconscious, his fingers and toes began to stir, prefacing his recovery. Some very credible people will swear to this. They will also swear, using many spooky examples, that he can indeed see.

For the soul aficionado, the real sorcery of Stevie Wonder arose in and endures from the 1970s, a decade he owned. Much is made of Bruce Springsteen's concurrent double exposure of the covers of *Time* and *Newsweek* in 1974. In that same year, Stevie also was given the covers of both of those magazines, and within two years, articles in *Esquire*, the *New Yorker*, and the *New York Times Magazine*, plus the cover of *Rolling Stone.* He had the good timing to burgeon artistically just as the warriors of the 1960s had grown weary. As John Lennon cut back and then cut out, Paul McCartney turned to silly love songs, and the Stones became country and disco dilettantes, Stevie took up the cudgels. Indeed, to real Stevie-philes there is genius aplenty in even lesser-known works of the early and mid-1970s that were never released as singles or even B-sides—"Big Brother," "Ebony Eyes," "It Ain't No Use," "They Won't Go When I Go," the last one of several mind-blowing numbers cowritten with his then wife and muse, Syreeta Wright. The collective body of Wonder-works from this period practically wrote the template of the incipient pop-funk constructions of the era, including, sadly, its bowdlerization by the disco beat. That Stevie was no captive to these formulae was obvious when he played against form with equal brilliance—say, "Village Ghetto Land," a symphonic feast in which he conducted a string orchestra with one instrument, a Yamaha GX-1 synthesizer, which was revived years later by George Michael at a 1988 Nelson Mandela benefit concert at Wembley Stadium, then by UB40's Ali Campbell on his 2007 *Running Free* solo album.

Not for nothing did Paul Simon, upon winning the 1975 best album Grammy, thank Stevie Wonder for not making an album that year. But Stevie didn't necessarily need to *sing* to weigh in on musical matters great and profound. Think of him as the musical equivalent of Kevin Bacon, only a few degrees away from any given soul song or performer. Consider Chaka Khan's "I Feel for You," the apotheosis of '80s pop-funk written by Prince. Khan's root, the soul group Rufus, was discovered by Stevie Wonder, while Prince was a Stevie acolyte. More directly, the harmonica on the track was played by Stevie Wonder.

A final point about influence: Stevie's incursion into reggae may have been regarded as too precious by half among a few island purists, but not to Bob Marley and Peter Tosh. In just one of a thousand and one Stevie Wonder milestones, the Wailers opened for him at a show in Kingston, Jamaica, in 1975—which was the last time Marley, Tosh, and Bunny Wailer played together. From that gig there is an amazing eight-minute bootleg tape of Stevie and Marley on "I Shot the Sheriff" and "Superstition." Stevie's 1980 posthumous tribute, "Master Blaster (Jammin')"—Marley was to have opened for him on tour that year—was pop-funk nirvana, with a pitch-perfect vocal done in the nearly impossible-to-ape Marley cadence. (Fittingly, "Blaster" itself was elegized by the Algerian-born raï singer Cheb Mami, yet another acolyte, for the song "Enfants d'Afrique," featuring the Canadian singer Corneille.)

There is, in the interest of full disclosure, the concurrent, not mutually exclusive "other" Stevie Wonder—the buffed, just a bit too airbrushed pop music purveyor whose unbroken chain of commercially disarming soft ballads and rollicking bluesbreakers seem to exist on an endless tape loop, no doubt playing at this moment somewhere, anywhere, on the globe. If in Mojo Nixon's polemic "Elvis is everywhere / He's in everything. . . . Elvis is in your jeans / He's in your cheeseburgers," Stevie Wonder can beat that. His music is in your radio, in your

TV—among the endless train of commercials using his songs: Chase Bank ("Higher Ground"), Nike Air Jordan ("Overjoyed"), and Lee Jeans ("Sir Duke"), meaning he really *is* in your jeans—and basically everywhere music is used to soothe nerves and shake money loose from wallets, like doctors' and dentists' waiting rooms, elevators, and shopping malls. Is Stevie Wonder cool? Listen to the USA Network's beyond hip *Burn Notice*. Its theme? "Higher Ground."

But he is more than cool. He is *real*. Often too real. If Stevie hasn't let himself coagulate in simmering pain, he too has had his pitfalls that might be textbook examples of repressed loathing rearing up with Freudian fury, causing depression, visions of premature death (that very nearly came true), sexual addiction, and shrinking from grabbing the reins of his own life. For all his genius and dictatorial tendencies in the studio, or maybe because of the time and thought processes demanded by his brain's creative lob, he has ever since coming to Motown been at the mercy of lesser mortals, led around by the nose and willingly manipulated by people—some in his own family—with either intendedly helpful or racially myopic motives.

The Wonder of it all is how it could have taken this long for the story to be told in its complexity, majesty—and entirety. Stevie Wonder predates the Beatles and the Rolling Stones, had a number one hit before either, and has stayed an elite and influential presence ever since. These things can be said for no other human being in the rock-and-roll era. This book wasn't only overdue to the point of absurdity; it had to be written from the objective sightlines of an outsider with a passion for what makes great music tick and the circumstances of that music's derivation—and not as a genuflection, without critical analysis or truths that might sting. From the skew of knowing someone I have come to know almost personally as the subject of this treatment, I can even venture the bold assumption that Steve will appreciate that; for once, his life and spectrum of inner visions have not been whitewashed and doused with antiseptic in the name of hero worship. Indeed, he long ago expressed just such contempt for those who would vacantly polish the apple of his celebrity. He has, in the end, been nothing if not a man who has lived life looking up and looking down, and has told in his words and music exactly what it felt like from both angles. What's more, he began contemplating life from both sides now before most of us knew there was more than one side. Hell, he had to, in the crib, fighting not for his art but for his life. On some distinct levels, he still is.

1

A World of Hurt

Yeah, I think I see. . . . I'm almost sure that the forms I see look exactly like yours. I mean, even with the textures of skin, or the different colors of skin, you can touch someone and you can get a pretty good picture in your mind. I assume that when you see something, you see it right in front of you, but you also take that image and it's in your mind's eye. It's no longer coming from your eyes, it's coming from inside you.

—*Stevie Wonder, 1975*

Being blind, you don't judge books by their covers; you go through things that are entirely insignificant, and you pick out things that are more important. . . . I understand that when you don't hear anything and you hear this very high frequency, that's the sound of the universe.

—*Stevie Wonder, 1973*

There is no "Hardtime, Mississippi," in Stevie Wonder's lineage, but there is a Hurtsboro, Alabama, in his blood, which is close enough. In the metaphoric sense, in fact, if Hurtsboro wasn't a real place it would be one he might well have created in a song. It might go something like, "I got Hurtsboro in my heart but it's a pain in my ass." So even though he was never actually in Hurtsboro, Hurtsboro is in him, in its rhythm and its blues and its pain. Such may help explain why a boy born with dead eyes in an urban bathtub ring called Saginaw, Michigan, could sing a song that begins with the line, "I was born in Little Rock / Had a childhood sweetheart" and make it sound so convincing, like a lick from people who sang the blues named Sonny Boy or Howlin' or Muddy and couldn't have nailed it better than Stevie Wonder when he laid down in the same song, "I got empty pockets—y'see I'm a po' man's son."

Well, *that* part was in fact literal, a common denominator in Saginaw and all the ensuing years in downtrodden Detroit. But the real, live hurt of being black and in a place like Little Rock or Mobile or Birmingham or Hurtsboro in the Jim Crow South could only be told secondhand to him, in sorrow and pity, by a hardy woman with the name of Lula Mae.

Hurtsboro is a blip on the map just west of the Alabama-Georgia border. Named for its founder, a land developer unfortunately named Joel Hurt, the town barely exists today; the 2000 census placed its population at not quite three hundred people, its gizzards eaten away by decades of attrition and hopelessness. At its apogee, in the 1940s, it boasted around five thousand inhabitants, few of whom had anything to boast about. One of them was Lula Mae Wright, who was born there in 1930 and grew up in that dust bowl with one general store, one school, and one Baptist church. Nearly all the townfolk were sharecroppers, cotton-pickers who were only differentiated from their slave ancestors by the few dollars they received for working fifteen hours a day under the broiling Alabama sun. The men usually died young, leaving the women to work in the fields, feed large numbers of children, and grow old and stooped in shotgun shacks on tar roads, their salvation found in God, ham and hominy, and the blues they could hear fleetingly through the static of an old burnt-tube radio.

The livin' wasn't easy, but they made do, their quiet frustrations and snubbed dreams echoing in the throaty testaments of the Alabama bluesmen, from W. C. Handy to Big Mama Thornton to Wild Child Butler. History informs us that the first blues song to be put onto a vinyl record was called "Crazy Blues," composed by Mobile native Perry Bradford. In the 1920s and 1930s, the blues rolled through the state as its practitioners rolled out of it on the way to greener pastures up north, or so they thought. Their music stayed put, the radio belching out slices of life like Cliff Gibson's "Tired of Being Mistreated," Barefoot Bill's "Snigglin' Blues," and Ed Bell's "Mean Conductor Blues."

Lula Mae could only dream of being lucky enough to ride the whistle-stop Ed Bell sang of out of Hurtsboro. Her life was a classic Deep South scramble. Her mother had been a teenager who had given her up to relatives six months after she was born, leaving her only with the surname Wright; her father, a bounder named Noble Hardaway, didn't even wait for the birth to vanish, hightailing it all the way to East Chicago, Indiana. Lula grew up believing her aunt and uncle, named Wright, were her parents. Only after they died did she learn about Noble, who in the winter of 1943 agreed to take in the daughter he never knew. Lula was put on the Atchison, Topeka & Santa Fe headed for East Chicago.

She was thirteen then, suddenly with a new surname and a new father, and what she would recall of that journey through the barrier of time and reality was how cold her bones felt when she stepped off the train in Indiana, colder than she could even describe. It would get colder still. Noble Hardaway was by then married and raising two children in a suffocating tenement, surrounded by other southern black emigrants driven to East Chicago by the promise of a steady paycheck from the steel mills. The promise was never quite as bright as they expected; the pay was paltry, lodging cramped, frustration thick in the sooty air. Worse, Noble Hardaway was a snarling, uncouth man and a mean drunk who quit on his newly found daughter after two weeks, sending her to an aunt and her church deacon husband a few miles away to look after her. There, Lula felt some warmth for the first time in the North. Her aunt was a tolerant woman who allowed her to drop out of school to work in a textile factory. She was even permitted to hop the train periodically with her friends for the short ride to the "other" Chicago, the real one, where she once saw Count Basie's orchestra perform in a nightclub. Her aunt's only requirement was, regardless of where Lula was the night before, to be in church on Sunday morning.

Urban life was surely an education in itself. It wasn't long before her aunt caught the good deacon in a very compromising position with another woman, and when she pulled out her pistol, he bolted from bed into the street, stark naked, ducking the shots she fired at him. Fortunately, her aim was bad, but her judgment was worse; she stayed with him on his vow of probity. Lula herself was not unfamiliar with the wages of sin. An adventurous, restless girl, in 1948 she became impregnated by a man named—of all things—Paul *Hardaway*. The suddenly moral cheatin' deacon, unable to bear the stigma, threw her out of his home and she roamed from one friend's couch to another before gathering up enough money to move into a small flat of her own. A few weeks later, she delivered a son, whom she named Milton Hardaway despite the father not having stayed around for the birth. Taking pity on her, another relative, an uncle who lived in Saginaw, took Lula and Milton into his home.

A lumber and mining burg in decline, Saginaw sat forlornly on the bleak tundra one hundred miles to the north of Detroit, double-hammered by the "hawk," as they called the wicked winter wind, sweeping in from the Saginaw River and the huge expanse of Lake Huron fifteen miles leeward. The town was a relic of the short-lived black renaissance of the 1930s and 1940s when the overflow of the great migration from the South coalesced into a middle-class bourgeois culture, its main line warming the winter nights with hot jazz clubs. Now, though, like the mines, the culture had been stripped to the bone, causing employment to ebb and crime to soar.

One of the chronically unemployed was Calvin Judkins, the first wrong number that Lula Mae Hardaway—a surname that had come to fit her well, as she seemed to do most everything the hardest way—fell for in town. Judkins was a squat man with glasses, pushing fifty, and an unrepentant drunk; Lula would many years later call him a street hustler and craps shooter, and bad at both. But she also admitted she couldn't resist him. Oh, he was good-looking enough, but that wasn't it. He just seemed to her not a common punk, especially when he sat down and played piano wherever he could find one. At those times, he was an artist, a man with depth and feelings who could transfer his suffering for life into what his fingers were tapping out on a keyboard. He had something to offer the world, if only he would get serious, clean up, be a man.

The chemistry led them to his bed, early and often. In short order, she was again pregnant, and in mid-1949 came the birth of her second son, Calvin Judkins Jr. Calvin Sr., doing his manly duty, moved Lula and her two boys into his two-room flat, then had a relative stay with the infants for a weekend while he took Lula down to where it was warmer—balmy Columbus, Ohio—to elope. When they got back, he seemed to be fulfilling Lula's grand dream for him to straighten up and fly right, taking a job in a furniture store and earning the first steady pay in his life.

It didn't last long. Walking the straight and narrow line wasn't what Calvin was about; the lure of the street came calling again. Quitting his job, he took up his old hustling habits—but now with a beyond degenerate twist. Calvin, looking to turn pimping into profit, knew of only one sure shot he could put to work on the street. One day, stinking drunk, he clambered into the house with a "friend," informing a flabbergasted Lula that he wanted her to "take a ride" with the guy. Before she could even react, he grabbed her arm hard, so hard she knew Calvin meant business—literally. Not knowing which was worse—that he was pimping, or that he was pimping his own wife, and in front of his baby son—she feared, rightly, that she had no real option. As if in a sleepwalk, she followed the john to his car, performed oral sex, and stumbled back in a daze. Pleased, Calvin, clearly unconcerned with any moral issues, nor the depth of his cruelty, reached into his pocket and put five dollars in her palm.

That surreal ritual would play out many more times. Lula, turning herself numb to the humiliation and pain, seemed to justify it by invoking some twisted construction of love, and the responsibility of feeding her children, given that Calvin's handouts were the only money he put into his family. At times she endured beatings, from Calvin, from johns, one of whom nearly broke her jaw with his fist when she gave him some back talk. Eventually, she began to carry a switchblade, just in case. When she found cause to use it, though, it wouldn't be a john but her own husband who would feel the blade.

But first transpired several more years of this sham of a marriage, with both of them living as if nothing were remiss about the pimp-whore sidelight. They even grew the family; late in 1949 Lula conceived once more. However, unlike the first two times, this was an uneasy pregnancy. Her body's immune system might have been weakened from the cold, the beatings, the strain of staying with a man she at times loathed, or by the backroom couplings with other men sanctioned by Calvin. As well, the Saginaw winter was especially brutal that year, and cases of influenza and tuberculosis surged, putting all pregnant women and their unborn at risk.

Lula knew there was something to be concerned about. There was constant pain in her distended belly; some days she could do no more than lie in bed, drawing the wrath of Calvin, who still wanted her out prowling the streets. She felt sick all the time. Then, two months before her due date, contractions began. With not much empathy from Calvin, she got herself on the bus and went to the hospital, where she was placed on a gurney and rolled into the delivery room. Doctors were reluctant to dilate her, trying to give the baby as much time in the womb as they could. For hours she was on her back, given drugs to ease the racking pain. Finally, on the morning of May 13 they began to extract the child.

It was a boy, meager, weedy, just under four pounds, but he was generally healthy, and he was alive, wailing loudly when they slapped his bottom. Lula was barely able to get a look at him as he was whisked away to a ward down the hall where premature babies were placed in incubators. Scotch-taped to the side of his was a sign bearing the name Lula had chosen for him: Steveland Morris. Or was it?

The inscrutable mystery of what name Stevie was born with has begat considerable confusion through the years, and Stevie and Lula would do little to clear it up—or even to get their stories to agree. In the original edition of Lula's biography, *Blind Faith*, for example, the authors, presumably on Lula's word, insisted that the birth name was "Stevland Judkins." In fact, Stevie himself used this nomenclature when he "signed" the liner notes of his epic masterwork *Songs in the Key of Life*. However, in the paperback edition of *Blind Faith* it was changed to the more grammatically plausible "Steveland Judkins." Despite the "settled law" of the odd spelling, seemingly confirmed by Lula at least in one printing of the book about her, the apparently incorrect "Stevland" became prevalent in numerous reference materials, and can still be found in a large number of chronicles. Further, the surname can alternately be found as Judkins, Hardaway, as well as Morris, which if Stevie can be believed—not always a safe bet—is the one that was pinned to his incubator. He said in a 1973 *Rolling Stone* interview, "Well, Judkins is my father's name. But it's crazy to explain it. Morris was on my birth certificate and everything, but Judkins was the father. I took his name when I was in school."

Given Lula's tempestuous relationship with Calvin Judkins, and the always impending possibility that she would walk out on him, one can believe Stevie's take that Lula would have preferred not to saddle the boy with a name she herself used like a curse, through gritted teeth. Yet the cognomen "Morris" has never been properly explained, by either mother or son. In *Blind Faith* it makes a quick entrance and departure, when he signed his Motown contract as "Stevie Morris." "His surname was also legally changed to Morris," the book suggests, "an old family name, as a presumptive strike against any attempt by Judkins to cut in on their sudden good fortune." As for himself, Stevie has never gotten around to doing what Lula neglected to do: say exactly who Morris was. And she went to her grave in 2006 without having explained why Morris was the name on the birth certificate.

The only real question that mattered on that day in May 1950 was whether the infant named Steveland would survive. For days he remained locked in his incubator, clinging to life, a tiny oxygen mask over his face. After she recovered from the harrowing delivery, Lula was taken in a wheelchair to the window of the premature birth ward, where she kept a silent vigil for days, her nose pressed against the Plexiglas watching her son fighting to see the next day.

Sunday was Mother's Day, and Calvin, suddenly fancying himself a family man, brought the two other sons to the hospital to gaze with her at the new addition to the family, coalescing in a tight circle and praying up a storm for him. When Lula was strong enough to go home two days later, he was still incubating, oxygen still being pumped into his lungs. It would be why he lived. And why his eyes died.

Though the Saginaw doctors didn't know it right away, Steveland Morris lost his vision mere hours after coming into the world because of a disease few if any doctors there—or any doctors anywhere—knew existed. It was called retrolental fibroplasia, a term later to be displaced in the medical journals in favor of the equally tongue-twisting retinopathy of prematurity, or ROP. When Stevie Wonder was born, it had been only nine years since the first known diagnosis, yet from 1941 to 1953 a quiet epidemic of ROP spread around the world, seen almost exclusively in affluent countries with advanced health care. The cause and effect, confirmed only in later years, was the well-intentioned and otherwise beneficial flow of supplemental oxygen in those incubation tanks. When breathed in by a premature baby of under thirty-two weeks and weighing fifteen hundred grams or less, the oxygen can produce an irregular growth of blood vessels in the eye. This in turn may cause scarring of delicate retinal tissue, and possibly cataract growth and retinal detachment.

Most often, this blip will resolve itself quickly, and most cases don't reach the stage where blindness results. But if it reaches the tipping point, it's too late—or was back then. While today "preemies" are monitored closely for signs of ROP, and are often cured with the use of laser treatment, during the epidemic twelve thousand babies suffered its worst-case consequence. One of them was Steveland Judkins.

Over the years, when he has deliberated on the subject of his blindness, it has been brief, matter-of-fact, and shorn of any great emotion. Usually he has abridged the biology by saying, "I have a dislocated nerve on one eye and a cataract on the other," which "may have happened from being in the incubator too long and receiving too much oxygen," with the quick and possibly apocryphal addendum, intended as a parable, that there had been a baby girl born the same day who was put in the incubator alongside him. In this telling, the girl had died, rendering him from that day forward "the lucky one."

That exegesis, the arching lineament of his life, was cast in the ultimate irony: that he would not have lived if not for the oxygen that was the death of his eyes; that the fullness, the completeness, and later the genius of Stevie Wonder arose from what was behind those eyes, in a rearranged nexus of senses and impulses and imagination. But it would take time, and surrender to the defeat of May 13, 1950, before anyone would have the nerve to say Steveland Judkins was born lucky that day.

For Lula Mae Judkins, when the doctors told her he was blind, undeniably and irrevocably, it cut as deeply as a stiletto. That news came after Steveland had been confined to his incubator for a biblical forty days and forty nights. By then they had clearly noticed that the boy, who was healthy in every other way, was not responding to visual stimuli. They had tried everything, but whether they dangled objects in front of his face, made loud noises at varying angles, or shone a penlight into his eyes, he never trained his eyes in any manner, never blinked when he should have.

Lula, who was inconsolable when they delivered their verdict, could not understand how such a thing could have happened. At first she cried, then begged them to do something, anything. They were doctors, she screamed at them—baby doctors! They were supposed to deal with freak occurrences like this. Then she cursed herself for not being strong enough during the prior months, for allowing him to be born too soon. In her grief and pity for her newborn, there was not a reason under the sun why she should have believed the contrary: that history would one day prove that an American original was born right on time.

They took him home on the fifty-fourth day, to a home life not merely dysfunctional but on the edge of pestilent. Calvin Judkins, fleeting as usual, quickly returned to his bounder ways, letting Lula figure out how to raise a blind boy when she didn't even have enough money to feed and clothe their other two sons. One thing she realized was that to have any money at all she would need to go on walking the street; neither did Calvin have any objection to sharing his wife with any man willing to cough up twenty bucks, not while he had no intention of trying his hand at another job. To him, a third mouth to feed simply meant Lula would have to stay on her back longer.

But he underestimated the fight in her, which may have been dormant but was not buried. One day in 1953, Calvin ordered her out into the bitter night to buy him cigarettes. This demand, oddly enough, struck her as more demeaning than to go out and service other men, and for once she stiffened, telling him to get them himself. Calvin never did tolerate words like that, certainly not from a woman he thought weak, and he slapped her so hard across the face that she buckled to the floor, just feet from where Stevie lay peacefully sleeping. He then picked her up and bodily flung her across the room, where she crashed into a table, her nose spewing blood. The noise woke all the boys, who began squealing a kind of three-part harmony from different corners of the apartment.

Bleeding, her head pounding, the degradation of her life never more obvious, she drew the nerve to stammer that she was going to take the boys and leave his sorry ass. Calvin only smirked, then slapped her yet again. What he didn't anticipate was that Lula, possibly having had premonitions about just such a blowup, had begun to keep her knife under the waistband of her skirt even at home. As he was about to backhand her a third time, she reached in, grabbed the blade, and aimed it at his throat. He saw the gleaming metal at the last fraction of a second, reflexively raising his arm enough for the knife to slice deeply into the flesh of his forearm, nearly to the bone. Now his own blood began gushing, and seeing it the bully suddenly turned poltroon. Whinnying like a wounded muskrat and believing, rightly, that she was going to finish the job, he turned on his heels and stumbled out the door, a trail of red on the floor and the street.

Even more remarkable than this exhibition of bloody execration was that Calvin actually filed charges against *her*. When word got back to Lula of this, she bundled up the boys and hid out at friends' and relatives' houses for several days. Keeping her on the run, as well, were some bad checks she had passed around town, and the recipients were sure to come looking for her. All things considered, she decided it would be best to leave Saginaw while she could.

It would get stranger still—as it always seemed to. After a week or so, a sniveling Judkins weakened, dropped the charges, and came crawling back. When he found her, he took all the blame for what happened and begged her not to leave. No more able to resist his charms, whatever they were, she too weakened and agreed to take him back. However, the decision wasn't as simple as it seems. Her price was that Calvin would leave town with her and the boys. The dividend was that he knew people in the big city—Detroit—who could find them a place to live there. Lula figured she'd given Saginaw far too much of her life; a change was needed. It would do them all good and keep her out of more trouble.

Their loveless marriage now became one of sheer convenience. Using her continued attention as leverage, she laid down another condition—no more whoring. Promising that those days were over, he dutifully made calls to the Motor City, lining up an apartment for them in the teeming Brewster-Douglass projects on the east side. The complex was right by the bubbling but decaying downtown twin red-light districts called respectively, with bemused irony and perverse pride, Paradise Valley and Black Bottom, both of which were taken to be black Detroit's answer to the pulsating rhythms of Harlem.

To Lula, it all sounded exciting, rather like the excursions she used to make to the similar underbelly of Chicago. In places like these, life was a great swirl, a blur of motion and music. The streets were home to pimps, hookers, numbers runners, and hustlers of every stripe, and they all ran shoulder to shoulder with well-heeled patrons and hepcat musicians funneling their way into the dozens of jazz and blues clubs that mottled the wide concrete expanse of Hastings Street cutting right down the middle of the Valley and the grid of byways like John R, Beacon, St. Antoine, East Canfield, Russell, Beaubien, Gratiot, and dozens more. Lining this edgy pavement, the neon-burning marquees of clubs, ballrooms, and theaters—many sharing the block with a Baptist church that the preachers hoped would catch stray sinners repenting for the night before—were like seductive arrows pointing the way inside. It didn't really matter which club it was; the names changed constantly, among the most enduring being the Flame Show, the Twenty Grand, the Frolic, the Chesterfield, the Cotton Club, Silver Grill, Jake's Bar, Little Sam's, the Cozy Corner, Club 666, the Garfield Lounge, Broad's Club Zombie, Lee's Sensation, Bizerti Bar, and the only one to endure to this day, the Roostertail. If the booze and the music didn't run out, the joint would be jumpin'.

On this turf, one was apt to run into a Duke Ellington or Louis Armstrong once in a while among the local crowd of jazz-blues singers and musicians, who in the 1940s and early 1950s included Delta expatriates Sonny Boy Williamson, Eddie Burns, Washboard Willie, and, most famously, John Lee Hooker, one of the greatest of the electric guitar–playing bluesmen. Music was always in the air, in the mind, on the tongue, and increasingly on the street corner where the kids were crooning an updated blues idiom soon to be codified as doo-wop.

The Judkins family, for all its clefts, all loved music, especially it seemed little "Stevie," who almost from the day they brought him home was banging spoons on pots and pans and singing with his brothers. This was perhaps Calvin's only redeeming quality: frustrated musician that he was, when he did stick around home long enough to interact with his children he would teach them songs and conduct their pot-and-pan symphonies. Before Stevie could walk, Calvin had bought him a cheap set of bongos, which he would play all day in his crib and sleep with at night. Clearly, teddy bears and other common playthings weren't to his liking; things that made noises could be roughly defined as music, on the other hand.

Stevie Wonder years later told *Billboard*, "I got the thirst for wanting to know. 'What is that? What is it made of? I know how it sounds, but how does it look? Can I touch it? What's a radio? Where are the people? Why do they come out of the radio?'"

Not incidentally, Lula, invested with the blues back in Hurtsboro, always had the radio on, tuned to the stations from which came the nectar of her heritage, and her son's future. Music that was beginning to congeal into what was ever more being defined by the term "soul." As it happened, to history's great debt, this rhythmic crossroads coincided with the one faced by Lula Mae. It is not fair or accurate to posit that her course was determined or influenced by anything remotely concerning music. And yet it seems nonetheless something like providence that the more she thought about where she wanted to take her sons, the more the move to Detroit felt right.

2

Motorin'

I'm goin' to Detroit, get me a barrelhouse flat,
I would take my baby but I don't know where she's at.

—*Blind Blake, "Detroit Bound Blues" (1928)*

Sneaking out the back door to hang out with those hoodlum
friends of mine

—*Stevie Wonder, "I Wish" (1976)*

When the first warm breezes of spring came to Detroit in 1953, they brought with them the Judkins family, who moved into their new digs at 2701 Hastings Street. The three-bedroom ground-floor flat was not technically part of the Brewster-Douglass projects, but for all intents and purposes it was, standing just to the east of the four fourteen-story towers and two adjacent six-story apartment buildings in the massive complex that was named for the storied Civil War abolitionist. In fact, any edifice relatively near Brewster-Douglass seemed to share its éclat, which was why people streamed into the neighborhood, reckoning it an oasis at a time when urban blight was rusting most of Detroit.

Developers had broken ground on the Brewster project in 1935, with First Lady Eleanor Roosevelt wielding a ceremonial shovel for the first federally funded public housing development in the United States. With their smokestacks perpetually belching turbid smoke into the already hazy sky, Brewster-Douglass and the other neighborhood buildings were drab and dreary by all accounts—their brick and mortar more aesthetically piquant in Stevie's mind's eye than in reality. Still, many residents proudly wore the banner of the black bourgeoisie. Most of them had to prove their economic status to be able to live there, with W-2 forms and 1099s showing that the family had an aggregate yearly income above $10,000—no mean feat in the 'hood in the 1950s. That the children of Brewster-Douglass reflected upwardly mobile instincts would become obvious within the next decade, when the population—as high as ten thousand at its apogee—would include teenagers named William "Smokey" Robinson, Diane Ross, Mary Wilson, and Florence Ballard (and in a very weird anomaly, comedienne-to-be Lily Tomlin, who came from one of the few white families in the area). And of course, a blind preteen who would soon be called Stevie Wonder.

Needless to say, Calvin Judkins could never have proven a steady income, not the kind that could be enumerated with tax forms. Indeed, if the man did one thing right in his life, it was turning the trick of getting his family into 2701 Hastings. Here, in a social setting Stevie would playfully pinpoint later as "upper lower middle class," Lula Judkins could at last breathe easily that her kids might grow up with plebeian comforts in the company of swarms of neighborhood kids their ages, since wherever one looked across and beyond Brewster-Douglass was a tableau of happily chaotic youth. This was especially important in Stevie's case, as Lula believed he needed nothing better than a sense of normalcy and reinforcement of familiarity so as not to feel like a leper. One thing she resolved early on was not to keep him cloistered, locked away like precious china in a cabinet.

Such a laissez-faire approach was critical in his development and assimilation, because there were no lines of demarcation between him and his brothers. As he would say, from his earliest days he felt an independence, the slack to be allowed to "fall on my ass" like other kids on the block. He recalls being out and about all the time, participating in the usual childish swashbuckling with the other kids in the neighborhood. They would leap from one storage bin to another in the backyard of the building—sort of a primordial, imaginary train surfing, which he mastered by counting off the paces in between beforehand—or ride bikes, straddling the bar while either Calvin or Milton sat in the seat and acted as the rudder. At times he rode alone, again after memorizing the geometric grid of the sidewalks and the rough yardage between some landmark—a lamppost, maybe—and the front door.

It was all by way of discovery, via extrasensory perception, and worked so smoothly that he would say he never understood his limitations; they just didn't compute as frailties in the world he was coming to know in his meanderings. "I never really wondered about my blindness or asked any questions about it," he said in 1974, "because to me, really, being blind was normal; since I had never seen it wasn't abnormal for me [not to see]."

There were little blips for him. The one he would recall most stubbornly was how he would continually step in dog shit out in the backyard, sometimes plop headlong into the stuff, and not even know it. Lula, however, would know when she saw her carpet streaked brown. Then there were Milton and Calvin offhandedly saying how he was "blind as a bat," a concept he didn't really understand. Lula would take it on herself to sit him down sometimes and have a heart-to-heart, to fill him in so he wouldn't be naive if—when—as he got older people mocked or tried to take advantage of him. There was, she explained, a give-and-take for his blindness. On one hand, the Lord had made him "special," he was "a gift from the heavens," God had taken his eyes but would look after him. Even so, even Jesus couldn't watch out for him all the time. That was something only he could do for himself. "Your ears don't tell you everything," she noted. "Beware of what's around you, child."

During these sobering moments, he could perceive how hard it was for Lula—harder for her than it was for him. He knew her eyes would well with tears, knew she blamed herself, though he knew nothing of the circumstances surrounding the birth. He found himself needing to reassure *her.* "I know it used to worry my mother and I knew she prayed for me to have sight someday," he once related, "and so finally I just told her that I was *happy* being blind, and I thought it was a gift from God, and I think she felt better after that." But only until the next time she would become weepy about it; the fact was, she had to resolve a lot more about his condition than he would ever need to.

Although it would be years before he saw the heather of a creative inner vision, even as a child he became aware of the existence of such a vision, through the adaptive processes that heightened the span and scope of his other senses, most centrally his hearing. Certainly Stevie Wonder's ears are of a higher grade of sensitivity and nuance than those of most humans, out of necessity. In truth, we all have the ability to channel sound waves into illusory patterns that shoot across a spatial field, especially, it seems, when listening to music. Through head-phones in a pitch-black room, music takes on added dimensions; we can "see" instruments separated in a mix, even in mono. But we can only imagine what it sounds and "looks" like to a Stevie Wonder.

So if he didn't really miss having functioning eyes, it was because his ears were all he needed. It was why he was always confounding people. Emerging as something like a carnival sideshow attraction, he remembers entertaining visitors who would habitually "drop change on the table saying, 'What's that, Stevie?' 'That's a dime. . . . That's a quarter. . . . That's a nickel.' I could always get it right except a penny and a nickel confused me," because of the similar timbre of the sound they made hitting the table. It wasn't, he said, a matter of hearing better than anyone but rather "how much you use [the sense]. . . . See, about sound . . . sound happens all the time, *all* the time. If you put your hands up to your ears, if you close your eyes and move your hands back and forth, you can hear the sound getting closer and further away. . . . Sound bounces off everything, there's always something happening."

The application of these principles—which of course would be years in the making—was only lengthened and deepened by the undula-tions of rhythm and melody. "When I hear music," he said in *Rolling Stone* decades later, "I can see it, each instrument has its own color, the piano for instance is dark brown, and I can see each instrument playing its own part. It's like a puzzle, and when I fit all the pieces together, that's my high. It's like a person in church gettin' the spirit. You hear all those things happening around you and it just lifts you off the ground."

In his case, literally, such as when he'd mount those storage bins out back and lift off. In 1963 there'd be a fabulous shot in *Ebony* of him soaring from the top of the stairway in front of the building, frozen in midair, arms reaching higher into space; the vibe is of pellucid joy and not an ounce of fear. It was a familiar pose to neighbors on the block, and necessity to Stevie. Up there, he could see everything, seemingly indefinitely. Years later, when he would bound from an airplane, para-chute on his back, the first of several times he skydived, it was like a rerun of an old show; he'd felt what it was like before, all the time, turning imagination into real-world images and a curiosity for what else he might see. "My mind," he once said, "wants to see to infinity."

He would over time create all sorts of theories, some clearly fanciful, as sources for inner visions. At times he would think up one on the spot. Once, speaking with a writer, he veered into another abstract. "I bet you," he said, apropos of nothing, and with a great gush of enthusiasm, "there is a way where the hands can actually see as eyes, connect to the optic nerve. . . . If you think of a cake and you feel a cake after a while in your mind you're thinking about how it looks. I see it. . . . I see the full shape of the cake in my mind. I'm seeing it in my mind now, a round cake."

Another went like this: "I have an idea of what colors are. I associate them with the ideas that've been told to me about those certain colors. I get a certain feeling in my head when a person says 'red' or 'blue,' 'green,' 'black,' 'white,' 'yellow,' 'orange,' 'purple'—purple is a crazy color to me." Was it, he was asked, simply what the word sounded like? "Yeah, yeah," he agreed. "To me, brown is a little duller than green, isn't it?"

He also, by his reckoning, may have caught a break, in one respect. Having run across what he presumed to be evil instincts during his maturation into adulthood, he couldn't imagine being conned by a pair of lying eyes. Rather, in the cynical vein of the unforgettable Norman Whitfield–Barrett Strong song "Smiling Faces," he would come to share the educated opinion that the truth is in the eyes, 'cause the eyes don't lie though they sure as hell try. "Eyes," he said in a 1976 *People* article, "lie if you look into them for the character of a person. Man, if that's what sight is all about, I never want to see. Never."

If Steveland Judkins ever saw cake in his mind back in Saginaw and in the projects, it wasn't because it was in front of him on his plate. Of those times, Stevie Wonder would look back in the biographical classic "I Wish" and try to imagine a greater good than creature comforts—"My only worry was for Christmas what would be my toy / Even though we sometimes would not get a thing / We were happy with the Joy the day would bring." They'd have to be, since the family never scratched the surface of the black middle class, not that Calvin had any desire to change that. Usually he was out the door, smoke through a keyhole, a rumor to the family for days or weeks.

Within a few years, when Detroit rotted away, those allegedly middle-class blacks were left to rot with it. That would be when neighborhoods like Brewster-Douglass began to implode, the wail of sirens the sound Stevie heard outside his window and from down the block nearly every night—a sound he would faithfully and traumatically recreate in "Living for the City."

The Judkinses always knew what it was like to be left to fend for themselves. While Stevie can recall little else about his first several years, he can clearly remember when in the pit of a typically brutal winter Lula and his brother, with no one to watch him and more hands needed, took him along on a middle-of-the-night foray to a dry dock where piles of coal were being stored, and stole away with bundles of it in his baby stroller to stoke the flame in the potbellied stove in an otherwise unheated apartment. "To a poor person," Stevie once would reason, "that's not stealing. That is not a crime; it's a necessity."

Because someone had to pay the rent, an almost unimaginable hundred dollars a month in the early 1950s, Lula by default was the breadwinner, though it may have been debatable at times which was worse: walking the street or, as she did in Detroit, working long hours at a fish market and coming home, reeking, to get the boys from a neighbor or from Calvin's aunt Ilona, who would watch them if Calvin was nowhere to be found, which was most of the time.

As default head of the household, Lula never wavered in keeping them out of trouble, even if it meant personally administering the rites of punishment, her implement of choice the thick cord that plugged her iron into the wall outlet. She would double it up by looping it around, to the width of a leather strap, and tattoo them across the rump until she was satisfied they got the message. That Stevie was not spared out of pity he later confirmed with his wry description of the ritual, funny only in retrospect to him, as the "Magic Ironing Cord Whipping"—and, of course, with a kicky beat in "I Wish" recalling the failure of "tryin' your best to bring the water to your eyes, thinkin' it might stop her from woopin' your behind."

But then, he knew he gave her no choice but to "woop" on his behind, such was his feisty, precocious nature. Nor did he particularly abhor it. Rather it was as if having his hide tanned further erased the line of demarcation between him and the other boys, the "normal" ones. He was even, he would say in future years, grateful to Lula for making this dearth of pity possible, by her recognition of his restlessness.

"Your mother is your first love," he said later. "She's the one who brought me into this world, and I thank God for allowing me to come through her. She handled my blindness a lot differently than maybe other mothers would have. As much as my being blind hurt her in the beginning, she did not limit me to just being in one place. . . . She allowed me to discover."

Courting—even daring—the barb of the ironing cord, he paid little heed to punctiliousness. For example, there was mouth. Easily absorbing the vernacular of the street, he could suddenly become as salty as a sailor. Once, when Aunt Ilona was at the house, she watched aghast as he flew from storage shed one to the next, and ordered him down.

"Aw, fuck you," he retorted, a bit too easily for a boy of five.

That night, naturally, he paid for it with another whipping, and he might not have wanted it any other way, not if it meant he had earned her sting.

Certainly the "magic cord" didn't prevent some reckless behavior. There was, for instance, the time he and his brothers, left home alone, were playing cards at the kitchen table. They came up with the bright idea that Stevie might actually be able to see his cards if the room was more illuminated. Soon they were lighting matches—a no-no by Lula's rules—and dropped them into a garbage pail. Smoke and flames quickly filled the apartment, and the building might well have burned to the ground had not Lula just then arrived at the door, to douse the blaze with a hose. It took her hours to clean up the mess, though the damage to the drapes and carpeting would be irreparable.

That's when the "magic cord" came out, as the boys knew it would. But in Lula's system of values, even playing with matches was no more serious an offense than her boy smiting the Lord by using profanity. After all, how could she beg Jesus to give back the sight he took from Stevie, how could he have pity for the poor boy if her son acted so shamefully?

What she didn't know was that the very utensil of her disciplinary ways would one day be immortalized in song, as "I Wish" narrated the grown-up Stevie Wonder's wistful yearning for the simple, dirty pleasures of youth. One can take the song as a confessional, checking off the trespasses of childhood—church money traded for candy, smoking cigarettes, writing nasty things on the wall, playing doctor with the girls, and, more seriously, sneaking out the door to meet those "hoodlum friends of mine."

In fact, he broached some skittish turf. Some in the old neighborhood will tell you that Stevie first donned dark sunglasses when he was running with gangs, whose members did the same in the name of dark cool, though his primary urge being to cover the uncoordinated eyes that would tip off that he was blind. Lula constantly fretted that he would wind up a juvenile delinquent, or worse, a shiftless bounder like Calvin. It was fortunate, she would admit, that he had music to distract him from those bums he ran with.

For years, Lula held out ever more faint hope that God would do a make-good—or rather, in her guilt, that *she* could do so—for her boy having lost his sight when he was born. That drove her to faith healers, a rising breed of hucksters since the end of World War II. Several of the bigger-name healers had a huge following, and huge bankrolls, because of the success of their tent shows at which they would make the sick well with a divine sweep of a hand. Summertime saw the entire roster out on the hustings through Middle America, including William Branham, Oral Roberts, Jack Coe, A. A. Allen, and Kathryn Kuhlman. When Oral Roberts came through Saginaw during Stevie's second summer, Lula made sure to be under his tent.

She waited patiently and prayed on cue. Then, when the call came for poor and desperate souls to come forward and be healed, she clamped her hand around Stevie's and began fighting through a mob of humanity until she'd clawed her way to the pulpit of the stage, only to be turned away because there were too many up there already. "But my baby is blind!" Lula cried out, raising him above her head for all to see, inviting sympathy as people began to chant, "He's blind! He's blind!" That led Roberts to part the way for them.

Standing among a line of ill and crippled believers, she dropped to her knees on cue with the rest of them and waited for Roberts's rites of redemption to drive out the devil behind Stevie's eyes. Down the line Roberts came, one by one ordering disease and pestilence away, whereupon, again on cue, some threw away their canes and rose from their wheelchairs. Then he came to Lula, who was shaking like a leaf and clutching her boy to her bosom. Roberts put his hands over Stevie's eyes.

"I command you to see!" he bellowed.

Lula tried very hard to believe. Tears rolled down her face. The crowd, breath held, waited for the child to make like he could see. When he didn't, Roberts said something about how the Lord sometimes takes his time, and moved on. Lula, crushed, led Stevie back through the grandstand, feeling empty, dead, and even more guilty than before. God had surely healed everyone else on that stage, but he still had it in for her. Worse, she would repeat the process with other healers. But God never answered.

Having been too young to remember any of this, being told about it by Lula years later only made Stevie angry. The healers, he has said, "talked that shit but they are crazy, man. They can't wake up the dead."

As risible as the healers were, Lula kept on blaming herself for Stevie's plight. It may well be she never felt completely sanguine about it. But she would always put up a brave front, saying variations of things like, "God blessed me with Stevie," and "God have blessed Stevie. He blessed the whole family and I'm really happy." Certainly she agreed that what the Lord had taketh he had giveth back, in her son's musical talent. That, she said convincingly, was "a gift."

Not that she didn't continue trying to make points with the Almighty. Every Sunday without exception she would trundle the boys onto the Detroit city line bus that rode up 26th Road toward Fenkell Street, the location of the White Stone Baptist Church. According to her memoirs and Stevie's, that was her sanctuary, and Stevie's real salvation. There he began to sing in the choir, something he loved, and he was easily the most distinguishable voice, high and joyous, with a neat little vibrato quake in it that fluttered the notes of the hymnal. As he sang, his body reflexively moved to the rhythm, his hands clapping in time, his head craning up at a near ninety-degree angle, making it look as if his eyes were trained on something far above the chapel ceiling. He quickly earned a reputation as the best thing about those Sunday services.

That weekly liturgy was his second incubator, where he gained confidence in who and what he was, where he could sing and show off and really feel like he was flying, a sensation that always came when he could lift his voice.

In order for Stevie to fly as high as he could, though, Calvin Judkins had to be banished from his life. While that seemed to be Lula's aim when she made her compact with Calvin to bring her to Detroit, their living situation remained frozen in limbo for three more years. He would be with them sporadically, then evaporate for weeks. Once in a while he would come by, so drunk he could hardly stand erect, and bring the boys a gift—admirably, seeing Stevie's affinity for music, he would buy him toy instruments: bongos, a plastic harmonica, a toy piano, each of which Stevie would have mastered by the time he visited again—or demand sex from Lula, a demeaning exercise she eventually refused to comply with.

Before he left, it seemed he always became so enraged at some real or imagined grievance that he would raise his hands to Lula and the boys, usually indiscriminate about which one he would pick on. Lula wanted nothing more than to be rid of him, but was afraid to ask for a divorce for fear of what he might do. Instead, she waited and waited for him to be gone long enough to legally declare abandonment.

Through the years, Stevie would have very little to say about Calvin Judkins, and absolutely no comment on his drunken outbursts. He would have no droll witticisms about Calvin's fists as he did about Lula's ironing cord. One rare reference seemed to hang heavy with what is *not* said. In 1974 he rather haltingly spoke of a "frightening" time when he was eight and Calvin, who had by then abandoned the family, suddenly came by the apartment when Lula had left his brothers to look after him. Calling him, awkwardly, "the, uh, father of me," Stevie recounted in *Esquire* how, almost like a stalker, Calvin asked him, "You want to go, Stevie, with me? We gonna go and get some candy and stuff . . . ride the bus and . . . C'mon!" Excited, Stevie left with him and they wound up in Calvin's new place, where, he recalled, there was a piano and a saxophone that Calvin let him noodle around with.

"I stayed there for a while, we stayed together," he went on. "Then one day, I remember him having to go off somewhere and he stayed away for a long time . . . and left me alone.

"That was the first time I got upset and I started to cry about that. But after a while I just said, hey, forget it, and I just went to sleep. I was just afraid because the surroundings weren't familiar to me."

He went no further into this episode, and Lula in her autobiography avoided mentioning it, as she did Calvin's violent, even psychopathic impulses toward his children. Could this have been because both wanted to keep the innocent, feel-good vibes of the Stevie Wonder story free of such a stain? Considering what Stevie would confide to some at Motown, we can assume that to be the case. According to one confidant familiar with the above tale, the truth—beyond Stevie's shrugging spin—was that Calvin had actually tried to kidnap Stevie that day and was foiled when Lula called the cops and tracked down Stevie.

Stevie may well have had Calvin Judkins in mind when, turning existential about the concept of inner hurt, he cryptically said to *Ebony* in 1972, "You don't know what happiness is unless you've experienced being sad." That bauble of wisdom must have surprised anyone led to believe in the 1960s that Stevie Wonder was an adorable wind-up toy without a care or a bad memory in the world. In retrospect, *that* Stevie Wonder was one hell of a front.

The music began to get earnest when the toy drums, harmonicas, and spoon-on-pot kitchen symphonies were replaced by real instruments. Providentially, a piano owned by a woman neighbor at 2701 Hastings Street who had allowed him to come by and run his fingers up and down the keys became his when she moved and said he could take it. A Hohner chromatic harmonica came as a similar bestowal from his barber down the block. A real drum kit was suddenly his when after he banged on it at a local Lions Club, the lodge elders threw a Christmas party for blind children and surprised him with a free door prize.

It wasn't only that these people were nice to him, or pitying; it was that he had, with remarkable self-taught skills, been keeping them entertained on those instruments. Indeed, Stevie Judkins was not just a happy, smilingly radiant novelty act from down the block—he *was* an entertainer, wherever he could be one. Certainly the kid got around, something confirmed by Kim Weston, one of Motown's most underlooked and underappreciated divas, her most memorable songs being her 1965 original version of "Take Me in Your Arms (Rock Me a Little While)" and her 1966 duet with Marvin Gaye, "It Takes Two."

Still living in Detroit today, where she does a soul music radio show, she said when contacted, "Funny you should ask about Stevie. I'm getting together a Stevie Wonder tribute show right now." She first came upon him when he was around nine and she twenty, in the church they both attended—though Weston insisted it was not White Stone Baptist but the New Corinthian Baptist Church on Tillman Street on the west side of town, a citation not found anywhere in the Stevie Wonder literature or in the written memories of Stevie or Lula Mae.

"Oh yes, it was the New Corinthian, that was it," she says. "In fact, the last time I talked to him I asked him, 'Stevie, do you remember New Corinthian Church?' He said, 'Of course!' I asked him, 'Do you remember me from New Corinthian?' And he said, 'Yes, I remember you!' See, Stevie remembers everybody, he has a photographic memory.

"And I clearly remember him, just as anyone who ran across him does. I remember that when he came in there would be a bunch of children following behind him, kids his age and younger. That's why I called him the Pied Piper. I remember Lula very well. I never met his father, don't think he ever came in with them.

"What I remember was that he'd sing in the choir, but then after the first service of the day he'd hang around and come in between the services and ask to play the piano. And I was in charge of the music at the church so I was the one that he would have to come to. Of course, I'd let him. 'Cause that boy could play! He'd play for a couple of hours, all kinds of songs, gospel, blues, everything, and I'd sit there listening in amazement at the talent he had. We all sat there like that, the people in choir from the afternoon service, who were there to rehearse, they'd listen. The pastor, Odelle Purdoch, he would listen. Whoever came in, they'd listen. Stevie always had an audience, even then.

"The thing about Stevie was, everything about him was advanced. He may have been nine but his senses were . . . they were so excellent. I don't know if he smelled the people and could distinguish them that way, but he knew who you were before you got to him."

Lula was only too happy, of course, to indulge his growing musical habits, herself astonished by how self-assured, even haughty, he could be about it, but the overall effect was that he felt so good about himself because of it that she could worry less about him, and dote less on him. When he was six and able to get around without her help, using Milton and Calvin Jr. as his guides, she had begun to work the graveyard shift at the fish market, from midnight to dawn, then overtime until midafternoon, furiously hoarding her wages so she could move them out of the ever-decaying projects and into a house. In the interim, she eased into the transition by moving them to a three-bedroom flat in a nicer neighborhood on Horton Street.

Stevie was by then going to Bagley Elementary School, which had special classes for blind students. There, he quickly chafed because he was well beyond the level of the curriculum in his music classes. To the teachers, his know-it-all bent wasn't precociousness but arrogance. When Stevie has reflected back on those classroom blues, he's had little but contempt for them. "People at school," he once told the *New York Times*, "told me I would end up making potholders instead [of being a performer]."

If this massively insensitive slight indeed emanated from people who were supposed to be lifting such stereotypes from the backs of blind children, it might explain why he became fixated on proving how wrong they were. Indeed, soon his talent was inordinate. One summer when he was eight, Lula took the boys to a picnic in a park on Belle Isle, a venue of heavy symbolic value in black Detroit. In 1943 racial tensions had broken out into violence on the island, and ultimately spread downtown. The incident left thirty-four dead and eighteen hundred arrested, the vast majority of them black. Great numbers of African Americans filled the park each summer in a festive atmosphere with bands playing deep into the night. Of course, whenever Stevie was taken to these reveries, he would dance around in his ostentatious way, as close to the stage as he could get, his arms and legs all akimbo and his harmonica spouting along with the tunes played by the band.

Doing so, he drew the attention of the disc jockey hosting the show, who leaned into the audience and asked him who he was. "My name is Stevie," he said into a microphone, his voice reverberating to the far reaches of the picnic ground, "and I can sing and play drum." This bit of unsolicited information, as he reckoned it would, led the jockey to take the obvious step of bringing him up onto the stage and depositing him behind the drum kit. As the band played the next tune, the sinewy blues ballad "Pledging My Love," he settled into a smooth backbeat, spiked by a few well-placed solos.

For his work, the disc jockey put three quarters in his palm, the first time he had ever been paid to perform, and it seemed like all the money in the world to him. But he still came off the stage disappointed. Given the tempo of the slow song, he told Lula, he couldn't execute the wild, long drum solo he had wanted to do.

"I really wanted to drive them people crazy, mama," he said on the bus ride home.

As he got older, the edges of these sounds were smoothed and their corners rounded by another form of self-tutoring, the nighttime ritual of falling asleep to the lullabies of the radio on the end table. As it happened, in 1956 a new station, WCHB, began broadcasting from suburban Inkster. It was one of the first black-owned stations in the country and its DJs, people like Martha "the Queen" Steinberg, Larry Dixon, "Senator" Bristol Bryant, and Joe Hudson, became heralds of a generation just now hearing the music of their Delta roots and how it merged with jazz, swing, and gospel to birth doo-wop.

Wonder has frequently cited the galvanic properties of a Sunday night program on the station called *Sundown*, where one was likely to experience Louis Armstrong, John Lee Hooker, B. B. King, Jackie Wilson, Hank Ballard and the Midnighters, Little Willie John, and Andre Williams within the same hour. "Oh, the music!" he once waxed. "Jumping around and dancing . . . *Honky Tonk! Bad!* Bill Doggett . . . the Coasters, the Dixie Hummingbirds, the Staple Singers . . . oooh, God! That Mavis Staples! I swear to God, I've been in love with that chick for so long." He called the effect of the moving sidewalk of voices like that "hypnotic," such that when he would later on meet Mavis Staples on the circuit, it was as if for all the world he could see into her eyes. "I could never see them, of course, but I felt the presence. You could feel them shining on you."

Similar soul-stirring was being felt all around town in the late 1950s. Detroit, despite all its visible faults, was happening musically.

The big record labels had little presence there. Instead, in a frenetic nest of musicians, performers, writers, and producers in which everyone seemed to know everyone else, records were cut in ramshackle studios and apt to come out the next day on one of a swarm of local labels, most fly-by-night (one, H.O.B., carried those initials because it was run out of the back room at the House of Beauty parlor), some more salient, the beau ideal for now being one operated by blues singer Johnnie Mae Matthews, Northern, which would be where the first incarnation of the Temptations took flight, as the Distants.

The alternative—and the best hope—was to shop a record to big labels in outside cities that could accrue some national airplay and sales. That trick had been turned by a select few, such as Hank Ballard's risqué blues-rockers like "Work with Me Annie" (less coy ones like "Sexy Ways" and "Open Up the Back Door" were taboo on the radio), and the gospel-heavy doo-wop of the Falcons, such as on their 1958 hit "You're So Fine." The last was a victory for another important, if now obscure Detroit music figure, Bob West, who owned the Flick and Contour labels and produced and managed the Falcons, into which he would later put two Detroit natives, Wilson Pickett and Eddie Floyd, both of whom would a decade later be riding high with the Memphis-based soul label Stax/Volt.

Nobody, however, seemed better at playing the record-shuttle game than a man on the make named Berry Gordy Jr. In fact, he had already played it so well that he was able to create Detroit's next new thing, which by the first days of 1959 was known to a good many people in and out of Detroit by one word—Motown. Before creating that budding dynasty, and for a time after, Gordy was pawning off records he had produced wherever he could, to any music-industry panjandrum he could court. Doing so helped him raise crucial capital for his quixotic venture as a black music entrepreneur.

Stevie knew all about Motown and, through the grapevine, Berry Gordy, who was a rather shadowy figure with a double-edged reputation, an impeccable arbiter of music talent and a man with connections but, as word on the street had it, a ruthless SOB who would exploit talent without paying them. Whether that meant anything to nine-year-old Stevie Judkins at the time is doubtful, but in any case the notion of presenting himself to Motown, or any other label, wasn't in his purview.

He just wanted to sing wherever he could, because that was what made him feel good.

But fate was about to conjoin them, forever. Indeed, things like that just seemed to happen to Stevie Judkins when he sang and played his instruments, things that nothing in the world could possibly keep from happening. And happening fast.

3

"That Shit Is Just Fantasticness!"

I decided to become a sinner . . . to follow my love of R&B.

—*Stevie Wonder*

Fortunate things just seemed to happen to Berry Gordy Jr. as well, at least since 1957 when he tapped into a nifty mother lode by cowriting songs for Detroit homeboy Jackie Wilson after the flashy singer quit the Drifters to go solo. Gordy provided Wilson's debut hit, "Reet Petite," and kept the chain going with bigger hits like "Lonely Teardrops," "That's Why," and "I'll Be Satisfied." Prior to that, he had reeked of failure, as a middleweight prizefighter, a Ford assembly line worker, and the owner of a jazz record store. As he gravitated more toward music, the stocky, rough-hewn Gordy was regarded within the tightly knit music scene as a talented but undisciplined and roguish ne'er-do-well, making him the black sheep of one of the few wealthy black families in Detroit. By the mid-1950s, in his mid-twenties, he was one among a flotsam of street hustlers, married with three children, but booted out by his wife for serial adultery and alleged physical abuse. Amid all this discord and confusion, he found his big break. Or rather it found him, since he did little to earn it. By dint of dumb luck, two of his sisters, Gwen and Anna Gordy, happened to run the photo booth in the Flame Show Bar, the most hoppin' joint on John R Street. For Gordy, it was a target of opportunity, perhaps his last best one, because the manager of the Flame Show was a man named Al Green, and he also was the manager of Jackie Wilson. Gordy hung out regularly at the bar, trying in vain to get Green's attention. He then begged his sisters to make the introduction. Gordy conned—er, convinced—Green that he had exactly what Jackie needed, and then against all odds went and proved it, delivering Wilson a clutch of big national hits.

However, he was gypped out of those songs' considerable royalties, which were hoarded by Green and then, after Green's death, by an even more cutthroat manager, Nat Tarnopol. Gordy, who no one could deny had the stones to do it, issued an ultimatum to Tarnopol: pay up or I quit. Tarnopol took maybe three seconds to tell him not to let the doorknob hit him on the way out. Gordy then appealed directly to Wilson, who cravenly told him, "Berry, I love you and your family, but I can't go against Nat."

But while he was not rich in the pocket, the Wilson imprimatur gave him some sway, not only around town but with his family. He created his own record label, called Tamla Records—for no reason other than that Gordy loved the Debbie Reynolds movie *Tammy and the Bachelor* and appropriated the name, which he had to alter slightly because of copyright issues. Needing seed money to get it up and running, he called together his parents and older sisters and hit them up for an $800 loan taken from the family's real estate investment fund, against future earnings from Tamla recordings. After some initial skepticism, the brood kicked in, and the germ of Motown began.

Haltingly but surely, with his label established, Gordy cobbled together a clutch of teenage singers and songwriters who would remain loyal to him, some to this day. One of these protégés was a tiny woman with powerful lungs, Raynoma Liles, who was so charmed by the nervy music vagabond with big dreams that she made room for him to live with her and her three-year-old son in her town house, freeing Gordy from years of crashing in his sisters' homes, unable as he was to afford any lodging on his own. At the start, they were on a platonic basis, but she would fall hard for him, despite some of his skeevy activities. One of these became apparent to her when he came home weary and cranky, complaining, "I have to get out of this business." When she inquired what he meant, he told her, "I have a few girls," but that he couldn't go on doing what he was doing—meaning, of course, pimping—because of unnamed "sick motherfuckers" who he said regularly beat up their girls. Raynoma wasn't shocked as much as amused by this revelation that her man was a pimp, given that Berry Gordy must have been the worst-dressed and least-equipped Superfly in all of Detroit, one who, lacking a car, had to improvise. "What kind of pimp," Liles asked incredulously, years later, "rides the bus?"

And yet, much as Lula Mae had literally laid her body down for Calvin Judkins, Raynoma—though without telling Berry—decided it would be helpful if she went out and became one of his "girls." She admits she turned one trick, to raise a few dollars. Not clear is how long Gordy's moonlight serenade as a poor man's procurer lasted, but it was fortunate that the Motown venture soon after began to round into shape. In that venture too, he was aided and abetted by Raynoma, whose powerful voice and wide range prompted him to form a group around her, the Rayber Voices, the name a portmanteau of their names. They were a loose phalanx of Gordy retainers whom he used as backup singers on his records; for a fee, the Voices would sing behind any vocalist who wanted to cut a record, and Gordy would usually swing a side deal to produce it.

From these hired-gun profits he amassed enough to make more ambitious moves, which he did with his posse of young, talented, and absolutely loyal talent, including brothers Eddie and Brian Holland, and of course Smokey Robinson, whose almost ethereal falsetto voice and impishly clever songwriting were impressively unveiled on a number of Gordy-produced records in 1959, such as "Got a Job" and "Bad Girl," released under the new name for Smokey's group, the Miracles, at times informally Smokey and the Miracles.

Through his connections, Gordy was able to put out several of his records by leasing them to big labels such as the Chicago R&B giant Chess Records—again with no small debt of gratitude to his family, as his sister Gwen had opened a label of her own, Anna Records, with her new husband Harvey Fuqua, the former lead singer of the Moonglows who had ties to Chess. For the Miracles, he scored a deal with George Goldner's New York soul label End Records, which was part of Goldner's stable that included Frankie Lymon and the Teenagers, the Chantels, Little Anthony and the Imperials, and the Valentines.

Gordy's debut record on Tamla—now regarded as the first Motown record—was Marv Johnson's "Come to Me," released in January 1959. Still unable to pay for nationwide distribution, he again went the lease route, placing it with United Artists. When the song went Top 30, he followed up with two Top 10 hits, "You've Got What It Takes" and "I Love the Way You Love," and a Top 20, "(You've Got to) Move Two Mountains," all within the span of eighteen months. These works, all backed by the Rayber Voices, were cut in Gordy's brand-new studio in the basement of a formerly abandoned A-frame row house on a relatively upscale, tree-lined street just west of Henry Ford Hospital. The address of the place—2648 West Grand Boulevard—would before long become as well-known as 1600 Pennsylvania Avenue, but when Gordy found it, it was a ramshackle wreck. But it was *his* wreck, one he deemed suitable to house his pipe dream of a self-sustaining enterprise of black capitalism. By then, too, he had married Raynoma Liles and had a son with her, necessitating larger digs.

In 1959 he made a $3,000 down payment toward a total price of $23,000 for the house at 2648 West Grand where he and Raynoma relocated, living upstairs as he went about converting the downstairs into an office suite and the rat- and roach-infested basement into a recording studio. He also had enough seed money to begin a second label, which he named by abridging the street-jive cognomen for the city of Detroit, also used as the corporate title of the organization— the Motown Record Company, Inc. Informally, the label was called "Hitsville USA," the trademark Gordy had spelled out on the portico of the house above the bay window on the frescoed porch. With this, Gordy was setting forth more than a cool-sounding trade name. It was no less than a mission statement, his plan being to roll out not only good R&B records but, like the ones he wrote for Jackie Wilson, records with mass appeal, the implication being that white record buyers would sop them up. For Gordy, it was all about crossover, which in industry-speak is the flow of black-made records onto, and hopefully up, the pop chart. That was where the money was.

The only color he really cared for was green, and the perfect epigraph for his designs was written into one of the first records he produced at his new domicile at 2648 West Grand Boulevard. Randomly tinkling piano keys in his new basement studio, he came up with a line that went, "Your love gives me such a thrill." When his teenage receptionist

Janie Bradford instinctively added the rejoinder, "But your love don't pay my bills," they hashed out a song in that cheeky vein, which Gordy recorded with an obscure singer named Barrett Strong and leased to his sister Gwen's Anna Records label. Early in 1960, it went to No. 23 pop, No. 2 R&B. The title of the song—which was what really should have been tacked onto the new Motown headquarters—was "Money (That's What I Want)."

Like Motown, Stevie Judkins was coming of age precociously in the early 1960s, with considerably less emotional drag now that the dreaded Calvin Judkins was gone. When he was ten, Lula saved enough—literally in her mattress—to move her and the boys again, this time to their first house, a modest four-bedroom row house on the west side at 3347 Breckenridge Street, just off 23rd Street, once again situated on the periphery of a suffocating housing project. At a price of $8,000, it was anything but modest for Lula, who had to fork over nearly every cent she had to make the $800 down payment. When she did, Stevie no longer had to surf storage bins, nor did he suffer the indignity of coming back inside covered in manure.

But a big house, any house, wasn't big enough to hold him. He seemed less blind than ever. And more mature, by God. He was now going to the Fitzgerald School for the Blind, a special public school that had been attended previously by Leon Ware, a future Motown songwriter who was blinded for two years by a childhood accident. Bused to and from the school, Stevie quickly mastered Braille and took an interest in world history, picking through the carcasses of grand but doomed empires and their twisted, demented leaders. This, he would say, helped him see clues and lessons when he turned his gaze outward to the broad schisms within the underbelly of the American empire and the reluctance of its leaders to see the same lessons in how "the whole thing crumbled . . . because of the missing links, the weak foundations," which he feared "could happen here, very soon. That's basically what 'Big Brother' is all about." And: "I speak of the history, the heritage of the violence, or the negativeness of being able to see what's going on with minority people." Most of his cannon fire, of course, would be trained on Richard Nixon.

Clearly, the education of Stevie Judkins cut in many directions, more of it occurring outside the schoolhouse door than inside it, and much of what he learned on the street immediately set on a collision course the secular and the holy. It was a battle that the saints could not hope to win. While Stevie seemed to be a gift of the angels singing in his white robe in the White Stone Baptist Church choir every Sunday, apparently he heard little in the reverends' sermons to separate him from the call of the wild. Certainly the killjoy admonitions of the apostles and in the words of the Psalms didn't seem to apply when he was sneaking out the back door and running with the thugs. Indeed, if we can read anything into his few words on the subject of sex over the years, it is that he was locked and loaded remarkably early. Wonder, indeed.

"We listened to Redd Foxx [albums] and did all that stuff!" he gleefully recalled in *Rolling Stone* in 1975. "We tried to sneak and do it to little girls. I used to get into a lot of shit, Jack! I got caught trying to mess with this girl. I was about eight years old. It was the play house trip. And I really was like taking the girl's clothes off and everything. I don't understand how I did that stuff, you know. I mean, I was *in* it! I had her in my room with my clothes off. And she gave it away 'cause she started laughin' and giggling 'cause I was touching her."

If by "gave it away" he wasn't speaking of a candy apple, and if he indeed lost his virginity at the ripe old age of eight, his music may only be Stevie Wonder's *second* most incredible achievement. What's more, this is actually plausible given what sex must feel and look like inside the mind's eye of a Stevie Wonder. The colors—by God, the *colors*!

"I mean, you just have to get in there and *do* that shit, you know," he went on, no doubt tingling. "That shit is just fantasticness!"Apparently this was not fey bravado. According to one of Stevie's neighbors and buddies, John Glover, who was three years older than Stevie and lived on 25th Street, "Stevie was always crazy about the girls. Always had lots of girlfriends, even back then. Girls would listen to him sing and play, and they'd wanna get next to him. There was this girl in the neighborhood— my sister knew her; I think she was like twelve, thirteen—and she was Stevie's girlfriend back then, when he was like seven years old. I'd be the one to take him over to her house when her parents weren't there, and they'd mess around while I waited outside."

Lula, of course, never knew about any of this, though she may well have wondered why some of those iron-cord "woopings" didn't seem to wipe the smile off his face. Not only was he skilled at keeping his delinquent misdeeds hushed, but he was also far too smart to put a budding career as a performer at risk by ruining the Stevie shtick: the adorable, wholesome, God-fearin'—Ha! If only they knew—blind savant people wanted to hug when he'd air out those gospel hymns or the feisty rhythm and blues on the stoop. At those times, he was properly chaste, even if his deviations into the music of the devil struck some as problematic. That not everybody in Detroit reveled in the openly raw, sexually bristling music of the Delta was evident, for example, on the rides to and from the Fitzgerald School, when his transistor radio filled the bus.

"Like I was the only black kid on the bus," he once recalled, "and I would always turn the radio down, because I felt ashamed to let them hear me listening to B. B. King. But I *loved* B. B. King. Yet I felt ashamed because—because I was *different* enough to want to hear him and because I had never heard him anywhere else." But he was not ashamed enough to turn it off, and not doing so, as he extrapolated later in the story, was no less than empowering. "Freedom," he went on, "begins in the simplest things, even in such things as feeling free enough to turn on a radio to a particular station. You have to sense that for yourself and then demand that kind of freedom from others."

Soon music grew into a serious pursuit, requiring precision and confederacy. Stevie wanted to jam with other musicians so he could blend harmonies and instruments, the parts for which he could arrange by ear. By the time he was ten, he was hooking up with John Glover, whose mother, Ruth, was a friend of Lula Mae. John played an instrument Stevie had not yet tried, guitar, and he could sing pretty well, mainly as an adjunct to Stevie.

"That's why we became friends," Glover recalls. "Stevie, he found me, sought me out. He'd know all the kids in the neighborhood who could play or sing, and he came to me and said, 'Let's jam.'"

The duo informally dubbed themselves "Stevie and John," and they held jam sessions on the stoop with Stevie on harmonica. Soon they were also writing songs, if they could technically be called that.

"They were really more like little song fragments," Glover says. "We had one called 'A Man Ain't Supposed to Cry,' another one was 'Lonely Boy.' We just made up a few lines and put 'em with a melody. 'Cause with Stevie, any song was just a jump-off point, it gave him a

melody and he'd take that melody and make up his own lyrics, just fly
with it all over the place until he was finished with it, which could take
a while. Stevie never seemed to run out of air, or ideas for songs. We
just never finished 'em."

With their repertoire of cover songs and original "fragments,"
they made the rounds of friends' front porches for impromptu jams,
whereupon passersby—"pretty big crowds of people," as Stevie
remembered—would stand three deep and watch, their bodies moving
in time.

"Oh yeah, we were an attraction, people would come from all
around and wait for us to come out and do our thing," Glover notes.
"And, I mean, he knew everybody in the business in town, not personally
but who they were. He knew all about Berry Gordy, Smokey Robinson,
everybody. And I have a feeling he knew something about *me* when
he befriended me, something he thought might be, let's say, valuable."
That "something" was the fact that John's cousin was Ronnie White,
one of Smokey Robinson's cohorts in the Miracles. If Stevie knew this,
he didn't let on.

"Stevie didn't say, 'Hey man, you're cousins with one of the Miracles,
let's play for him,'" says Glover. "He was too cool, too smart for that.
He let me tell him, and bring that up myself. Because that was something
I was going to do, anyway." Finally, in early June 1961, the Miracles
came home and John made contact with White, asking him if he and his
blind friend could come to White's house and do some songs for him.
"He was doin' me a favor, doin' it for the family. I'm sure he didn't expect
to be knocked out. But I knew he would be. Everybody who saw Stevie
always was."

When the young pair arrived, Ronnie was with his fellow Miracle
Bobby Rogers. When they saw the scrawny blind kid with his big
sunglasses going through his head-swiveling movements, Ronnie was a
little nonplussed. Not knowing how one is supposed to make conversation
with a blind person, he almost comically raised his voice, as if Stevie
were deaf instead. "I heard you're a pretty good singer," he yelled.

Stevie, who no doubt had dealt with such overreaction before, easily
parried, politely replying, "Yes sir. I can sing real good." Then, in the next
breath, he gushed, "I can sing badder than Smokey."

Rogers, all these years later, laughs and says, "I never saw a kid as
confident as Stevie was. Usually kids were in awe of us, they'd swallow

their tongues. But Stevie had no fear. You couldn't help but like him. He was a funny little kid. But we had no idea he had so much talent."

Stevie had decided it would be hackneyed to sing Miracles songs back at the two men. Instead, he and John started riffing with their "fragment" "Lonely Boy," with Stevie singing to John's acoustic guitar strumming and adding some sharp harmonica tooting.

"That was cool," Rogers says, "how he accented with the harmonica, like it was extension of his voice. Ronnie and I were impressed, no question about it."

But singing and playing was only part of the Stevie experience. Between songs, Stevie would wax about how much he loved the Miracles' songs, but offered the unsolicited criticism that they could be even better. Recalls Rogers, "Here was this little kid layin' on us that we should've done this or that. Then he'd sing parts of the songs in different keys and tempos and stuff. Ronnie and I looked at each other, like, why are we listening to this little blind kid tellin' us how to do our jobs?

"There was no doubt he knew what he was talking about. And, Stevie, he was a little conniver, he knows how to get in your head and make you remember him. We really didn't know how he could fit into Motown, because Berry was strict about kids finishing school before he'd sign 'em. And he was blind, so we didn't know how that would work. But Ronnie told Stevie he'd come by his house the next day and take him to Motown."

It's telling that Rogers only mentions Stevie as the object of White's attentions, though he actually took both Stevie and John to Motown. Being lost in Stevie's bright light, and generally forgotten, would be something John would become accustomed to, and accept with no hesitation.

"I had no problem with it. I knew Stevie was really the act, not me," he says. "Stevie obviously knew that, but he wouldn't have gone for an audition without me. You know, many years later he sang 'That's What Friends Are For,' and that's Stevie, that's what he's about. He wanted me to audition. In fact, we went there as an act, Stevie and John. He didn't go there that day with the idea of being a solo star."

In truth, being signed at all was the longest of long shots. Record companies rarely offered contracts to anyone their ages, and Berry

Gordy had a particular aversion to signing acts who were not at least seventeen and in clear sight of completing high school—having rejected the future Supremes in 1960 for that very reason. His reasoning was twofold. First, from a purely legal perspective, signing minors by law required that he become their de facto legal guardian until they reached eighteen, a headache he didn't need given that creative people like Gordy often can barely manage to take care of themselves. Then there were the attendant matters of schooling, nannies on the road, insulation from the scabrous lifestyles of the music crowd—among whom there were no altar boys. Maybe worst of all was the meddling of stage mothers.

One such mother, of course, was Lula Mae Judkins, who naturally accompanied Stevie when he came to Motown with Ronnie White the day after the impromptu audition. She was dubious about the whole thing when Stevie breathlessly told her of the opportunity to audition for this Berry Gordy. Not only was she not impressed, having never heard of him, but she shared the reservations of the industry honchos about how showbiz might dampen his education.

Still, how could she have stood in his way of a dream like making records? If it worked out, if he could make a few and have some transitory success as a novelty act, it might even raise some money to pay for him to go to college. And so she let him go to Motown—just as long as she was there to meet this big shot he kept telling her about, to check him out, make sure he was on the up-and-up.

The way auditions worked at Motown, almost nobody got to see Gordy right away. That was normally the last step after a screening process in which one had to pass muster with underlings one or two levels below the summit. On the day Stevie and John came in, September 23, 1961, they, along with Lula Mae and Milton Hardaway, were ferried to 2648 West Grand Boulevard in Ronnie White's Cadillac. Once there, the group walked across the weedy lawn. Stevie, guided by Milton, heard the crunch of new-fallen leaves under the feet of a hectic chain of people coming and going. He could hear the faint sound of harmonized voices coming from open windows upstairs. Once inside the building with the "Hitsville U.S.A." sign, White steered them into an office occupied by Brian Holland, who would have first pass on the kid. Still just twenty years old, the babyfaced Gordy protégé had earned privileges such as this one when he emerged as Motown's third-ranking songwriter—after Gordy and Smokey Robinson. One of the compositions Holland had collaborated on, the Marvelettes' "Please Mr. Postman," was just now entering the *Billboard* Hot 100 chart, en route to its eventual place at No. 1; it was the company's first number one hit and the first Motown single to simultaneously make the top of the pop and R&B charts.

Holland, whom White had told about Stevie, was similarly knocked out when the kid voiced an a cappella facsimile of the Miracles' "Bad Girl," filling the lyrical gaps with saucy harmonica riffing. It earned Stevie a trip to the next level, to see Mickey Stevenson, no less than Gordy's second in command. Stevenson was the head of A&R, which in industry-speak stands for "artists and repertoire" and means the scouting and signing of talent but in Stevenson's case meant, well, everything, including writing, producing, arranging, assigning songs to producers and artists, hiring musicians, and completing others' work that was wanting.

An edgy sliver of a man who will never need a megaphone to be heard, Stevenson was only in his mid-twenties yet had been around the block, once a kid singer himself, when he was nine, before hooking up with jazz bandleader Lionel Hampton's backup vocal group the Hamptones, who shared a marquee at one show with Frank Sinatra. In Detroit, he floated around the clubs and back alleys, running with the same music crowd as Berry Gordy, with whom he teamed up on several records that went nowhere. When Gordy founded Motown and needed a smooth, fast-talking hepcat to be his frontman and shield, Stevenson became his first hire. Other than Gordy, only he had the authority to sign up a new Motown act on the spot.

"Listen, I saw hundreds—no, thousands—of youngsters looking for a break," he says. "I think there were only two or three acts I can remember specifically. The Temptations were one, 'cause I loved those guys. And I remember Stevie because that was a Ripley's [Believe it or Not] thing. Someone brought him into my office and I thought, 'Is this *The Ed Sullivan Show*?' It was like, what's next, the singing mouse?'"

Stevenson, however, perhaps because the details of even that audition are a little fuzzy, seems to believe it wasn't Brian Holland who ushered Stevie in but rather Clarence Paul, his assistant and a swingin' denizen of the Detroit blues scene.

"See, I'm under the impression that Clarence was the one who found Stevie and brought him to me. Clarence was my man, my main man.

We had sung together. Clarence taught me the blues, because I was a jazz guy. He was a very talented guy so I made him my assistant at Motown. And I remember he kept bugging me all the time about this Stevie kid who could sing the blues and play congas and this and that. And I'd tell him, 'Get out of here.' 'Cause, shit, that was too young for me to be dealing with a kid.

"But Clarence, I owed him something because he had really taken me under his wing in the fifties. He was an older cat, like ten years older, and he hadn't produced a hit record for us. He'd taken Stevie on as a project, he believed in the kid. He said, 'Mick, I need something to work with and this is it.' So I said, okay, let's see what he can do."

This chronology departs from previous accounts, in that no one else has placed Clarence Paul that early in the Stevie Wonder stream of events. However, Stevenson may well be right. Asked when she first encountered Stevie, Janie Bradford, the cowriter of "Money (That's What I Want)," says, "Let's see now, he was out on the front lawn with his mother and Clarence Paul. That was before he signed with Motown, before he ever auditioned. I'm sure of that. Clarence was in a position to bring Stevie in to Motown."

Indeed, Paul was such an omnipresent fixture on the city's blues scene that it was only natural that he caught Stevie Judkins from the local talent shows, and if so would have been aware of the young man before Ronnie White had seen him, and got him to Motown first. In any case, whoever opened Stevenson's door that day, there is no debate about the result.

"That little guy, he was really something," Stevenson says. "His talent was out of this world. I'd been a kid singer and he was far and away better than what I was. He was on an adult level with what he could do. He started singing, oh, I don't remember what, but he had his bongos with him and he played 'em like a pro.

"The funny thing is, I didn't even realize he was blind! Not right away. Clarence hadn't told me that part, maybe because he thought I'd sour on the idea before I could see him. And when he came in, he didn't act blind, didn't bump into things. He was wearing those dark glasses, but a lot of guys did because it was the cool look, and he looked at me when I was talking, he knew where I was. I guess he had his brother and his mother with him but he didn't act like he needed help to get around.

"When I realized he was blind, I said, 'Oh shit, how are we gonna handle that?' 'Cause we had stairs in there, upstairs, downstairs. What if he'd fall down the stairs and hurt himself? Berry would kill me. But after he performed, all I knew was he had all kinds of talent. I told Clarence, 'Okay, buddy, he's yours. We're gonna sign him up, it's up to you to get a hit record with him.' "

Normally, that might have been enough to get a Motown contract out of the desk drawer, but there were a myriad of complications because of Stevie's age. Stevenson wouldn't make the final call; Berry Gordy had to sign off on this one. In his 1994 autobiography *To Be Loved*, Gordy recalled that he was eating breakfast on that morning when Stevenson "burst in" and, fairly panting, gushed, "BG, you got to come hear this little kid *now*!"

"I hurried down to the studio," he went on, "and found a young blind kid that Ronnie White of the Miracles had brought in for us to hear. He was singing, playing the bongos and blowing on a harmonica. His voice didn't knock me out, but his harmonica playing did. Something about him was infectious . . . he was only eleven years old and people were already saying he could be another Ray Charles."

With no prompting, Stevie found his way from one instrument to another and, to the amazement of everyone, including Lula Mae, diddled a few random notes on each. It was during this interlude that Gordy apparently made up his mind to sign him—sign *them*, since both Stevie and John were given Motown contracts.

"Yeah, the contracts read 'Steven and John' as the name of the act," Glover points out. "It wasn't like I was chopped liver. I could sing and play, too, just not anywhere near how Stevie could. Besides, I was like 'family' at Motown. It was like how when David Ruffin was signed, so was his brother Jimmy. Martha Reeves's sister, Lois, came in and sang at Motown. It was like that there; if you were family and you had some talent, you'd get a break.

"But, again, their interest was in Stevie. They were gonna let me hang around while I went to school, but they wanted Stevie to do things right away."

Gordy had contracts readied, a process that would take several days while the Motown lawyers codified the approval of the state Labor

Department; under child labor laws, Gordy would need to provide for both boys' education. Under those laws, they would not be paid directly. As with all teenage performers, any royalty and live concert earnings would be deposited into an escrow account and held in trust until they each turned twenty-one.

At no time during the process did it occur to Lula Mae or Ruth Glover to hire a lawyer to represent families' interests, just as it never occurred to parents of any teenage performers in the industry then. This was not only because most young artists and their families were too poor to afford a lawyer. More centrally, few believed they needed one, the assumptions being that Stevenson and Gordy were the credible custodial guardians of the artists' interests that they claimed to be and that making money for one's self naturally coincided with making the company money; thus they all would prosper together.

The ponderous, legalese-heavy details of the contracts were something to be glossed over while training a pen on the dotted line under their names. Indeed, the attendant corollary of this equation was that merely asking a question about something that didn't seem quite right in the contract language might create static, causing the benefactors to perhaps take back the offer. Certainly, the flock that found a home under the Motown roof, all thrilled to no end to be embraced by a man like Berry Gordy, had little doubt about his paternal concern for them. What's more, he could make a salient point: In the hands of these impressionable youngsters, whatever bread was due them would almost certainly evaporate; they would blow it in no time. In contrast, by sinking the cash in a safe and secure lockbox supervised by wise adults who specialized in making financial decisions, the record executives could ensure that the money would be there for them when they were older and presumably wiser.

Gordy was also correct in making the case that his recording artists could only grow if Motown did as a whole. And early on, the company walked a perilously shaky wire; indeed, Gordy had a lot more to lose than the artists. For the first several years of Motown he was essentially broke, having committed everything he made from royalties back into the company; the fact that Gordy didn't claim a profit was the only reason Motown survived. Considering the ancillary costs, it's a wonder he didn't drown in red ink. His enormous overhead included salaries, expensive recording equipment, disbursements to record distributors and promoters, outlays for full-page ads in the music trade magazines (a mandatory precursor for records being given notice and favorable reviews), and for less aboveboard services, to "shmear" the palms of Teamsters bosses to keep record pressing plants running and an uninterrupted flow of records shipping from the docks down by the Detroit River.

The latter arena of activity would for years stoke gossip—never proven—that Gordy was in with Mafia types who, as the speculation went, were cut in on Motown profits, at the risk of Motown being shut down. Then too, as did all record honchos, Gordy by rote lavished "gifts" to radio station program managers and disc jockeys to get Motown product heard on such shows as *Sundown*—which might have been called payola had anyone with authority ever wanted to make an example of Gordy, as they had of Dick Clark in the late fifties for accepting similar charity. That no one did so led conspiracy theorists to wonder if Gordy had perhaps shmeared eager palms on both sides of the law, though it is also true that by the mid-1960s he no longer needed such help. Motown was too big and too self-sustaining by then.

At the beginning, while Gordy outwardly bowed to the necessity to spit-shine Motown's image by buffing his own—such as with a fleet of Cadillacs for himself and his top brass (but not any of his artists)—he was leveraged and invested to the eyeballs. This is not to say that Gordy did *not* rip off his "children," nor that he was alone in that practice. As he had learned from how callously he was treated while writing for Jackie Wilson, showbiz was not a province for altruists.

In lieu of royalty and advance payments—which instead went regularly to the writers and producers—Motown paid its performers with a nominal salary, generally $200 a week. For those under twenty-one, there was less formal remuneration, a couple hundred bucks a month out of Gordy's pocket, payable to an underage artist's guardian. Even so, the pool of royalties due these performers held in escrow would be subject to deductions unspecified by the company for the cost of every recording session at which master tapes would be made, whether they became records or not, as well as for the pressing of any and all records, even those that would be shelved and never released.

Motown, then, was akin to a company store, to which its employees owed their souls. Every one of its artists, from wildly successful to inconsequential, was by contract obligated to Motown as their manager, agent, booker, lawyer, accountant, and whatever else Gordy and his sister

Esther Gordy Edwards could think of. Performers' tax forms were each year filled out for them, which they would promptly sign before the figures were added. Access to the company books was restricted, seemingly under penalty of a slow and painful death, meaning that no performer under contract ever knew exactly what they were earning—a condition that endures to this day, Gordy having survived a myriad of back-royalty lawsuits over the years.

Against this background of plantation-style disparity between have-nots and have-mores entered Stevie Judkins, wide-eyed, naive, and uninterested in these fiduciary details.

According to Lula Mae's version of what occurred after Stevie's audition at Motown, Gordy handed the ball back to his hipster-in-chief Mickey Stevenson, who, she claimed, tried to rush her into accepting the standard five-year Motown agreement. John Glover and his mother signed his copy without delay. But Lula Mae, later saying she was turned off by slick Mickey Stevenson's hard sell, resisted. The paltry salary was one of her concerns. But the biggest was the matter of the trust fund. She asked why she couldn't be the executor of her son's money.

"'We're uncomfortable with that,'" she quoted Stevenson as saying, which she took as an insult, a euphemism for "We don't trust you," which of course was the very same way she felt about *him*. Finding no satisfaction, she said she'd had enough. Grabbing Stevie by the hand in the same way she had gotten him out of Oral Roberts's faith-healing rally, she marched him out the door, leaving the contract unsigned on Stevenson's desk.

This scenario prompts a Stevenson rebuttal that goes like this: "All those conversations took place in Berry's office. I don't think I had any part in that. But I'll say this: we had to dot every 'i' and cross every 't' on that contract to keep from violating the Jackie Coogan Law [on the hiring of underage performers], which went back to the thirties. You had to be extremely careful with these kids.

"As I recall it, if his mother was upset, it wasn't about signing the contract; it was because the contract wasn't ready fast *enough*. I think she had it in her head that Stevie would be in the studio making records that first day.

"Look, I didn't need to con anyone. We were looking to protect him, that's why we had all the lawyers work it all out. Once they did, she came runnin'. That's the truth of it."

Running or not, Lula Mae did indeed return to Motown days later to proffer her signature in Gordy's office, which was crammed with lawyers. Whether she did so because the lawyers had vetted it and it was ready by then, or because Stevie, as she told it, was unrelenting in his pleas for her to change her mind, the important thing was that the standard five-page Motown agreement was under the pen she held in her hand. Stevie, too, was required to sign as the minor party, and he did so by scratching his marker—a big "X"—under the typed-in name of "Steveland Morris," that curious "family name" that Lula Mae never quite explained, the real import of which was that it was *not* Judkins, erecting a legal wall between Stevie's future earnings and the possible clutches of Calvin Judkins Sr. should he stake any legal claim to them.

As laborious as the contract process had been, now that it was done and Stevie Morris was a Motown asset, for Gordy and his collaborators it was the easy part. Now would come a question no one at 2648 West Grand Boulevard seemed prepared to answer: What in God's name were they going to do with him?

Even so, he was there, and that was not an inconsiderable milestone of history. Neither was it small news in his neighborhood.

"I'd lost touch with him because he was gone from church," says Kim Weston. "The next thing I knew, he was with Motown. And when I got to Motown in 1963, he was already a star. A *big* star. Stevie sure didn't waste time, did he?"

4

Jazz, Soul, and Grab-Ass

At first we were told to stay away from [Stevie] because we might be a bad influence.

—*Martha Reeves*

Stevie was a terror, man. You couldn't hold him back. He wanted to do it all. He wanted hits, he wanted girls, wanted . . . wanted the world!

—*Mickey Stevenson*

Tangibly, Stevie Wonder can be called case one in support of Berry Gordy's point about having a salutary, even lifesaving effect on the ghetto fodder that fed his ambitions. No one man, woman, or child ever received as priceless an education in music and life as did the blind kid from Breckenridge Street—an enlightenment that would one day add up to a price tag Gordy never imagined he would pay, but one that would be recouped many times over by Motown. That no dearth of cases supporting the opposite conclusion would be amply demonstrated during Stevie's Motown years—cases with names such as Florence Ballard and David Ruffin, and later Marvin Gaye—is what makes Motown such a confounding and equivocal historical exemplar.

Growing up in this crapshoot of fate, within which a very few would break the bank and very many would come away with little but fleeting fame, no one in the stable had any idea where they were headed, nor how long the journey would last. As Motown took on breath and breadth, however, Stevie Judkins was miles behind the rest of the pack. Kim Weston may be right that had Stevie not been annexed by Motown, he would have reached the same lengths. Still, it was Berry Gordy's benevolent dictatorship, with its talented steerage class, that would breed the most stable and enduring entertainer of the last half century.

It began with a contract that could be the definition of chattel. Artists were due a 3 percent royalty on 90 percent of the retail price of each record sold (reflecting the discount at which records were sold), minus taxes and "packaging costs." In the market value of the times, that would translate to approximately two cents per record sold at seventy-five cents. Thus, for a record that would in a best-case scenario sell one million copies—again, by Gordy's word alone, with no outside auditors to verify it—the artist's share would come out to roughly $20,000. Gordy would pocket the rest—a whopping $730,000—plus whatever else he deemed to cover expenses and costs. A Motown contract—*any* record company contract—was hardly a ticket to ride for anyone but Gordy, who rode on golden wheels.

What's more, the contract terms were harsher for those who could write a good song, a commodity Gordy was always seeking. Songwriting ability, in fact, was the immediate reason why the Marvelettes were signed; they had brought in "Please Mr. Postman," which was written by one of the girls in the group—though when it was released its label also carried the names of three Motown writers, including Brian Holland. Mary Wells was booked passage to Motown when she came in with a song that would become her first hit, "Bye Bye Baby." She was credited as the songwriter, but as with any song written by a Motown employee, including those by Smokey Robinson, Mickey Stevenson, Brian Holland, and Janie Bradford, all its publishing rights, present and future, were given to Berry Gordy's publishing company, Jobete Music. Further, while being credited theoretically meant a writer would be the recipient of royalties, few ever saw any, as monies were held and deducted for expenses.

Whatever a composer of a record made from it was more or less what Gordy was disposed to pay from his own pocket. And by the time it came out, the songwriting credits might be crowded—if in fact the original writer was even still among them. Clarence Paul, who died in 1995 at age sixty-eight, looking back at some of the more unsavory aspects of the company, told writer David Ritz ten years earlier, "Just about everyone got ripped off at Motown. The royalty rates were substandard. Tunes were stolen all the time, and often credit wasn't properly assigned."

As Paul would come to see firsthand, cribbing credits on Stevie Wonder songs would become a common practice. While Stevie would deal with it cleverly, and get more than his share of writing credits, he would exist within the general framework of a closed club, at Gordy's mercy. As Marvin Gaye once explained, "As far as business went, Berry had the publishing wrapped up from the beginning. You could write songs at Motown, but you'd never own any of your copyrights. You'd get paid as an employee—paid very little—but no one except Berry kept any ownership of the songs. We were all helping Berry build his catalogue [which] he understood [would be] the key to his personal wealth."

Like Marvin, Stevie would be no more than an entry on an asset sheet, working not technically even for Motown but rather something called, with anodyne innocuousness, International Talent Management Inc. However, there was nothing innocuous about ITMI—four letters that could send cold shivers down people's spines all around Hitsville. As the unquestioned authority for all matters involving company artists, ITMI, which operated under the auspices of Esther Gordy Edwards, was by default manager and talent agent for each act. In the historical looking glass, ITMI was a monumental conflict of interest, given that its mission was to make the employer rich at the expense of its employees, who were entitled to no outside representation.

Not that in the maw of the times many realized this, or, if they did, that they cared or were prepared to buck the system, which could be grounds for immediate dismissal, at Gordy's whim and subject to no review. Gaye, describing the general sense of fear and loathing within the Motown "family" atmosphere Gordy constantly portrayed it as to the press, was really speaking of the headlock applied by ITMI when he described Motown as a "gestapo. It was a loving gestapo—because Berry is a loving cat—but it was still the gestapo. I was the one guy crazy enough to argue with [Gordy]. Though we were fighting on the same side, I resented his power."

Stevie would take a far more prudent tack in dealing with Motown's "fuehrer"—to whom he would always pay proper deference in interviews, with adjectives like "cool" or mandatory references like "the father of us all." Not that he too did not bridle, silently, at the peonage, or fail to grow increasingly miffed that things would not change for him, materially, for a good decade. His salary of $200 a month, paid to Lula, made no more than a small dent in the family's financial straits, what with nearly every dollar of Lula Mae's salary going to pay the mortgage at Breckenridge Street, yet Gordy would not raise the allowance until the mid-1960s, and then only by a hundred dollars.

Indeed, having obtained a divorce from Calvin Judkins, Lula decided to turn for comfort, but mostly aid, to Milton's father, Paul Hardaway, who now was divorced and bringing up another son named Larry. After rekindling their past relationship, they would marry in 1962, with Paul and Larry moving into the house. Soon after, she became pregnant, and gave birth to a daughter, Renee, late that year.

By then, Stevie had become almost a stranger there. Between school and Motown, where the bus would drop him every day after school, he wouldn't come back in until late at night when one of Gordy's chauffeurs would take him home. Lula Mae would try to lay down the law to him, and he would promise to be home at a decent hour, but he simply couldn't tear himself from the musical milieu on West Grand. There, he had quickly fused into one of the crowd, providing Lula Mae good reason to worry. Having observed the denizens of Motown more than a few times, she could rightly believe that Stevie had exchanged one set of hoodlums for another.

The grizzled, hard-bitten Motown sidemen considered themselves indentured servants. They made little more than union scale—$11 per session—and Gordy worked them, as he did his artists, over long and grueling hours. To make matters worse, the dungeon-like atmospherics they labored in—far from the spotlight and rarely praised or even mentioned in public by Gordy—made Studio A seem like a leper colony.

Most of them habitually sucked on an endless chain of unfiltered Marlboros and Lucky Strikes, told the filthiest jokes, and had pistols tucked into their waistbands, a defense mechanism carried over from the clubs where after-hours was often a walk on the wild side. Of them all, the most enigmatic was the utterly peerless bass player James Jamerson, a scowling young man with a mustache who plucked the thick strings of his big upright or electric Fender Precision Bass, eccentrically, with nothing more than the index finger of his right hand, which he called "the Hook," and with no other instruction needed than to control the beat as he wished, which he did with a vascularity and itchy brazenness that found not only the beat but the bone and marrow behind it, propelling a song to its sonic capstone. Yet for all his innate genius, or perhaps *engendering* it in overcompensation, he stayed clammed up, as if in a trance, lost in private thought, sucking dry one bottle of whiskey after another. No one really knew why he was so tortured (he was known to be embarrassed at having a clubfoot), nor did anyone care to ask. Such reticence may have been wise, given that a story made the rounds about the time someone tried to mug him, only for Jamerson to whip out the gun he carried in his waistband and wind up robbing and pistol-whipping the mugger.

The wildest of the sidemen, however—and, as it happened, Stevie's favorite—was drummer Benny Benjamin, a monster on drums who could nail a beat blitzed on booze, heroin, or both, as he was likely to be when he could make it into the studio, a feat he managed with decreasing frequency as the years passed. Benjamin could ladle the beat with jazz- and Caribbean-rooted overtones, rolls, flourishes, and fills of every kind, his round, scarred face contorted into a terrifying glower interrupted by an occasional burst of incoherent babble. One day in the studio, apparently in delight after a kicking take, he blurted out a faintly Spanish-sounding word, something like "papacito!" Stevie happened to be in the studio at the time and took to repeating it, without a clue what it was supposed to mean. Then he began address-ing Benjamin as "Papa Zito," which soon became the drummer's moniker. Benjamin, in turn, pegged Stevie as "Little Papa Zito."

Over the years Stevie would pay homage to Benjamin only fleetingly, once allowing that he was "a cat who took me under his wing." But in truth the effect the drummer had on him burrowed deeply into his musical palate. In the 1970s, when Stevie did drum tracks on some of his album sessions, the metered cadences of the snare would be, to those who could perceive such things, eerily reminiscent of Benjamin's own. Benny took such a liking to him that often the gnarled hepcat and the emaciated blind boy could be seen together, eating lunch or combining on improvised riffs in the studio, Benny either tapping out a beat to Stevie's voice or Stevie taking the sticks, seated in the big man's lap, his hands being guided through the beat. Observers would giggle at the incongruity, how the boorish Benjamin would curtail his gruff and bluff ways when the kid was around. Some would wince, thinking about what Papa Zito might have been teaching Little Papa Zito, not about the drums but about, well, God only knows what.

All of the Motown acts shared the Funk Brothers, but each had its own producer in the studio. The first assigned to Stevie was another music maven he respected, Clarence Paul. Born as Clarence Otto Pauling, Clarence and his brothers formed a gospel group as teenagers in North Carolina that later reformed as the blues-oriented "5" Royales, who in the late 1940s scored a No. 1 R&B hit, "Baby Don't Do It." Paul, who truncated his name to establish an identity separate from his brothers, served in the Korean War and upon his return settled in Detroit, writing and recording blues tunes through the 1950s before hooking up with Mickey Stevenson as a duo. His life spent mostly on stages, in recording studios, and in blues clubs, by the time he got to Motown he was in his thirties, and well acquainted with the sum and particularly the substances of the music lifestyle.

In recalling Paul, Stevie would ennoble him in brief homilies, such as the time he said, "I worked with a gentleman named Clarence Paul," adding that Paul was "the first one to really spend some time working with me. Clarence was like a father, like a brother, and a friend. . . . [He] loved me like I was his own son."

This is essentially Paul's epigraph. Though he would work with virtually every big Motown act, including Marvin Gaye, the Supremes, and the Temptations, he never found the right alchemy with anyone other than Stevie. Accordingly, he would endure in history as more than a producer or mentor. Choker Campbell, the bandleader on most of the Motown road tours, in Nelson George's 1986 Motown chronicle *Where Did Our Love Go*, said that "Clarence [was] like Stevie's daddy. They should recognize Clarence as being the man that really guided Stevie the right way." Surviving Motown spectators recall Paul with minor variations of that theme. To Kim Weston he was Stevie's "surrogate father," to Janie Bradford his "caretaker," to the sole surviving Temptation, Otis Williams, his "chaperone."

Paul cultivated that deep a relationship by forming a connection with Stevie's family. "That was important to his mother," says Mickey Stevenson, "and she was the key to it all because Stevie really loved his mother and whatever she said was the law to him. So she had to be convinced constantly that we were doing right by him, and Clarence did that.

"Clarence would constantly talk to her, tell her what he wanted to do with Stevie, brought her into the planning and everything. He even suggested she should write songs with him. Now that was damn smart, 'cause it made her feel like she was a Motown person, too. And damn if she didn't actually write songs with him, too. He would bring 'em in and want to record 'em."

Paul, who seemed to know that his work with Stevie was likely his only chance to rise on the Motown company ladder, threw himself into the job. Within weeks of Stevie's entree at Motown, he was bypassing Breckenridge Street altogether to stay in an apartment with Paul, who was at the time newly separated from his wife, Barbara. Paul would get it on with lots of women while Stevie noodled on the keys of a piano in the living room, patiently waiting for Paul to finish his other business. When the fireworks were done, Clarence would come out in his bathrobe and go back to working with Stevie on chord progressions and blues singing.

Having been assuaged by Paul about his plans for Stevie, Lula worried less that Stevie would fall in with the wrong people at Motown. As she saw it, Paul was the one redeeming factor that could put her ease about what Stevie had gotten into.

She wasn't alone in her admiration for the man. As Otis Williams recalls, "What I remember most about Clarence Paul was how cool he was. I mean, he'd been around the block and back, he had that swagger about him, that strut, you could tell he knew what he was talkin' about. For me, meeting him was a real thrill, more so than meeting Berry, because I had grown up listening to Clarence when he was with the '5' Royales, and I loved the '5' Royales.

"I always liked being around Clarence because he wanted to help out all the acts. And he knew that the Temptations were struggling in '61, '62. He came to us with a song, a blues song, a cover of Nolan Strong and the Diablos' "Mind Over Matter," and he went in the studio and cut it on us. He even had it released not as a Temptations record but with us as the Pirates. We even went onstage dressed in these pirates' costumes with the puffy shirts and patches and all that. Clarence came out on the road with us when we'd go and sing it.

"Yeah, the pirate thing didn't work, the record tanked. The whole thing was embarrassing and we quickly went back to being the Temptations. But you know what? I still give him credit for shakin' it up, doing something different. Clarence even did a country-western album with the Supremes when they were struggling. He was full of ideas, and not all of them worked, but he made you think—you had to, 'cause Clarence was a highly opinionated man. But he was a very nice man, too."

Williams lets out a laugh. "I don't know where he got all them ideas, but I'll tell you one thing, Clarence smoked a lot of weed—a *hell* of a lot of weed. But then we all did that back during those days."

Lula Mae didn't know about Paul's pot-smoking habit, and that might have changed her mind about him. In 1985, Paul came clean about his and his cohorts' proclivities. "There were lots of drugs around Motown in the early sixties," he told writer David Ritz, "just like there were lots of drugs around any black neighborhood. Marvin [Gaye] and I did our fair share of cocaine beginning in the early sixties. We were into it early on."

Holding little back, he went on to chronicle that "Marvin's nasal membranes were funny and he couldn't snort as much blow as some of us. He'd get a freeze by rubbing it over his gums, and then he'd eat it."

No matter. Gaye became as hopelessly hooked on blow as Paul. As he too would fess up to Ritz, "I've been tooting for a good twenty-five years," and "I like the feeling. No one will ever tell me it's not a good feeling. A clean, fresh high, 'specially early in the morning will set you free—at least for a minute."

Paul did make a pointed exception about his former protégé. "Other artists, like Little Stevie, hated the stuff," he said, though even those words were passively damning, since they meant that Stevie sampled the white powder as well, though exactly when was left unsaid.

As it happened, Stevie never did become a slave to drugs, mainly because of several terrifying experiences in future years. Some of his most intensely personal songs would have harrowing drug imagery and themes of horror and dissipation, and were recorded roughly at the time Clarence Paul and Marvin Gaye were defending their unconditional surrender to coke. As it happened, Stevie did give in to addiction, of the sexual variety, but this was easily kept buried, one of the rewards reaped by Motown from its early marketing strategy that positioned Stevie as cute, incorruptible, unthreatening, and antiseptic—white America's favorite little black boy.

Surely, no one on the outside would ever have imagined that Motown's soulful altar boy had ever touched a drug, a boob, or an ass in his adolescent years. "Let's put it this way." says Mickey Stevenson, "we made Stevie into an image. It was up to him to live up to it."

With Gordy, everything was about image. His own was as a patriarch, or at least a benevolent despot—Big Daddy with Big Brother tendencies. He hung in his home a cheesy wall-sized oil painting of him in the guise of Napoleon, his face transplanted onto the body of the French general, his hand jammed into a brass-buttoned waistcoat. He would often play the part by lecturing his young and frisky troops about upholding the Motown public facade of class and cleanliness, so that they could be cast as a new generation of inner-city blacks, clued in and aware of the world around them but nonthreatening to the white majority in voice and manner. By doing so, he could dream and plot about putting those black artists on stages in high-toned supper clubs and Las Vegas hotels.

In 1962, Gordy adopted as the commercial trademark for Motown "The Sound of Young America"—pointedly not "Young *Black* America," the face of Motown being black in pigment and innate rhythm, not intent.

Yet he was no one to talk about morals and values, being an unreconstructed philanderer and gambler. And because he was, Motown took its moral cues from a man Marvin Gaye called "the horniest man in Detroit," who "married blacks and fooled around with whites," and who "you'd think was working, but he might be freaking with some chick right up there in his office."

It was as if his sleaze was the plasma of their blood. As Marvin Gaye put it, "Berry liked to play, and since Berry was the leader, we followed the leader," though Gaye was actually, for a time, the exception to the rule, rather shy and insecure about sex and assiduously faithful to Anna

Gordy, who at seventeen years his senior was more of a maternal presence than a wife, until their marriage fell apart in the 1970s.

That was not the case for Gordy's adjutants Smokey Robinson and Brian Holland, whose marriages were the last thing on their minds when they were prowling for warm and willing females. In time, all three would wind up having affairs with one particular female, who not entirely by coincidence would wind up as Motown's biggest ever star and the biggest diva in the world. This, of course, was Diana Ross, who in 1961 was known just as Diane Ross, another bit of flotsam in the Motown ocean, floating with her bandmates Mary Wilson and Florence Ballard in a struggling girl group, the Supremes.

The Motown cast aside, Martha Reeves's observation that Motown artists were admonished about becoming a "bad influence" on Stevie is a hoot. If anything, given Stevie's experiences on the street and in the catacombs of 2648 West Grand Boulevard, such a fiat might have actually made more sense the other way around.

In 1961, Reeves, who with her group the Vandellas had come to Motown with acts like Marvin Gaye, Lamont Dozier, and David Ruffin from Gwen Gordy and Harvey Fuqua's Tri-Phi label after it went under, was awaiting her break by working as Mickey Stevenson's secretary. An oft-repeated story is that she agreed to "babysit" Stevie for a few bucks a week. But Reeves disputes that was the case.

"I never was Stevie Wonder's babysitter," she says vehemently. "Like everyone else, I liked being around Stevie, and he liked being around me because he loved to be around singers." She recalls that he would "come over to my house after sessions at Motown. He knew and loved my family just like [his own]. It wasn't like he was a little blind kid. Stevie would beat everybody up. He was taller than most of them [and he would] tear my mama's house up."

Mickey Stevenson enjoys a good giggle at the babysitting canard. "Listen" he says, "I gotta believe that if he let Martha take him home, it's because he thought there was something good waitin' for him there, if you know what I mean."

Stevie certainly knew. In fact, it seemed that to the kid no Motown woman was off-limits. He had indeed grown by leaps and bounds, shooting up just in 1961 to around five feet eight, though still skinny as a thimble, and as Otis Williams says, "Stevie liked the girls." Actually, "liked" is a little mild, as could be discerned watching him interact with the women of Motown.

"Stevie had roving hands," notes Williams, "He would grab girls' behinds or their breasts. They'd say, 'Stevie, stop that,' and he'd go, 'Oh, I'm sorry, I didn't see you there, didn't know you were standing there.' And, you know, he was little Stevie so he could get away with it. He'd walk away with a big, shit-eating grin on his face."

Or as Mary Wilson put it in her 1986 memoir *Dreamgirl: My Life as a Supreme*, "Stevie Wonder was immediately accepted into the Motown family, and he came into the studio all the time. Learning every inch of the place, he eventually got to the point where he didn't need help getting from room to room. Stevie always seemed to know who was standing near him, and one of his favorite pastimes was to run up and pinch young ladies on their bottoms."

Because, as the refrain went, it was merely Stevie being Stevie, and as Wilson says, "Everybody loved him," such miscreance was taken as harmless gamboling, which to Stevie was like a free pass to an amusement park. What's more, it was impossible to get pissed off at the happy little tyke with the outsized talent.

"I don't think any other guy could have gotten away with what Stevie did," says Janie Bradford, who was an eyewitness to his full routine from the reception desk. "Stevie was a cut-up, a prankster. If one of the girls, like Mary or Martha, were in the room Stevie would stroll over and say, 'Oh Mary, that's a pretty yellow dress. Love that little bow on the shoulder.' He must have had it all planned out, conspired with Clarence or somebody where they'd tell him what she was wearing. It would freak people out because he did it so naturally. He'd have people whispering to each other, 'Do you think Stevie can see?' I mean, I figured out what was going on and *I* wasn't sure he couldn't see.

"Stevie targeted me a few times with his pranks, too. I used to have a big jar filled with pennies on my desk. Stevie knew it from our conversations—he could shake the jar and have a pretty good idea how much was in it. And one day he was standing there and all of a sudden he grabbed the jar and ran. He was outside in the front yard before I could catch him—he knew those stairs and doors better than I did with my eyes wide open. When I caught him and took the jar, he said, all pitifully, 'Janie, you're not gonna take a poor little blind boy's money, are you?' And people are lookin' at me, like, how could you do such a thing? Again, he had it all figured out, but he didn't get away with it, not that time."

Given free rein to come and go as he pleased, he sometimes would wander into the studio, not knowing the "do not enter" red light above the door was lit. On one such occasion, Mickey Stevenson was in there conducting a session. "He came bursting through the door," Stevenson recalls, and when the kid realized what was going on, "he started making funny faces at me and turned the place upside down."

Stevenson can laugh about such intrusions now. Back then, like for other Motown producers, they caused much friction, and entreaties were made to Gordy to keep Stevie's movements somehow tethered. Even Clarence Paul, when working in the studio with other artists, blew his top when it happened. Years later, with a bit of euphemistic slack, he told *Newsweek*, "He was a pest. He'd come by at 3 every day after school and stay 'til dark. He'd play every instrument in the place and bust in on you as you was cuttin' somebody."

Paul another time insisted he had actually not been as sold on Stevie as everyone believed, and that he began working extensively with him mainly because "didn't nobody else want to be bothered." He went on, "But I would listen to him. He'd start something on the piano and I'd show him something else to try. He started paying attention, because every time I'd tell him to do something, it sounded good. Then I started going in the studio [with him], letting him do drums and organ and things like that."

Gradually, in these incremental steps, the sum and substance of Little Stevie Wonder began to coalesce. Once that happened, his know-it-all attitude only worsened.

"One day in the studio," Paul recalled, "I was at the piano trying to teach him a tune and he was singing it, but he was playing another tune on the high end of the piano. I made him quit that. Then he started blowing another tune on the harmonica while playing a different one on the piano, and I took that away. Boy, he was mad. He was mad enough to cry."

In the tunnel of history, this sort of empirical improvisation can today be seen as the genesis of techniques used not only when the Motown sound grew more sophisticated—with separate musicians playing different ends of the spectrum on the same instrument, such as piano or bass—but also in Stevie's highly experimental 1970s compositions. Back then, however, it was seen as no more than an annoying waste of time as producers went about trying to crank out two or three finished songs in an hour of studio time.

For Stevie, such time constraints simply did not exist. "The thing about Stevie," says Mickey Stevenson, "was that you couldn't get him to go home. He wouldn't leave Motown. You'd almost have to drag him out. He was like a lot of the kids then, Motown really was his home. It wasn't only for the music. These kids, a lot of 'em, had problems at home and at Motown they had a family that cared about them.

"We didn't know much about Stevie's home life, but, you know, you'd hear things. Evidently there was some static with the father. But when Stevie set foot in Motown, that was in the past. It was a relief to be there, he was comfortable from day one."

Already fielding complaints on a regular basis, Gordy had his own reason to be irritated with the little wonder. Stevie, "being Stevie," would sneak into Gordy's office and, knowing exactly where the phone was, issue edicts over the intercom, speaking in a dead-on imitation of Gordy's high-pitched, singsong voice. Looking back, Gordy could laugh, something he didn't do in real time. Stevie, he once said, would call the studio and, posing as Gordy, tell them to give Stevie one of the portable tape recorders kept there for the use of producers and engineers. Stevie took home two of the machines and lost them both. Hip to the scam by now, Gordy bought him a cheaper model, for which he docked him an "expense."

Stevie, though, would not let up on the imitation, and would do it so often in front of Motown people that it unnerved Gordy, so accurate was Stevie in reproducing his semiliterate manner of speaking. Remarkably, for a prominent songwriter, Gordy had not learned to read or write on a high school graduate level. Just as remarkably for a man with strong ties to the civil rights cause—he would release an album of Dr. Martin Luther King's "I have a dream" speech, and in later years record spoken-word albums by Langston Hughes and Amiri Baraka—he knew alarmingly little about world history. Once, when a discussion turned to the Holocaust, he was genuinely surprised to learn that six million Jews had perished. "Really?" he asked. "Did that happen?"

While Stevie had not an ounce of malice when he'd launch into his Gordy impersonation, Gordy always felt as if he had been exposed as some kind of ghetto hood masquerading as a corporate executive and, more importantly, that others would see him that way. Stevie, rarely for him, didn't pick up on these vibes, but it may have played a part in Gordy's impatience about seeing whether the kid really did belong on the Motown roster after all.

That John Glover wasn't to be a part of the plan for Stevie could have been a sticky issue for Stevie, if not anyone else at Motown, had not John made it easy for them. Fully knowing that Gordy had no real use for him, John took the graceful way out.

"Like I say, Stevie was the act, and Stevie was the ambitious one," he says. "And I went along really to get Stevie goin', so he'd have a break. My whole thing was to get some future attention at Motown, and here I had a contract at thirteen, fourteen years old, which was more than I could ever have dreamed about, so I was happy with that. I could wait. I went to school, got better as a musician. Besides, I wanted to do my own thing, not just be in Stevie's shadow. He had to make it his way, and I had to make it my way.

"I was at Motown, anyway, all the time. I'd hang out, play guitar sessions—including some of the early Stevie Wonder sessions. I knew I'd have my own Motown career. But for Stevie, the time was now."

The first Stevie Judkins recordings were booked for Studio A in December 1961, with considerably less enthusiasm from Gordy than when he signed him. Gordy, in fact, had become convinced that Stevie's voice, which had a tendency to whine and crack at the higher registers, was too watery to carry the weight of a song. Instead, he would inflate into gimmickry the kid's versatility as a musician. For this schema, Gordy believed the usual three-chord, four-by-four R&B beat would constrict too much of Stevie's virtuosity. The more limber and freestyle digressions of the records he used to sell in his defunct jazz store offered a better showcase, and he put Clarence to work composing some of the only jazz, or at least pseudo-jazz, songs Motown would ever record, all earmarked for Stevie.

Paul disagreed with the entire concept, and with hiding Stevie's vocal abilities, and the two men engaged in loud arguments about it. But a soldier like Paul had no chance against Napoleon, though he did extract from Gordy a commitment for a series of such recordings, making the case that they couldn't possibly release a jazz single by an unknown black kid. What they needed, he said, was an entire album with which they could present Stevie as a formidable artist, not a one-shot novelty.

Paul's proposal would turn on its head the normal procedure for releasing an album—most albums, at least on the rock side of the ledger, were a reward for having a hit single, and would be slapped onto a hash of filler—but Gordy assented. Paul also persuaded him to fudge the title a bit so as not to shut out Motown's prime audience, but the title they settled on—*The Jazz Soul of Little Stevie*—was an awkward oxymoron, a mystifying force-fit of two nearly mutually exclusive idioms.

Paul, to his credit, attacked the project head-on, and, wanting Stevie to be more than a bystander in its development, gave him a far greater role than most Motown artists had when material earmarked for them was composed. Though Stevie was not a student of jazz, nor of writing music, he embraced it as a challenge and wrote a couple of songs with Clarence that would make it onto the album.

Another collaborator was the obscure Marvin Gaye, who had become tight with Stevie and whose own Motown apprenticeship under Clarence Paul was slow and indecisive—his debut recordings, still months away, would have him cutting Broadway show tunes and pop evergreens, so insecure was he about how to sing soul music. Gaye was also writing with Paul, and one of their songs, "Soul Bongo," found its way onto the Stevie album, on which Gaye also played drums on some of the sessions, continuing the role he had aced on the Marvelettes' "Please Mr. Postman."

Of the nine tracks on *Jazz Soul*, four were cowritten by Paul and Hank Cosby, a horn player and arranger who performed both of those jobs on the sessions, the latter particularly crucial since he would need to transcribe clinical sheets of notes and chord changes into arrangements with a "feel" of a generational wunderkind, all fresh and new and swingin'. The last track would be a Berry Gordy tune, "Bam."

Gordy was a laissez-faire kind of producer, who let sessions take on fuel and fire according to the instincts of the veteran musicians culled from the Paradise Valley clubs. Far more detail-oriented and particular, Paul was not content to rely on Stevie to memorize lyrics simply upon his reading them to him—which was necessary to do, since Stevie could only read Braille and no one at Motown knew how to write it. Instead, Paul rigged a crude telecom system comprising a microphone that linked directly to one earpiece of modified headphones worn by Stevie when he would lay down his vocals. In the isolated room used for vocals, Paul would stand as far from Stevie as he could, so as not to have his voice picked up by the live microphone, and whisper lyrics, two or three lines ahead, as Stevie sang. Adding to the acoustic confusion of this division of his attention, Stevie would be listening to the recorded instrumental track in his other earpiece. How he could concentrate on getting the words thrown at him while keeping the groove of the melody is, well, a wonder.

But even Stevie would complain that it was too unwieldy a system, and that he sometimes couldn't hear or understand what Paul was whispering to him. Fortunately, by the mid-1960s Motown chief engineer Mike McLean would build a better mousetrap, wiring up a remote audio connection from the producers' control booth to Stevie's headphone, meaning that Paul could stay in the booth and loudly call out the lyrics.

As far as Stevie's playing went, Paul gave him the freedom to tailor his parts on harmonica, piano, organ, or bongos as he saw fit. To the astonishment of the hard-boiled pros in the room, Stevie seemed to know and be prepared for every chord shift and progression.

"See, Stevie just worked so hard, 'cause he had to, bein' blind and all," recalls the guitarist Eddie "Chank" Willis. "Everyone else had the chords, the lyrics, everything on paper. Stevie had to memorize it all and Clarence would have gotten all the different little changes in tempo, beat, whatever.

"Clarence was the one who really spent a lot of time with Stevie. I remember in the beginning, Stevie would always have his mother with him. She'd bring him in and stay there all day waiting for him to be finished with what he was doing. But then, after Clarence took him under his wing, he was his caretaker, the mother stopped coming 'round. And all the time he was with Clarence, Stevie would be learning something.

"I'm sure Stevie could have played with us. But Clarence didn't want him to be under that pressure, and also didn't want him to be buried by the other instruments—remember, this was before all that separate tracking, everyone played on one track basically and the vocal would go on another, maybe they'd put the bass or a guitar part on a separate track but that was it. So Clarence had Stevie play his parts later and then overdub onto the master tape, which they called 'ping-ponging' back in them days, 'cause you'd bounce a track from one tape machine onto another tape machine, mixin' it all together.

"And Clarence did a great job, 'cause if you listen to that album you'd think Stevie was right there in the room playin'. But then too, that was how good Stevie was. He had to listen to the track through head-phones and play his harmonica or bongos or whatever with the same feel and same tempo, and blend in with Benny on drum and me on guitar. That's not an easy thing to do. It's hard enough for guys who've been around a long time. It took years for the Funk Brothers to mesh to where we could anticipate what, say, Benny was doing and not miss a beat. It took Stevie like one session to do it.

"Yeah, working with Stevie was a trip [big laugh]. *Really* a trip—'cause Stevie would be trippin' over chairs, microphones, amps. He'd be walkin' into walls, walkin' around in circles, and it was funny. It was always a lot of fun with Stevie, and he'd laugh at himself. 'Cause all he wanted to do was be in the studio. The kid would never go home. He *hated* to leave. So he was there a lot, learnin', always learnin'. And you'd have to say it paid off, now didn't it?"

Jazz Soul, if a tad uneven, came out as a cohesive, high-octane product. Working off the thematic epistle of the title, Paul and Cosby didn't try to create genuine jazz, merely a "jazzy" rendering of blues-rock faintly approximating soul. Most tracks were perfectly infectious, seasoned by Benny Benjamin's saucy Caribbean beats and the by-now-manda-tory Motown signatures—a deep and nervous bass at the bottom and stabbing horns at the top, all of it echoed into a dewy slab of rhythm. While technically an instrumental album, its calling card of youthful exu-berance was punctuated by sundry shouts, hoots, and sometimes brief exhortations of impromptu, incoherent lyrics.

The opening track, the Cosby-Paul "Fingertips," was big-band-style foam that parted for, of all things, a flute solo. Hard to fathom as it is given the subsequent version of the song that would define him, Stevie does *not* play harmonica on it, doing a turn on the bongos. The harmonica is saved for the Cosby-Paul "Some Other Time" and "Paulsby," which begins with a harmonica solo, on Paul's "The Square," and on Gordy's bluesy "Bam," and on each of these it peals with a froth and spine that even today seems indivisible from the full bloom of Wonder's later harmonica work. Stevie's drumming is tight on the Cosby-Paul "Manhattan at Six," his organ nimble on "Paulsby" and on one of the numbers he'd composed with Paul, "Wondering." On the other of those, "Session Number 112," he alternates from piano to organ to harp.

Pastiche that it was, the LP hung together well, and Paul placed Stevie's parts on a separate track within the primitive three-track recording scheme, so that there would be a degree of isolation to them even as the band played all at once, as was common until more sophisticated multitrack technology became the industry norm in the mid-1960s. *The Jazz Soul of Little Stevie*, when heard today, is a bracing, refreshing curio that seems like a perfectly reasonable unveiling of a preteen prodigy. Bruce Eder and Ron Wynn of the superb Allmusic Internet database call the work "still an amazing musical document," "rich and diverse," and "extremely sophisticated instrumental music for its time," adding that "the 'jazz' reference in the title is not a matter of optimistic convenience or self-aggrandizement—a lot of this is legitimate jazz."

In real time, however, Gordy, whose idea it was, gave it orphan treatment. He could see no real upside to releasing it, there being no track he could first send out as a single to fuel its sales—a requirement he had after all agreed to waive when he gave the go-ahead for the album. Paul took the decision to shelve it for now, or until he could come up with a single worthy of release, as a betrayal, but there was an upside for him. Given the green light for another album project for Stevie, now he would be able to get his voice on tape, wailing the blues.

"The blues was Clarence's meat," says Mickey Stevenson. "He taught me what it was all about in the fifties. And it ain't as easy to sing as the young kids thought. Clarence taught you what he called the 'colors' of the blues. You'd start with gospel and take it to different places while keeping the main color the same.

"That was the root of all Motown songs. I like to say that Motown never released a blues record, that all Motown records were pop records, and it's true. But there's more to it than that. We didn't make pop records, either—we made *hit* records. What I mean by that is, we made pop records into hits by using rhythm and blues elements, not the usual white teen idol kind of trash. We always had the blues element, because after all that is our heritage; it's mine, it's Berry's, it's Stevie's. Making it fit into pop, that was the trick, that was the *real* Motown formula, and nobody else could get it.

"The fact that Stevie was schooled in the blues by Clarence went a long way to shaping what he would become. And Stevie was ahead of the game to begin with, because he can see colors in his own way. But even with Stevie, as with most of the artists, it took time."

For Stevie, it would take more time. Because, in another blow to Paul, Gordy again rode herd on the concept for the next album, which would not be straightforward blues but another loopy gimmick—introducing Stevie as a scion and legatee of the most famous black singer and musician in the world, simply by virtue of his color and handicap. Gordy's title for the project, *Tribute to Uncle Ray*, seemed to Paul something less than a tribute to Stevie, and an oddball move for sure, since Ray Charles was neither a Motown artist nor was his repertoire of jazz, big band, and country-flavored blues any way commensurate with Motown.

Though Paul couldn't see how this concept would behoove Stevie, Gordy's order was inviolate, and Paul in early 1962 accepted the unenviable chore of choosing Ray Charles songs both hits and otherwise amenable to adaptation by an eleven-year-old street blues singer.

By the time he and his fledgling returned to the studio, a more critical adaptation had taken effect. When Stevie came in, it was with a new identity.

5

"Take a Bow, Stevie"

Listen, Stevie operates on a different plane than everybody else.
He didn't mean to be a pain in the ass; he was just a different
breed of cat. You can't understand Stevie Wonder unless you're
Stevie Wonder.

—*Otis Williams*

In 1962, when Clarence Paul and Stevie returned to the studio
to begin work on Stevie's second album, it was still well before
there was something as quantifiable as a Motown "sound." Yet the conditions, the process, and the raw material were there from the start, as
was obvious in the deep echoes and ringing chords smoothing out the
rough, granular textures of such early records as the Miracles' "Shop
Around." That record, released late in 1960 on Gordy's Tamla label,
one of the first to be distributed nationally by Motown itself, became
the company's first Top 10 pop hit and first No. 1 R&B hit (and first
million-seller, at least according to the Motown publicity releases), and
carved the template for all Motown writers and producers.

Gordy, who demanded an authentic R&B kick to his early product,
at first had artists sing live right along with the band. Soon he would
move Motown toward state-of-the-art equipment and multitracking
techniques, making it easier to hear just what the musicians were doing
and how incredible they were, but no matter how polished and technically perfect the record, they would never lose the "live" feel. This live
jazz and blues rooting explains why those primordial Motown grooves

still activate wild foot-stomping and shameless sing-along impulses in people, who are simply unable to act their age when Motown is on the radio.

By the time Stevie came through the Motown transom, the label had at the very least fused a new kind of R&B, and was putting out records by gifted artists almost as soon as they were signed. Within a few months, Stevenson signed up Mary Wells. Smokey Robinson would write and produce her, taking both Wells and Motown to lofty heights.

That year as well came two acts with clear promise. One was a group of four teenage girls, the core of which, three girls named Diane Ross, Florence Ballard, and Mary Wilson, had grown up only steps from Stevie Wonder, in the Brewster-Douglass projects. The other was a male quintet for whom Ross, Ballard, and Wilson had been originally alloyed to sing backup, though that never happened as the two groups went their separate ways. These were the Primettes and the Primes, respectively, who after they were signed were promptly rebranded as the Supremes and the Temptations.

The third leg of what by the end of the decade became the three legs of the stool that was the Motown empire came into being when the somewhat irritating but always wondrous blind boy was handed his new persona.

As Berry Gordy tells it, the recasting of Stevie Judkins/Morris can, like most things Motown, be laid at his office door. "I don't really remember it, but Esther [Gordy Edwards] told me that one day in the studio, watching Stevie perform, I said, 'Boy! That kid's a wonder,' and the name stuck," he wrote in his memoir *To Be Loved.*

However, like most things in Gordy's memory bank, the retrospection is rather gauzy, and is contradicted by other voices. Elsewhere in Motown literature, the dawn of that new day in American pop culture was ushered in by Clarence Paul, who in booking some early gigs for Stevie in the local talent shows and sock hops had him billed as "the eighth wonder of the world." One day, engaged in shop talk with Mickey Stevenson, so another story goes, he said, "Mick, we can't keep calling him the eighth wonder of the world," then had an alternative: "How about Stevie the Wonder?"

As usual, Stevenson has his own take. "What happened was this," he begins. "At the beginning Clarence was always saying, 'Mick, you gotta see this kid,' and I'd tell him, 'Okay, okay, bring this wonder kid in here.' So when we were looking for a name we could record him under, I remembered that, about the wonder kid."

He recalls the conversation going like this:

Stevenson: Why don't we call him "The Wonder Kid"?
Paul: "Wonder Boy."
Stevenson: There's already a Wonder Boy. Batman got him.
Paul: "Stevie the Wonder Boy."
Stevenson: Sounds more like a circus act, like he's gonna pull a truck with his teeth.
Paul: Maybe we should just keep callin' him "Little Stevie."
Stevenson: How 'bout "Little Stevie the Wonder"?
(After a pause, in unison): "Little Stevie Wonder"!

Then there is Paul's version, given in the 1980s. In this take, it was he who came up with the new name during a session with Stevie recording a song Paul had written with Stevenson, "Thank You, Mother," apparently as a paean to Lula Mae, though it would later be changed to "Thank You (For Loving Me All the Way)" when it was used as the B-side of one of Stevie's early singles. A few days later, on a Sunday, the tale goes, the two men accompanied Stevie to what would be his first live performance, at a Saginaw resort called Shay Lake, where the "show" took place on the back of a pickup truck. In introducing Stevie to the "crowd" of a few dozen, Mickey applied the "Little Stevie Wonder" tag for the first time in public. Whatever its origins, the new sobriquet seemed almost providential—among the tracks on *Jazz Soul* was "Wondering." While Gordy wondered if perhaps it was a bit too contrived and cheesy for a prospective top-line act—an object lesson seemed to be an original Motown artist who was saddled with the name Singin' Sammy Ward, which did nothing to lift him from obscurity—Gordy was anything but certain that Stevie Judkins Morris would amount to much no matter what the embellishment.

So Gordy signed off on Little Stevie Wonder. The cover of the Ray Charles homage would bear the title *Tribute to Uncle Ray* in large letters, with the last two words lit up in red, a kingly crown atop the "R." Underneath was a color picture of Stevie seated on a stoop against an antiseptic background, in black slacks and a white shirt, a harmonica held at the ready under his chin, the mandatory wraparound smile on his face, huge dark glasses over his eyes—a mini-Ray in every detail. To the right, in letters half as large as those in the title, it read "Little Stevie Wonder."

That Calvin Judkins could not have been held in any lower esteem or higher contempt than by Lula Mae was borne out in the book *Blind Faith*, which dealt with Stevie's abhorred father as one would with ringworm: once cut out of the pith of the Judkins family in those pages, he ceases to exist, until almost as a forget-me-not wraith many years later. This left the impression that he may have knocked around somewhere beyond the periphery of their lives, never again to intrude; neither has Stevie ever been moved to venture any supplemental detail of the father he has recalled only skeletally.

Record-keeping is sometimes hazy and incomplete for black men of the day who made little of themselves and lived from bed to bed. Given such a vacuum, it is possible that Lula, with Stevie's help, created a tidy, charitable record for Calvin that would tie up his time on earth with a nicer bow. In *Blind Faith*, his sudden reentry, on the next-to-last page of the book, has the authors reporting that "everyone turned out for Mr. Judkins's funeral in 1976, including Lula," and that Stevie had generously "bought his father a new Cadillac" three years earlier. Lula, letting bygones be, was quoted saying, "I still say he's the best-looking devil God ever put on this earth."

However, according to death records and obituary notices, it seems not everyone turned out for a Calvin Judkins Sr. funeral. In fact, no one may have attended, as there may not have even been a funeral. Not then, anyway. Certainly, there is no trace of Stevie saying anything about it in interviews from 1976 and beyond. It is possible, therefore, that if Calvin did not intrude through the years, it could have been because, strange as it seems considering the later scenario, his fate had been sealed earlier.

John Glover, for one, has an entirely different story of Calvin's last mile, or at least its last few feet. "I don't exactly know when it was, I think it was early, just after Stevie had been signed to Motown," Glover says. "It was all over the neighborhood. Stevie's dad was crossing the street, got hit by a car, and was killed. It was only about two or three blocks from Stevie's house on Breckenridge. I don't know if [Calvin] was living in the neighborhood or not, or if he had any kind of relationship at that point with Stevie, because Stevie never, ever talked about him. I never knew anything of what happened between them until much later. That was something Stevie put out of his world. When kids would get to talking about their fathers, Stevie would tune out. It was like his father didn't exist."

If this take is the right one, perhaps Lula Mae thought it too tragic to relate. But at the time, there must have been a bit of what-goes-around-comes-around irony in the fact that he had breathed his last lying broken and helpless on a cold street not far from the streets where he had forced her to sell her body. And yet she evidently wasn't so coldly indifferent to Calvin that she would have been prepared to let city authorities simply dump the man she once loved into the bowels of a potter's field with the other bums. There *was* a funeral, as Glover also recalls that Lula arranged for a proper service, and brought her sons to see him lowered into the ground—which they likely did with little emotional investment, though for Stevie there had to be memories and a few fleeting tears for the father he should have had, the man who had taught him music and brought him candy before he would clench his fists and betray his craven, empty soul.

Such an involuntarily residual attachment may well have been why all the songs Stevie had had a hand in writing until now bore as a writer's credit the name "Stevie Judkins," which of course he had eschewed at Lula Mae's insistence when he signed his Motown contract. Asked about this anomaly years later, Stevie would say, referring to Calvin, "I signed the [early] songs contracts in his name but I don't know why." Henceforth he would sign them "Stevie Wonder."

Gordy's goal was to prime Stevie's public acceptance as a familiar kind of blind act. It was cynical, and undersold Stevie's talent, far more than Clarence Paul believed was wise. But, given his orders, Paul again threw himself into the assignment, though in his hands it would be more primal in its blues undertow than Charles's jazzy orchestral renditions.

"With Clarence, the blues was always the bottom line, which sometimes put him at odds with what Berry and I wanted Motown to do, which was not to release blues records," says Stevenson. "Berry believed, and I backed him up, that a blues record would never become a number one hit on the pop chart. We didn't want Motown to become just another black blues label putting out records heard by three people, just for the sake of making 'black' music.

"So Clarence had to adapt, and what he did was, he would create 'colors' of the blues, keeping it lighter but keeping it real. He'd always have these passages of hard, gritty blues underneath the pop hooks. It's a tricky thing. Sometimes it works. Sometimes it doesn't."

Paul gleaned six Charles-penned tunes—"Hallelujah I Love Her So," "Ain't That Love," "Don't You Know," "Drown in My Own Tears," "Come Back Baby," and "Mary Ann"—and sprinkled in undistilled blues numbers, one by him and Stevie ("Sunset"), one by Gordy ("My Baby's Gone"), along with the traditional folk song "Frankie and Johnny" and the 1939 standard "(I'm Afraid) The Masquerade Is Over."

Once more, Paul and Hank Cosby navigated with care some un-Motown-like turf, greasing the way for future Motown "tribute" albums marrying Marvin Gaye to Nat King Cole and the Supremes to Sam Cooke. In fact, *Uncle Ray* was a rousing trip, with Stevie busting a gut amid Cosby's arrangements of pealing brass, booming drums, and Charles-style jaunty keyboard runs, as well as a dead-on copy of the Raelettes' gospel-flavored backing vocals by the Motown background trio, the Andantes. (Another element, intriguingly for blues and jazz applications, was an ethereal flute that ducked in and out of most of the tracks.) Stevie merrily careened from torchy ballads to up-tempo stompers, trying hard to emulate Charles's characteristically choppy cadences and garrulous growling notes but straining to hit some notes in too-high keys. In "Sunset," cut in doo-wop style, his emotive wailing made him sound just like the leather-lunged Arlene Smith, the lead singer of the R&B girl group the Chantels, especially on lines like "I turn my head to hide the tears in my eyes." On the jazzy "Hallelujah I Love Her So," he transposes himself for Charles, with a musky murmur repeating how his girl whispered in his ear, "Stevie, everything's all right."

That he was hormonally ready was evident, and he was more than up to this not quite logical project, just as with the previous one, in the space of two albums expertly splitting his time as a multi-threat instrumentalist and a kid who could stand toe to toe with no less than a man called "the Genius." And for all that effort, he still had gotten exactly nowhere. To Gordy, the results only reinforced how much the kid deserved his new moniker. But Gordy was in the same bind as before: no cut on *Uncle Ray* was discernible as a marketable single. "Sunset" was deemed the best shot, and made it to one of the regular Friday meetings of the inner circle, when the latest records faced a group vote on possible release, subject to Gordy's final decision. When Paul was told it didn't make the cut, he was livid.

And why not? After having worked so strenuously with Stevie, he became convinced that Gordy was playing games with him and his twelve-year-old charge. It was as if Gordy's cold feet about Little Stevie Wonder were more accurately a matter of a cold heart, that Berry just didn't believe he could sell Stevie, and that there was no place for Paul in a burgeoning Motown dominated by younger writers and producers.

But Gordy had his reasons for being reticent, worried as he was that Stevie might lose his cuteness—and, with it, his appeal—when puberty hit full force, the way Frankie Lymon's nascent voice lost its sweetness and most of its melodiousness in his midteens. Even if the public went for the high-pitched girlish tonality of Little Stevie Wonder, would they stay with him as just Stevie Wonder? Would it not be better to wait to hear what he sounded like at thirteen or fourteen? All that Gordy had done with Stevie so far had been the result of playing hunches. Putting the boy on the shelf now could have been another, done swiftly with a cold lack of emotion. However, Mickey Stevenson says this was not a real possibility.

"Berry was a big believer in timing, that you couldn't force something if the timing wasn't right," he notes. "But understand something. It's not that he didn't believe in Stevie. He did. We all did. We knew we had something special. That's why he was trying different concepts for Stevie. Okay, they didn't work, but we kept on trying, maybe find something that would fit his voice better. That's the thing. We never stopped trying. With Stevie. With the Supremes. With the Temptations. All you really want to do during a development period is to keep the act alive, keep its name alive and out there, get 'em on a record every once in a while, while you waited for the right thing to click."

And so Gordy moved ahead with the Stevie franchise, such as it was, shifting strategy to seek a stand-alone song that could be released as a single independently of an album. Both Gordy and Stevenson were adamant that Clarence Paul continue overseeing him, and that the single be in his hands. Paul, in turn, took an ambitious step of his own, creating a "concept" 45 rpm record by cutting the same song in diametrically different ways on each side.

The song, cowritten with Hank Cosby, was called, cheekily, "I Call It Pretty Music (But the Old People Call It the Blues)," though technically it was neither. Rather, it was a middling pseudo-blues riff recorded at a fever pitch on the "pop" side of the disc, as if raw volume could overcompensate for its shallowness. Stevie, of course, took it to the max, his zealous vocal keeping up with a bombastic rhythm section, this time with Marvin Gaye on drums doing his shuffle beat. The rapidly paced pop version—"Part 1"—was the A-side, and it followed the template of most early Motown songs with its strict verse-break-verse structure and eminently danceable beat.

Stevie's polished vocal could elevate such pabulum like the opening lines: "I was sittin' in my classroom the other day / Playin' my harmonica in a mellow way." If he kept it real with some gritty harmonica blasts and an exuberant "whoooo" on the break, it was really on the B-side— "Part 2"—that he let loose with full-blown blues, amid a tempo slowed to a crawl and his harmonica playing sad and mournful. Taken together, the two sides of the record are a virtual primer of blues in transition into pop—the hybrid creature that would by the mid-sixties fuse into the vernacular as "soul music."

Released on August 16, 1962, with the catalog number Tamla 54061, Stevie Wonder's debut single loitered just beneath the interest level at which disc jockeys would spin it regularly, but was played just enough to put it on the *Billboard* singles chart, coming to rest one notch out of the Hot 100 in the early fall. It wouldn't make it to the R&B charts.

For Gordy, that was a reasonably rewarding near miss. In fact, as a first single, "Pretty Music" did better by far than those of the Supremes, Temptations, Marvin Gaye, the Miracles, and Martha and the Vandellas, none of which left any mark at all on the pop or R&B charts. Thus even a tepid charting now led Gordy to dust off the two shelved Little Stevie Wonder albums and send them onto the market, hoping the embryonic word of mouth about Stevie would keep growing.

With a three-quarters shot of a laughing Stevie looking ultra-cool in a white cardigan over a black dickie, *Jazz Soul* was released in September, quickly followed a month later by *Uncle Ray*. Striking hard, Gordy also rushed out, on October 3, a follow-up single with yet another new concept, pairing Stevie in a duet with Clarence Paul on a pop-blues song written by the latter, "Water Boy." The label of the disc carried both names as the artists, while the flip side, Paul's "La La La La La La," was listed as Stevie's alone. This confusing, schizoid proprietorship hardly helped cement Stevie's budding persona. "Water Boy," a tamer, more jumbled derivative of "Pretty Music," was dead on arrival, never to scrape the chart.

Not waiting for the results, Motown on the day after Christmas issued still one more Stevie record, "Contract on Love," backed with the song Paul had believed so deeply in, "Sunset." This was perhaps not by accident, since in choosing "Contract" Gordy looked away from Paul, trying to buy Stevie some luck by alloying him with the hot Brian Holland, who had done so well for the Marvelettes, and giving "Sunset" some daylight was quite likely a sop to Paul. (Who may not have been entirely mollified. Three years later, producing an album for Motown's top act, *The Supremes Sing Country, Western and Pop*, he had them cover none other than "Sunset").

The assignment of Holland to write a Stevie Wonder record, in fact, is a significant signpost, it being one of the first times he collaborated with Lamont Dozier, whose failed singing career had led Gordy to shift him to the songwriting-producing side. (The first product of their union was perhaps the Supremes' "Time Changes Things," the B-side of the trio's fourth Motown single, "Let Me Go the Right Way," released, and soon to flop, as a single in November 1961.) Both men were strong melody-makers, and though Dozier could come up with a song idea from a stray phrase either verbal or at the keyboard, neither was an accomplished lyricist. Needing help, they went to the young woman who had fleshed out the lyrics of "Money (That's What I Want)," as well as "Time Changes Things."

"Actually, as I remember it," recalls Janie Bradford, "when Brian and Lamont called me in, the song ['Contract on Love'] wasn't being written for Stevie. It wasn't written for anybody. Most of the songs written at Motown at that time weren't. We'd write them just to write a good song, and later we'd sit around and say, 'Well, maybe this sounds like so-and-so would be good for it.' Maybe for Brian and Lamont, they had Stevie in mind, but for me it was just another generic song. There was nothing special about it, there still isn't."

She wasn't alone in that judgment. Even sweetened with background vocals by the original cast of the Temptations, pre–David Ruffin, "Contract" was a dud. Not pop as much as pap, it buried Stevie's strained vocals in the mush of a bossa nova beat that had by then become a boilerplate Motown affectation, peppered with a New Orleans-style honky-tonk piano *and* an organ line. Assuming the role of a cad, an out-of-character Stevie sang, "Now that I know the score / No one's gonna hurt me no more."

It was a curveball, all right, but to no effect. The personification of "bad boy" Stevie appealed to no one, and "Contract" was here and gone in a few weeks. Now, after a year and a half of varying strategies, Gordy was at an impasse. If there was an upside to the act, it was that Stevie was killing out on the hustings, in concerts that had progressed from sock hops to one-nighters fanning out from Detroit to Cleveland and eastward to D.C. and Philadelphia. Accompanied by Clarence Paul, who served as his handler and musical director, he would rack up reviews, full houses, and ample box-office receipts that Paul would bring back to Gordy (the money going not to Stevie but to his trust fund, less "expenses"). All this opened a new avenue of viability. It also quite probably saved Stevie Wonder's career.

Stevie's ascension as a live performer came with impeccable timing. That very fall, as it happened, would see the inauguration of the ambitious Motortown Revue, a bus caravan of Motown's top acts into big cities and through the hinterlands. The Revue, as it was assembled under the aegis of Esther Gordy Edwards, would cover familiar inner-city stages on which black entertainers had performed for years, while adding mainly white suburban venues like armories, high school gymnasiums, and American Legion halls. It would also traverse the perilous turf of the Jim Crow South, a real risk for Gordy—though nowhere near the real peril faced by the young black troupe on those back roads—but critical to Motown's crossover designs given the buzz, and sales, the shows could generate in each sphere the tour passed through.

That maiden tour set out on October 23, 1962, for a fifty-six-day trek that would blow through thirty-six cities, a brutal itinerary that would leave only four days without a show. Forty-five performers, musicians, roadies, and assorted other Motown personnel climbed aboard two old, wobbly buses and set sail for the first gig, three days later at the Howard Theater in Washington, D.C. By the time the tour reached its ornamental climax with ten days of shows at Harlem's venerated Apollo Theater, it would seem like they had lived several lifetimes.

But the revue would be of inestimable value. Some acts would break out, none bigger than the Contours, whose screaming dance record "Do You Love Me" was lifted into a smash hit along the way, and Marvin Gaye, whose sexually turbocharged, pelvic-thrusting theatrics made women in the audiences act insanely.

It was also a molto big deal for Stevie, whose electric stage act qualified him for a seat on the bus, though in an adjunct role, listed not individually on the theater marquees but among the lesser lights identified only as "And Others"—which included the Supremes and Martha and the Vandellas. Another, the Temptations, would only get a call for the Apollo shows, to sing backup for Mary Wells. Actually, Gordy didn't realize the trouble he'd be getting into by putting Stevie on tour for two months, away from his schooling, and should have known better considering the legal hashing that had had to be done in signing him.

In effect, Gordy dumped the prickly logistics of Stevie's navigation throughout the tour in Clarence Paul's lap. Paul would go along as Stevie's caddy and musical director, and it would be his responsibility to know which cities had ordinances prohibiting underage performers from going onstage after a certain hour; in those that did, Stevie would have to be moved up in the order. As it happened, though, Paul's main function would be to keep Stevie from hogging too much stage time. Once he was onstage, Stevie paid little attention to the one-song-and-off orders. He'd almost always be so carried away with extended harmonica solos that the next act, waiting in the wings, would take to frantically motioning to bandleader Choker Campbell to cut off the music, though even that would not have stopped Stevie from pushing ahead.

Because the audiences would be so caught up in Stevie's reverie, Campbell would refuse to stop the band, leaving it to the overburdened Paul to sheepishly amble out onstage, grab Stevie, and yell in his ear to cease and desist. When Stevie would ignore the command, as he usually did, Paul would have to take him firmly by the arm and lead him offstage, earning a cascade of boos and catcalls. It was a ritual both

Stevie and Paul hated, and it caused friction to grow between them. As much as Paul tried to explain that the shows were really geared for the big-gun acts like Smokey and the Miracles (who were even allowed to skip the tour bus and ride in their own Cadillac), the Marvelettes, and Mary Wells—they were, after all, being paid around $400 per week during the sojourn, nearly twice as much as the rest of the acts—Stevie wouldn't get the logic. "But look at 'em, *listen* to 'em," he would whine, meaning the audiences that went wild over him.

Those bigger acts had their own feelings about the crowd's reaction to the kid, and they were not felicitous. For all of Gordy's bromides about the Motown "family" esprit de corps, where everyone was supposedly pulling for everyone else, it did not go over well with many that Stevie was stealing shows. Now he was less of a team mascot and more of a rival. On the bus, the usual good-natured ribbing of him turned more acrid as the tour stretched on. Stevie, whose energy never gave out and who never seemed to sleep—unlike everyone else, his rest cycles were not conditioned by sunlight giving way to darkness—would shift restlessly in his seat, fingering his harmonica, playing tunes in the darkened bus.

While this might conjure up a kind of old-time, front-porch blues aesthetic, for his fellow Motown travelers trying to get some shut-eye it was just plain irritating. And it never seemed to subside. Otis Williams, whose Temptations weren't on the bus for that first Revue, tells of the exact same kind of nocturnal static occurring on subsequent Motown tours.

"Oh, man," he says, "it would be two or three in the morning and Stevie would be in his own world, it's like he was the only one on the bus in his head. And we would really get pissed off. We'd yell at him, 'Stevie, cut that shit out! We got a show tomorrow, we gotta get some sleep.' He'd just laugh and go on playing—sometimes he'd even play his bongos! People would call out, 'Stevie, I'm gonna kick your ass if you don't stop.'

"Eventually, he'd cut it out, he'd get it that people were upset. See, I just think if he had a melody in his head, he had to play it, 'cause then it would be stored in his memory or something. Again, Stevie is on a different wavelength than everybody else. You don't try to figure him out; you can't."

• • •

That there was some tension in these interludes was not unusual, considering that nerves and tempers became frayed in conditions suited for a cattle car. The heaters on both buses conked out early and several in the troupe caught colds. Others became nauseous from the bumpy ride on rusty axles. Progressively, the buses in fact felt and smelled like cattle cars, with stenches, known and otherwise, choking the air. From the back, where the musicians spent the long hours playing cards, came clouds of reefer smoke. Because the buses ran on a tight schedule and were always late, they stopped only sporadically for food and bathroom pit stops.

While there was some canoodling between Motown men and women right from the get-go, in spite of the warnings from the middle-aged matrons sent along as chaperones, by the end of the first leg of the journey, through the Northeast, most of the company were pretty much tired of one another. However, when the road led them south of the Mason-Dixon Line they were grateful they had one another in places where they could feel sentiments ranging from chilliness to outright loathing from outside the bus.

Suddenly, they began seeing "Whites Only" signs at restaurants and gas station bathrooms, forcing them to hold it in and stay hungry and thirsty until facilities could be found in the "po' folks" section of town. At concerts in some towns, police tape or ropes segregated whites and blacks in the audience.

If Motown's mission was to unite the races through the medium of music, such surreal scenes proved it was quixotic in 1962, and it would remain that way for years to come. It was still a year before Mississippi would see the murders of Medgar Evers and civil rights activists Michael Schwerner, Andrew Goodman, and James Chaney, whose car was dumped into the Bogue Chitto swamp after the three men were shot to death. It was three years before the Civil Rights Act and a decade before lynchings were outlawed in much of the South. Indeed, Martha Reeves would tell of the eerie feeling on the bus when the Revue hit the very ominous-sounding Lynchburg, Mississippi, and she recognized from history books the infamous "Hanging Tree" on which hundreds of blacks died. "There was not a leaf on it," she said, as if confirming the tale that, as she added, "no leaves had grown on it for twenty years."

Adding to the sense of unease, they weren't only riding over the tracks of the Ku Klux Klan on many of these roads, but doing so in the ultimate symbol of the civil rights battleground, in which blacks were ordered to the back seats and "uppity" blacks rode as "Freedom Riders" in protest. In fact, since few rednecks had a clue about what the "Motortown Revue" banners on the bus referred to, the entertainers were sometimes taken for hordes of Freedom Riders.

This was exactly what Gordy had feared would happen when he gave the go-ahead to the tour's promoter, the Atlanta-based Henry Wynne, to book dates in the South. And at times things became very dicey. Once, after they pulled into a gas station to use the john, the flannel-wearing attendant welcomed them by saying, "Y'all niggers better get out of here," then went and got a double-barreled shotgun to speak for him. By pure, divine luck, two cars driven by state troopers came upon the grim scene and, if not exactly acting heroic by overruling the red-neck, at least gave the riders safe escort back onto the highway.

Even more terrifyingly, in Birmingham, Alabama, shots seemed to ring out in the night after a show at the National Guard Armory—a happy event indeed, as it was the first time the audience there was integrated. Some believed the sound was just rocks being thrown hitting the side of the bus, but when Choker Campbell screamed, "Them's bullets!" everyone scrambled to get aboard the buses. Mary Wells, who had fallen on the bus steps and couldn't get up, was nearly crushed in the stampede and kept moaning, "I'm shot! I'm shot!"

Stevie, luckily, was standing with Clarence Paul or else God knows how he would have gotten on the bus in the rush of human flesh. After driving a few miles, the driver stopped and got out to check the bus. He noticed two holes in the "Motortown Revue" banner on one side—with a bullet inside each hole. In relating the episode, Stevie noted that the shots "just missed the gas tank." If they hadn't, the bus they hit would have been a fiery tomb for half the performers of Motown, including Little Stevie Wonder.

The southern nightmare wasn't over yet. On November 20, two days before Thanksgiving, the tour was in Greenville, South Carolina, when the tour manager, Thomas "Beans" Bowles, and a roadie named Eddie McFarland left in a car to do advance work at the next stop, in Tampa. McFarland fell asleep at the wheel and collided head-on with a truck, crushing the entire front end of the car and killing himself instantly. Bowles, riding in the backseat, was pinned by twisted metal and chrome and when pulled out was barely alive, both of his legs and one of his arms broken, a flute he'd been holding jutting from the back of his neck. It would require months of hospitalization before he was taken off the critical list, whereupon he fully recovered.

Upon hearing of the deadly accident, the troupe was dazed and almost numb, and many just wanted to go home. Back in Detroit, Gordy seriously considered canceling the rest of the tour. But there was just too much to lose by doing that. The Revue was a cash cow, to be sure—Bowles and McFarland, in fact, had been riding with $12,000 in cash, proceeds from the last show, in a satchel that, incredibly, was recovered from the wreck with not a scratch on it. Canceled dates would mean forfeiture of thousands in fees, thousands more in box-office receipts, and an incalculable loss in potential record sales. And so the tour went on, and at Christmastime the tattered and battered performers rolled into New York for the Apollo run and managed to put on ten days of spectacular shows in the mecca of black entertainment.

That engagement itself was buffeted by the pressure of high expectation and the burden of low endowment. After checking into the Hotel Theresa, they rolled up to the famed theater and as they got to the stage door a black guard greeted them by asking, "Who the hell are you black motherfuckers?" Other black people on the street, seeing the "Motortown" sign on the buses, grumbled about the "Detroit niggers." Apparently, they learned, regional racism didn't only apply to white regions; it existed among their own as well. The Apollo itself was a shock. The landmark where Duke Ellington, Count Basie, Louis Armstrong, James Brown, and others members of the black entertainment elite had played to rabid crowds for decades was in disrepair, a dimly lit, fetid-smelling mausoleum with peeling wallpaper and dirt wherever one looked. The lower-billed performers—Stevie among them—were assigned dressing rooms that required a five-story climb up a narrow staircase. As Clarence Paul led Stevie up that exhausting incline, rats scurried at their shoetops. If some could appreciate the grime and crud as a kind of romantic sediment from their forebears, most only saw grime and crud.

Stevie was among the former—though it was clearly to his advantage that he couldn't see what the Apollo looked like from the inside, his perspective carved entirely by the ghostly vibes he felt bouncing off those dirty walls. This stage had been the site of recordings by the bluesmen he revered, which he heard on *Sundown* all the time. Stoking his sense of excitement was that Gordy would be recording, on film and audiotape, the Revue during the Apollo gig, for a concert movie to be shown in theaters and a live album.

Not that Stevie needed any inducements beyond simply going out on a stage, any stage. But his performance on the grainy black-and-white films and rough, poorly recorded albums of the Revue at the Apollo show him in full Stevie mode. Clad in black slacks and shoes and a light jacket, he was led out on the arm of Clarence Paul to a spot in front of a chair at stage center. With Choker Campbell and his big band massed behind him, he would begin with a minute of extemporaneous harmonica fiddling. (Campbell had given up trying to get Stevie to play a specific tune when he came out, so often had he strayed from the set song to do his own thing, and had simply instructed the band to vamp as best they could with what he was playing.) Then Paul would return, picking up a set of bongos that had sat on the chair as he lowered Stevie into it and jamming them between his knees so seamlessly that Stevie lost not a beat replacing the harmonica-blowing with bongo-tapping as he launched into whatever song had been chosen for the show.

At the Apollo, Stevie was slotted between the high-energy Marvelettes and lower-energy Mary Wells—a placement she hated, having to follow two firecracker acts. The song alternated from show to show between "Pretty Music" and "Don't You Know," the latter from *Uncle Ray.* For these shows, too, Gordy had ordered, with no ifs, ands, or buts, that Paul keep him to no more than a minute of run-on time after the song was supposed to be over. But that was the rub. Because Stevie was hip to the order, he would intentionally *not* end it, instead going into his extended harmonica solo *before* the final verse, meaning he would have to return to it sometime.

Gordy, who flew to New York for the Apollo engagement, like the Motown performers who had waited in the wings during the tour wildly waved his arms, not at Choker Campbell but at Paul.

"Goddamn it!" he yelled. "Drag him off!"

Some who were there can recall when Paul literally had to do that, clutching the collar of Stevie's jacket with one hand, the other hand pushing so hard at the small of his back that Stevie's feet would almost be dangling off the floor as he was cradled by the much larger Paul. It would happen so violently that the bongos and harmonica would be left strewn on the floor in their wake.

Stevie always lit into Paul when he did that, and would in spite seem to dawdle even more at the next show, as if daring Paul to come and get him. It became such an obvious undercurrent that many in the audience began to assume it was part of the act, a bit of shtick borrowed from James Brown's signature encore ritual of having a guy come out and drape a shawl over his shoulders and begin to lead him away, only for him to break away, throw off the shawl, and go right on wailing the daylights out of a song.

But it was no joke to Gordy, Paul, or Stevie; it was a real bone of contention. Gordy was so adamant about getting Stevie off the stage in a prompt manner that beginning in 1963 he'd have Paul onstage from the start, ostensibly as Stevie's personal bandleader, but he was actually situated mere feet away so he wouldn't have to walk out, which always made it look like a setup and opened Paul up to the mandatory boos from the house.

Indeed, with clever calculation as usual, Gordy now planned to use the dynamic of the act, the spillover in time and the interruption of it by Paul included, for commercial gain. As it would turn out, *big* commercial gain.

During the first five months of 1963, Gordy had Paul take Stevie into the studio and cut more songs, none of which either man deemed worthy of release. In the afterglow of Stevie's Apollo performance, the window of opportunity to cash in was left open because of the movie and album made of the last show in the run, but it would soon close if no Stevie product hit the streets. And so, half in desperation, half in opportunism, Gordy went back to the tape.

He surely had lots of it on his shelves. Gordy often recorded his acts doing live performances, his reasoning twofold. First, he could judge how "real" they were as soul-based performers, and how well they connected with audiences; and second, he was constantly seeking to build up stores of live material for possible release, as with the *Motown at the Apollo* albums, which would be issued from 1963 to 1965 and with a finale in 1969. It was just such tapes of Stevie's earliest live gigs that had helped convince Gordy to send him out on the Revue.

Now, reviewing those nearly six-month-old tapes, he listened long and hard to one that had been made at a trial-run Motortown Revue show in mid-June 1962 at Chicago's Regal Theater, a regular stop for Motown acts since 1960. The Regal, sitting in the heart of the Windy City's "Bronzeville" jazz/blues-club corridor, at 47th and South Parkway, was the midwestern version of the Apollo, a columned, Byzantine structure with impeccable and very "live" acoustics. As such, it was an ideal recording environment, with sound waves coming off the walls being fanned into different directions. Musicians compared the sound in the hall to the explosion of a giant water balloon.

Stevie, who at the time was completely unknown by the audience, it being a month before "Pretty Music" was released, was introduced by Motown emcee Bill "Winehead Willie" Murray, who briefed the crowd about "the young man who is only twelve years old" who "is considered as being a genius of our time," asking for a "nice ovation as we meet and greet Little Stevie Wonder, how about it?" After Clarence Paul had helped him into his seat and headed over to conduct the band, Stevie began to intone in his girlish voice, "Yeah, yeah," and announced he would be doing "a song from my album, *The Jazz Soul of Little Stevie*. The name of the song is called, uh, 'Fingertips.' I want you to clap your hands. Come on, yeah! Stomp your feet, jump up and down. Do anything that you *wanna* do!"

But there was a new wrinkle to "Fingertips" tonight. After making his little peroration while tapping on the bongos, he put them aside after only seconds and began wailing on the harmonica, replacing the passage of the song that had given it its name with long and sophisticated harmonica bursts that perfectly meshed with the red-hot, horn-heavy constructions of the band, which included Marvin Gaye on drums. Clearly this had been a decision made beforehand, possibly by Paul, who never was content with the bongo bottom line on the song after he'd recorded it in the studio, believing it made the song sound like a hokey semblance of Caribbean jazz-lounge music.

After around three minutes, Stevie suddenly interrupted his playing by injecting some contemporaneous pseudo-lyrics, crowing the soon-to-be-immortal church pulpit command "Everybody say yeah!" followed by a collective "Yeah!" from the audience and the extended byplay that streamed on as if it were a sweaty tent-show revival meeting— "Say yeaaah!" ("Yeaaah!") *"Say Yeaaah!"* ("*Yeaaah!*"), "Yeah!" ("Yeah!"),

"*Yeah, yeah, yeah!*" Then came, "Just a little bit of sou-ou-ou-ou-oul, yeah yeah yeah yeah yeah yeah . . . Clap your hands just a little bit louder . . . Clap your hands just a little bit louder," and a brief a cappella turn when, accompanied only by rhythmic clapping from the crowd, he went on, "I know, I know, yeah, everybody had a good time . . . just one more time when I come by, so be advised."

Then, after the orchestra peeled away, leaving only the metered clapping of the audience to the ghost of the beat, Stevie launched into an impish harmonica morsel of "Mary Had a Little Lamb," with a little wiggle on the last note, to howls of laughter from the crowd, especially the little girls.

Now, as the band struck up a final chord, emcee Murray bellowed, "How about it! Let's hear it for him, Little Stevie Wonder! Take a bow, Stevie."

The orchestra played a crescendo and Clarence Paul ambled out and began leading Stevie away, only to have him break free and return to center stage, where he resumed airing out his Hohner. The band, which had begun playing off-music, stopped for what would be a few very confusing seconds—and music history bliss. As each act had its own musicians, Stevie's began to gather up their instruments and sheet music, but seeing him come back, they sat down again and picked up the beat, joined by several members of Mary Wells's band, one of whom, bass player Joe Swift, looking bewildered as he plucked errantly at his strings, asked no one in particular, loud enough to be heard, "What key? What key?"

As the musicians got themselves together, Stevie broke into some more unscripted verse—"Come on! Back to back, back to back, back to back to back. I'm gonna go now. Gonna go yeah and dance . . . just swing it one more time."

It was now around eight minutes into this number, and Stevie showed no sign of wanting to quit. But here Murray once more stepped in, repeating what he'd said a few minutes before: "How about it! Come on, let's hear it for Stevie Wonder!"

Paul was there again now, again leading him off, and this time Stevie went along, waving and beaming to the audience he had left limp and drained—no doubt to the consternation of Mary Wells. For his trouble, Paul was given an encomium by Bill Murray: "The other young man who was responsible for the arrangement, and conducting, was Mr. Clarence Paul."

It was surely a strenuous ten minutes, something like spontaneous combustion—or was it? For decades now, speculation among Motown academics has had it that the whole shtick was in fact concocted, the ad-libbed lyrics indeed scripted, even the surprise encore and the changing of the bands done for effect.

Mary Wilson came away with no doubt that Little Stevie's set at the Regal was a "choreographed ploy," though not necessarily on Stevie's part. His breaking away for the unscheduled encore, she says, was really not a breakaway at all. Rather, Paul had actually "pushed Stevie back onstage."

For his part, Paul, holding to the theme of an extemporaneous chemical reaction, looked back years later and explained it this way: "Man, I'd never heard noise so loud. It scared me. I picked him up and took him off the stage. But them kids were hollering and he wanted to go back onstage. He jumped right back out there."

Neither has Stevie Wonder deviated from that exposition about what went down that night at the Regal. Nor should he. The Immaculate Conception endures without need of further review, too.

Whether parts of the show were recherché, Gordy was stunned when he heard the tapes. Although he wanted more discipline out of Stevie on future Motortown Revue tours, the raw aural power and puckish image of the kid stayed in his mind. Now when Paul could find no new single that aroused him, he came up with yet one more concept for Little Stevie Wonder: a *live* single, a most rare commodity in the record business, both then and now, which would be the centerpiece of an ensuing live album, whittled from recordings made at the Regal and other venues.

Given the length of the number, Gordy was able to split the record into—à la "Pretty Music"—Parts 1 and 2, each pared to a manageable run time of around three minutes. Part 1 was nipped just before "Mary Had a Little Lamb," at which point Part 2 began. The latter was the side that mattered, as it showed off Stevie's bluesy call-and-response lines and the nervy excitement and "confusion."

With Gordy listed as nominal producer, Motown on May 21, 1963, released "Fingertips—Part 2" (maybe the only single ever on which the flip side was officially the one designated to be played). Generating nothing but buzz wherever it was played, its infectious grooves caused a nationwide stir. By the week of July 7, it had broken into the *Billboard* Top 40 chart. By the week of August 10, it was ensconced at No. 1, replacing the Tymes' "So Much in Love." The second Motown record after "Please Mr. Postman" to be king of the vinyl mountain, and the first live record to get there, period, like Stevie when he was on a stage it refused to move, staying there for three weeks before being pushed out by Lesley Gore's "My Boyfriend's Back." At the same time, it sat at No. 1 on the R&B chart, a first for Little Stevie Wonder.

This was nirvana in Gordy's crossover dreams: a "race record" powerful enough in what it *didn't* need to say to make an important statement to African Americans, such as the hundreds of thousands who gathered on the Mall in D.C. to hear Dr. Martin Luther King that month and danced to the tune when it was played over loudspeakers, and at the same time endearing on a mass scale among Caucasian Americans. And yet Gordy expected none of it, admitting decades later in his memoir, "We're not sure why the record was such a big hit," though leaving in the "mistake," as he called the improvised encore, helped imbue it with . . . something. "It didn't hurt," he allowed. "There are certain kinds of mistakes I love. They sometimes give things extra life and magic because of their raw, real quality."

Whatever it was, it made Little Stevie Wonder a household name in neighborhoods of every demographic stripe. On the upcoming second edition of the Motortown Revue tour, he would share top billing, never again to be relegated to the lowly status of an "Other." He would appear on TV, and make solo tours.

And yet nothing about his immediate future, and whether it would even come at Motown, would be anywhere near as smooth as the path of his first, titanic hit.

6

No Wonder

You really had to start paying attention to Stevie after "Fingertips." No matter what else you might be doing, you'd always know that Stevie had a superior musical intelligence and was learning just as fast as you.

—*Marvin Gaye*

Fingertips" **was the gift** that kept on giving. The album featuring the song—all six minutes and forty seconds of it on one track, along with six other similarly frenzied cuts (including Marvin Gaye's "Soul Bongo")—was titled *Recorded Live: The 12 Year Old Genius*, the sobriquet by which he was routinely introduced at his stage performances, and another bit of cadging from Ray Charles, known of course as "the Genius."

It was released the same day as the "Fingertips—Part 2" single, eight days after Stevie's thirteenth birthday, making the title somewhat dated at the outset, not that it mattered. By summer, it had vaulted past the competition into the number one spot on the album chart—the first Motown album to do so. It was an astounding feat, more so because a child had done something no one else ever had, not even Elvis: taken a single and an album concurrently to the top. Since then no one so young has racked up a number one album and single, which sold over one million copies, according to Motown. While this figure cannot be confirmed because of Gordy's quarantining of the account books, the record was clearly a nationwide smash.

Just as clearly, "Fingertips" made a star out of the lecherous, sometimes irritating, but always engaging kid from Breckenridge Street. In July, as the song and the album shot up the charts, Stevie earned his first national media exposure with a fluffy pictorial in *Ebony*, an important step forward for both him and Gordy, such coverage in the biggest black magazine being a precursor to similar attention in the white press.

Under the headline "The Wonderful World of Little Stevie Wonder" and the subtitle "Public acclaim catapults blind recording artist, 13, into exciting new environment," the story's angle was to facilely contrast the "glittery, tinseled world of show business" with "the world he knew as a little boy lost in a big city [with] poverty, a broken home, a father he rarely saw, and a mother burdened with four other children." Motown, attested Stevie, to Gordy's hearty approval, "was the best thing that ever happened to me."

The spread was festooned with photos of Stevie at work and at leisure, a happy, peppy puppet posing with Gordy, with Ray Charles, at sock hops, playing bongos on his stoop, and the aforementioned picture of him soaring through the air. The slim text slyly mentioned that "Stevie's backers guard his income," noting he was being paid an allowance of $2.50 a week, the paltriness of which must have made many readers do a double take. To underscore the point, the magazine quoted a Motown hand named Ardenia Johnston, apparently in all seriousness, saying that "sometimes Stevie spends it all and then he whispers in my ear, 'I'm broke,'" and that "we hope to teach him to use his money wisely, to avoid champagne tastes."

That would surely prove to be magnificently ironic a decade later.

In the summer of his fourteenth year, Stevie Wonder was not so little anymore. More knowing, musically, than just about anyone else his age, and capable of a wider range of musical idioms than any other Motown act, with Marvin Gaye running a close second, his anatomy was now catching up with his intellectual age, not to mention his already ripe amatory instincts that so unnerved Motown women.

In just the last few months, his growth spurt was more of a gusher. He now stood around five foot nine, seemingly a head taller than Berry Gordy. His face had shed its chubby cheeks, his jawline and once bulbous nose tapering into a taut, handsome semblance of real masculinity. The sprigs of a budding mustache grew over his upper lip. No longer did the boxcar sunglasses overwhelm his face; no longer force-fit, they simply *fit*. When Clarence Paul would shepherd him onto the stage, the two were at eye level. Just like that, "Little" Stevie Wonder became an anachronism.

Gordy had anticipated this circumstance with dread, in light of the ominous Frankie Lymon parallel and the double edge of Stevie's ineffable success as a preciously pubescent wunderkind with a pipsqueaky voice and a number one record. In fact, even as "Fingertips" was being played continuously on radios and Victrolas all over the place, it was already the kind of song he could no longer do with the same believability. After two years of experimentation to find a song that suited him, there had to be another search for one that was right for him *now*.

And the search wasn't going well, judging by the series of songs Paul had tried with him that came up flat. Examples of two of these misfits were "Lois" and "Don't You Feel It," cut respectively in 1963 and 1964, neither of which were released (and would stay unreleased until the 1986 retrospective compilation album *Never-Before-Released Masters: From Motown's Brightest Stars.*) Both, as with the other duds, tried to find a middle ground between youthful exuberance and a more mature, tempered sensibility, toning down the volume and brassiness of the arrangements to swath a more refined vocal from Stevie. But all that was really tempered was the elusive jolt of natural excitement.

With Stevie Wonder once more a conundrum, and faced with a need to keep riding the temblor of "Fingertips" when summer gave way to fall, Gordy and Paul had no choice but to go with the "safest" bet, a Paul–Hank Cosby tune called "Workout Stevie, Workout." This was a raw, flat-out gospel blues number that began with Stevie, in a lower key than usual, solemnly intoning, to a humming choir, "Every time I feel a little groove coming on, I just have to move," before the musicians cut loose, with Stevie wailing on harmonica between frenetic calls like "Do you *feeeel* it?" answered by the massive choir's "Yeaaah!" plus repetitions of the title and delirious hand-clapping.

It was another fiery Stevie trip. But if Gordy wanted—needed—to take him into a more mature pop fold, the song did anything but, undercutting what had been accomplished with "Fingertips."

Released on September 13 and backed with a trifling tune called
"Monkey Talk," it was heard, albeit fleetingly, as the same kind of
amiable novelty as his ersatz Ray Charles phase, although the lingering
taste of "Fingertips" carried it to No. 33 on the pop chart (it was shut
out on the R&B chart). And if going Top 40 didn't seem half bad, in the
still burning afterglow of the "Fingertips" madness it could just as easily
be construed a failure.

For now, however, and for the foreseeable future, even after the
embers of "Fingertips" had gone cold, the imprimatur of that song
was enough to keep Stevie's popularity intact. Indeed, for the second
Motortown Revue tour set for the late autumn, his days as one of the
"And Others" would be over, his status elevated to sharing top billing
with the likes of Smokey and the Miracles, Mary Wells, and Marvin
Gaye—that is, *if* he would be on the tour. In September, that was far
from clear, as was the very notion that Stevie Wonder would even be a
Motown artist at all.

So caught up was Gordy and everyone else at Motown in the Little
Stevie Wonder phenomenon that all of the original concern about satisfying the Michigan child labor laws had seemingly been forgotten in the
pandemonium. As Stevie's long hours spent recording or just hanging
out at Motown mounted, and his road trips for personal appearances
multiplied, little thought was paid to how much time he was missing at
the Fitzgerald School.

In effect, his entire fifth grade term was a washout. Even on the
rare occasions when he did make it to class, there was static. Stevie
would later recall that his teachers never let up on their browbeating
him that showbiz would be his ruination—even after he had a number
one hit, which they regarded as a fluke, a cruel promise that would
never again be met. "They told me," he said, "that I should stop pursuing
music and continue my education"—something they could say since
Steve had all but made it a choice of one or the other. What's more,
they could legally compel him to stay in school instead of in the studio,
if in their judgment his career was turning him chronically truant. That,
naturally, would spell the end of his days at Motown, as he would not
be permitted to sign a contract there or at any other company at least

until he had graduated from high school, when he likely would be no more than a faded echo.

Along with the hectoring and lecturing came a continuation of the old, bizarre remarks by teachers of the blind that without a high school degree the future held only the promise of making potholders. Another insult that stayed in his mind was when one of them said, "I had three strikes against me, because I was poor, black, and blind." Not by coincidence, such slurs and pressures only fed his appetite to stay away from school, out of spite. And when he was there, the Stevie who sat in the classroom was not recognizable as the happy Motown mascot but rather a surly, frustrated youth, a chip heavy on his shoulder. It didn't help that schoolmates could hardly be called fans. Once, after a kid—"a big guy, a bully," he recalled—called him, derisively, "Wonders," Stevie, sizing him up by the sound of his voice, pushed him down a flight of stairs. He would remember the incident proudly, as proof he could always fight his own battles. But he couldn't fight the school when administrators told Lula Mae that he would have to redo the grade when the new school year began in September 1963. He had no choice; if he didn't keep to a regular schedule, the school would move to void his Motown contract.

Lula Mae had in fact been worried sick about Stevie's missing so much school, and blamed herself for not being more vigilant, for letting him twist her around his finger, telling her why this or that impending session or concert was too important to disrupt. Now, blaming Motown for leading her son astray, she was ready to beat the state to the punch by ending the whole Motown nonsense herself. Marching into Gordy's office, she told him Stevie was through, contract or not.

Gordy knew he'd screwed up, and was contrite. If that's what she had to do to get her son an education, he said, she had every right. However, compounding her guilt, he reminded her that it would for all intents and purposes be the end of Stevie's dream. Seeing her weaken, he proposed a compromise, which had presented itself after Gordy, because of the Fitzgerald School's threats, canceled an appearance Stevie was scheduled to make in Louisville, Kentucky, but relented when the promoter of that show put him in touch with a Louisville tutor, a matronly white woman named Helen Traub, to teach Stevie his lessons while he was in the city.

Gordy flew Traub to Detroit to meet with Stevie and Lula Mae, who were so impressed with her that they asked, and gained, approval from the Michigan Board of Education for Stevie to go to Kentucky under the tutelage of Traub. He then offered Traub a salaried job to continue on in the capacity on a steady basis. This eased the brouhaha, but after a few trips with Stevie, Traub felt it was inappropriate for a woman to accompany a pubescent boy on the road. To continue the arrangement, she queried the superintendent of the private Michigan School for the Blind in Lansing about a male tutor who could spare that kind of time, who turned out to be a former student there, a recent Michigan State University graduate named Ted Hull.

Hull was remarkable in his own way. Partially sighted and legally blind, he had made numerous trips around the world and had earned not only a driver's license but a *pilot's* license (actually a copilot's license because he wasn't permitted to fly solo, not that this made it any less notable). At the time he was working as the program director at Detroit's Penrickton Center for Blind Children, but he was up for the more challenging position that brought him to Motown. The gangly, bespectacled Hull had no idea what he was in for, but came aboard at a salary of two hundred dollars a week. Part of the bargain, too, was that Stevie would now enroll at the Michigan School for the Blind and study a curriculum that Hull coordinated with his teachers.

When he packed for his first trip, Hull's valise was stuffed with Braille textbooks, slates, and writing tablets. The trip was to Chicago in early October 1963, not for a gig but, curiously, a recording session Clarence Paul had scheduled with the twenty-eight-piece Chicago Symphony Orchestra string section, the tracks from which would be used on Stevie's next album. They rode in a clanking station wagon driven by a Motown hand named Gene Shelby. En route, they pulled into a roadside diner, whereupon Stevie's fame could be measured in microcosm when a young white man recognized him and asked for an autograph.

For Stevie, it was something of a threshold moment, but also a bit embarrassing since he had not mastered how to write his name—hence the "X" that he scratched onto his Motown contract—and up to now whenever his autograph was called for, such as on Motown publicity photos, someone else had signed for him. Now, a bit nonplussed, he didn't know what to tell the fellow. Seeing his discomfort, Hull quickly stuck a pen into Stevie's right hand and with his own hand guided Stevie's over the paper through the contours of the signature. Today, Hull delights in telling how Stevie "squealed with excitement" and believes that to Stevie this seemingly simple achievement meant much more, that it represented "the ability to take control of a little larger part of his life."

Clarence Paul was also grateful for Hull's arrival. Now it would be Hull with whom Stevie would share hotel room, and who would be his guide everywhere but onstage. For Paul, this was a large relief, if for no better reason than it freed him to happily get loaded on booze, weed, and coke in his room, and entertain playmates whom he had previously had to stop at the door. And now Stevie would be able to get to where he was expected on time, not whenever Paul got around to it, a habit that had led Motown people to say that Paul had such a vague awareness of the clock that he ran on "CP time."

Hull, noticing what everyone else already knew, recalled that "Clarence was a real carouser," and that he "represent[ed] absolutely everything you wouldn't want a young boy exposed to." Giving credit where it was due, he did give Paul props for "always treat[ing] Stevie with respect and never try[ing] to involve him in anything harmful."

So Hull was now the one sacrificing his time. Soon after he began the job, he found he needed a little break from Stevie and sent him to stay one night in Shelby's room. When Hull came by Shelby's room the next morning, he found Stevie asleep in one of the room's twin beds, and in the other a naked woman with whom Shelby had shared his mattress. Years later, Hull is still astonished that Shelby, as he said, "didn't see anything wrong with the situation, since Stevie had his own bed. I didn't quite see it that way. Stevie was blind, but he wasn't deaf. And he was way too young and too smart to be exposed to Gene's act as a ladies' man." That night was "the last time I let Stevie spend the night with anyone else," at least until Stevie was around sixteen and could stay in his own room.

Paul and Shelby were effective tutors for Stevie in their own right, in the art and science of philandering. And because not even Hull could keep an eye on Stevie all the time, there was ample time and opportunity for a growing, hormonally raging teenager to use the lessons he'd been taught. As Stevie would coyly put it, "I was surrounded by older people all the time, and there were temptations."

He didn't mean the singing group, either. Around Motown, the subject of how Stevie succumbed to the "temptations" became water-cooler fodder. During 1963 and 1964, it was said, a crafty Stevie once slipped away from Hull at a motel where several acts that had performed at a show were staying, to party with the female gospel-R&B duet known as the Soul Sisters, Tresia Cleveland and Ann Gissendanner. Another time, he evidently eluded Hull long enough for one of the traveling musicians to treat him to an hour with a call girl, donating his room for the occasion and picking up the tab. Hull would look around for him, knocking on other performers' doors, until Stevie appeared at his door, nonchalantly and no doubt satisfied, explaining that he had been going over songs with Paul or someone else on the tour and lost track of the time.

Some believed that it could have been during any of those absences that Stevie lost his virginity. If they only knew what Little Stevie had been up to on the streets running with the hoodlums when he was *really* coming of age sexually. If they had, it would have been Stevie doing the tutoring.

Indeed, among a male population of Motown driven as much by sex as by music, he fit right in, an adorable boy with the drives of a horn dog. Even then, he had a hard-on for Motown women, though the practicality didn't really mesh with the reality of such a coupling. Of one such enticing entity, he once related, "The first time I met Diana Ross, I used to be in love with that chick, Jack. I don't know if I wanted to do it to her, 'cause I was too young, but I sure was in love with that chick. I loved her to death. I had a fantastic crush on her. Loved her voice. Her talking voice. I used to listen to [the early Supremes song] 'Time Changes Things' over and over again, for thousands of hours."

Pining away for a woman whose own amatory hours were kept on reserve for powerful Motown men who could help her climb the company ladder did nothing to limit his thirst for any woman whose scent he caught. Junior Walker, the brilliant sax-playing soul singer who came to Motown in 1961, would be amused when Stevie, looking to make a booty run, waylaid him in a hotel lobby and begged him to take him out on the town with him.

As Walker told it years later, he would respond, "Uh-uh, Stevie, you gotta stay in, you're a kid." However, that didn't mean Stevie couldn't get some, regardless. When Junior happened to mention during one hotel conversation, "I seen a little chick out there that dug you," Stevie's ears pricked up.

"You go get her and bring her back to the room," he said.

In such ways did a thirteen-year-old boy get big Motown stars to act as his personal procurers.

What Stevie recorded with the symphony string section in Chicago was yet one more wrinkle for him to try to ride into a "fluke" hit. Clarence Paul had produced an album to wrap around "Workout Stevie, Workout," its tracks in the same vein as the grittily gospel title cut that would also be the title of the album. But the failure of the single obviated the need for the project, which was shelved, forever. And with so many misfires with R&B material since "Fingertips," Paul now turned 180 degrees and steered Stevie to classic middle-of-the-road fare. It was not designed to shake and stir such music with R&B into a new hybrid of soul, but rather to broaden the soulful gospel-blues pop star most record buyers knew into a purveyor of Tin Pan Alley pop.

If Paul, who brainstormed the idea with Berry Gordy, didn't know this was a long shot, he need only have consulted his other primary act of note, Marvin Gaye, who had been there and done that, fruitlessly. But again Paul dove into a daffy project. Choosing nine songs for an album that could easily have been titled *A Tribute to Tony Bennett*, he decided on happy or sentimental suds such as "When You Wish upon a Star," "Make Someone Happy," "Get Happy," "On the Sunny Side of the Street," "Give Your Heart a Chance," "Smile," "Without a Song," and "With a Song in My Heart," the last of which became the album's actual title. Paul cut the instrumental tracks in the early autumn, but beyond what he'd gotten done in Chicago in one day there was no time to lay down more of the vocals before the second Motortown Revue shoved off in late October. That meant that although Stevie would be one of the headliners of the tour, he'd have no new song to pump, with "Workout Stevie, Workout" having burned out.

•   •   •

But then the Revue was a downer altogether. After the troupe rode the buses through another unnerving expedition through the South—Ted Hull still winces at the plethora of Confederate flags he saw along the route and even in some of the arenas—it came home for a Thanksgiving respite before heading off for the climactic ten-day run at the Apollo Theater. On the morning of November 22, while the troupe was home, radios in the Motown offices crackled with the horrifying news out of Dallas that brought the nation to a halt. At Motown, Gordy was regarded as a kingly analog of John F. Kennedy, overlord of his own brand of Camelot, thriving in the same ether of a New Frontier—its youthful optimism, idealism, and racial transformation refracted through the narrow funnel of crossover soul but applicable to much broader cultural themes.

After Kennedy died of the gunshot wounds that rang out in Dealey Plaza, everyone at 2648 West Grand Boulevard wandered around in a fog, many crying hysterically. Gordy canceled all business for the day and sent them home. But before he could leave, he had to endure a scene in his office with Marvin Gaye that gave new meaning to Gaye's classic song "Ain't That Peculiar." Gaye was there arguing with Gordy over a money issue, and even the assassination of a president didn't deter him. Gordy, trying to placate him, told him to "be a good boy, okay?" At that, Gaye exploded irrationally. "See! See, BG! That's a whole bunch of bullshit. You think I'm a boy just like the white man!" Gordy could take no more. Angrily sweeping the top of his desk clean, he shouted, "Don't you realize the president was killed today?" Then he shoved Gaye aside—some accounts have it that Gordy pinned Gaye against the desk and for a few tense moments tightened his hands around Marvin's neck—and went home.

Stevie, who that morning was in his classroom at the Michigan School for the Blind, was taken home by Ted Hull after classes were let out, and with his family camped in front of the television during the long, mournful weekend of the funeral and the surreal chaos of Jack Ruby's murder of Lee Harvey Oswald—a chain of events that only seemed to confirm Stevie's early visions of an American apocalypse.

Gordy considered calling off the December Revue dates, but he relented when faced with the financial toll. And so, in the sheath of gloom that caused industry-wide record sales to suffer that holiday season, the buses went rolling eastward, to do much good helping audiences along the route heal and reclaim a sense of normalcy through the restorative powers of music. Gordy had told the troupe to play and perform their asses off, and by Christmastime the grimy walls of the Apollo were shaking with some of the wildest Revue shows ever given.

In the old grainy films made of the final Apollo show, it is clear that this tour was really Marvin Gaye's coming-out party. As if he were plugged in to an electric current, there was almost an audible buzz around him. Wearing a waist-level busboy jacket and skintight pants, as he sang "Hitchhike" he pulled female audience members onto the stage to bump and grind with him. Screeching "*Yowwww*" to punctuate the verses, his confidence swelling, he seemed to float on air as Martha and the Vandellas, singing backup offstage, sang piquantly, "Hitchhike, Marvin. Hitchhike, children."

To Stevie's great misfortune, he had to follow Gaye on this excursion, and while no match for the raw animal magnetism Gaye could muster, he had his own supply of voltage. Bill Murray cued him much the same way as he had at the Regal, saying, "I'd like to introduce to you an outstanding young man considered to be a genius of our time, and he happens to be thirteen years old. Meet and greet the thirteen-year-old genius himself, ladies and gentlemen, Stevie Wonder!" Entering from stage left on Clarence Paul's arm, modestly clad to match the garb worn by the band—light jacket, black pants, tie and shoes, and a natty hankie in his jacket pocket—he was lowered into a chair on which the bongos sat, and as Paul turned to lead the band Murray all but pushed him into the chair. Without a pause, he neatly wedged the bongos between his knees and began tapping on them, emitting a saucy "yeeeaaah." Then, duplicating the prologue of the original recording at the Regal Theater, as if it were still fresh, "Ladies and gentlemen, I'd like to do for you, from my new recording from my live album. The name of the song is, uh, 'Fingertips.'"

Now, as the audience took on energy, he went into the "Stevie rap," preaching, "Now I want you to clap your hands, stomp your feet, jump up and down—do anything you want to do!" followed by a primal "*wooooo-eeeee!*" at which he rose to his feet, bongos replaced by a harmonica, puffing the now familiar melody and moving to a solitary dance, knees churning, shifting from one foot to the other, the moves imitated by the band, which got up on their feet, swaying with him in a tight formation. Next came the exhortation that had become his calling card—"Everybody say yeah!" and the rudimentary verses broken up by harmonica bursts capped by the "Mary Had a Little Lamb" riff.

When Paul took him by the hand and led him offstage, with a crisp bow by Stevie; there was no encore and no calls for one, just polite applause. In a wink, the Marvelettes were onstage doing a frenetic rendition of "Please Mr. Postman." Clearly, as Stevie had learned, following Marvin Gaye at the Apollo could take much of the air out of any act.

Stevie had his revenge, though, only days later, getting another shot at Gaye once the Revue returned home and the acts were thrown right into an even more rabid proving ground: the annual Motown Christmas show at the Graystone Ballroom.

A cavernous hall, the ballroom had been a popular hotspot in Detroit since the 1920s. In 1962, Gordy bought it for Motown's use, mainly for recording occasional large-scale string arrangements and the Christmas shindig, which always sold out. During the shows there, the centerpiece of the show was a mano a mano competition between acts of Gordy's choosing, pitted in a two-round "match" judged solely by Gordy, the old boxer. It became a matter of enormous pride for an act to take home the "title," and Gordy only savored the fact that those of his own "children" picked would work themselves into a frenzy—even a mutual hatred—that heightened the competition.

On this night, the chosen warriors were Gaye and Stevie, and the atmosphere inside the Graystone grew more fervid. Stevie, up first, did a torrid version of "Workout Stevie, Workout." Gaye countered with "Hitchhike," showing that he had given the contest some thought. Trying to one-up Stevie, he whipped out and began blowing into a melodica, an oversized harmonica played like a keyboard, as he danced about the stage. Gauging the crowd reaction, Gordy gave round one to Gaye, forcing Stevie to have to turn it up in round two, leaping into "Pretty Music" but tacking onto it the incitements of "Fingertips," keyed of course by *"Everybody say yeaaaahhh,"* and lengthening—and lengthening—until the crowd was limp, and the round his.

Now it was Gaye's turn to sweat. As he proceeded to belt out "Stubborn Kind of Fellow," however, a strange vibe began to surface in the house. Instead of getting into the groove, some booed. One person yelled out, "Marvin, you should be shame o' yourself takin' advantage of a little blind kid!" to cries of "Yeah!" from the crowd. Gaye pushed on, now met by hissing and more booing. Even the notoriously tough crowds at the Apollo had never treated him like this. Totally thrown, unable to concentrate, he looked toward Gordy for help.

Still shaken years later, Gordy recalled that "the smile on [Marvin's] face couldn't hide the pain." Realizing now that the match had been a terrible mistake—one that *wasn't* beneficial—he climbed onto the stage, halting the show. As recorded music was played over the loudspeakers, the lights were dimmed and the crowd instructed to file out. As it did, many were still booing, now at Gordy, for cutting the festivities short.

But to Gordy, and Gaye, there was nothing festive about the dark mood that ended the evening, caused by Gaye being put in the unenviable position of competing against a "little blind kid." As soon as Gordy left the stage, he found Gaye sitting alone, his head buried in his hands. Despite all the static that existed between the two men, Gordy felt nothing but pity for him now. He put an arm around Gaye's shoulders, saying nothing but already having resolved that there never be a rerun.

"Though I still felt competition bred champions, I could also see that it had a downside," he wrote of the night. "And in this particular case of putting a grown man against a little blind boy, I had blundered badly. That was the last Battle of the Stars at the Graystone."

Stevie too felt badly about the whole unsettling episode. Catching up with Gaye later that night, he consoled him by saying there was no way in hell that he could have ever beaten him, on that night, on any night.

As the new year of 1964 began, it was apparent, and urgent, that Stevie needed more than one megahit to keep moving forward. A larger problem was that his voice had changed so much that when he was scheduled to finish laying down vocals for *With a Song in My Heart*, Clarence Paul found that the instrumental tracks were even less suitable, recorded in a key too high for Stevie to handle without straining and yelping like a hoarse coyote. Normally in such a case, a producer would try slowing down the speed of the tape, but Paul was loath to do that, fearing it would nullify the bouncy beats he wanted to liven up those old groaning tunes.

The only option—other than canning the project, which had already cost a good deal of money (all charged to Stevie's escrow account) and thus was ruled out—was for Stevie to slog through it. As ever, he did it admirably, his deft and subtle inflections reminiscent now not of Ray Charles but Nat King Cole. Squeaks and all, he warbled his way through some rather drippy passages heavily coated with strings, horns, and background choirs, holding notes until they echoed into the mist, sometimes with quivering, Ronnie Spector–style vibrato, and biting off the last syllables of certain words, Cole-style.

He did well to get through it. As a work, it was altogether pleasant, and altogether irrelevant. Released on December 28—as the first album to bill him as simply "Stevie Wonder"—*Song* was dead on arrival, never to come near the charts. The timing of that flub was amplified when, testing the waters of a Motown expansion abroad, Gordy sent Stevie on a brief journey to London for a few nightclub gigs and radio and television appearances, including one on the BBC TV show *Thank Your Lucky Stars* on January 11. Although "Fingertips" was just then beginning to find an audience across the pond, and by now Stevie could perform it with gusto in his sleep, to the reliably ecstatic reaction of any audience, he had no other songs in his pocket that could keep the fire burning. In general the trip didn't do much to establish a foreign market for him, nor a Motown beachhead.

One indicator that Gordy had zero expectations for the album was that, without waiting for its imminent death, he had yet *another* concept for Stevie to try, though it was so minor in the grand scheme of Motown that it didn't involve Motown proper, or even Clarence Paul, but instead doings two thousand miles away, in La-La Land.

Out in Los Angeles, Gordy was just starting to organize the skeletal structure of a "Motown West" operation, to establish at least a presence in the motion picture and TV community for future reference. By 1964, the operation, run out of a cramped office in a one-story building on Sunset Boulevard, consisted of three writer/producers, Frank Wilson and the team of Hal Davis and Marc Gordon, and one artist signed out of L.A. and being recorded there in a local studio, a drop-dead gorgeous thrush named Brenda Holloway. Gordy put the office to work mainly cutting instrumental tracks for use as filler on prospective albums. But he also had made an early incursion into the movie arc, sort of, by striking a mutually beneficial deal in the fall of 1963 with producers Samuel Z. Arkoff and James H. Nicholson, whose production company, American International Pictures, began production on a new genre, if it could be called that, of film called "muscle beach movies."

The first, *Muscle Beach Party*, set into motion a formula that would go unchanged, no matter how much money any of the movies made: it was produced on a shoestring budget, with grade-Z actors behind the two main "stars" of the franchise, Frankie Avalon and Annette Funicello. The entire concept was a giant anomaly, not merely because the stars were has-beens and nobody's idea of cool, nor because the "plots" were no more than an endless tease of nubile, skimpily clad (for then) people wanting to but never actually having sex, but because the music that was to anchor these lead balloons was the "surf" and "car" rock that by 1964 would be ebbing in popularity.

Lightweight or not, a movie was a movie, and Gordy considered it an entree into the sphere where he wanted to take Motown, and himself, in future years. He also figured, correctly, that it would be nice exposure for Stevie (though again, the appearance fee from American International was never paid to Stevie himself). And today, as horrifyingly bad as these flicks are, the filmed images of him singing—actually lip-synching—in this and one more such flick are likely the best performance videos of Little Stevie Wonder (as he was billed in both), and likely the only ones in color dating back to the early and mid-1960s. Unfortunately, the songs were bottom feeders. In *Muscle Beach Party*, clad in jeans and a powder blue polo shirt, he lip-synched a low-grade Davis-Gordon song, "Happy Street," bomping and clapping his hands as the low-grade actors got up and did the twist on tabletops. The song was reprised during the closing credits, a grooving, bongo-playing Stevie on one side of the screen, a go-go dancer gyrating on the other.

Thinking ahead, Gordy wanted to milk the idea, and kept Stevie in L.A. long enough to cut a spin-off song, the Davis-Gordon-Wilson "Castles in the Sand." At least it was supposed to be a spin-off, but in truth it wasn't really a beach-idiom song at all. Produced by Davis and Gordon not as a happy, brainless tune but rather a sobering, reflective semi-ballad of lost love, the song is notable as the first time Stevie was permitted to sing in a lower, more adult range, and for plaintive, syntactically challenging lyrics, such as: "There might be another song / But all my heart can hear is your melody."

Though it was something of a muddle, Gordy issued "Castles," the last single to bill him as "Little Stevie Wonder," backed with the long-ago-recorded "Thank You (For Loving Me All the Way)," on January 15—hardly an optimum time for a beach song—only to suffer another disappointment. Coming off the failure of *With a Song in My Heart*, it climbed only to No. 52 on the pop chart in mid-March. Still not deterred, he also went ahead on an album for Stevie that Gordy sought to market as a "surf rock" product, titling it *Stevie at the Beach*, which included sand-under-the-feet titles like "Castles," "Beach Stomp," "The Party at the Beach House," "The Beachcomber," as well as instrumentals such as "Ebb Tide," "Red Sails in the Sunset," "Sad Boy," and a cover of Bobby Darin's recent hit "Beyond the Sea."

Greasing the way for a summer release of the album, one that would coincide with the opening of *Muscle Beach Party*, Gordy launched a Stevie Wonder frontal attack on the public. Pushing hard, he was able to book Stevie for a May 3, 1964, guest shot on *The Ed Sullivan Show.* This was a gig of monumental importance for Motown, which had thus far succeeded in placing only one act on the venerable, top-rated Sunday night CBS TV show, the Marvelettes on March 5, 1962. What's more, it would come barely three months after the Beatles had set off pandemonium, and something close to electroshock within the American music industry, putting on a deathwatch the Broadway-based coterie of fat-cat song publishers and their staff writers that dominated pop music, their metaphoric seat of power being the Brill Building.

That Stevie would go on as Gordy's major competitors were near panic-stricken pondering how to keep themselves extant in the soon-to-burgeon era of self-contained rock bands singing self-composed songs was not incidental to Gordy, who always saw the compound implications in every decision. Motown, he wanted to put the industry on notice, was here for the duration, its product resistant—no, immune—to extinction by virtue of its self-reliance and self-determination. Now, he posited, the new order Motown had wrought by alloying black and white idioms would be no less than the salvation of American pop music. And Stevie Wonder would get the first crack to show why.

Of course, he did as expected, hammering out a routinely dynamic rendition of "Fingertips." For many around the country, it was the first time they could attach a face and persona to the groove of that now eleven-month-old hit—and two-year-old recording. Even in the dusky black-and-white monochrome of millions of TV screens the sinewy images of the blind wunderkind in his suit, skinny tie, and sunglasses were nothing but vivid. Gleefully hopping from the well-worn lyrics to the fiery blasts of his harmonica, the song ended moments after the "Mary Had a Little Lamb" tittle, as it had in rehearsal, with no encore.

Stevie, smiling broadly, head tilted up as if peering into the mezzanine, took a brisk bow. Then the camera was off, before Clarence Paul came for him. It wasn't the Fab Four; but to Gordy, it was sublime, a great leap forward for the fortunes of Motown Record Corporation, and secondarily so for Stevie Wonder.

Eighteen days later, on May 21, Gordy put out as a single one of the other cuts from *Stevie at the Beach*, "Hey Harmonica Man," another showcase of Stevie's skills with a Hohner, in a loud, bouncy hash of percussion, hand claps, and male backup singers who at times drowned out his part-sung, part-spoken vocal. A month later, *Stevie at the Beach* was released.

The album was, of course, a very strange concept for a Motown artist—an inner-city-bred, gospel- and blues-singing scion of Ray Charles having reason to hang out, sing, and work on a suntan at the beach. Yet that was the very image used as the cover on the album and on the jacket sleeve of "Hey Harmonica Man": Stevie sitting cross-legged on the sand in swim trunks and a flowery cabana shirt blowing his harmonica, the peaceful ocean lying behind him.

If a tenuous case could be made for it in America, it couldn't in England. There, music devotees revered hard-core American R&B singers and cringed at sellout projects like this, leading the Stateside label that distributed the record to retitle it *Hey Harmonica Man*. Over here, the single was palatable enough to catch the wave of *Muscle Beach Party* and ring in at No. 29 on the singles chart, but the album wiped out without smelling the chart. Later that summer, Stevie appeared in the follow-up film, *Bikini Beach*, in which he performed a trifling number called "Dance and Shout," percolating in Ray Charles mode, "Yeah, yeah, yeah, what did you say?"

For Arkoff and Nicholson, the muscle beach flicks turned into a mint. But if Motown was a player in the creation of a new movie genre, it never really found a compatible crossover fold with its own ersatz beach fodder.

Gordy could accept that trade-off. He was hardly hurting, not with a thriving Motown having grossed over the million-dollar mark in sales in 1962 and multiples of that figure each year from then on. Long gone were the days when he'd had to declare zero income because every dime was reinvested in the company, and when he had to live with his family upstairs at 2648 West Grand Boulevard. Nor did it matter that his personal life was as grimy as a pulp novel. One night Raynoma Liles, learning he was fooling around with a woman named Margaret Norton, confronted Norton, pulling a gun out of her purse. Smokey Robinson, who was luckily there, saw her reach for the gun and yelled to Norton, "Run!"—possibly saving her life. Banished by Gordy to oversee a fledgling Motown sub-operation in New York that never got off the ground, Liles was soon busted by the FBI for pawning Motown records at a deep discount to record stores (an early, illegal form of "bootlegging"), whereupon he stripped her of her Motown stock in exchange for not pressing charges. After he obtained a Mexican divorce, he and Norton began living openly in a colonial home on chichi Outer Drive, and would move on up in the mid-1960s to his first of several mansions, all equipped with an indoor and outdoor swimming pool, movie theater, and tennis court.

As for Motown business, with Mary Wells pumping out one Smokey Robinson–produced hit after another, including the leviathan "My Guy," which zoomed to No. 1 in the early spring of 1964, he was able to weather a bum record or two. He had an assembly-line-like combine that now cranked out hits by numerous sub-labels, including the one called Motown that featured big guns like the Supremes and Wells—at least until later that year when the latter, claiming her contract was illegal because she'd signed it as a minor, walked away from Gordy for a lucrative offer from 20th Century Records. While this was a painful blow for Gordy, he got a measure of revenge when, suing Wells and 20th Century for breach of contract, he was awarded nearly one million dollars in damages. A sweeter reward was that Wells, sans the Motown music machine, never again had a substantial hit. For all appearances, Berry Gordy's power seemed endless, and endlessly puissant.

With the Wells example as a cautionary tale of what might happen to them, Motown artists marched to his orders. The prophecy of a "family" growing famous and fat together seemed to be on the edge of fulfillment. Besides the singing talent, the songwriting/producing team of Brian Holland and Lamont Dozier, rounded into perfection by Eddie Holland's cheeky lyrics written in the voice and vernacular of lovesick young girls and guys—and, increasingly, adult women and men—solidified into Motown's meal ticket. Right behind them, almost equally successful in mining the Motown "sound" into chart gold, were Smokey Robinson and then Norman Whitfield with the Temptations; Harvey Fuqua and Mickey Stevenson with Marvin Gaye; and Johnny Bristol with Junior Walker and the All-Stars and, later, the early Marvin Gaye and Tammi Terrell records.

Motown, then, in every aspect that mattered, was the empire Gordy had alone envisioned in 1959. Still, in the narrower lens, after three years of myriad incarnations and experimentations, the Stevie Wonder investment had paid only partial dividends—inarguably, some quite big. Of his seven singles, two went Top 30, one a No. 1. Another just missed the Top 30, one more the Top 50. And of course "Fingertips" was still a resounding sensation, though its echoes were gradually fading.

On the flip side, there was the chain of failure post-"Fingertips," a trend that showed no signs of changing well into 1964, giving rise to the possibility that Stevie Wonder still could not find a consistent niche at Motown. It was not coincidence that, as a corollary, Clarence Paul had not been elevated to the heady stratum occupied by those other writer/producers, some of whom arrived on the scene long after him but had passed him by.

Indeed, the stagnation of Stevie Wonder would become a vexatious topic at Motown, where hard decisions would have to be made about the whether the Stevie Wonder brand was worth the trouble in keeping it alive.

1

The Motown Way

Stevie increasingly resented Motown's nonchalant attitude toward his career and, frankly, he had every right to feel that way.

—*Ted Hull*

You'd have to be a fool to believe that, at thirteen years old, or any age, you knew better than Berry Gordy how to make yourself a big star at Motown.

—*Mickey Stevenson*

No one detested Motown's descent into beach blanket bingo madness more than Stevie himself. The whole affair left him miserable and feeling insulted that Gordy had compromised his talents to chase the carrot of crass, short-term commercial gain. Good soldier that he was, he did what he was told, only to come away embarrassed, even embittered. His true feelings could be gauged by the flatness and listlessness of his voice on several tracks of *Stevie at the Beach*. Years later he would confirm that those sessions were the nadir of his career, far more burdensome than the jumbled but still impelling works like the Ray Charles tribute and the live album. The interim spent in L.A. recording the gruel that he did, he confessed, was the first time in his life that he lost his ardor to sing.

"You couldn't blame him," says Otis Williams, who caught Stevie's feedback on subsequent Motortown Revue trips. "I remember Stevie telling me one time, he said, 'Man, why don't they just let me sing my own songs? I'd be doin' a lot better if I can sing what I wanna sing.' But at Motown, you couldn't make those decisions yourself. You just had to wait it out. Motown was a big machine, man. You can't fight the machine. You're only one part of the machine."

Clarence Paul, who was feeling his control of Stevie beginning to slip away with each passing failure, also bridled at being forced to do what he intrinsically knew was wrong for Stevie. The worst part was seeing Stevie lose his edge because of it. "He'd get ticked off," Paul once said, "but he'd end up doing it because that was the only way. Everybody else there did. They were getting their records out by doing what people said to do."

Although Ted Hull noted that "Clarence was one of the few adults in Motown willing to listen to Stevie's creative suggestions," Paul too came in for his share of criticism when Stevie was blowing off steam to Hull. In fact, the tutor would have to act as a buffer between Stevie and the Motown establishment, easing his fluttering before Stevie could say something he'd regret to the wrong person. Even so, sometimes Stevie would crack.

"Once in a while," Hull recalled, "he'd get surly and argue points." At times like that, Hull's role would be that of, as he puts it, a "Dutch uncle. I'd have to let him know he was out of line. I'd remind him to just be cool, that the people he was working with really did know more than he did."

And so he would take another hard swallow and go on, frequently hating what he was doing.

In this, Stevie Wonder's first depression, Motown became less of a home and more of a call to drudgery. The irony was that his mood was lifted only by the habitat that by 1964 had replaced 2648 West Grand Boulevard as his sanctuary, the Michigan School for the Blind. Having been so out of sorts and prickly at the Fitzgerald School, for Stevie the Lansing campus was a major revelation and a sinecure allowing him to think less about what he considered Gordy's unfocused, incoherent handling of his career.

The grounds there were as wide and green as a country club. Students could swim in a kidney-shaped pool, go boating in crystal-blue lakes, skate on them in winter. There were ball fields, basketball and tennis courts. Stevie would begin to spend much idle time running laps on the track team, the long distances passed in solitary thought hatching fragments of new songs, or working off his excess energy doing take-downs on the school wrestling squad.

Moreover, the music department was a paradise. Though he'd been in the middle of the bustling Motown scene, absorbing the procedures of big-time productions, he had little practical knowledge of music theory, nor how to read and write musical arrangements. Now, enrolled at Lula's insistence under the name of Steveland Morris—which, according to Hull, caused Stevie distress, as he had never heard of the surname until the day he signed that "X" to his Motown contract and to him it was "one more indication his life was taking him in directions he'd never anticipated"—he eagerly took courses in a myriad of musical subjects, burying his nose in the Braille textbooks and listening for hours to records of symphony orchestras and operas.

It could almost seem as if he was lost in the crowd, something he never was at Motown, and the lack of Gordy-induced pressure was a blessing. The school's choir director, Yvonne Wainwright, recalled him as just one of forty-five kids taking her direction, not trying to give it, as he had back at the churches. He became the featured singer of the choir for a Christmas pageant not because of who he was—the school administration had directed there be no special treatment—but because of how he tore into "Ave Maria" and "White Christmas" at the audition.

Stevie was so gratified by the place that he actually would juggle his Motown commitments to be able to spend more time in Lansing. Rather than jumping into Hull's car and hurrying back to Motown after school, he would accede to other students' requests to hear them sing and give his opinion. He made friends at the school that would still endure decades later—a far cry from Motown, where other than Marvin Gaye most everyone else became disposable.

It may have been, surmises Hull, the first semblance of a normal life, mercifully removed from the convulsions of home, the barracudas on the street, and the "family" bullshit of Motown, and as such it provided him, as Hull said, "physical, emotional, and mental breaks" from the mouse-in-a-maze bind Gordy had him in. As importantly, to the benefit of his craft, he could "let his mind synthesize what he was hearing as both a professional and as a student."

Thus he would in time bring the mountain to him, persuading Benny Benjamin, Chank Willis, and other Motown house musicians to make the trek up for music symposiums. Hull would make the arrangements, sometimes adding musicians from clubs around Lansing.

"All I had to do," he said, "was ask, 'How'd you like to spend a few hours working with Stevie Wonder?' It never failed."

No human on earth spent more time with Stevie during his teenage years than Hull, including Lula Mae and Clarence Paul. Soon, he and Stevie were staying on the campus in a residential dorm so Stevie wouldn't have to crisscross the state. If Stevie had to go to Motown to record for a few days, he'd usually stay in Hull's apartment, where the tutor would transmute the day's curriculum. Before long, the overfamiliar sight of the blind teenager and the professorial-looking white man gave rise to some intracompany buzz about what the latter's role really was, as it seemed to extend beyond merely a tutor to that of a rabid watchdog.

While Stevie could slip away from him, no one seemed to be able to penetrate the wall Hull built around Stevie. The understanding was that Hull was charged with keeping Stevie's nose clean in the company of wolves. Not begrudging that function a bit, when talk on the bus tours got too loud or smutty, artists like Smokey Robinson or Diana Ross would pipe up, "Shhh! Be quiet, Ted's trying to teach Stevie." However, Hull could be magisterial about it, pulling rank over big-name stars with stated warnings to "keep it clean around Stevie." A stray curse word would draw an icy stare from him, no matter who said it.

If anyone waylaid Stevie in a hotel for longer than a few minutes, Hull would stare from across the lobby, impatiently tapping his foot. In restaurants, he would insist that Stevie place his napkin in his lap and use the proper type of fork or spoon, and would instruct him to scoop his soup from the back of the bowl. Though Hull maintains that these procedures were simply a process of transferring what had been instilled in him as a child, when other Motown artists were dining in the same halls, watching such habits, Hull bluntly says, they "made some of the others feel awkward for having few table manners drilled into them as children."

The unease grew in early 1965 when Gordy officially ceded Hull more sovereignty, including the authority to collect box-office receipts after Stevie's concerts, book musicians for shows, solely determine Stevie's allowances, and choose hotels where they would stay, supplanting the duties previously performed by Clarence Paul. Presumptuously, to many, Hull began to identify himself as Stevie's "manager," drawing snickers from those who knew all too well of Motown's unconditional jurisdiction over all performers through ITMI—not until 1967 would Gordy loosen its grip enough to allow anyone to hold the title of manager for any act, and then only someone of his own choosing, answerable to him.

To some in the Motown shop, where there was always a quiet but palpable rumbling about Gordy's confederacy with white business executives at the top of the company ladder, Hull's race, magnified by his stern, imperious manner and southern heritage, became a peripheral issue, undercutting the respect he had cultivated as Stevie's mentor and rudder. Martha Reeves, for instance, could barely mask her contempt for him. Reeves, Hull says, "clearly let it be known she resented my white presence in a black organization." Once, when Hull and a black Motown executive went with Stevie to see Wilson Pickett perform at a local club, Reeves dropped into a seat at their table. Tipping a glance at Hull, she sneered, "What's *he* doing here?"

Their racial divergence was another factor in the delicate and complex relationship, one that seemed to have little upside for the white "outsider." On trips to the South, for example, Hull's skin color could open doors closed to blacks at restaurants, hotels, and public toilets. On the other hand, when he was riding in a station wagon with Stevie and Gene Shelby, that same skin color led rednecks to wonder if Hull was another of those white liberal "nigger lovers" who came to the South to cause trouble. Often, Hull would shudder with fear, believing he might not make it back to Detroit but rather would be left in a shallow grave, as James Chaney, Michael Schwerner, and Andrew Goodman were in 1964.

Hull, who was born in Chattanooga, was no redneck, and, a bit naively, was astonished at the depth of racism he encountered while in the company of a black entertainer in mid-1960s America. Often he would feel the sting of it, such as when some jackass would start verbally threatening Stevie or some other Motown star. Then, he recalls, the bile would be redirected at him, "I guess because I was a safer target," at least when the original target was someone like Marvin Gaye or one of the Temptations, all of whom stood over six feet.

But Hull was perhaps most flabbergasted when, in London early in 1965 for a brief stay to do that guest shot on the BBC TV show *Thank Your Lucky Stars* and a round of radio interviews, he and Stevie ran into the American rocker Del Shannon, whose song "Runaway" was indeed a runaway hit the year before. Appearing on the same BBC radio show as Stevie, the Arkansas-bred Shannon seemed to enjoy meeting Stevie, but when Hull extended his hand to Shannon, he was left holding air. Said Hull, "Del gave me the distinct impression he didn't approve of a white man living and working so closely with blacks," which united Shannon with a good many blacks at Motown.

Hull and Stevie could bicker with each other as well. Culturally and politically opposite, they differed over politics and the cause of social activism. Their debates about such issues and about the escalating war in Vietnam, which Stevie foresaw as an impending disaster and Hull as a patriotic imperative, also escalated, at times rancorously. Though it wouldn't affect the general collegiality and loyalty they had for each other, it was clear that Stevie wasn't completely comfortable with Hull as his eyes to the world.

Adding to their complicated interdependency, Hull also began to write songs with Stevie, and Stevie insisted on giving him a writers' credit on a couple of songs he recorded. He had learned well the ways of the industry, one of which was the dispensing of writers' credits like Halloween candy to favored stooges or business allies. He did this for Lula Mae as well, which few around Motown took as anything other than largesse for the mother he was seeing less of and may have felt guilty about. In truth, Lula Mae could barely read or write, yet as Berry Gordy had proven, these failings did not necessarily preclude being able to write a good song.

Later that year, Gordy offered Hull the option of being paid according to a percentage of Stevie's earnings, in lieu of a salary. For Hull this might have seemed a quite deserving recompense—albeit one that had some risk too, what with Stevie's declining record sales— given that he'd had to tailor his life around Stevie's daily routines, in the process sacrificing any semblance of a personal life of his own. Then too, no reward might have seemed generous enough for having to put up with Lula Mae's constant henpecking and meddling.

She may have been seeing less of Stevie, but she made up for it by becoming more and more volatile. Not a day passed, it seemed, that she wasn't calling Hull, Gordy, Stevenson, or whoever had the misfortune of being the last to have her calls passed to and complaining about some real or imagined grievance about what was being done to Stevie. The normal end point of these rants was a threat to take him away from Motown forever. The common procedure was to rejoin each complaint with, "I understand, Mrs. Hardaway," or "It'll be taken care of, Mrs. Hardaway," and then simply ignore it. Usually Lula Mae would forget what she'd called about anyway.

For Hull, who bore most of her psychodramas, Lula Mae's interference would often lead him to seriously contemplate quitting. The most serious breach came on what was planned by Gordy as a working vacation and pleasant, relaxing diversion for Stevie following the completion of the rigorous projects *Muscle Beach Party* and *Stevie at the Beach* in mid-December 1963. By then plans had been made for a two-week excursion to Paris where Stevie would perform at the famed Olympia music hall during the Christmas holiday, and would also bounce across the Channel to do a few appearances in England on BBC television and radio as well as some interviews by the rabid Brit music newspapers—all important stepping-stones for Gordy building a market for Motown in Europe. From L.A., Stevie—for whom Gordy had obtained a passport in the name of Steveland Morris—and Hull were flown cross-country for a connecting flight to Paris.

In New York, they were met by Esther Edwards, Wade Marcus, a Motown hand who would act as Stevie's musical director for the Paris show, and Lula Mae, who had been adamant that she would not allow Stevie to fly all the way across the ocean without her being at his side. But, as Hull already had seen, Stevie was never in a relaxed state when she was around him, fully anticipating that she would blow a fuse over nothing. Hull came to dread those outbursts, too; as he noted, "No one ever knew what might set her off."

As soon as the plane was off the ground and en route to Orly Airport, it was clear that Lula had cast a pall over Stevie, evincing the strange dynamic of interwoven love and dread he had when he was with her. As he did during those times, he receded into her shadow, seeming to lose his otherwise ever-present froth and smiling face. Sitting beside her in stony silence, listening to her yammer about this and that, he fitfully squirmed in his seat and, according to Hull, "wrench[ed] at a clump of his hair," a nervous habit that worsened around Lula Mae. By the time they landed, he'd plucked a bald spot the size of a dime.

Because Lula Mae never ceased bad-mouthing Motown, Stevie's mood was hardly mellowed in Gay Paree; rather, even in the midst of all the attractions of a city he had studied in his textbooks, her static, as Hull recalls it, "fueled cynicism and moodiness." It only worsened when he began to feel pain in his throat when he sang. A ready induction was that it was some sort of psychosomatic reaction to the pressure that was exacerbated by Lula Mae. Whatever the reason, as the two-week Olympia engagement went on, he was unable to hit the high notes of his songs, which of course were mainly high notes. The audiences' lukewarm responses to an act that was the headliner of the shows, and the French promoters' grumbling, led Esther Edwards to take drastic action. For the Christmas Day show and thereafter, she pulled Stevie out of the "cleanup" spot—the last onstage, with the job of bringing the house down—moving him up to a supporting act for the new headliner, a young Dionne Warwick.

Crushed by the demotion, Stevie moped around Paris muttering to Lula Mae's loud agreement that Motown was "against me." The day after the humiliation, Stevie's frustration spiked in neurotic fashion when Hull presented Lula Mae with a bottle of expensive wine as a Christmas gift. Stevie reached for the bottle and dropped it on Hull's foot, breaking one of his toes.

As Hull winced in pain, Lula lit into Stevie, seemingly irrationally, for dropping it on purpose.

"Lula, it was an accident," Hull told her, only to realize by Stevie's unconcerned look that she was right: in his anger, Stevie saw Hull as one of "the enemy."

Later, his foot in a bandage, Hull was so fed up with the noxious atmosphere that he had it out with Stevie, wanting to clear the air of the "paranoia and distrust" being sown by mother and son. Blasting Stevie for his "arrogance," he said that unless Stevie changed his attitude, Hull was gone. "I'm not going to invest my life in a situation that's not going to work," he said. "I've got my own life to live."

Stevie uncharacteristically said nothing and the two of them barely conversed for several days. Only after Esther had a private talk with Stevie and Lula Mae, apparently to lay the law down to them, did they come to Hull and urge him to stay on. Toward the end of the trip, Hull and Stevie restored their bond, going off on their own to share the mutually profound experience of visiting Paris's National Institute for the Blind, where Louis Braille had studied and invented the reading system named for him.

But while he stayed on the job, with every right to a larger bounty for all he had to tolerate, Hull was torn about Gordy's royalty compensation offer. Because there'd be some who would regard it as a power play on his part, "it was imperative to me that Stevie, his mother, the Gordys and everyone at Motown know my actions were based on what was best for [Stevie], not my own self-interest." Yet merely that the supposition would exist—as well as his desire not to fuddle the moral lessons he tried teaching Stevie, one of his favorite being the need not to become a slave to the god of money—caused him to turn down the offer, one that would have eventually made him hugely wealthy, and something Hull need not be reminded of.

"Looking back from my financial position today," he says, "I sometimes wish I'd accepted, although I've never regretted it."

But neither did he regret walling Stevie off from the Motown crowd, something he admits "I caught a lot of flak for." His student may have been mature and knowing beyond his years, and incredibly functional for his blindness, but he was still vulnerable, perilously so when he found himself in large crowds. At those times, Hull had to be like a one-man SWAT team to pull Stevie through the mass of clutching hands of wild-eyed little girls trying to embrace him. More than once, he lost him in the crush for long, terrifying minutes, before somehow fighting his way through the mob to reclaim him. After a show in San Francisco's Cow Palace, they were separated and, peering through the crowd with his limited vision, Hull saw Stevie being pushed into a car, the slamming door just missing being closed on his hand. Hull was frantic, believing he had just seen Stevie Wonder kidnapped right before his very eyes, until he was told, much too late, that the car was that of a security detail hired by Motown without his knowledge. That only angered Hull more, because it confirmed how casual and erratic Motown was when it came to protecting Stevie—and why he was so overly vigilant about doing that. Making his point, he quotes an unnamed "Gordy assistant" whom he claims once told him, "Who cares about crowd control? We don't need it."

To Hull, that relaxed attitude seemed to quantify Motown's thinly disguised indifference to Stevie's career. Judging by the sapless records they were having Stevie make, the notion became inescapable to both mentor and protégé through almost all of 1964 and 1965: with Stevie's Motown contract due to expire a year later, Motown may have simply been waiting for those crowds that kept streaming to his concerts to cool down and thin out before deciding to cash in its Stevie Wonder investment.

It turned out that the pain in Stevie's throat was caused by the growth of two nodules on his vocal cords. Doctors diagnosed it after he'd gotten home from Paris in mid-January 1964 and surgically removed the nodules a few weeks later. Forbidden to sing, or even speak, for two more weeks, he had little to do but fret about how the operation might affect his voice—an already problematic issue because of his changing hormones—which only stressed him out more. The problem grew more magnified over what would be a nine-month recovery until, fortunately, no complications ensued and he was able to sing again without pain or inhibition.

By then it had been nearly a year since his previous recordings, though in the interim his "beach" album and singles filled the void and kept his star afloat, if not with the most buoyancy. Now, returning to the studio, he found no swell of new, quality songs waiting for his vocals. In fact, what was there seemed no better than before, another indication to him that Motown was not exactly working overtime on his behalf. One of the songs he cut, which was scheduled to be his next single, was called "Pretty Little Angel." This string-laden glob of fluff was reminiscent of Bobby Vee's ornate teen-pop fare of the early sixties, with Stevie trying to tame his still squeaky voice and odd twang at the direction of Clarence Paul, who tried to produce it as pure white pop, with no harmonica or any other R&B touches.

The result, however, could be summed up by the title of the intended B-side—"Tears in Vain"—and Gordy canceled its release. It took another four months to find a decent replacement, one on which Stevie hardly sang at all. Going back to the Ray Charles trough of jazzy R&B, Gordy chose "Kiss Me Baby," cowritten by Paul and Stevie and produced by the former as another swingin' harmonica showcase, with Stevie seductively purring, "Kiss me baby—sugar kiss" on the intro and then screeching "Oh yeah!" at intervals over the jazzy arrangement.

By now, though, these kinds of "Fingertips" clones had become cliché. Released on March 26, 1965, backed with the revived "Tears in Vain"— six months after "Happy Street"—"Kiss Me Baby" stiffed, shut out on both the pop and R&B charts.

Coming just as Gordy had rolled the Motortown Revue, Stevie included, all the way across the Atlantic, the lack of success for "Kiss Me Baby" was not particularly helpful. Gordy's salvo against raging Beatlemania and the ensuing British "invasion" of America was taking Motown right into the Fab Four's home turf, where the company brand had been slowly building. This move was nothing but logical, inasmuch as American blues and R&B had long been a major influence on budding Brit rock-and-roll singers. The Beatles, in fact, revered Motown, covering a number of its songs on their early albums, which wasn't just a compliment to Gordy but a vital fount of relevance and acceptance in the new order of rock and roll, and the Rolling Stones and Yardbirds recorded note-for-note reduxes of the likes of Muddy Waters and Elmore James, couched in hard rock and psychedelia.

That Motown, its debt paid to its musical roots, was now in the process of devolving from overt R&B to mainstream pop incidentally sung by blacks was seen by some critics in the notoriously harsh British music press as a "sellout," a word that Gordy would soon have thrown in his face in America too. But in 1965 it didn't do any damage to Motown's credibility as a "ghetto" idiom, which fascinated the monochromatic English poseurs by letting them pretend they knew what it was like to be black and oppressed by listening to black music (to the amusement of the American soul artists who played there, such as Sonny Boy Williamson, who toured with the Yardbirds and issued the immortal smackdown, "Those English boys want to play the blues so bad—and they play the blues *so* bad.")

An important breakthrough came when soul music moved from narrow corridors to broad bands when "pirate" radio stations broadcasting from offshore boats broke the putative "embargo" by the BBC on "foreign" records, which many believed was aimed at American "race music." The government stations were, by early 1965, playing Motown and other soul hits with increasing frequency, greasing the path for the Supremes' "Baby Love" to hit the top of the British pop chart in November 1964, one of the very few American "race" records to do that, or *any* American record. Thus the timing seemed right for Gordy to export not only his vinyl but actual humans across the Atlantic.

The tour was set for March and April that would take the troupe—Stevie, the Supremes, Smokey and the Miracles, Martha and the Vandellas, the Temptations, and a sextet of Motown musicians fronted by pianist Earl Van Dyke—through towns large and small, and with side trips to Germany and the Netherlands before a climactic finale at a locale that made Stevie's stomach hurt—the Olympia in Paris, which like the Apollo finales would be recorded and filmed for theatrical and album releases. Gordy ratcheted up a lavish and expensive PR onslaught to pimp the tour, which was at least implicitly headlined by the now red-hot Supremes. They were in the midst of what would be *five* consecutive number one hits, which began when Holland-Dozier-Holland had them cut "Where Did Our Love Go" the previous summer and, with HDH as their sole overlords, continued apace with "Baby Love," "Come See About Me," and their newest, "Stop! In the Name of Love."

It would have been advantageous if Stevie had even one hit of that magnitude, or anything close to it, post-"Fingertips." In fact, not only was he not on that stratum, but he'd been left in the dust by Marvin Gaye, who was on a roll of his own, with his first four Top 10 hits, the latest being "I'll Be Doggone," written and produced by Smokey Robinson. And yet, curiously, for the most ambitious Motortown Revue of all, Gordy made the decision to leave his brother-in-law home, despite several wildly popular guest slots in the past by Gaye on British TV. Gordy's reasoning was that solo acts weren't selling as many records as the groups (never mind that the top single of 1964 was Louis Armstrong's "Hello Dolly"). This rash verdict would nearly destroy Gaye's confidence, prompting him to record over the next three years mainly in duets, first with Kim Weston, then Tammi Terrell. Neither did it seem to bode well for Stevie.

Except that Gordy had made an exception for him, inviting him along as the only solo act on the bill. Maybe it was a reward, or pity, for a kid who'd worked so tirelessly and agreeably on so many dreadful Gordy projects. Or just that Gordy, who had a funny way of showing it, wanted to show that Stevie was still in his favor. As Mickey Stevenson observed, Gordy liked to play hunches, which came to him spontaneously. One day he could be down on Stevie and high on someone else, only to invert those opinions the next. As the Revue flew off to Paris, he seemed to have elevated Stevie and relegated Gaye.

To Stevie's noticeable relief, Lula Mae was not invited on this flight over the ocean. But one consideration in Gordy's suddenly renewed faith in Stevie was that he had gone to lengths to placate her, upping the ante of his investment in her son. Most patiently, he had given in to Lula Mae's grousing about her crumbling walls and floors on Breckenridge Street, paying $18,000 for a spacious four-bedroom house on Greenlawn Avenue in northwest Detroit, in a very tony neighborhood that made for culture shock all around. When the Hardaways moved in, they became just the third black family to inhabit the block. (Gordy probably did not mention to her that the cost would be deducted from Stevie's escrow trust fund account.)

While she tended to furnishing her new digs, with yet another child, a son named Timmy, to raise, she coincidentally kept a safe distance from Motown, to the relief of everyone there. With far less tension, Stevie took off for Europe not pulling his hair out but instead optimistic for the first time in months, Gordy having reassured him that there'd be a fresh round of better-quality recordings when he returned. His voice was strong, very close now to settling into a natural, lower register that wouldn't crack when he shifted into the higher notes—exactly what Gordy had been waiting two years to find out.

The problem was that, wedged between so many hits from the rest of the Motown cast, he was all but lost in the shuffle. After all, everyone else on the stage came armed to the gills with gold. In addition to the Supremes' hoard of it, the Temptations had broken out early in the year with the Smokey Robinson gem "My Girl," a No. 1 pop and R&B hit. Martha and the Vandellas, on a two-year roll stoked by Holland-Dozier-Holland fuel such as "Come and Get These Memories" and "Heat Wave," and Marvin Gaye and Mickey Stevenson's epochal rock-and-roll battle cry, "Dancing in the Street," now had on the fire another HDH ruby, "Nowhere to Run." Smokey and the Miracles, always money in the bank, were riding their latest hit, the ultimate makeout song, "Ooo Baby Baby," into the Top 20.

Within this grand buffet of soul and pop, Stevie had to make do with table scraps of stage time, which he made the most of. Yet since

"Fingertips" was too distant for reprise now, when he was performing songs unfamiliar to audiences the halls could lose some of the heat that had been fanned by the hitmakers. At those times, more than one person in the Motown troupe probably wondered why Stevie was there and not Marvin Gaye. This drop-off in ardor can be gleaned by viewing what is now a timeless, indelible marker of the tour, and of that nexus of history when Motown was at its utopian apogee as a stable of roughly egalitarian acts in full bloom. This was a special produced by the hip BBC television music program *Ready Steady Go!* called "The Sound of Motown," hosted by the British thrush and Motown acolyte Dusty Springfield, who had pitched the show to the BBC after being on the same bill as the Revue at a Christmas show at the Brooklyn Fox Theater hosted by the New York DJ Murray the K.

Taped and broadcast early in the tour, on March 18, it crammed a profusion of hits, mostly in truncated form, into an hour, with a pace so breakneck that one act would dissolve into the next without a pause. Stevie got on during a round robin of medleys by the other acts; squeezing in a minute or so of "Pretty Music," he was perched in a chair on a platform raised six feet above the stage and undulating go-go dancers below, letting rip his usual high-energy arm-flailing and harmonica wailing, but was gone before many may have realized he was on. Later, introduced by Springfield as a "fantastic talent . . . and he's still only fifteen," he sang "Kiss Me Baby" while standing in front of a microphone, bobbing and roiling. Long and lean, he was as tall as the dancers that pranced around him, but no less childlike in his glee. But the tepid song almost made it seem like this was a lull in the show. In the show's closing jam, he was again up high, clapping, the platform shaking, as the cast joined in on the Miracles' "Mickey's Monkey."

The configuration of the company during that last number was an augury. Onstage, while Smokey and his group did the song, all the other acts were lined up stage left, while the Supremes alone were given stage right. This was not an accident; the entire English tour was devised to elevate Ross, Wilson, and Ballard, rendering everyone else the "And Others." From the start, the trio was ferried about in Gordy's stretch limo while the "others" rode a bus, and were put up in luxury penthouse suites stocked with champagne bottles in ice in London's posh Cumberland Hotel, literally and symbolically above the rest of the troupe, who were consigned to the lower floors. Not that the Supremes needed hotel rooms; throughout the tour, while the troupe hunkered down in cheap motels in working-class towns like Bristol, Manchester, Portsmouth, Cardiff, Wolverhampton, Leicester, and, mandatorily, the Beatles' breeding ground of Liverpool, Gordy and his pampered pop princesses often stayed in castles and palaces as the guests of British royalty.

For Gordy, squiring the girls, and Diana Ross in particular, through this storybook that lacked only for Prince John and Emperor Contalabutte, he seemed to redefine the intended goal of the trip, from doing the European market to doing Ross. The two of them, notwithstanding their fifteen-year age difference, had been doing a barely concealed mating tango for the past year, with Gordy trying for once not to think with his fly and keep a professional distance from the brazenly ambitious Diana, but as powerless to resist as had been his "boys," the married Smokey Robinson and Brian Holland. When Ross, who clearly knew where her bread was buttered at Motown, set her sights on the big boss, as she had from the beginning, the only question was where and when.

The where turned out to be Gordy's hotel room in Paris, in the wee hours after the Revue's grand finale at the Olympia, a blessed event Gordy would remember as "Ecstasy to the tenth power! And after that night it only got better."

Actually, in some ways it got worse, as the two of them carried on a near psychotically erratic "secret" affair (which not a soul at Motown didn't know all about) that at times was something more out of Sade than Balzac. Even before Paris, however, that Gordy had stacked the deck in favor of the Supremes begat hard feelings lower in the ranks. Looking back at that fateful tour—which in the end was a financial disaster, played to many half-filled houses and with no real boost in record sales—Martha Reeves, up to then a vital part of Gordy's strategems, says sadly, "I never questioned his directions or his motives—until this trip to England," whereupon the change in the wind at Motown left her and her mates, and more than a few others, feeling out in the cold.

If Gordy heard any of these rumblings, he was too obsessed with milking the Supremes to care. Nor did he have any conscious qualms that the Motown the world had known had ceased to be. Now it would become primarily a Cinderella fable, times three, bathed in glitter, gowns, and galas. At the same time, Gordy hired a charm-school pedagogue to instruct the Supremes and, by his order, all Motown acts—even the male ones (Stevie, mercifully, earned an exemption)—in methods of poise and sophistication. He brought in Cholly Atkins, a hard-driving choreographer who with partner Honi Coles had tap-danced on the Broadway stage in the 1930s, to "class up" the fancy but still rough-hewn footwork manifested at Motown shows. To some, Atkins's real marching order was to strip the "blackness" from those dance steps. Gordy also called in Maurice King, the esteemed bandleader for years at the Flame Show Bar to coach the performers on how to ad-lib witty and engaging patter onstage in the gaps between songs.

Among Gordy's steerage class, these protocols typically were derided, out of Gordy's earshot, as offensive—and worse, if one could infer in them a dynamic of racial self-loathing.

It was inarguable that the Motown purview *did* change dramatically, and with it the racial fundament and ligature to the ghetto that had carried the company to its fruition. There is no clearer line of demarcation in Motown history than July 29, 1965. On that night, the Supremes became the first black act of the rock-and-roll era to play New York's Copacabana nightclub, the essence and epicenter of 1950s and '60s swingin' "Rat Pack" white cool, thus breaking the seal for other Motown acts, and other *black* acts of the era, to follow. Soon, the Temptations, Smokey and the Miracles, even the "downgraded" Martha and the Vandellas and the resurrected Marvin Gaye would preen onto the floor there, to intermingle the Motown hits with decidedly soul-free Broadway and show tunes.

As it turned out, the Motown talent roster had no major objections to the new, whiter wind blowing at Motown, which after all carried more profit for them, too. The only rub was that they had to bide their time on the back burner waiting to follow the Supremes into this room or that casino. Accordingly, the "new" Motown was not the one with the spirit of sharing growing dreams, and in its wake few new or holdover Motown acts would catch fire during the second half of the decade, until the arrival of the Jackson 5. For those five years, Motown *had* no promise, no mission statement beyond making money, and no room at the inn for anything fresh to develop.

The irony, then, is that one Motown, the one that had had to wait the longest and with the most patience, would only now, without any real logic to it, begin to flourish. In the periscope of history, those ancient

"Sound of Motown" tapes reveal a fifteen-year-old boy on the precipice of enduring stardom. And yet in real time, not even Gordy could have played a hunch on that.

Not unless someone could come up with that long-elusive hit for him would that be possible, nor could Stevie Wonder's place at Motown be anything close to secure.

For Stevie, England was a bummer, not for garnering too little attention but rather too much, though for all the wrong reasons. Dispensing interviews liberally with the Brit media early in the sojourn, he had to tolerate repeated questions not about music or Motown but the "issue" of his blindness. Bizarrely, thanks to the greasy London tabloids that pushed brain-dead gossip, rumors had been going around that Stevie was not blind at all, that it was all a gimmick engineered by Motown for maximum public relations value. This no doubt grew out of the same cheesecloth that always had people atwitter at how he could do so many things, play so many instruments, and get around so effortlessly—and still be sightless. The especially gullible on the Fleet Street rags may also have bought the folktales told by Motown wags, such as about how Stevie could "see" what women were wearing, without the part about how he set up that con with accomplices.

Stevie had a good time playfully and coyly dealing with the charge, even pulling the same ruse on the Brit reporters. "Where'd you get that shirt?" he'd ask, before denying a little too much that he really, really couldn't see. Not so amusing, though, was a related story that Stevie wanted to undergo surgery on his eyes to restore his vision but, as the scuttlebutt went, was being prohibited from doing so by Motown because he wouldn't be as profitable.

There was actually some truth to this story, in a circuitous way. Its genesis could be traced to a female reporter in London, described by Ted Hull as a "sexy young black woman . . . as charming as a black widow spider," who in private had told him about such an operation and who *herself* had made that assumption about Motown, in such a leading way that Stevie was inveigled to agree with her, precisely what she had wanted for the sake of the story. In fact, Stevie had previously discussed with Hull whether a surgical procedure existed that might restore at least some of his sight, with Hull not wanting to encourage him. "[I told him] nothing could be done about his blindness, and I thought such notions had been dispelled," he recalled. Now he was parroting the sexy reporter, with Hull remembering Stevie saying he wanted to try an operation, "but Esther won't allow it, because if I could see, then I wouldn't be a star for Motown. And they won't make money off me."

Again Hull had to dash his hopes, with a mixture of sadness and anger. "My heart went out to Stevie as I gently explained what he already really knew," Hull said, adding, "I was outraged that the woman could be so cruel as to lie like that." Stevie, though, would not totally let go of the myth, mainly as a parable of Motown and the Gordys. And when people at Motown picked up on the story—"Even Clarence Paul asked me if it was true," Hull said—and commiserated with Stevie about his plight and Gordy's motives, it only fanned what was now a simmering discontent not just about where Motown was taking him but how *it* could be so cruel.

Despite Gordy's forbearance in putting him on the tour, after coming home Stevie had no reason to believe there was any greater emphasis on finding him hit material. That is, if there was any material at all. Having tried to work seemingly every idiom under the sun, Paul was at an impasse, and with nothing on hand worthy of booking studio time, Gordy once more was rummaging through spools of concert tape to find something he could put out as the next single that might catch the same fire as "Fingertips. He went with Stevie's version of the much-covered 1964 hard-core blues rattler "High Heel Sneakers" by Tommy Tucker, taken from the final Motortown Revue show at the Olympia, with Stevie freely embellishing the "Put on your red dress, momma" riffs with the "Everybody clap yo' hands" doggerel of "Fingertips."

This cut is one Stevie had grown fond of, saying years later, with some hyperbole, that "it was the highlight of the show," and that the raw euphoria of the recording was due to the French musicians who spoke no English and "were just following along. It was a very spontaneous thing." But if this seemed to be an updated equation of "Fingertips," the single, released on August 2 (with the B-side a bluesy take on Willie Nelson's twangy "Funny How Time Slips Away," which Stevie was using as his show-closing number but was replaced on later-issued copies by "Music Talk," cowritten by Stevie, Paul, and Ted Hull), made it to No. 59 pop, No. 30 R&B, not horrible but nothing that justified Gordy's faith in him.

By the autumn of 1965, that sometimes wavering allegiance in fact seemed to be the only thread, and a thin one, that Stevie Wonder could grab on to. Murmurs could be heard that time was running out for Stevie. Because his contract was also running out, due to expire in May 1966, that date became a kind of unofficial deadline for something to break his way. A scant two years before, he had done a lot to put Motown on the map, and he was still turning the voltage meters up wherever he went. But now Stevie Wonder was on the clock.

8

Outta Sight

My sound wasn't really Motown as much as it was me, my sound. The first three or four albums I did mostly their suggestions, but after that I work[ed] with the producer and they did *my* suggestions.

—*Stevie Wonder*

Not at all surprising, given his acute awareness of what was in the air around him, Stevie heard the ominous scuttlebutt about his future. After "High Heel Sneakers" failed to rekindle the heat wave of "Fingertips," the idle chatter grew louder. Though no one, least of all Berry Gordy, ever sat him down for a heart-to-heart about the hard realities, to Stevie the threat wasn't just implicit, it was tangible. He could even name names of the headshakers, and at least one would-be executioner, who in retrospect he would only identify as a "guy at Motown [who] recommended that several acts be dropped" and wanted Stevie out on grounds that, as Stevie quoted him, "His voice is changing, he's getting taller, we gotta buy him new clothes." Intriguingly, Stevie let it be known that this gent had apparently produced him, that "he would call me in and ask me to sing with strings, he'd say, 'Sing over this' and I'd say, 'Make it a little lower. Man, my voice is changing.'"

One could presume he meant Clarence Paul, given that he'd been produced almost exclusively by Paul. He also added that the man "eventually got fired," and Paul did in fact split from Motown, but then so did many others, in an "I quit/you're fired" scenario, including Mickey Stevenson and Harvey Fuqua, each of whom worked with Stevie in the studio at one time or another. Whoever the "guy" was, his opinion was shared neither by the only Motown "guy" whose opinion mattered nor by Gordy's deputy Smokey Robinson, who dug Stevie to no end. Still, as Stevie's antennae told him, Motown had definitely pulled away from him.

The pullback was made obvious by the fact that he was now hearing his songs on the radio only fleetingly, left orphaned by a lack of promotional pushing. Although Stevie could point to the wild reaction by audiences to his act, Motown was a record company living off sales, not concerts, the latter being a means to that end, and reliant on no particular act. Indeed, in early 1966 the Motortown Revue was sent back out on a tour of college campuses, but not even the absence of the Supremes, who were busy doing their own road treks, kept the Revue from selling out every show. Stevie Wonder was a valued team player in those appearances, but with a paucity of chart hits, if he was cast out, few might have even known, or cared. Not immaterial to the discussion was that Motown had thirty-four chart hits out of the roughly sixty releases that year—a truly remarkable ratio—and chalked up gross sales in excess of $40 million. Bottom line: Gordy didn't *need* Stevie Wonder.

Indeed, as Gordy would tell it, it was Stevie, not any of the Motown song purveyors—and certainly not himself—whom he held responsible for the failure to build on "Fingertips." Having "opened the doors" for Stevie, he maintained, his inability to walk through them "was a no-no for our company. As far as I was concerned that was a sin."

Thus the leverage Stevie had curried with Gordy was shaky. Whether or not the clock would indeed have run out on him when his contract expired is something only Gordy knows. However, Mickey Stevenson insists it was nowhere near midnight in mid-1965, despite the negativity of some in executive offices. "There was no way we were thinking of letting him go," he says. "He was fifteen! That would've been stupid. He was still fucking green. We felt that we'd just started to scratch the surface with Stevie. It was the same with the Supremes and Temptations. We knew what we had in them but they couldn't buy a hit until it clicked.

"That was my job: to find the right combination. And you just keep releasing records to keep an act alive, keep the name alive, knowing you won't get a big hit out of it. That's what we did with Stevie. We didn't put a lot behind some of those records, but we kept him out there until it happened for him. Sometimes it's a matter of coming up with the right writer and producer. Sometimes the artists themselves come up with the right idea. With Stevie, it was both."

Stevie himself didn't seem to be overly worried. John Glover, who had reinserted himself at Motown in the mid-1960s as a songwriter and producer for the Originals and Jimmy Ruffin, describes his old running buddy as if he was preparing for his breakthrough, and hardly waiting for the ax to fall on his neck.

"If anything, Stevie was working harder than ever," Glover says, "because he thought he'd have to play a bigger part, take charge more of his own affairs. He was traveling around so much, he was never home, and during those travels he was really growing up, physically and musically. He was writing all the time, in a style more attuned to his changing voice and more mature musical tastes. He'd tell me, 'Hey man, I got all these song ideas and nobody to tell 'em to.'

"That's really what he needed, someone to translate and build on what he was thinkin', take those little fragments, you know, and make them what he had in mind for a song. Clarence taught him a hell of a lot, but he had moved beyond Clarence. He needed someone, a new face who could understand new ideas."

If Stevie believed Motown was looking in all the wrong places for his material, he didn't think it was necessarily wrong for him to dabble with themes and concepts outside the Motown orbit, ones for which he had more affinity. As he once admitted, "I had the independence because I was somewhat distant," given his schooling in Lansing and his "bubble boy" existence enforced, most of the time, by Ted Hull. In trying to develop his own material, Stevie paid no heed to what a Motown song was supposed to sound like, or what *he* was supposed to sound like, at least according to the Motown establishment. For some reason, Motown hadn't accepted or adapted to the new, deeper comfort zone of his voice, which sounded *better* than ever; his phonic timbre had ripened without hollowing, finding greater depth and range and blending subtle inflection with pure down-home, gospel-choir bombast. It was, as Gordy marveled in his memoirs, "a controlled, powerful, versatile instrument." Yet either Berry didn't fully know that or else wasn't moved enough to utilize it, as if doing so would, in the grand worldview of Motown, risk the residual sales, live concert, and marketing value of "Fingertips." Of course, the Catch-22 here was that future sales would not likely pick up until "Fingertips" was eclipsed by a current, more keenly crafted tune.

Aching as he was to kick his way out of the box Motown had him in, Stevie's sessions had become trying affairs, with Stevie sometimes snapping at Paul, who in turn grew more testy himself and less willing to hear what Stevie had to say. "The people who produce me," Stevie said later, cutting Paul a break by not fingering him as a perpetrator, "used to say, 'Now come on, Stevie, I want you to scream on this part, 'cause that's you man.' And so I used to scream my head off. Then I thought, 'Shit, maybe, maybe not. If I feel it, I'll do it. But don't make me scream before the break on every song.'" Clearly, the relationship between them was fraying at the edges, another reason for some of the Motown brass to waver about keeping him.

Paul, on his part, was ready to cut his tether. "I had exclusive production on Stevie," he recalled in the 1970s, "but we were cold. I didn't have no hits. I couldn't think of nothin' and he couldn't think of nothin.'"

Glover's recollections cast doubt on Paul's attempt to make Stevie complicit in that dried-up well. Just as likely was that Stevie was brimming with ideas, ones that Paul quite obviously didn't care to hear. But was there anyone who would?

When Paul drew back from the task of overseeing Stevie's recordings—he'd continue as his conductor and musical director on the road—Gordy gave the role to Hank Cosby, who of course had been arranging and writing some of Stevie's songs from the beginning. But the horn man was not the sort of collaborator Stevie needed; he did not have the same ear for melody and for the young, happening vernacular that Stevie spoke. The entrenched narrative for the transition has long been that, with no one else clamoring for the job, a still fledgling Motown songsmith named

Sylvia Moy—whose own future at the company was in doubt, with very little of her work being committed to vinyl—stepped forward. With nothing to lose, Gordy gave his assent. In some tracts, credit is freely given to her for thus "saving" Stevie Wonder's career.

This claim might gild the lily a wee bit, since as Glover points out, Moy was employed at the time as Hank Cosby's apprentice and, he says, "Sylvia kind of was like a throw-in. I think she'd actually written some stuff with Stevie, so I don't know that she volunteered to 'take over' writing with him as much as she already was. But I guess it sounds good."

Stevenson surely had no objection to them teaming up. "We liked Sylvia," he says, "her style of writing. At that time, the sound was changing. Clarence was an older producer and guys like Holland-Dozier-Holland were taking us in a different direction, very swinging and happening. Listen, I didn't care who was writing what, just get the damn thing done, 'cause I was payin' my musicians by the hour, so it was like, get your shit together and bring me a song."

Stevenson would take an active role in making "that song" into a record, as it turned out, after hearing a demo that came out of those writing sessions. The tune cribbed a melody from the Rolling Stones' monster summertime hit "(I Can't Get No) Satisfaction," which itself had been modeled on the hard-driving Motown four-by-four rhythm, with a snare drum strike on each beat instead of every other, on the backbeat. Using this beat, Holland-Dozier-Holland created a lively, nervy edge to their songs. (And not incidentally, going for massive crossover appeal was structured around the theory that whites tended to clap on every beat, as opposed to blacks who did so on the backbeat.) Around it, Moy erected a lyrical framework peppered with "Stevie-isms," pet phrases he had picked up from the emerging vernacular of cool in the vein of "far out" and "groovy," the most obvious being "outta sight!" Another one he liked to spout was "uptight!"

As the composition was stitched together, Moy filled syllable space by using the rhyming expressions in conjunction, forming a nice hook that went, "Baby, everything is alright. Uptight, outta sight," and whipped up a teen tableau with a social message that actually cut rather deep, the protagonist a poor boy crowing about winning over a rich girl—who, if anyone thought about it, was too rich judging by the lyrics to be a *black* girl. To those who would take it that way, it would not merely be the wiping away a class barrier but a racial one, and more centrally, perched on the third rail of interracial dating and sex.

Any such theme would be playing with real fire in 1965, and to this day Stevie hasn't really said if he wrote the song as a conscious provocation, or with motives more ingenuous. But one can assume that he and Moy knew they had to tread lightly, tilting toward the class perspective much as had the Four Seasons the year before with two huge hits, "Dawn" and "Rag Doll." Stevie, channeling his own background, sang, believably, in his lower voice, of proudly being "an average guy, no football hero or smooth Don Juan," with the "empty pockets" of a "poor man's son," but still able to win over the "pearl of a girl" from "the right side of the tracks" who lived "in a great big old house, full of butlers and maids."

When Hank Cosby in mid-September went in to cut the first of many tracks of the song, which was given the very cool-sounding if, to many, contradictory title "Uptight (Everything's Alright)," Stevenson was in the booth with him, perhaps as a sentry to make sure it would be produced with no "message" in its grooves other than to compel teenagers to get up and dance—though, intriguingly, Stevenson can't confirm this because he seemed at a loss when asked about his role in this signal Motown song.

"Hmm, I remember that, somewhat," he says. "It's a long time ago." A laugh. "If it says I was a coproducer, then I coproduced it. To be very honest with you, I don't remember many of those songs [for which he was credited as a producer], or what part I had in them."

Stevenson pauses, evidently to ponder about how what he'd said might be taken—namely, that Motown producing credits, like the writing credits, were at times doled out to executives as spoils of the job, regardless of merit. (Producers customarily received a one-third royalty of a song's earnings.) Quickly, he backtracks.

"I got a royalty off everything," he goes on, "every song, no matter what, as the A&R director. I got paid on every hit, that was part of my deal. That's why, if I wrote a song and you wrote a better one, I'd go with yours. 'Cause we'd *both* make money off it. I didn't need no fuckin' ego rub. Same goes for producing. I didn't go around braggin' on myself for doing that. If I was listed as a producer, then, man, it means I was in the studio as it was going down. I was on the case."

Stevenson could have been there to coach Cosby on the finer points of the Motown sound, a template that had generally not been used for Stevie's previous songs with their "fly it live" feel. For "Uptight," it had been decided to go with the pomp and care that had refined the R&B-rooted grit and gruff of most Motown songs into smooth, punchy pop with a bone-shaking deep bottom and rattling percussion at the top. By now, too, while Studio A was still a "snakepit," as the musicians called it, its airless and dungeonlike aesthetic crucial to the musicians' mind-set of playing hot, authentic licks, state-of-the-art equipment had been installed in the control booth and instruments walled off from each other and recorded on an eight-track recorder that could separate sounds within the general Motown blast of massed rhythm. And vocals were being recorded in a discrete booth independently of the instrument track.

Armed with these advantages, Cosby and Stevenson could coat "Uptight" with loud, exhilarating horns, strings, and Benny Benjamin's thunderous drum rolls, which probably not incidentally all but obscured the subject matter. To be sure, it is the most clamorous Stevie Wonder record of all, more so even than "Fingertips," and it restored the element that had gone missing from the records he'd made since: naturalness with unforced excitement and agitation.

Even navigating with circumspection around the parlous lyrics of "Uptight," however, the "poor man's son" refrain would still be heard in many ears as a slyly bold racial statement, or at least a socially conscious one, which could be said about few Motown records up to then. And though a timorous Gordy and his yes-men were wary about the consequences of such a reaction, they prospered despite themselves. Released on November 22, 1965, with "Purple Rain Drops" (credited to Ted Hull and Clarence Paul) on the flip, it hit the Top 40 in late January and soared to No. 3 on the pop chart, and all the way to No. 1 on the R&B chart, two months later, almost certainly clearing one million copies sold, though only Gordy and his accountants knew the real numbers.

Its handsome financial return aside, "Uptight" was a pivotal record, not only in Stevie's now-assured longevity at Motown but in the substance of Hitsville's musical catalog. Not that there would be any less emphasis on the Supremes' "high-toned" trope, but even they would be deemed suitable to front a "serious" message, Gordy himself two years later being one of the writers of the self-consciously venturous and supremely successful "Love Child." The same year would yield Marvin Gaye's almost unnerving rendition of Norman Whitfield's mordantly dark-hearted "I Heard It Through the Grapevine," which would become the company's top-selling record of the decade. Moreover, in this new phase of the Motown evolution, Stevie Wonder would not be a bystander or free rider. Trusting only his own instincts, he would be a major energy cell.

"Uptight" also guaranteed that Sylvia Moy, who had been trained as a classical pianist, would never again have to worry that her future would be as a music teacher. Her foreseeable future was going to be soldered to Stevie Wonder. The most immediate exigency of her dawning was one with a good deal of pressure: to somehow match the success of a record that had made such an enormous impact—the failure to do exactly that after "Fingertips" had nearly cost Stevie his Motown career.

And so Stevie and Moy chose the safest course: reheating a savory and profitable stew for a second helping. The song they penned, "Nothing's Too Good for My Baby," was once again coproduced, according to its label, by Hank Cosby and Mickey Stevenson, the latter of whom remembers as little of this assignment as he does "Uptight." Recorded just after the new year, the arrangement reprised almost note for note the same hard-driving beat of "Uptight," from the drum and bass intro working into the same font of honking horns, nectarous strings, Benny Benjamin's nonstop array of drum rolls and shuffles, and clanging guitar backbeat. There was even the same citation by Stevie of the "pearl of a girl" and the "ha ha ha ha ha *yeah*" burbling on the fadeout.

What was *not* there was any crumb of deeper meaning to the love-letter lyrics about the "sweet and kind" girl who "tells me she's mine all the time." Whether or not this defanging was at the insistence of a still nervous Gordy or Stevenson—who this time gained a writer's credit too—the sanitizing and desensitizing of the throbbing nerve of "Uptight" took the edge off the ballistic punch of a melody and Stevie's infectious and easeful vocal. While "Nothing" was hardly that, it was something not nearly as big as "Uptight." Released on March 24, backed by "With a Child's Heart," it ran just as fast up the R&B chart, landing at No. 4 in early summer, but stopped at No. 20 on the more important pop chart, plausibly, because a more mature Motown audience was left unmoved by the (literal) whitewashing of a song that could be assumed to be a sequel to "Uptight." As well, in a sure sign that radio DJs weren't smitten by it, and were turning the disc over, "With a Child's Heart" broke off for a chart run of its own, scraping the bottom of the pop list at No. 133 but hitting a strong No. 8 on the R&B.

In no way was Stevie contented with these results. Indeed, "Nothing's Too Good for My Baby" marked the last time he would cheat himself by copycatting any of his hit records. As he charted the course of what he wanted to release next, he resolved immediately to go as radically against the grain as Motown would allow, even if he had to *make* them allow it. At sixteen, with a rasher of ideas and concepts that didn't naturally fit into the Motown scaffolding, he was now far ahead of the field there in audacity and self-sustaining intellectual fuel. If Marvin Gaye was so cowed by Gordy's imprecations about "solo acts" that he couldn't bring himself to demand the studio for a work of personal and, tangentially, social significance, Stevie had no such equivocation. He'd endured, paid his dues, engineered his own renaissance. He was in it for the big picture now, for what he wanted to say—for what he *saw*. Which was getting more and more piquant, restless, and issue-driven by the day.

As Ted Hull tells it, the business of Mickey Stevenson producing or not producing those Stevie sessions was part of a larger Motown label-credit scam, one that cost Hull his status as a sometime writer in its employ. He first learned how the game was played as a beneficiary: when "Music Talk" supplanted "Funny How Time Slips Away" as the B-side of "High Heel Sneakers" because, since the flip sides were entitled to all the royalties earned by the A-sides, Motown, albeit tardily, sought to keep the royalty pot in its pocket rather than in Willie Nelson's.

A far bigger plum came when another Hull tune, "Purple Rain Drops," was chosen as the B-side of the far more profitable "Uptight." It would be a real pot of gold for Hull. However, it turned into a contretemps when "Rain Drops" was released with Clarence Paul gaining Hull's credit as cowriter. Hull, who had composed the song while in college, insists that Paul's only contribution to the recorded version was that "he suggested I change the tune slightly," earning for him a 50 percent split on the royalties he would reel in when the song zoomed—in addition to his one-third royalty cut as its producer. "No one," Hull said, "had discussed such an arrangement with me. . . . What I didn't know was that it was customary to share credit with anyone [who] helped get a piece produced. It was a lesson I learned the hard way."

By the rules, Hull was expected to keep mum and be grateful for the alms he got. One day, before he knew "Rain Drops" would be so vested, he and Stevie were with Stevenson and Kim Weston, whom Stevenson had recently married, in a limousine going to the airport when Mickey piped up, telling Hull, "I understand you're getting a free ride on the flip side of my record." Hull, who foolishly believed it was *Stevie's* record, took the remark to mean he would get no more "free rides" if he groused about sharing credits.

Hull was right, but he did grouse about it. And it was the last time a song of his was released by Motown—or even rereleased. While Motown would soon issue, only six months apart, two Stevie Wonder albums, each using sundry B-sides as filler, some several years old, Paul evidently agreed to keep "Rain Drops" off them to spite Hull. On the other hand, "With a Child's Heart," the song Motown chose as the flip of "Nothing's Too Good for My Baby," was written by a nonstaffer, but one who happened to be a hot young woman from New York named Vicky Basemore, one of Paul's harem of willing women. She too had to make room on the label, so that Hank Cosby could take a cowriting credit.

A corollary lesson to be learned, then, was that if Clarence Paul had ceded control of Stevie to Cosby and Moy on new material, with the handoff had seemingly come a quid pro quo: he could pick a credit, any credit, or someone of his choosing. Hull had a word for it, one he uses ruefully when he says, "Looking back now, I wouldn't care how many names were added to mine on the label, or who got a kickback [if it meant my work would have been heard]."

Hull insists that Motown's spite was ongoing. That year, at the annual Motown Christmas gala at Detroit's Fox Theater, Gordy handed out envelopes with company bonuses. Hull, for all he had done keeping Stevie schooled, and in school, reckoned that Gordy surely owed him something—figuring in Gordy's notorious penury, he says he would have been happy with fifty bucks—but was left with an empty palm.

Then there was the sad case of Beans Bowles, the man who had nearly been killed toiling for Gordy on the Motortown Revue. A favorite among the Motown crowd of artists and musicians, especially of Stevie, he nonetheless was robbed silly by Paul, for no apparent reason other than that he could. It seems that Bowles had created the melody for "Fingertips" but with Paul calling the shots on credits, none was given to Bowles, despite Paul's repeated assurances that he would personally see to it that Beans got royalties. Pitifully, almost comically, Bowles once related that after getting nowhere with Paul, he was comforted by a sympathetic Stevie, who, Bowles once recalled, "said he'd give me some money."

Bowles laughed at the memory, knowing that Stevie himself was little more than Motown chattel, and would be even after rising in rank. "Ha! He was only twelve. He didn't have any, and he didn't have enough control to give me any money. [And] I have yet to get one penny from 'Fingertips.'"

Motown surely must have been a mercenary, cutthroat operation for a man who literally had nearly given his life for the company to be treated so shabbily.

In the brave new world he was seeing in his thoughts, Stevie now looked beyond Motown for inspiration, far beyond, all the way to Bob Dylan. Stevie had been turned on by the scraggly, folk-singing bard for some time now, recognizing a rising new wave in pop music sensibilities in Dylan's orphic, updated Beat Generation verse set to sparse instrumentation, accented by a bluesy harmonica perpetually harnessed around his neck.

While Stevie had been well aware of the allegorical properties of "Fingertips" in the soundtrack of the civil rights cause, he hadn't yet walked through enough of life to own a ripe political agenda. Even so, his early affright of an American apocalypse was heightened by the escalation of war somewhere in Southeast Asia called Vietnam, where the population was being incinerated and Americans left dead every day. A kind of cold, soulless apathy about it all was just now melting into anger that would cleave the country along class, age, and racial lines. As a small microcosm of the debate was beginning to rage, he and Ted Hull frequently went at each other, with the tutor tenaciously shilling for the war with the usual jingo about "supporting the troops" and "America, love it or leave it," and Stevie unrealistically pushing for immediate withdrawal before the country would bleed Vietnam and itself to death. They'd get so worked up, Stevie would hear himself called unpatriotic and dub Hull a racist, before each would cool off and apologize.

Unlike most everyone in the record business, Stevie could think of no good reason why this debate shouldn't extend to the music of a no longer innocent culture. Although the industry preferred to avoid taking sides and risking the loss of any market subset—witness the jittery nerves around Motown by the mild societal exposé of "Uptight"—a major benchmark was carved in 1965 when Barry McGuire's unflinching Armageddon prophecy "Eve of Destruction" hit No. 1, as did, six months later, its "answer" record, Sergeant Barry Sadler's "Ballad of the Green Berets." The rabid home-front civil war was certainly out in the open now, with all hell to break loose on the streets, and in another year or so, flames, insurrection, and the enforced retirement of a president.

Apocalypse, indeed. And Stevie Wonder couldn't sit still about it—not that he could for anything. As a kid weaned on the joyous noise of rhythm and blues, he was hardly the type to sing "Eve of Destruction"; pedantry and sledgehammer lyrics weren't his bag. That was where the Dylan model came in. Over the past year, Stevie had begun performing "Blowin' in the Wind" in his stage act, as a duet with Clarence Paul, whose yearning blues burr abetted Stevie's rearrangement of the midtempo, folky original from Dylan's 1963 *Freewheelin'* album to one similar to the quietly intense Peter, Paul and Mary cover, itself an enormous hit, going to No. 3 later that year.

The irony is that the song—partly derived from the Negro spiritual "No More Auction Block" and the Book of Ezekiel—actually was a diss of liberal pedagogues with impractical solutions for world peace, the real answers for which, Dylan seemed to rue, were lost in the elusive wind. Yet the dreamy fatalism made it the perfect all-purpose protest song. Stevie's own touch was to make folk folksy, by decorating plaintive lines with some swinging embellishment—interjecting, for example, "Whoa yeah, let me tell you" in mid-sentence while begging that the flying cannonballs be forever banned. Indeed, Stevie was so affected by the song's prescript to stop dreaming and comb that blowin' wind for answers that he had Ted Hull write a preamble to that effect that he'd intone before singing it onstage.

The number played so well that Stevie replaced "Funny How Time Slips Away" with it to close shows. When Gordy signed off on him cutting the tune in the studio, Clarence Paul, the logical choice to produce it, changed nothing, keeping it a semi-duet and the Motown sound less ornamental, a fat, jumpy James Jamerson bass line driving the simple midtempo melody and the rest of the band mixed at low volume. It was simple, pretty, moving, maybe a tad precious, but undeniably compelling. Hearing it, Gordy's biggest objection was Paul inserting himself in the vocal, though Stevie insisted on it.

But for the bloom of "Uptight" and its clone of a follow-up, Gordy likely would have killed it as a single. As it was, he was far from sold on its viability as a Motown product. But Stevie had an éclat now, and power that was nearing inviolate, or so he believed. And on this one, he had read the currents wisely. Released on July 28, 1966—backed with the fittingly titled Stevie song "Ain't That Asking for Trouble"— "Blowin' in the Wind" blew up the charts, finally nestling just inside the Top 10 by late summer. And as if that weren't impressive enough for an antiwar song with a Motown beat, it took a white folk protest song deep into the inner city, going to No. 1 on the R&B list.

Not waiting for the fate of the song, Gordy had rushed to cash in on the two previous hits with an album that would milk them further. Mandatorily titled *Up-Tight Everything's Alright* (the first word spelled differently than on the single), it came out in May and, with the fresh impetus of "Blowin'," which was included on it, rang in at No. 33 on the pop chart, though the real payoff came when it ran all the way to No. 2. on the R&B chart—the first appearance there of a Stevie Wonder album.

Stevie wasn't waiting, either. With the early buzz of "Blowin' in the Wind" all good, he went back into Studio A over the summer to cut another hummable quasi-protest number, "A Place in the Sun," the title not a nod to the 1951 Elizabeth Taylor movie but to the later Lorraine Hansberry play and movie starring Sidney Poitier about a black family's ambivalence fleeing their ghetto neighborhood in Chicago, *A Raisin in the Sun*. It was cowritten by a new Motown hand, Ron Miller (with a partner named Bryan Wells), who Mickey Stevenson had found singing in a Chicago club and was now the only white writer on the Motown roster—a highly ironic turn given the song, which Stevenson took to Stevie. He, in turn, was almost in a trance listening to it, not so much for its ingenuous lyrics—"'Cause there's a place in the sun where there's hope for everyone / Where my poor restless heart's gotta run "— but for its viscerally soothing reassurance that, as Sam Cooke had sung, a change is gonna come.

Everyone who heard the song took it as a metaphor of ghetto grit and pluck, capped by a killer hook that went, no doubt to nodding heads, "Movin' on, movin' on," which really meant "movin' on up." Singing those two words, Stevie's soulful, mellow vibrato ranging effortlessly over several octaves was so memorable that many would think they were the song's name.

It not being a Cosby-Moy song, Clarence Paul again got the gig, producing a subtly powerful ballad awash in strings, soft jazzy licks, and a female gospel choir. In another reminder that the strongest statements are made without raising one's voice, Stevie made the whole thing glisten with his emotive but sapid midrange tenor, which he had fully grown into. Released on October 24 (Moy and Cosby were mollified by being given the B-side, the eponymous "Sylvia," which they cowrote and Cosby produced), "A Place in the Sun" moved on to No. 9 pop, No. 3 R&B.

It seemed Stevie could do no wrong now, with talismanic qualities for Gordy, who hurried onto the market yet another album before the end of the year, *Down to Earth*, completing a kind of macrocosmic trilogy—wind, sun, and earth. The LP, which included "A Place in the Sun," was filled out by, let's say, an *eclectic* grab bag of items from the Miller-Wells title track to covers of Dylan's "Mr. Tambourine Man," the Supremes' "My World Is Empty Without You," Sonny and Cher's "Bang Bang (My Baby Shot Me Down)," and Tennessee Ernie Ford's "Sixteen Tons," as well as Stevie collaborations with Paul ("Hey Love") and with Sylvia Moy ("Thank You Love").

Perhaps most diverting was the album cover, on which Stevie sat on an alleyway curb, ankle on knee, contentedly blowing his harmonica, the alley's walls streaked with graffiti—the kind of ghetto scene never before seen on a Motown record jacket. During the first few years of the company, its black faces were kept off covers altogether. Now it seemed Stevie had made it safe for Motown to admit what a black neighborhood looked like. Thus Gordy grudgingly inched his way to songs and images of reality, while going full speed ahead taking the Supremes into the whitest neighborhoods, his reticence underscored by the fact that *Down to Earth* was where the album went, getting no higher than No. 72, though it was salvaged by going to No. 8 on the R&B chart.

Its failure to launch signaled to Gordy that Motown wasn't a folk-protest vehicle after all, and that it was time for Stevie to bag the peaceful, easy feeling and get back to making Motown soul-pop.

Stevie was committed to cutting two more tunes by Miller, who happened to live in the same apartment building as Ted Hull and would often sing new material for Stevie before anyone else. In October, he went into the studio with Clarence Paul to cut "Someday at Christmas," a preachy Miller-Wells song that would be released as a Christmas song. In truth it was really "Blowin' in the Wind" with a Christmas motif, its lyrics merging mirth with mawkishness, wistfully dreaming of a future Christmas when "men won't be boys playing with bombs like kids play with toys."

It was certainly ahead of its time, an intriguing foretoken of latter-day conscience-gnawing Christmas songs like John Lennon's "Christmas (War Is Over)" and the 1980s superstar jam "Do They Know It's Christmas." But in its time it was no more than a notable curio; released in November with the more traditional "The Miracles of Christmas," it didn't come close to making the holiday charts. But it did convince Gordy that Stevie was worthy of a Christmas album, a genre Motown had gotten into in 1965 with the Supremes. Stevie's would come out the following year as *Someday at Christmas*, the title track carried over and buttressed by several other, more conventional Miller-Wells Christmas songs and well-worn holiday standards.

In early 1967, Stevie cut Miller's "Travelin' Man," which lifted the title of the 1964 Ricky Nelson hit for another quiescently shimmering piece, this time of personal not political introspection, again produced by Paul. When it flopped, Gordy had second thoughts about another soft ballad penned by Stevie, Paul, and Motown staff writer Morris Broadnax and recorded in late fall, "Until You Come Back to Me (That's What I'm Gonna Do)," which he decided to put on the shelf (where it sat until Stevie's 1974 *Anthology* album, two years after Aretha Franklin's cover of it went Top 10). Instead, Gordy ordered up material in the rollicking "Uptight" mode, leading to a new round of collaboration between Stevie and Sylvia Moy.

However, by now, Moy found it increasingly frustrating to work with him. It had never been easy. From the start, she'd had a hard time with the crude communications relay system that Clarence Paul had instituted in the absence of lyric sheets in Braille. Stevie had become comfortable with it, and appreciated its side benefit, the edgy semi-spontaneous feel of hearing a line in his earphone only seconds before he had to sing it. But Sylvia couldn't get it to work as smoothly, possibly because of his chronic lack of concentration, necessitating dozens of time-consuming takes.

Neither could Moy determine which of his song fragments Stevie felt most strongly about, since there were so many of them (by his own count, he later reckoned that he was at the time writing around 150 songs a *month*) that he'd bounce from one to the next, forgetting what he'd left behind. Moy, Stevie once conceded, with great sympathy, "had to do a lot of writing," with his contribution at times being as little as "a basic idea, maybe a punch line [from which] she would have to write the song." In general, he said, after beginning work on a song, "I was so interested in getting down another tune, I'd give it to someone else to finish it up." When Motown would choose to record one for which he had diminishing affinity, his enthusiasm flagged. Trying something, anything, Moy would call people from the hallway into the studio to give him an audience, that always being the "fix" he needed to enjoy his art.

"He had to feel the presence of people," she said. "If there was no one around, his vocal was just dead."

Upon reaching his seventeenth birthday, then, he was not simply the adorable if sometimes annoying wind-up toy, driving people to exhaustion with his nonstop ideas. He was far more into his studies, a startling development to Lula Mae, and much less eager to make the trip from Lansing to West Grand Boulevard—even less so after Gordy had no use for songs he'd put the most time into, such as "Until I Come Back to You." Another he had recorded early in 1967, "My Cherie Amour," was one of the new crop of material written with Moy. Clearly chipped off the Beatles' "Michelle," it reflected Stevie's worshipful fascination with the Fab Four as oracles of pop music craftsmanship.

"Oh definitely, Stevie loved the Beatles, mostly Lennon and McCartney for their writing," recalls John Glover. "That was where he saw their genius, not their performing—in fact, he didn't think they performed some of their songs as well as he could do it; that's why he would cover so many Beatles songs and later work with Paul, so he could show 'em how it was supposed to be done [laughs].

"He thought their best songs were the ones like 'Michelle' and 'Yesterday,' with their simple, gorgeous melodies and perfect hooks. The later stuff, the 'Sgt. Pepper['s Lonely Hearts Club Band]' and 'I Am the Walrus,' he thought was taking them away from their real strengths for the sake of being 'heavy.'

"That was something he never did. He always stayed true to keeping the structure of a song simple and clever and *melodic*. If it didn't have that, to Stevie it sucked.

"To be honest, I don't think Stevie felt he was getting to that next level working with Sylvia or Clarence or Ron. Even the big hits they made left him feeling like he missed, like just by an inch maybe, of being able to compete with Lennon and McCartney. He was never completely happy with them, and he wouldn't be until he could record exactly what he wanted to, not what Berry did. He'd say, 'John, I'm biding my time. You just wait till I'm twenty-one.'"

The irony was that, having been on Motown's clock before "Uptight," his ascendance had inverted reality. Now Motown was on *his* clock.

But while that clock ticked, Gordy made the calls, though his former Cassandra knack for knowing a hit when he heard it was ebbing. That same year, he killed the song intended as Marvin Gaye's return to the singles market, "I Heard It Through the Grapevine," which Norman Whitfield wrote and produced as a slow boil of mounting rage over an impending lover's breakup, causing a brooding Marvin to confess, or threaten, "I'm just about to lose my mind." It was by miles Motown's most noirish record, and Gordy again played it safe—but only until Whitfield's jazzy up-tempo revision with Gladys Knight and the Pips was given the go-ahead and became the top-selling Motown record to that time. Gordy then put out the Gaye original, which went on to rack up even greater sales.

"My Cherie Amour" also seemed to prove that Gordy had lost his golden ear. In melody and verse it was a near replica of "Michelle," with Hank Cosby recreating the easy, jangling canter of the Beatles' record with swirling violins, a tinkly jazz piano line, and a dash of proto-funky guitars. Stevie's restrained yearning from afar for a girl "lovely as a summer day" yet "distant as the Milky Way" was the whipped cream.

Beautiful and lush a confection as it was, however, Gordy thought it would be met as a flat-out rip of "Michelle" and shelved it for now, causing Stevie to drop hints that he'd rather be composing symphonies and not pop, no doubt hoping this passive threat would get back to Gordy.

Still, such was the ingeniousness of his "punch lines" and Moy's ability to write in his voice and say what he would if he had the inclination that they and Gordy would only prosper. In early spring, Stevie cut a song titled "I Was Made to Love Her"; the writers' credits would include the name of Lula Mae Hardaway, perhaps not just out of a residual filial debt and/or guilt but because she may have been why it saw the light of day. With Hank Cosby's rhythm track in the can, Motown hurriedly scheduled Stevie's vocal, no matter that it conflicted with his school hours, and thus came into Ted Hull's crosshairs. After Hull rebuffed numerous Motown entreaties to reconsider—"If I give in this time," he told them, "tomorrow's going to be the same thing"—it turned to an unlikely ally, Lula Mae, who Hull said "tried to charm me into changing my mind." Having borne the brunt of her usual "charms" in the past, he enjoyed hearing her not badger but beg.

"Ted," she cooed, "if you'll make an exception just this time, I'll make sure you get your reward."

Hull, who of course believed he was being kept from gaining writers' credits on Stevie's songs, regarded such a promise of unearned spoils as risible. Yet, feeling the heat, he says, "I gave up and gave in," but as for Lula's affiance, he adds with a chuckle, "I'm still waiting."

Gordy had good cause to put a rush on "I Was Made to Love Her." Based on what Stevie has since claimed was his first love back in the projects, a girl named Angie Satterwhite, the song's ebullient adolescent love theme busted out of the gate with that indelible opening line, "I was born in Little Rock / Had a childhood sweetheart / We were always hand in hand." Cosby's track was a grill sizzling with loud, ringing guitar chords, tambourine, and vibes, and for a bluesy feel reintroduced Stevie's harmonica on the bubbly intro ushering in the "Hey, hey, hey" chorus that was the song's hook, preceded after each verse by Stevie's covenant that "I was made to love her, built my world all around her."

It was a gas all the way through his vow on the fadeout that "Stevie ain't never gonna leave her, *nooo!*" and a benchmark of 1960s pre–funk-rock. Released on May 18—the "reward" went to Cosby, Clarence Paul, and Mickey Stevenson as the credited writers of the flip,

"Hold Me"—it soared to No. 2 on the pop chart (and No. 1 on the R&B) the week of June 24, kept out of the penthouse by Aretha Franklin's cover of Otis Redding's "Respect," en route to a fourteen-week run in the Top 40. That run begat, in late August, an album of the same name that Stevie, tired of the Motown M.O. of stuffing albums with low-grade filler, turned into a real blues project, with covers of "My Girl" and Marvin Gaye's "Can I Get a Witness," as well as "Respect" and Ray Charles's "A Fool for You," James Brown's "Please, Please, Please," Little Richard's "Send Me Some Lovin'," and Bobby Bland's "Pity the Fool," along with several fresh Wonder-Moy tunes.

The album, though, was a letdown, dying at No. 45 on the LP chart (though No. 7 R&B), dealing another blow to a work Stevie believed in and fought for, and the search for a follow-up to "Love Her" became a labor as he began to turn his focus on the new school term in Lansing.

Indeed, that summer was ebb and neap, his mood succored by the huge hit, then battered when Detroit came perilously close to going up in smoke.

In the beginning, Motown found Stevie a name but not a set niche, trying to present him as an R&B hybrid, a mini Ray Charles–Calypso kid, and a white-tie and white-tailed Van Cliburn.

Of all Stevie's Motown mentors, the most important were drummer Benny Benjamin (second from left) and his first producer, and "surrogate father," Clarence Paul (standing behind Stevie), under whose watchful eye and loose morals Stevie both flourished and chafed.

After two fitful years came the first jackpot—"Fingertips (Part 2)," a raucous, live No. 1 hit, and a No. 1 album that certified Stevie as the world's newest, and youngest, musical genius. The world hasn't been the same since.

Running with the A-List Motown crowd was outta sight. Even among the Temptations, Smokey and the Miracles, the Four Tops, the Supremes, and Martha and the Vandellas, shown here in this typical Motown publicity shot, Stevie was the center of attention—though the women had to be wary of his roaming hands.

Rewarding Berry Gordy for choosing him over Marvin Gaye for the Motortown Revue's crucial 1965 tour of England, a sizzling Stevie blows up a storm on the British TV show *The Sound of Motown*, as the Supremes sway in the background.

"Little" Stevie played a very big part in making the ramshackle row house at 2648 West Grand Boulevard live up to the sign "Hitsville U.S.A." He would be the only major Motown artist to remain under that banner through the years and to this very day.

Dragging Motown into socially conscious themes, Stevie recorded important songs like "Blowin' in the Wind" and "A Place in the Sun" on his 1966 *Down to Earth* album. The ghetto street scene on the album cover was a first for the always cautious company.

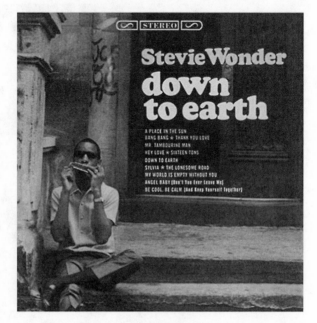

Glad-handed by President Richard Nixon (left), Stevie was honored with the Distinguished Service Award in a ceremony in the Rose Garden in 1969, his mother, Lula Mae, proudly beaming at his side. Stevie grinned and bore it, putting aside the loathing he would later express in scalding anti-Nixon anthems like "He's Misstra-Know-It-All" and "You Haven't Done Nothing."

Stevie and his new bride, Syreeta Wright, toast each other in the autumn of 1969. Even though the marriage ended within three years, Stevie would suffer enduring guilt for the failure of the union and later insist that Syreeta was the only true love of his life, composing songs confirming the truth of the claim.

The label of the original 45 rpm single of "Signed, Sealed, Delivered I'm Yours" (1970), the smash hit that earned Stevie his first Grammy nomination. Successes like this one kept Stevie moving toward his goal of complete control of his music, which he would soon have with his next album, *Where I'm Coming From*.

Where I'm Coming From (1971) set the stage for Stevie's domination of the decade, far removed from the old Motown crowd. Though not a major success on the charts, the album convinced Berry Gordy to pay $13 million, a record amount at the time, to keep Stevie on the company's thinning roster.

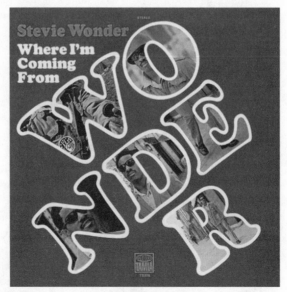

Mick Jagger and Stevie perform an unforgettable encore on the Rolling Stones' 1972 North American tour. As the opening act for the Stones, Stevie irked Mick and Keith Richards for repeatedly stealing the show and, in a pot-meet-kettle charge, for his band's wild carousing. Still, Mick insisted Stevie remain on the tour.

Stevie performing with Bob Marley. After opening the doors of rock and roll to soul and funk, Stevie also merged soul with reggae by inviting Marley to open for him on several tours. Later, a year before Marley's death, he wrote "Master Blaster (Jammin')" (1981) about the Jamaican reggae legend.

Recording engineers Robert Margouleff (left) and Malcolm Cecil (right) man the control room board during intense sessions for the 1972 *Talking Book* album at New York's Electric Lady Studios. They were the unsung heroes of Stevie's 1970s superstardom, paving the way to turning synthesized sound into beautiful music, until they had a falling-out with him. *Photo courtesy of Malcolm Cecil.*

The triumvirate of Wonder, Margouleff, and Cecil made TONTO (The Original New Timbral Orchestra) come alive by programming it before the music even began, as they are doing here during the *Talking Book* sessions. TONTO, the means and method of Stevie's genius, was a massive block of synthesizers that required its own room. *Photo courtesy of Malcolm Cecil.*

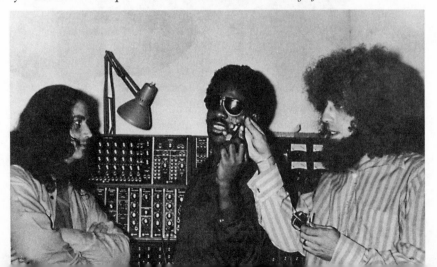

TONTO, pictured here in this 1973 shot from the Record Plant Studio in Los Angeles, grew into an enormous operation, looking much like the Starship Enterprise. Stevie, Margouleff, and Cecil were all that was needed on the "bridge" to bring TONTO into action. *Photo courtesy of Malcolm Cecil.*

Talking Book (1972) was the first of Stevie's eight gold/platinum albums and the first of his four straight Best Album Grammys. Its synthesizer-driven funk and soft romantic grooves included "Superstition"—the Song of the Year—and "You Are the Sunshine of My Love."

At one time, Gordy considered cutting Stevie from
Motown, but by the 1980s. Stevie was his only real
asset. Here Gordy is only too happy to get up and
boogie with a funked-out Stevie as he shakes his
moneymaker during a stage performance.

Back when a Stevie Wonder
album came out nearly every
year, with an unbroken string
of genius, *Fulfillingness'
First Finale* (1974) revealed
a more introspective Stevie,
with groundbreaking cuts like
"Boogie On Reggae Woman,"
"You Haven't Done Nothin',"
and the scary "Creepin'."

Arguably his best work, *Innervisions* (1976) seamlessly fused the seething anger of "Living for the City," the spirituality of "Higher Ground," and the optimism of "Don't You Worry 'Bout a Thing." Eerily, Stevie survived a near-fatal car accident just as the LP was released.

The sublime 1976 double-LP *Songs in the Key of Life* has sold over 10 million copies, with "Sir Duke," "I Wish," and "Isn't She Lovely" among its classic grooves. But the flip side was that, with it, Stevie reached his creative peak, never again to hit those heights of genius.

9

You Met Your Match

It seemed like Stevie was only doing so-called soft songs in those days, but we [the Temptations] were following what he'd done with "Blowin' in the Wind" and like that. We got into heavy shit, and Stevie really helped put that on the plate. But Berry had him do a little bit of everything, because he *could.* When Marvin got heavy, he was expected to be heavy, *say something.* Stevie could do that and then make the greatest pop song ever recorded. That's an amazing thing. *Nobody* has ever done that.

—*Otis Williams*

For Detroit, the long hot summer of 1967 was anything but the Summer of Love. If in San Francisco people had flowers in their hair, in the Motor City they had matches and Molotov cocktails in their hands after a July 23 police raid on an after-hours club on 12th and Clairmount streets—answering a long-asked question on the streets, which was not *if* a conflagration would happen but *when* it would. Such was the stench of desperation and implosive anger that had been rising in town for years.

No American city had hit the skids faster or harder than Detroit, where the casualties of everyday life could be measured in high crime rates and body counts of victims both innocent and not, and mass arrests by the police trying to deal with it all, as well as by the abandoned ruins of a once proud society. Not least affected were the hoary blues and jazz clubs of Paradise Valley, almost all of which were bulldozed, along with the wide boulevard of Hastings Street, to make room for a nexus of superhighways. In the process, as Detroit cops responded with mass arrests and anecdotal evidence of horrific police brutality—according to Beans Bowles, "They were like cowboys, quick draw artists, and they practiced on black people"—the town had become a symbolic ground zero for a growing black militancy. Early in July, the Black Panthers' "Justice Minister" H. Rap Brown famously avowed that unless America, and Detroit in particular, didn't make radical changes, "we're gonna burn you down." It was no idle vow.

The raid on Clairmount was the match to the tinderbox. Outside the club, a seething crowd began vandalizing stores, looting, and setting fires. The carnage raged unabated for forty-eight hours, turning the daylight sky black and night sky fiery orange. No street was safe, including West Grand Boulevard and the avenues where the clubs were still open and humming. With the mobs on the march, Earl Van Dyke and several other Funk Brothers were in the middle of a set at the Chit Chat Club just down the block on Clairmount. Beans Bowles was playing his horn at the Fox Theater. Apprised of what was happening, they and everyone else in the clubs scrambled onto the dark streets and ran for cover.

At Motown a few hours later that morning, some of the musicians, not aware of the growing mayhem, had arrived for sessions as usual, but as the sound of gunshots got closer, and not knowing if they'd be incinerated in that basement studio, they were told to go home and the place was padlocked. Tambourine player Jack Ashford, hearing the shots from outside, and fearing more for guitar player Joe Messina than himself, covered Messina's head with his sport jacket and rushed him into Ashford's car. "We were afraid Joe would be shot in the street for being white." he says. "Hell, we didn't know if we'd all be shot."

Although smoke billowed from burnt-out buildings along West Grand, Motown itself was spared. The only damage it incurred happened days later and, ironically, from a National Guard tank, which fired a shell from across the boulevard that crashed through a window and out the roof, leaving a two-foot hole. That it escaped the torch gave rise to an urban myth that this was not by accident, that out of some unspoken oath of allegiance to and gratitude to the company, the rioters let Motown be—a fanciful notion that doesn't begin to explain why scores of other black-owned businesses were not deemed worthy of mercy. By the time the National Guard and the 82nd Airborne quelled the violence, the toll was grim: forty-three people dead (thirty-three of them black), nearly twelve hundred injured, over seven thousand arrested.

As it happened, Stevie was far from Detroit when it fell into Hades. On that first night, he was in Baltimore where he'd performed hours earlier on a bill with Ray Charles and Dionne Warwick. He and Ted Hull heard nothing about the eruption back home, and routinely caught a return flight a day later. Still not aware of the carnage when they landed, it was only on the cab ride from the airport that Hull, seeing and smelling the acrid smoke hanging over the skyline, asked the driver where all that smoke was coming from. "It's the riots," came the matter-of-fact response. "The whole city's burning. Didn't you know?" Suddenly, both Stevie and Hull were sick with fear, wondering if their families had made it through. They had reason to worry, since the Hardaway home on Greenlawn Street was mere paces from where the riots had originated, and Hull's flat in the Chatham Apartments only twelve blocks away. Recalled Hull, "Our panic grew as the cab made its way through the smoldering nightmare. We had no idea what we'd find at home, or if we'd even be safe getting there."

Fortunately, neither residence was damaged, and they stayed hunkered there for the next several days, when a curfew was in effect from dusk to dawn and almost all the city's business and food markets were closed, many boarded up, some with their owners standing guard on the rooftops with shotguns pointed at anyone who came close.

Berry Gordy wasn't in Detroit either at the outset of the riots, and with the airport closed down he couldn't catch a flight back for days—a perfect metaphor for his separation from and the dread he felt for his hometown. In truth, though he wouldn't have admitted it, he had already privately resolved to flee it for the high life of L.A., where he could groom Diana Ross for impending movie stardom and not have to countenance the community that had made his empire possible. In fact, Gordy was out of town during that fold of time because, as usual, he was with the Supremes at one of their high-profile gigs, at the Flamingo Hotel in Las Vegas. But in another barometer of deepening dissension at Motown, one of his chores on that jag was to fire Florence Ballard, the culmination of her escalating booze intake and weight gain matched only by her open loathing for Gordy, who had been progressively bullying her from the group she had founded.

Gordy must have felt besieged on all sides. When he returned home and saw that hole in the roof from the tank shell, he shuddered at how vulnerable the company was. At once he began selling off the row of additional town houses on West Grand Boulevard that Motown had been using for secondary business. He also leased space in a fortress-like office building nearby on Woodward Avenue and moved all the administrative offices there, though all recording would still be done in Studio A. Indeed, long after Detroit stopped burning and Motown had continued apace, Gordy was up to his mustache in all manner of crises that had been festering for months, even years, the inevitable result of his reign as a feudal lord in an enterprise that made scads of money for no one but him.

A major bone of contention was his stubborn refusal to split any of his Motown stock—which was worth a cool $5 million in the late 1960s. This was only logical to Gordy, who was fond of saying, "I make the money, it's *my* money," and to prove it, organized Motown as a Subchapter S corporation under the IRS code, meaning he was responsible for every dime of its tax bill and would pocket every dime it made or lost. Even later, when in the 1970s he dispensed token shares to his sisters Esther, Gwen, and Anna, and to Smokey Robinson (but not even a single share to his "children" like Stevie Wonder, Marvin Gaye, and Diana Ross), he still owned 4,494 of 4,995 shares.

Down below, in steerage, Motown executives and its writers and producers, who were treated better than the acts who were far better known, were subject to Gordy's largesse or penury. The first to call Gordy on it were Holland-Dozier-Holland, who of course had no stake in the copyrights on their own songs. While the trio had made a small fortune, not being cut in as shareholders, as well as Gordy brusquely rejecting a large loan, led them to split at the end of 1967 to start their own label, sparking half a decade of contentious, costly courtroom warfare between them and Gordy that ended in a settlement favorable to Gordy, though he could never recoup what he'd lost in creative juice when they walked.

HDH weren't the only good soldiers to go over the hill. By mid-1967, Mickey Stevenson, Gordy's first hire at Motown, was also rebuffed on stock, as well as his aim to make his wife, Kim Weston, a star. When Gordy wouldn't release more of her records, Stevenson made a deal to produce her with a West Coast label and the both of them took off.

As did Harvey Fuqua, once Gordy's biggest yes-man, who, after he divorced Gwen Gordy and felt her brother giving him the cold shoulder, bid him adieu. While Motown would fill these holes easily enough and continue to reap big, important hits, its heyday was over, its importance as a driver of the cultural cuisine ebbing.

As it was, Motown had fallen behind in the soul music derby to the more authentic, stripped-down brand pouring out of Memphis and Muscle Shoals from Sam and Dave, Otis Redding, Wilson Pickett, Eddie Floyd, and Aretha Franklin. Without a single number one record—other than Aretha's "Respect"—their labels, Stax and Volt, and their distributor overlord Atlantic through 1968, would close out the decade rewriting the soul that Motown had once made seem so fresh and new, making Berry Gordy seem old and tired. At that summer's epochal Monterey Pop Festival, soul was represented not by Marvin Gaye, the Temptations—or Stevie Wonder—but by the magnetic Otis Redding, and by blues-based acid rock, which Motown didn't deign to do, the funk of Sly and the Family Stone and the electric wizardry of Jimi Hendrix.

Motown would make an attempt to update itself, though Gordy would need to be dragged into it. As with Gaye's "I Heard It Through the Grapevine," in 1968 he would recoil at the Temptations' psychedelic-funk gem "Cloud Nine," as a far too obvious parable of drug use, before Norman Whitfield convinced him the sky wouldn't fall. To say the least, it didn't; in 1969 the song would garner Motown's first Grammy, for Best Group R&B Performance (such fusion of black idioms not yet recognized as mainstream pop). In the new dawning of rock and roll, Motown was surely an outrider.

It was also a lonelier place than it used to be. Not only had the top brass been thinned out by attrition, but its roster, whittled down from over a hundred acts in 1965 to half that two years later, now mattered for only a handful, with all others having faded in ennui and neglect.

And for at least one in that elite, there was hardly any reason left to pledge allegiance to Berry Gordy.

Working within this morass of disillusionment, in an environment that had become cold and rather sterile, the old "family" kinship now unrecognizable, a now less impressionable Stevie Wonder was not immune to squalls of personal pique that belied his carefree stage image. Indeed, mirroring Gordy's falling-out with his trusted lieutenants, Stevie's relationship with Clarence Paul had gone south. This was something few at Motown could see coming, probably because the brass still perceived Stevie as they did in 1964, when Esther Gordy Edwards remarked that Paul was not Stevie's "surrogate father" as much as his analog. They were, she said, "both 14-year-olds, and Clarence is the one who's never gonna grow up." As correct as she was about Paul, three years later Motown seemed to be the last to know that Stevie had moved beyond, way beyond. One of the upshots of this was that he couldn't stand being around Paul. Tellingly, at seventeen, Stevie felt as if *he* was the grown-up to Paul's feckless recreant.

Paul apparently greeted Stevie's maturation as license to be less chary in keeping his night-crawling booze, drug, and sex habits away from him. Frequently now he would take Stevie on road gigs in his boat-sized Chrysler Imperial. On the front seat was a leather pouch that he'd pick up and squeeze, sending a stream of booze or wine into his mouth, even while driving at breakneck speed. And that was his *responsible* behavior. According to Ted Hull, when Paul gave the wheel to Gene Shelby or someone else in the traveling party, "he would get flat-out drunk whenever he had the chance" and wind up passed out cold, unable to be revived until bare minutes before he was to go onstage with Stevie, hungover but able to hide it. After one such close call, the promoter, unaware of Paul's condition, slipped him a fifth of whiskey, ensuring a repeat performance the next night.

Just as out of control was his fly. As Hull puts it, Paul "just couldn't keep his thing in his pants." That was of course something Stevie had known, and wanted dearly to emulate, but he couldn't abide that Paul would strut around in his shorts to the delight of young women he'd invited backstage, sometimes as he was going over charts with Stevie.

Despite Gordy's hypocritical lectures to his troops about upholding Motown's honor and classy image, his laissez-faire approach to such conduct was a given. David Ruffin's prodigious cocaine use, as another example, had been tolerated for years because his raw nerve of a voice delivered hit after hit for the Temptations; only when he began missing shows was he dismissed in 1968. In fact, Gordy's far greater beef with Paul was the way he had inveigled that duet on "Blowin' in the Wind," though it was Stevie's idea. Mainly because of that, Paul in late 1966 had been briefly fired as Stevie's musical director, but when Wade

Marcus couldn't motivate a diffident Stevie before shows the way Paul could, Hull asked for Paul's reinstatement. Esther Edwards agreed, with a proviso.

"You know what you're getting into," she said.

Paul didn't prove her wrong. The worst of it was that his old pep talks were now laced with profanity and insults, resulting in an ugly and very rare outburst of anger one night in Philadelphia early in 1968. Although the details may have been hushed up by Motown, years later Otis Williams became aware of the contretemps when Ron Tyson, who in 1983 joined the Temptations, related that he had actually been in the audience that night.

"Ron said he saw Stevie slap the shit out of Clarence Paul on the stage," Williams recalls. "Ron's from Philly, and he was like ten, eleven at the time, but he said he'd never forget it. He said Stevie turned around and hauled off on Clarence. I said, 'He did *what*?!' Ron said, 'Otis, I ain't kiddin'. It was the craziest thing I ever saw.' Man, I wish I'd seen that."

Unclear is why it may have happened, but a rumor began to make the rounds that around that time Paul had either struck Stevie, or came close to, with some sort of stick. When it got back to Lula Mae, she rang up Gordy and demanded Paul's head on a stick. Gordy then dutifully called Paul into his office and informed him, "You don't go back out with Stevie anymore," the reason being that "Lula doesn't want you on the road with him. She heard you swung a stick at him."

Stung and stunned by the charge, Clarence was near speechless. "Who'd ever believe that?" he managed to say. "They got to be out of their minds," adding, "Berry, knowing Stevie, if I'da swung a stick at him, he woulda ducked."

Paul, his pride scarred, refused to dignify the allegation by defending himself. "There wasn't no sense in even arguing because it was so stupid," he later told Ted Hull, who for his part never saw or heard from Stevie anything about a stick—or the slap, for that matter—and instead believed the rumor had been contrived by Motown horn player George Bohannon, who Hull said had a personal grudge with Paul.

Whatever the truth, and whomever the culprits, Clarence Paul was gone from Stevie's arc, replaced now for good by Wade Marcus. For Stevie, it was a family tie necessarily broken. Fast approaching his eighteenth birthday, the last thing he wanted or needed was the vestigial influences of a past life. Yet, the demotion of Paul aside, Gordy still seemed unwilling to let him grow up.

Stevie's formal coming-of-age happened squarely between the murders of Martin Luther King and Robert Kennedy, a metaphorical confirmation that he was caught in a maelstrom from which he couldn't escape, certainly not by making pretty music even he couldn't call the blues.

The follow-up to "I Was Made to Love Her" was "I'm Wondering," *not* the Stevie-Paul "Wondering" from *Jazz Soul* but a bouncy, engaging Stevie-Moy R&B riff with a doubled lead vocal produced with few flourishes and room for Stevie to wail, "How can I make you love me a little more than you loved him," and to sprinkle in the harmonica in midsong. But it was undeniably trivial—precisely Stevie's concern about the feel-good/say-nothing pop Motown wanted him wedded to.

Even so, "I'm Wondering" rose on the echoes of "I Was Made to Love Her" to No. 12 on the pop chart, and more significantly a repeat No. 1 on the R&B chart—the latter a product of a curious surfeit of regard for Motown product among black record buyers (as opposed to "purists" who were the most vocal critics). Within this market, Hitsville's ever whiteward drift was balanced by its black birthright, a reflex mechanism that would keep most Motown singles at or near the top of the R&B list. At the same time, among whites, it was cool in the late-1960s cultural churn to *feel* black by buying black records. This win-win situation was what led Gordy to have the Supremes "do" the ghetto, at least temporarily, and sing about a "love child" being "born in poverty," and for Marvin Gaye to lyrically equate falling in love to being "chained."

Such pungent tropes, it was understood, were off-limits to Stevie, who had to privately bleed for community wounds all around him—and he bled heavily after King was gunned down on the balcony of the Lorraine Hotel in Memphis on April 4. That afternoon, Stevie was picked up in Lansing by Gene Shelby. Half asleep in the backseat, he heard the ghastly news in a bulletin on the radio. Having experienced a similarly scarifying moment as a thirteen-year-old when Malcolm X met his death by a bullet, Stevie was left numb. Recalled Ted Hull, who was also in the car, "Gene clicked off the radio and no one said a word."

Stevie reached his hand out. Hull grasped and held it until the car got to Greenlawn Street.

Stevie, who'd met King in 1966 at a Southern Christian Leadership Conference event in Chicago, desperately wanted to attend the funeral in Atlanta the next day, but Gordy quickly planned Motown's representation. Since he was in New York for a Supremes engagement at the Copacabana nightclub, he and the girls—who performed a poignant rendition of the song "Somewhere" in King's honor that night on *The Tonight Show*—would fly to Atlanta and be front and center among the celebrity mourners. Stevie would get to pay his respects three months belatedly at a benefit concert for the People's March to Freedom, the project King had been working on, a symbolic procession from Atlanta to D.C. At the concert, for which Gordy also brought the Supremes, the Temptations, and Gladys Knight and the Pips, Stevie movingly sang "Blowin' in the Wind," alloying a song to a seam of history as he had when "Fingertips" filled the air above the March on Washington.

As circumstances had it, Stevie was only a few blocks away when on June 5 Robert Kennedy was slain in the kitchen of the Ambassador Hotel. Playing a concert that night in L.A., he was booked into a room at the same hotel and was on his way back there when the shots rang out. Stevie had wanted to get there before Kennedy left the hotel for a prearranged handshake photo op. Pulling up to the entrance, Hull had to weave him through a thicket of people screaming and sobbing. Hearing what had happened, Stevie begged Hull to lead him to the ballroom where the senator had given his victory speech upon winning the state's presidential primary, wanting to, as he said, lend some "positive energy." But there was nothing but bedlam in there so he went to his room, sitting zombie-like in front of the TV until the next day when Kennedy died.

On the flight back to Detroit, he dictated shards of potential songs about the fallen icons into a recorder. He was beaten to it by Dion's "Abraham, Martin and John," a huge hit in the fall, but it's highly unlikely Gordy would have put out such a benediction on his label. In fact, his reaction to the double kick to the solar plexus that spring was to palliate it with pop, not philippics. Motown's soul was pretty much spent by now, and its social conscience had never been much to begin with.

•   •   •

Thus there'd be no interruption of Stevie's assigned rounds that spring and summer, which was touring in support of his *Greatest Hits* album (which went to No. 37 on the pop chart, No. 6 R&B), and his next single, "Shoo-Be-Doo-Be-Doo-Da-Day," one of the most portentous and overlooked songs of his Motown maturation. Indeed, one can instinctively mistake it today as something out of his '70s funk trough—a manifestation of how far ahead of the curve he was when left to his own devices. Far ahead, too, of where funk was in 1968, with Sly Stone as the major influence in soldering traditional horn-driven R&B and acid rock. It made for a paradigm shift—the compatibility of pot, pastel bell-bottoms, and Afro Sheen—but Stevie's idea of funk was less barbed. He just wanted a new, better dance groove; not mind expansion but *sound* expansion. To do that meant finding a new kind of phonics, from sources likely, blues, R&B, big band, swing, rock, and unlikely, instruments not previously configured in those idioms.

As such, Stevie was poles apart from Holland-Dozier-Holland, Hank Cosby, and most of the big producers. He could but preferred not to chart a song by chord changes. Rather, he would fly it live, and when a groove happened, then people who did the chord sheets would codify it on paper and Cosby would take over. In this way, he *was* his own producer, though not quite yet nominally.

Another example of this dynamic was that for the "Shoo-Be" session, he had Cosby, who had cowritten the song with Sylvia Moy, hire a Clavinet player, a first for Motown and possibly for any rock session. Stevie had heard this rather New Age electrified keyboard in classical and folk songs, was smitten with its spiny, slinky, almost metallic coil of sound much like an electric guitar, and wondered how resonant it could be plugged into an amplifier. He found out at the session, to his delight, and it became the focal point of the track, doubled and even tripled so as to sound like a kind of supernatural computer argot. To this sonic base was added conventional keyboard playing and the usual Motown bells and whistles.

"That's what Stevie was looking for, new ways to make a beat sexy," says John Glover. "Not necessarily by what the lyrics would say but the sound, what the sound would say. It was like he said later in 'Sir Duke'—'You can feel it all over.' That's what he wanted to happen, and it's what he wanted even when we were little kids."

The clue to his intention was the title of "Shoo-Be," no more than an old-time jazz scat line that defined the immateriality of the lyrics.

From the start, the song was an electric boogie ride, stirred by that tinny "sex organ" that was not merely the focal but the *vocal* point—so seminally emphatic and enduring that it is today nearly indistinguishable from the same Clavinet undertow on "Superstition," "Higher Ground," and many others. In retrospect, it was the first blush of the *real* Stevie Wonder, not as a harmonica cat but a keyboard king, and as bad a funk master as he wanted to be, when and *if* he wanted to be.

Gordy surely admired the results, and had no problem putting it out, as he did on March 19, giving it a run up the chart to No. 9—and No. 1 R&B. Then, with a follow-up mandated, came another revelation, and benchmark—the first Stevie Wonder record to carry his name on the label as the producer, shared with Don Hunter, an ambitious young Motown staffer who had recently been made his road manager and apparently factored into the record in yet another Motown credit scam.

The song "You Met Your Match"—a title that is temptingly easy to see as an epistle from Stevie to Berry Gordy—was a regular patronage pie, its writers officially being Stevie, Lula Mae, and Hunter though clearly it was all Stevie's. And he busted a gut on it, including—in another glimpse of the future—playing many of the instruments himself, with conviction, infusing more funk fusion and frisson. Kicked into gear by a bone-shaking James Jamerson bass lick, the multiple-tracked Clavinet, drum, and string rhythm backed Stevie in giving no quarter to a fickle paramour who "tried to make me look like a fool."

But if this seemed a propitious time to keep out in front of the funk curve, the diminishing returns on the new sound—"Match" went to No. 2 R&B but only No. 35 pop—and the dual convulsive tragedies of spring had him retrenching, casting aside sexually charged innovation for calm, peaceful restoration. And so the flowering of Stevie was diverted, first to mesh with Gordy's new Hollywood pandering, which itself bloomed when in 1967 the Supremes landed the title track of the film *The Happening*, a No. 1 record despite the flick bombing. Now he fancied Stevie covering Dionne Warwick's two-year-old "Alfie" from the hit Michael Caine film of the same name—with the twist that Stevie would do it as an instrumental.

Stevie could dig it; the haunting Burt Bacharach–Hal David song was by turns piano-bar intimate and lushly orchestral, and Stevie, who was not wedded to any idiom but rather to virtuosity he could control, was eager to have at it. Indeed, as Gordy knew, doing an instrumental had been on

Stevie's mind, his having just composed one for the brilliant jazz guitarist Wes Montgomery, whose butter-smooth licks on reworked pop hits had yielded several popular albums. Stevie loved his craftsmanship—especially his use of octaves, or the same note played on separate strings an octave apart, which Stevie had the guitar players do on "Shoo-Be" and "Match"—and his song for Montgomery was a mellow bonbon called "Bye Bye World," which turned sadly prophetic when the guitar legend died suddenly on June 15 at age forty-five.

After Stevie presented the song to Montgomery, the two had discussed collaborating on an album that Stevie would produce for him. How this could have been squared with Motown was left moot. Gordy's subsequent interest in an easy-listening instrumental may have been a way for Stevie to bring the concept to Motown, and may have carried a clue about how Gordy would have handled Stevie producing on another label. When "Alfie"—a straight orchestral piece with a sly, laid-back harmonica—was released in August, the name on the label was "Eivets Rednow," a reverse eponym meant to fool no one but that might have been a way for Stevie to moonlight. It also in effect branded a "second" Stevie, the soft yang to the funky yin.

Enough buyers saw through the thin disguise to bring "Alfie" to No. 66 on the chart, and for Gordy to continue the gentle ruse, allowing Stevie to cut his "Wes Montgomery" album of instrumentals under the same pseudonym, which would also be its title. While some of the Motown literature has passed off the work as a Gordy folly foisted on Stevie, in truth Stevie pushed hard for the chance to be an orchestra conductor, in order to, as John Glover puts it, "stretch out."

Boasting "Alfie," the LP seamlessly wove a nine-song sedative that was, depending on the listener, dreamy or soporific, applying the identical harmonica-and-string formula to accommodating blues-light victuals such as the Bacharach-David "A House Is Not a Home" "Grazin' in the Grass," "Ruby," "Which Way the Wind," "More Than a Dream," a "Never My Love"/"Ask the Lonely" medley, as well as "Bye Bye World" and a new Stevie song, "How Can You Believe." All of them were lightly covered in a diaphanous mist that bore no traces of funk, more Mancini than Motown. Reflecting the motif, the cover had a montage of a drum kit, keyboard, and saxophone, each semitransparent and seeming to blend into one another. An impish line in the right-hand corner read, "How do you spell Stevie Wonder backwards?"

It was one of the loopiest of Motown albums, and like previous Stevie "concept" works, fell off the earth. Released on November 11—not, as were all other Stevie records, on Tamla but on the Gordy label, so as to further milk the "is it Stevie or not?" gag—it didn't dent the pop chart and just scratched the R&B chart at No. 37. The benefit to Gordy was that, yet again, Stevie had quenched his musical wanderlust. And true enough was that Stevie was so grateful by then that he would have done about anything Gordy wanted, which was the usual Motown pop fare.

"Berry was smart in that way, he didn't invest much into albums like that," says Otis Williams. "We had a couple of throwaways like that, too, so did the Supremes. Berry would keep you from getting bored, or pigeonholing you, by having you cut something he didn't want to do anything with. And with Stevie, Berry was letting him do all that stuff he wanted, letting him write, produce, play, whatever. By doing that, he could make Stevie happy and fresh when it came to the other material, the A material."

Jimmy Ruffin, who sang one of Motown's most unforgettable hits, "What Becomes of the Broken Hearted," in 1966, agrees that for Stevie there was no downside to occasional deviations—adding that Gordy actually had progressively less to do with steering him.

"The thing people don't realize is, Berry didn't really know what was happening at Motown," says the older brother of the troubled David Ruffin. "See, Berry was obsessed with the Supremes, he had that tunnel vision, he saw only them. It was really [Motown vice president] Barney Ales who ran the store from the mid-sixties on, and he would let Stevie do his thing. And he should have. Because Stevie was a master of everything he tried, and he wanted to try everything.

"Listen, I knew Stevie from way back and he always was like that. He was always askin' me, 'Hey, how do you do this, how do you do that?' He did that with everybody. He was a real pain in the ass—I say that with love [laugh], but I'm still sayin' he was a pain in the ass. That's how he learned all he did."

Eivets would endure as a felicitous lark, and a precious sidebar, for Stevie. He would delight in telling a possibly apocryphal story in which a buddy of his, having heard some of the cuts of the album, commiserated with him, frothing that "this Eivets dude needs to be sorted, Stevie!"—meaning put in his place, because "he's trying to copy you."

Meanwhile, Stevie's self-stated "independence," based on the fact that he had grown "distant" from the Motown culture, became the envy of the rest of the crowd. "I think a lot of our artists," he went on trenchantly to *Rolling Stone* in 1973, "could have been more sustained if they had other writers, besides Holland-Dozier-Holland, because then they would have found their identity—and that's what everybody needs."

By now, too, his identity could withstand any drop-off in the curve of his hits, such were their consistent train that kept on chugging in the fall. Even as the *Eivets* sessions proceeded, Motown was able to dip into the vault for another, one that was a complementary mellow jazz rocker. The song, "For Once in My Life," cowritten by Ron Miller and Orlando Murden in a slow, writhing tempo, emerged in 1966 when Miller, testing Motown's hegemony, produced a version with a non-Motown singer named Jean DuShon and leased it to Chess Records. When Gordy found out, he pulled rank and brought it out at Motown first with lounge singer Barbara McNair, then had the Temptations and Stevie cover it, though Stevie's was shelved when Gordy disliked Stevie's up-tempo take, produced by Hank Cosby. In the interim, Tony Bennett also did a cover, which went Top 10 on the new *Billboard* easy-listening chart. (In time, among its plethora of covers were those by Frank Sinatra, Ella Fitzgerald, Bobby Darin, and James Brown.)

Gordy—or, if Jimmy Ruffin is right, Barney Ales—revisited Stevie's version in October 1967, which overflowed with schmaltz, its layered orchestration kicked off by a boffo dual electric guitar intro fusing into a thundering bass, frenetic tambourine, tinkling piano, and Stevie's swingin' harmonica break. The vocal was unhurried, almost casual, with only marginal flights up the scale, as Stevie waxed ecstatic: "I won't let sorrow hurt me / Not like it hurt me before," and about having "someone who needs me." It could not have been more convincing—with some of those sentiments of loneliness and sorrow coming from deeper within him than anyone realized—and that Gordy had held back this polished gem spoke volumes about his withering musical ear. Indeed, when "My Life," released on October 15 with the Stevie-Moy-Cosby "Angie Girl" on the flip, ran to No. 2 pop and R&B late in the year, it was kept out of the summit by Marvin Gaye's "I Heard It Through the Grapevine," which of course Gordy had also originally killed.

An equally fumbled decision was the follow-up record, on which Motown slapped Stevie's year-old "Michelle" knockoff, "My Cherie Amour," on the back of a tune called "I Don't Know Why," the credits of which, like "You Met Your Match," listed Stevie, Don Hunter, and Lula Mae (along with Motown arranger Paul Riser); the production credit went to Stevie and Hunter. In fact, the latter seemed to have moved into a real position of power vis-à-vis Stevie—to the consternation of many, including Cosby and Moy, whose own influence was gradually waning.

Another was Ted Hull. He detested Hunter from the start, regarding him as a weasel and opportunist, and as Hunter began to co-opt some of Hull's duties like collecting box-office receipts and making hotel and travel arrangements, Hull, after years of escalating responsibilities, was back where he had come in, just a tutor. And with Stevie now in his senior year in Lansing, Hull sensed that Hunter wanted him out altogether. Tension between the two on the road grew thick as Hunter seemed to wall Stevie off from just about everyone.

Although isolating Stevie was pretty much what Hull himself had done, the difference, he says, is that Hunter was "a deceitful, unprincipled manipulator who'd lie if it was to his advantage," and that he had "a hidden agenda. . . . Gene Shelby noticed it, too, and neither of us knew how he was allowed to get away with it." The agenda, says Hull was that he "saw controlling Stevie as a way to become a songwriter and make some money"—which, of course, had panned out, with Hunter garnering valuable credits on several records.

After Ted took his complaints to Esther Edwards, to no avail, Hunter apparently retaliated by alleging to Ewart Abner, a recently named Motown vice president, that during a gig in New York at the Green Door club, Hull had thrown a "noisy party" for "a rowdy crowd"—absurdly, as they were some of Stevie's teachers and classmates from the Michigan School for the Blind—and paid for it with money "stolen" from Stevie. Never having been embraced by the Motown honchos, Hull had to defend himself to a stern Ewart when he returned home.

Hull grew paranoid about Hunter. Late that year, when the Motortown Revue toured Japan, Stevie pulled him aside in the hotel room one night, whispering, "I want to show you something." It turned out to be a tiny listening device Stevie had somehow discovered under a night table. Hull's first reaction was that it was a Stevie prank, but when it became clear it wasn't, Hull thought it could have been planted by Japanese police, a reflection of anti-Americanism in the country during the Vietnam War. One day, when he and Stevie were walking around the streets, they were stopped by cops, asked to show their passports and explain what they were doing in the country, and escorted back to the hotel.

If not the Japanese, then maybe it had been the CIA, which during the war routinely and nonsensically spied on American artists when they journeyed to the Orient. But his pet theory centered on someone else. "I wouldn't have put it past Hunter, whose room was next door, to have thought he could eavesdrop on Stevie," he says.

Stevie, as always, was caught in the middle, unable to control warring factions around him by choosing sides; he would be led along by whomever got his ear, as Hunter clearly had. But the festering wounds, as well as being bummed out by the unending instances of moral delinquency engendered by the war, left him insulated, stand-offish, trusting no one; as Hull put it, "not acting like his normal self." Ultimately, Hull mentioned it to him.

"Stevie," he said, "you're not acting right. You seem to be thinking about yourself in a way that's not good. You've got to snap out of this and start trusting again."

Stevie listened, then nodded meekly.

"I'll try," was all he could say.

Hunter, meanwhile, moved deeper into the inner circle, cashing in with "I Don't Know Why." The song, a languid, sinewy ballad with a dark, gothic organ intro, blended gathering horns and high, funky guitar riffs suggestive of the Stax/Volt sound and a breathy, scratchy Otis Redding–style vocal that had Stevie testifying, "You threw my heart down in the dirt / You made me crawl on this cold, black earth, baby." Released on January 28, it would hit No. 39 on the R&B chart in the early spring of 1969, but as it weakened, "My Cherie Amour" found life, with DJs flipping over the record to the near-hypnotically soothing ditty and sparking a separate, emphatic run to No. 4 on both the pop and R&B charts.

It was a bonus for Stevie, one that temporarily thwarted Don Hunter's incursion. By Motown canon, the follow-up had to go to Cosby and Moy. But now a hitch developed that would derail Stevie. For months, he had been having a recurrence of past vocal cord problems, unaccountably so since doctors could not find a regrowth of his surgically removed nodes. With increasing anguish, he tried all sorts of remedies. When he was in D.C. for a series of shows, one of the musicians suggested he should fill a sock with salt and keep it on his throat overnight, only he thought that meant putting it *in* his mouth, which he did until he nearly gagged.

It's possible Motown went back to find "For Once in My Life" and "My Cherie Amour" because Stevie was laboring on his vocals. That he wasn't quite right was apparent when, only months after doing his second guest shot on *The Ed Sullivan Show* on December 15, 1968, with boffo performances of "Once" and "You Met Your Match," he made his debut on the glitzy Saturday night variety show *The Hollywood Palace*. The March 8, 1969, episode was hosted by Diana Ross and the Supremes (their official name since 1967). While Stevie was able to finesse informal duets with Ross on "Once" and "I'm Gonna Make You Love Me," a recent Supremes-Temptations hit, he stood stiff-kneed in his natty tuxedo, struggling with the higher notes when he did his only solo turn, on "I Don't Know Why." Looking rather dour, he never flashed his signature smile, and at the end of it he seemed annoyed, standing inert as the audience applauded.

While his vocal woes didn't keep him from making a tour of England in March, he clearly was not up to recording. He gave it a shot, cutting a song called "Never Had a Dream Come True," but Motown couldn't dress up his compromised voice with studio tricks and its release was canceled, and no single would go out until autumn. The void was filled by two Stevie Wonder albums, *For Once in My Life* (No. 5 pop, No. 4 R&B) over the winter and *My Cherie Amour* (No. 34 pop, No. 3 R&B) in the summer, leaving Stevie to busy himself with his classwork in Lansing, from which he would graduate in June, ceremonially, in front of his family, a number of Michigan state politicians, dozens of press photographers taking pictures that would run in newspapers statewide, and a single representative of Motown, Ewart Abner, now the president of ITMI. The program for the festivities featured a full-page shot of Stevie seated at the school piano.

There were also several high-profile honors he received during the winter and spring, one leading him all the way to the White House. First he was honored as Michigan's Disabled Person of the Year by the governor, William Milliken. Then he was nominated for and awarded the Distinguished Service Award of the President's Committee on Employment of the Handicapped. Those rites were held on May 1 in the Rose Garden, with the recently inaugurated Richard Nixon handing the award to him, saying Stevie was "an inspiration to all handicapped citizens, particularly the younger ones," and that he "demonstrated what we mean when we say it's ability, not disability, that counts."

Stevie, who had made fund-raising appearances during the campaign for Hubert Humphrey with other Motown acts at Gordy's behest, tightened his jaw at the empty bromides and would have loved to put Nixon on notice about Vietnam, poverty, race, and a million other matters. Instead, flanked by a beaming Lula Mae and a Motown emissary named Junious Griffin, he bit his lip, smiled hard, and shook hands with a man he would soon enough hold accountable for too many more apocalyptic visions to come, and eviscerate him for it in words and music.

Unknown to most at Motown, part of Stevie's blues had to do with the sort of misery he rarely sung and wrote about in the hopeless romanticism of his endless love songs—love gone bad. Not at all "uptight outta sight" was the romance he'd been pursuing with Angie Satterwhite, the "Cherie" of that song and "Angie Girl." As much as he wanted it to work, by early 1969 his long absences cooled her desire for him and they ended it. He had no problem finding replacements, carrying on with, among others, teenage sisters of Florence Ballard and Martha Reeves.

Chuckling at the regularity of these flings, John Glover says, "Stevie never flaunted them, but when I'd hear people asking if Stevie was doing it back then, I'd think, he was doing it at ten, why wouldn't he be doing it at nineteen? The better question was, when was he *not* doing it? I know, because I was the one who drove him to all those girls' houses. Stevie was still living at home but he was never there. I remember the thing with Lois Reeves. Stevie always loved Martha, but I guess if he couldn't have her, he'd take her sister."

He then started up with Earnestine Pearce, the lead singer of a non-Motown girl group trio, the Flirtations, who were on the bill during the tour of England. Getting wind of it, a typically rabid British music paper ran a story headlined "Stevie Wonder to Marry a Flirtation," and called the romance "the best kept secret in pop." It also ran a photo of the two, wearing matching sunglasses and smiling rather sheepishly.

"Yes, we definitely want to get married," Stevie told the paper, and Pearce—whose age was given as twenty but was several years older—dreamily related how Stevie passed up his limo to ride in the bus with her, snuggling all the way. "We both believe in the stars," she noted. "I'm Cancer and he's Taurus. That means we're mates." But while they spoke of her meeting Stevie's parents after the tour, the "engagement" was over by then, with a good many believing it was all another classic Stevie ruse, designed to punk the gossip-mongering Brit press that had bedeviled him in the past.

In reality, he didn't find what he was looking for until he got close to Syreeta Wright, a burgeoning Motown diva who was being groomed as a possible replacement for Diana Ross after her impending break from the Supremes—perhaps not yet "prime" but surely close to it. At twenty-two, she was tall, sultry, and deeply talented. From where he sat, Wright, who'd begun as Brian Holland's secretary, was every bit as good as Sylvia Moy at writing and conceptualizing his songs. They began to spend long hours side by side on a piano bench, noodling songs and getting very familiar. By the summer, both were sure it was real love.

Syreeta, beneficially, sparked a renewal in Stevie's songwriting, which had lately become more valuable to other Motown acts than to Stevie himself. Of those, Marvin Gaye cut "Try My True Love" and the Vandellas "I'm in Love (And I Know It)." No less than four were cut by Smokey and the Miracles, the most notable "The Tears of a Clown," cowritten with Smokey and Hank Cosby; it first appeared on a 1967 Miracles album, three years before the single would go No. 1 pop and R&B. He and Wright had also composed a brassy screamer of a song for the Spinners, "It's a Shame," which was, ironically in light of their blushing romance, an acrid indictment of a cheating paramour, with Angie the likely retro-inspiration for verses like "Why do you use me, try to confuse me / How can you stand to be so cruel." Keeping his studio chops in order, he produced it in mid-1969, giving the group its first substantial hit when it went out a year later.

As for new Stevie Wonder product, it could only be heard in minor doses, as filler in the two albums such as "I'm Satisfied," "Do I Love Her," and "I'd Be a Fool Right Now" on *Once in My Life* and "Somebody Knows, Somebody Cares," "Give Your Love," and "I've Got You" on *Cherie Amour* (which also included his cool, gritty cover of the Doors' "Light My Fire"). And, problematically, his supply of new material wasn't yet up to snuff. With the clock ticking louder in the fall, Motown once more reached into the drawer, pulling out a track he'd cut two years before, "Yester-Me, Yester-You, Yesterday," a melancholy ballad of love's broken dreams written by Ron Miller and Bryan Wells that made "It's a Shame" seem carefree. Produced by Harvey Fuqua just before he split from Motown and the veteran Motown creative hand Johnny Bristol, it was a glossy, orchestral pastry along a slow, dolorous beat and wrapped around wistful lyrics recalling when "life was warm and love was true" but how in the end that love was "just a cruel and foolish game we used to play."

By the time the song was salvaged, such pleadings as "What happened to the world we knew?" and "Where did it go, that yester glow?" mirrored Stevie's growing sense of isolation and paradise lost—not about love but Motown. As he figured it, if the company wanted to script his last teenage year and last single release of the 1960s in that mournful light, at least he wouldn't need to fake the mood. And it was inarguably a winning strategy. "Yester-You," released in late September backed with the Wonder-Moy-Cosby "I'd Be a Fool Right Now," shot to No. 7 pop, No. 5 R&B by the turn of the decade; it also made it onto the *Cherie Amour* LP, fueling its shelf life.

Motown had every reason to want to keep him rooted on this terrain, and he would, all the while thinking of the upside of, as he'd once sung, "moving on, moving on"—as in, beyond Motown.

With a year and a half left on a contract due to expire on his twenty-first birthday—at which point he'd be due his escrow trust fund and Berry Gordy would no longer call his shots for him—there had been a remarkable turnaround from the last time he was on the clock. Now Stevie held all the cards. When it came to his place in Motown's future, he could make *them* sweat. If he didn't come right out and say it, he surely must have said it to himself: Ain't that a bitch?

10

Pretty Heavy

When I was struggling for the right of the Motown artist to express himself, Stevie knew I was also struggling for him. He gained from that fight, and the world gains from his genius. Don't get me wrong—Stevie would have made it big without me. His talent is cosmic. But as it turned out, Stevie's really a preacher like the rest of us. I like to think I helped show him the light. Now every time I hear him, in between my twinges of jealousy I thank God for Stevie's gift and the privilege of feeling his energy at such close range.

—*Marvin Gaye, in* Divided Soul: The Life of Marvin Gaye *by David Ritz, 1985*

All around Stevie now, things were indeed moving on. After Stevie's graduation, Ted Hull believed he still might have a role at Motown, given that he'd been broached about teaching remedial reading to company artists, many of whom needed it. However, Stevie had about had it with the prissy preceptor, though Hull had loosened his tethers on him. He even indulged Stevie's daredevil thirsts by allowing him to take the wheel of his car at times on quiet streets (something that had been verboten since 1965 when Stevie smashed into a parked car, an incident that was hushed up when Gene Shelby paid off the owner of the other vehicle). He'd also let him briefly take the controls of the small plane Hull sometimes flew as a co-pilot to nearby concerts.

But Hull had not loosened up his control of expenses. Even now, he had Stevie on an allowance of five dollars a week and when Stevie asked him to squeeze money out of Gordy for a boat, he refused. Stevie threw tantrums for days.

Hull had peeved Lula Mae, too, by counseling Stevie not to, as she was pushing him to do, go to college. Heeding her, Stevie, interviewed on *The Mike Douglas Show*, stated that "I plan to go to USC." Hull's advice wasn't easy, but as he says, "Stevie was an average student who, with my tutoring, was able to maintain a B average." College, he reasoned, would not only have been a "struggle" for him, but the time commitment would have killed his career. Lula Mae blew a gasket at that, and ran to Gordy demanding that he send Hull packing. Hull could at least be relieved that Lula Mae hadn't come running for *him*; during a recent road trip that she came along on, he would recall, "she'd gotten angry at someone and hauled a pistol out of her purse. Lula was not a woman to be messed with."

Hull could see the writing on the wall. After he had accompanied Stevie to D.C. for the meeting with Nixon, he was told to remain at the hotel, stunned that he was forbidden to be at Stevie's side in the Rose Garden. Then, in late spring, he was summoned to Gordy's mansion. As the Motown monarch was being dressed by a houseboy, he told Hull to surrender his Motown ID badge. The surreal moment come when he was dressed down by the old street hustler turned fop—a transition that could explain much about why Motown lost its way—left Hull with a bitter aftertaste.

"I'd have much preferred," he says, bitingly, "to say goodbye to the boss at work, with both sleeves rolled up, instead of watching as a houseboy put on [Gordy's] socks."

Stevie barely acknowledged Hull's departure, nor his seven years of thankless work enduring the kid with the pistol-packin' mama. And when he was canned, he was given an "insulting" $1,000 in severance pay. "What hurt most," he said, "was that no person, not even Stevie, said, 'We'll miss you.'"

Stevie may have owed a residual debt to Hull. Before they parted, Hull gave him an album of classical music set to rock called *Switched-On Bach*, by Walter Carlos and Benjamin Folkman, which employed a radical new rock tool, the electronic Moog modular synthesizer—the instrument that would switch on a whole new musical mien for Stevie Wonder.

Another postscript, of course, was that Stevie took Hull's advice to heart, dropping his USC "plan" in order to keep his career on track, though with a certain nagging liability about it that would lead him to personally accept almost any honorary degree that nearly any university would offer him.

Stevie himself was moving on, to the higher ground of autonomy. Indeed, for years now, he had been growing within and without Motown, in quite nearly two discrete orbits. There was good soldier Stevie, following the orders of the Hitsville joint chiefs, laying down prescribed vocals over formulaic Hank Cosby tracks, and reaping the whirlwind of hits. And there was generalissimo Stevie, building the infrastructure of his own duchy, even if he had to do it almost all by himself, at least until Syreeta Wright came along.

Rarely did the twain meet; Stevie's work was so proprietary that when he now went in to cut his pet projects, neither Cosby, Moy, nor even the Funk Brothers—not even James Jamerson—were invited into his studio. In recording "It's a Shame" with the Spinners—whom he chose expressly because they were not high in the Motown caste, and thus not bound to any idiom—and their subsequent album, he arranged the tracks himself and played bass, drums, guitar, and keyboards on the sessions, dubbing and redubbing them on the twenty-four-track recorder now in use there, the coolest toy he'd ever played with.

He was in early 1970 doing the same on sessions he was producing for his own work, intended for an album of material by himself and Wright, deviating from it for the follow-up to "Yester-Me." It was a similarly easygoing ballad called "Never Had a Dream Come True," which because his voice was not quite back to peak timbre led Hank Cosby to compensate by cutting the busy arrangement of string, horns, and funky guitars at earsplitting levels, to give him cover. Something of a flat soufflé, the record, paired with the credited Wonder-Hunter "Somebody Knows, Somebody Cares," flatlined on the charts, making it to No. 26 pop, No. 11 R&B in the early summer of 1970. It also was the last Stevie Wonder single to carry the names of Cosby and Moy.

Stevie's timetable for the collaborative album with Wright, though, was altered when one of their early tracks was heard by the Motown brass and requisitioned as his next single, the gulf between his domains bridged by a throwback R&B rocker amenable with all corners of the Stevie Wonder market. The song was "Signed, Sealed, Delivered I'm Yours," the genesis of which made for a crowded label, the writing credits being Stevie, Syreeta, Lula Mae, and Lee Garrett. The last was a crony who was also blind but knew his way around and took Stevie on some memorable all-night benders; once, as a gag, when the emcee crowed, "Ladies and gentlemen, Stevie Wonder," out came the tall, thin, shades-wearing Garrett.

According to Stevie, Lula Mae earned her credit by giving the song its very name. Hearing him sing, "Here I am, baby," as he played a skeletal version of an unabashed musical valentine to Syreeta, she called from across the room, "Signed, sealed, and delivered!"

He produced it in classic Motown style, embellished right off the bat by the coiled rhythm of a sitar. While this was not a new feel in rock since the Beatles had Ravi Shankar play it in their late 1960s "Maharishi" period, and the instrument had also been used in the Box Tops' "Cry Like a Baby" and B. J. Thomas's "Hooked on a Feeling," it was surely a new application for soul. Stevie didn't compromise on that, keeping the soul real, melding the sitar on the intro with a thumping bass and then into a stream of horns and funky guitars. He did eschew strings for a harder, more fisty groove, for which he himself kept the beat on drums, with rolling, tumbling flourishes. And he bulked up the vocal by having Syreeta double some of the lines in a pseudo-duet. The gospel-R&B backgrounds were shouted by what he had now formed as his backup group on the road, Syreeta, Lynda Tucker Laurence, and Vanetta Fields, who were called Wonderlove.

Thematically, the song mixed regret with cocky swagger at having been "delivered" by the love that "set my soul on fire." Looking back over the battlefield of love, he sang, "I've done a lot of foolish thing that I really didn't mean." Vowing fidelity everlasting, he concluded, "I know you're my heart's only desire"—a promise he may have known he would not be able to keep.

It came out restrained funk tempered by Motown familiarity, and as such it lit the same fire as had "Uptight" and "For Once in My Life." Released on June 3, it was backed with "I'm More Than Happy

(I'm Satisfied)," the last issued song credited to Stevie, Moy, and Cosby and the last one produced by Cosby, save for an old track that would be the B-side on a 1971 Stevie Christmas record. "Signed, Sealed, Delivered I'm Yours" sold more than any other Stevie Wonder record of the decade, well over a million copies, making it to No. 3 on the pop chart and No. 1 on the R&B in midsummer. It would also net him his first Grammy nomination, as R&B Record of the Year. Perhaps as a lingering payback for Gordy's snubbing of the Recording Industry Association of America, Grammy nominations were still rare baubles for Motown, which had until now received only three—limited, as with most black performers, to the R&B categories—two for the Supremes and one for the Temptations, who won the 1968 award for "Cloud Nine."

While he'd lose the Grammy to Clarence Carter's maudlin "Patches"—a face-off that pitted two blind soul men against each other, Carter a venerable Alabama soul guitarist—he was perambulating in the ether now, high above the Motown factory settings. He and Syreeta had leeway to go about their business according to their timetable, and Gordy could only hope they'd touch down and drop in once in a while at the shop. That summer, too, Stevie embarked on another tour of England, where his records had been selling well, sometimes better than at home—"Never Had a Dream Come True," for example, went to No. 6 on the Brit charts.

Syreeta, who by then had been bypassed as Diana Ross's replacement as the Supremes' frontwoman when Gordy picked Jean Terrell, came along as part of one of countless permutations of the Wonderlove road editions over the years. But that function seemed almost incidental when in June the Brit tabloids again were crackling with another Stevie Wonder engagement story, with Stevie making the announcement of a September wedding to his now favorite collaborator whom he credited with bringing serenity to a heretofore desultory, insignificant life with instructions in transcendental meditation and Eastern spiritualism. It was Wright, in fact, who had turned Stevie on to the sitar used to such brilliant effect in "Signed, Sealed, Delivered I'm Yours."

"I want peace," he averred in one interview. He meant for himself, but, parroting John Lennon, he regurgitated the word almost like a mantra, as if repeating it enough would force it to happen on a universal level. "There's a lot of people want peace," he went on unashamedly. "I want peace for brothers and sisters everywhere. The trouble today is . . . lack of communication. Young people can do so much for understanding and peace, because they're not set in their ways. And music can be used as a great force for bringing people together."

It was the kind of bromide-laden homily that would burgeon and morph into countless directions, all with good and sincere intentions if few limits on time and grandiosity, and marked the moment when the Stevie Wonder of the 1970s and beyond was born. The first manifestation was the follow-up to "Signed, Sealed, Delivered," which could not have departed more from the former's upbeat dance grooves. Conspicuously titled "Heaven Help Us All," it was penned by Ron Miller but perfectly reflected Stevie's higher calling. As produced by Miller and Motown crewman Tom Baird, it was more akin to the Edwin Hawkins Singers' "Candles in the Rain" than anything Motown. Stevie returned to his gospel roots, with measured, hypnotic preaching, spontaneously lurching into wailing backed by a swirling choir: "Heaven help the boy who won't reach twenty-one / Heaven help the man who gave that boy a gun."

Danceable it wasn't, but by now Motown was at his mercy— crossing him might well help drive him away—and when it went out in late September with the Stevie-Hunter "I Gotta Have a Song," with its mantra-like hook, "Show me to where there's music," on the flip, it surprised everyone by rising to No. 9 pop, No. 2 R&B by Thanksgiving. It also seemed to be something of a corrective after the *Stevie Wonder Live* album had tanked, coming in at No. 81 pop, and only No. 16 R&B. The ensuing *Signed, Sealed, and Delivered*, issued in August with the last songs on an original Stevie Wonder album ever to carry the credits of Motown writers besides Wright (the cover image of Stevie seated in a box labeled "Handle with Care" was his idea, and a subtle but clear hint that he might soon be headed elsewhere), was riding a wave to No. 25 pop, No. 7 R&B.

Still, he was in no great rush to file any new work—the start of another long-term habit—as he and Wright went about their business at Stevie's pace. But with the Stevie brand roaring, it seemed he could do no wrong. His next single, taken from the *Signed* album, a liberally reworked cover of the Beatles' now past-prime "We Can Work It Out," ladled on the funk with an anvil—actually an electric Fender Rhodes electric piano amplified to deep, fuzzy distortion and dueling high and low vocal yelps of "hey." A historical curio at best, it nonetheless ran to No. 13 pop, No. 3 R&B in the early spring of 1971.

•   •   •

By that time, Stevie had been married six months, having tied the knot with Syreeta on September 14, 1971, in Detroit's Burnette Baptist Church—although the ceremony was delayed when a nervous Stevie, ushered into the church by his brother Calvin, his best man, developed a nosebleed that he couldn't stem for almost an hour. Properly plugged, he came out of the bathroom and was married by a reverend named Caldwell in a candlelit service in front of a packed room with a full contingent of Motown luminaries, including Berry, Esther, and Gwen Gordy. The bride and groom looked splendid, Stevie dapper in his two-toned black-and-white tux, Syreeta dreamy in a white satin gown. A press photo ran the next day in newspapers of the Wonders in a limo afterward, all smiles, clenching each other's hands, Syreeta holding a full champagne glass.

The reception for three hundred guests, paid for by Motown, was at Mauna Loa Hawaiian restaurant, where they sang improvised duets between bites of pineapple chicken. A cake the size of an Alp was wheeled in, and Stevie carved slices for the crowd. Then they flew off to Bermuda for the honeymoon. Syreeta was amazed that Stevie, after getting an initial lay of the land, got around as if he knew where everything was. When they got back, they moved into a cozy three-bedroom ranch house worth $30,000 that Esther Edwards had picked out for them in suburban Inkster, where Stevie had told her he'd be able to think and work undisturbed by the traffic and police sirens that played a crude symphony on the streets in Detroit, even in Greenlawn. In the den he would convert into a makeshift home studio, there was a $5,000 Moog synthesizer, a wedding gift from a suddenly very generous Berry Gordy.

On the surface, it was all storybook—Wonderland in every way. But some were already skeptical the marriage was phantasmic. "Stevie was definitely in love with Syreeta, but I don't know if either of them were ready to marry or thought it all out," posits John Glover, Stevie's longtime peep who was a guest at the wedding and an early visitor at the new digs.

Clear to Glover, and others, was that a component of Stevie's desire to show his independence was needing to play house. Never having lived on his own, he surely had no intention of doing so depending on his family—what would be the point of moving? Logic told him that the only alternative to having Calvin or Milton move in with him would be to either shack up or marry a woman he trusted; better yet if it was one he loved. At the start, this sounded like a propitious arrangement for Stevie and Syreeta. But both fairly quickly learned that it did nothing to essentially wipe away the biggest bugaboo he had—one that Syreeta deduced. "It was only after I came to know Stevie," she would relate years later, "that I realized how lonely he was."

That she discovered this while living with him under the same roof was the first clue that the marriage in fact had little to do with lifetime commitment and everything to do with ephemeral comfort and convenience. For Syreeta, the doubts about the union grew as she watched him falling deeper into dark, silent aloofness that she could not snap him out of. Only when he had to show himself to the world outside did he brighten into the effigy of "Stevie," a trait she found rather remarkable. As she would say, "He never shows he's sad to anyone. To me he'll show his grievances but when he steps out he never shows he's angry or depressed. He feels life is too short to upset other people."

Thus he found more solace in the shadows on the road, if she wasn't with him. Then he would chase the loneliness away with whatever warm, willing female would be fetched for him. Long forgotten now was the attempted interdiction of such liaisons; as bluenosed as Hull was, as the years went on he had allowed Stevie whatever time he needed in his room to finish his mattress dances. On one layover in Canada in the late 1960s, Hull opened the door and was nearly trampled when "half a dozen teenage girls burst in. Stevie was seated on the edge of the bed, and they climbed all over it and him, rubbing him in some highly inappropriate places. He loved it, and giggled and chatted playfully the whole time. Every time I peeled one of the girls off, the others were on him again."

Hull didn't say what happened, nor did he need to, but he lived under constant stress caused by the obvious perils presented by under-age girls once Stevie turned eighteen—perils magnified by Stevie's prodigious appetites.

Motown was able to keep a lid on that side of the Stevie experience, avoiding major repercussions to his always clean-cut image, and the inevitable blowback has been minimal. If there were pregnancy claims, they were taken care of as Shelby did the owner of the car Stevie ran into, with cash. Apparently some did try to leverage such a claim for cash. One teenage girl, having somehow gotten Lula Mae's phone number, called her and said she was pregnant with Stevie's baby. Sensing it was a con job—and not for the only time in such a circumstance—Lula Mae called the bluff. "Honey, if it comes out black, blind and playing the harmonica, then I'll believe you," she said. The girl hung up, never to call back.

More than marriage, then, music was his stabilizer, to give voice and ideation to alienation. Submerging his feelings of inadequacy, his work with Wright was intense. Yet he had a gnawing sense that it wasn't saying quite what he wanted to, that he was caught between rock and a hard place—Motown—that he wasn't saying what Marvin Gaye was. In fact, so seismic was Gaye's 1971 awakening as a deeply sententious artist that it obsessed Stevie, even taunted him that Marvin had gotten to that high ground first, even as both had been following the same blueprint, annexing more sovereignty in the seams of their Motown obligations. Taking a cue from Stevie, Gaye helped clear his musical cobwebs by writing for and producing, with great success, a lesser act, the Originals. As well, Gaye had his own buffet of personal torments, first when Tammi Terrell died of a brain tumor in March 1970, then when his marriage to Gwen Gordy hit the rocks.

Gaye considered quitting the business, and even tried out as a wide receiver with the NFL's Detroit Lions, before gathering his catalog of wits and self-inflicted tortures and scraping the viscera of his soul as if with a rusty nail in "What's Going On," the ultimate manifesto of high anxiety amid a world gone mad. Citing the bloodletting in Vietnam and unrest at home, he pleaded, "Don't punish me with brutality"—and, in the ultimate grievous irony, "Father, father, we don't need to escalate." Gordy, as with most songs that wore pain—real pain—on their sleeves, cringed, saying it was "the worst record I ever heard." When Gaye said he'd walk unless Gordy released it, "What's Going On" went to No. 2 pop and No. 1 R&B (for five weeks) early in 1971.

In the cyclical coexistence of Stevie and Gaye, where Gaye had followed Stevie's lead, his biorhythm was now higher. Stevie was paying close attention to Gaye's upward thrust and methods of elevation, looking for applicable directives. There was, for one, Gaye saying that "I realized that I had to put my own fantasies behind me if I wanted to write songs that would reach the souls of people." Stevie was getting there too, almost parallel to Gaye. Indeed, as the latter began work on the *What's Going On* album, Stevie and Syreeta Wright were ready to lay their masterwork on vinyl, with Stevie using the full extent of his leverage, ceding no artistic control to anyone at Motown, as Gaye had done. The difference was that the stimuli for Stevie's pain came from a different place—though of course the lacerations of their fathers were all too similar—and thus would not burn like salt in an open wound but rather cleanse and soothe it with mercurochrome.

The title of the work became like a pronunciamento. Originally he planned on calling it *Stevie Wonder the Man*, but because that would undermine all that had come before it as juvenile, he instead went with *Where I'm Coming From*, at once binding him to the high expectation not of age but momentousness. He furthered that notion by noting to a British paper prior to its release that he and Wright were "trying to touch on the social problems of the world today. We want them to be relevant, to mean something. [There'll be] songs of war, anti-drugs and the racial issue."

The tracks would solder a wide range of eclectic influences, mainly the endless derivatives of soul music reaching across the entire rock-and-roll landscape. Gaye was doing the same, but wouldn't have much to do with the hard and harder-edged funk of Sly Stone and Jimi Hendrix, stopping at the water's edge of carryover R&B funk that Curtis Mayfield took to the *Shaft* soundtrack.

Conversely, Stevie, master of the sensuous, stringed groove though he was, found more to mine in harder rock forms—believing that Hendrix, whose death in September 1970 left him seething at the Russian roulette of the drug culture, had only begun to tap into a blues-oriented acid rock orbit. Less of a grab for him was the soothing soul syrup of the Chi-Lites, the Moments, Tyrone Davis, and the luxuriously ambrosial Gambler-Huff productions at Philadelphia International with the Delfonics, Stylistics, and Billy Paul—which had all but replaced the Smokey Robinson Motown model of romantic soul-pop, and also made inroads into disco funk with the O'Jays and Harold Melvin and the Blue Notes.

Stevie wanted to bring on the funk, bring on the noise. Lately he had been studying on a microcellular level the work of Sly Stone; frequently, he would call Sly in San Francisco and the two would go on for hours about the shifting soul tides. He made several appearances at concerts to share the bill with him. He even looked like Sly now, dressing in flower-print shirts, bell-bottoms, and fringed leather vests. He had also developed a major hunger for Eric Clapton, and in his home studio tried to reproduce the slide guitar licks on "Layla," which he regarded as pure and brilliant blues caramel.

All of it had some place on the album, but for the life of him he could not loosen his grip on the mainstream pop-soul ballast. When he was ready to lay down tracks in Studio A—some of the last recordings made there before Motown officially renounced Detroit—he stayed closer to the Motown template than he might have, even hiring the Funk Brothers for the sessions (for what would be the last time). The act of faith could be traced to the good company man he had been, and the hope that Hitsville had in fact made an effort to bend to the winds of change. He liked to cite the Temptations' socially conscious hits like "Cloud Nine" and "Psychedelic Shack" as evidence of that. Adopting the en vogue term "funkadelic," he defined it, in his own words, as "a combination of R&B, psychedelic and funky African-type beat."

Still a sucker for a good pop hook, Stevie crafted *Where I'm Coming From* with studied balance, continuing his trend of throwing out the traditional LP format: a couple of strong songs ringed by factory seconds—for a collective "storybook," though with a better transitional flow—and barbed messages all around. It began with "Look Around," his "Welcome to my angst" preamble, a creeping ballad with an eerie *Addams Family* harpsichord sound—actually a doubled Clavinet—and deeper-than-deep bass and dirgelike annotations paraphrased from *Be Here Now*, the Ram Dass spiritual bible of that year, opining that "You will find / Searching for time / Empty is your mind."

"Look Around," a historical doubloon as Stevie's only real foray into psychedelia, was followed by the six-minute funk-fest "Do Yourself a Favor," a prickly caveat to bad bloods in the 'hood who "persecute your own pride" to "learn instead of burn"; the Vietnam obloquy "Think of Me as Your Soldier," embroidering with a Wes Montgomery–style guitar line a sentimental vow to "find the promised paradise," an ambiguous foreshadowing of either love, death, or both; a cool ballad of love's redemption, "Something Out of the Blue," in which a string quartet virtually weeps to treacle like "When hope was lost / love paid the cost"; and "If You Really Love Me," a frothy, jazzy gambol kicked into gear by a joyous Stevie yip and rolling on with continual beat and tempo changes that take the groove from that of a jazz combo to a piano bar, metaphoric of love's mercurial moods.

The back side of the record began with "I Wanna Talk to You," a seriocomical dialogue between a young black man and an old white man, both parts sung by Stevie, a none too subtle reminder that the struggle could be defined as much along age as racial lines. Then came "Take Up a Course in Happiness," a pseudomeditative séance retrofitted to big band and Beatles beats; the near-maudlin but gorgeous "Never Dreamed You'd Leave in Summer"; and the final track, the nearly-seven-minute chanty "Sunshine in Their Eyes," a schmaltzy paean to the hopeless cause that ghetto children would one day see the sun in their eyes as he could in his sightlessness, with an opening that checked off too-familiar vistas like fear, hungry faces, pain, and unchased dreams before pining: "Oh, I can't wait until the day there's sunshine in their eyes."

Stevie himself was aware that very little of this content was commercially viable, on any chart or radio playlist, and so could not have been surprised when Gordy's negative verdict centered on just that fact. To Gordy, it sounded like a whole lot of pretentious preaching and tomfoolery. What's more, Stevie was far from sure he had gotten it right. A few years later, he would tell Ben Fong-Torres in a *Rolling Stone* interview that the album "was kinda premature to some extent, but I wanted to express myself. A lot of it now I'd probably remix," and that the rationale for the work was no more complicated than that "I love gettin' into just as much weird shit as possible."

While one can dissect all sorts of brilliance in those grooves, perhaps even as the key to the ignition of all that would come after, the main problem with the work is that it failed to deliver on its promise: one could not possibly know just where Stevie was coming from. It had loose and long-form guitar passages like Clapton and Hendrix; Edwin Hawkins gospel fervor; gushing Chi-Lites romantic soul; Pink Floyd psychedelic space rock. It had a little bit of everything—and not nearly enough of Stevie Wonder.

Gordy wanted him to re-sign without pause, on Gordy's terms. Stevie, though, was determined to wait and judge the currents. The first order of business was to put out a single from the album, but Gordy could find nothing with any commercial grab. Reversing his usual M.O., he put out the album with no single to drive it, on April 12. A month later, as Stevie's twenty-first birthday—and the expiration of his Motown contract—came and went, the LP had gone nowhere. But as it sat stuck in inertia, a buzz did stir around "If You Really Love Me," which DJs were starting to rip from the album. That led Gordy to release it as a single on July 22, with "Think of Me as Your Soldier" on the flip. Already familiar, the song ran to No. 8 pop, No. 4 R&B, in the early fall. The album, however, never broke out, never rising above No. 62 pop, though it did beat a path to No. 7 on the R&B list.

But if Stevie had prospered from "If You Really Love Me," he got a bigger boost from an indirect ally—Marvin Gaye, whose own ambitious concept album came out a month and nine days after his. But while Gordy was right in Stevie's case, Gaye's work drew huge numbers of black and white ears to songs that, like the title track, bled with real pain, most notably "Mercy Mercy Me (The Ecology)" and the opus "Inner City Blues (Make Me Wanna Holler)."

These spurting grooves, drizzled with dewy and dreamy echoes and Gaye's own overdubbed harmonies, were part jazz and R&B, but far more gut-stabbing than Stevie's busy but curiously planar elegies, and nothing about them except the artist could remotely be tagged as Motown (though Gaye, blessedly, enumerated thirty-nine of Motown's long-shrouded studio musicians on the jacket). But unlike the sluggish response to Stevie's album, Gaye's flourished on the AM and FM dials, rewarding Gordy in ways he hardly deserved, going to No. 6 on the pop album chart and—for nine weeks—to the top of the R&B chart over the summer and selling two million copies. The next year, the follow-up, *Let's Get It On*, which replaced somber reflection with panting sexuality, did even better.

Stevie rightly acknowledged that Gaye had gotten it right where he had not, which was keeping it real and keeping it affecting on the first listen—as opposed to, say, a listen four decades hence, which with aural hindsight becomes a treasure (such as a review of *Where I'm Coming From* on the Allmusic Web site calling it "uniformly excellent" and "frequently astonishing"). Even so, he knew Gaye had created a shared right-of-way for them both. Because both works were on the market together, they ran as a kind of entry on the rock track, and were often yoked in reviews. One of those was an August 5, 1971, review in *Rolling Stone* by Vince Aletti, who wrote of the conjunction, "Ambitious, personal albums may be a glut on the market elsewhere, but at Motown they're something new. These, from two of the Corporation's Finest, represent a subversive concept, allowed only to producers, the overseer/stars of Motown's corporate plantation, as long as they didn't get too uppity. Both Gaye and Wonder have been relatively independent at Motown, their careers following their own fluctuations outside the mainstream studio trends, but these latest albums are departures even for them."

Stevie usually suffered in these comparisons. For Aletti, "Stevie apparently wanted an opportunity to loosen up outside the confines of the typical Motown single. But he blew it," the offenses supposedly being "sadly undistinguished" lyrics, "self-indulgent and cluttered" arrangements, "effects that too often obscure the utter virtuosity of Wonder's singing," and a surfeit of "thick studio veneer [and] double-tracking for vocal self-accompaniment"—which sounded an awful lot like saying Stevie *was* too uppity, inasmuch as "the most successful cuts, 'Think of Me as Your Soldier' and 'If You Really Love Me,' are short, unassuming love songs, pleasant vehicles for the Wonder charm, his off-hand intensity, his intimate heavy breathing, his joyous yelps [and] warm, sensuous style. In the end, though, even vibrant vocals fail to carry the album beyond its own excesses. Quite a disappointment."

Brutal as such a verdict could be, sharing a ride with Gaye hardly hurt Stevie's credibility. Indeed, Gaye would routinely give him huzzahs for inspiring him. Neither was it harmful that Gaye being played on FM radio opened that medium for other black artists besides Hendrix, Sly Stone, and the Chambers Brothers.

But he needed more than incidental attention. He needed to get "pretty heavy," as he put it. He needed separation from Motown, geographically in miles and artistically in light-years. It would be Gordy's call as to whether Motown would bend that far over for all this in order to keep Stevie Wonder on his attenuating payroll.

The night before Stevie's birthday, Gordy had thrown him a party at his sprawling estate on plush Boston Boulevard, which in addition to his usual palatial perks had an underground tunnel leading to the guest-house and a moat around the grounds. While the royalties brought in by Stevie and other successful Motown artists had built much of this free-hold, he had never before been invited to enter its gated portal—or, for that matter, rarely seen or spoken with Gordy directly for several years. Now Big Daddy wanted him to know how much he treasured the filial relationship they had shared through the years. Stevie, who couldn't possibly have passed up a chance to experience life on the other side of the tracks, brought Syreeta, Lula Mae, and the rest of the family. A good time was had by all. And not for a minute did he buy Gordy's charade.

The show of hospitality, he knew, was a caviar-dipped fillip for him to re-sign with the company and thus enjoy continued affection from a man who had all but razed the "family" he had always paid lip service to while secretly robbing many of them blind. In that midyear of 1971, Hitsville was almost purely a nostalgia juke box setting off memories of classic hits. Its roster had dwindled to a mere few dozen, most of them on paper only. Other than Gordy's favored children—Diana Ross and the Jackson 5—and his two prodigal sons with their wavy concept albums, little came from Motown that mattered. The iconic West Grand Boulevard landmark with the big bay window would soon be shuttered, most of the studio entrails put on trucks bound for L.A. A few of the Funk Brothers went west, too, but found the operation clean, coolly professional, and completely soulless. James Jamerson tried to fit in but was so corroded from booze that producers shied away from booking him; soon after, his precious sunburst Fender electric bass was stolen. The forgotten Martha Reeves didn't go, and if Gordy was removed from the quotidian demands of the record business while he hunkered at Bel-Air country club power lunches, he was still petty, demanding that Reeves repay him $200,000 in back "expenses" before he would let her out of her contract.

As Stevie approached his pivotal birthday, he had somehow hired an entertainment attorney whose office was in Omaha, Nebraska, but was touted to him as a tough-as-nails negotiator. Tabulating Stevie's share of sales and royalties held in escrow as best he could (given that the account books were off-limits to prying eyes), he estimated that if he had sold around thirty-five million records—a reasonable figure—and if, according to the terms of his contract, those sales would entitle him to around ten cents per record, Stevie was due no less than $3.5 million on his birthday, though this did not reflect the great equalizer of all record industry executives: deduction of expenses. The Omaha suit vowed to collect this bounty, and in the meantime said he would send out feelers to other labels about Stevie being receptive to offers. Big-money offers only. Stevie, his head swimming with those big numbers and bigger ones to come, followed his orders not to re-sign with Motown.

Then the lawyer *really* played hardball. The day following the party, Gordy took off again for MoWest. As he recalled in his autobiography *To Be Loved*, "Waiting for me at the office was a letter from a lawyer I'd never heard of disaffirming every contract Stevie had with us—effective upon his turning twenty-one. I couldn't believe it. I couldn't believe we could have been together the night before like we were and he [did] not prepare me for something like this. That was not Stevie. But if it was, I was definitely going to tell him about it."

In truth, such a letter was normal operating procedure in business negotiations, one that Gordy would have been very familiar with had he allowed his employees to retain outside legal representation. That he was so incensed about it was more a reflection of his own incubation and narcissism—never mind the hypocrisy of expecting blind loyalty from his financially undernourished "family." Steam coming from his ears, he picked up the phone and called Inkster. Stevie wasn't home but Syreeta answered, and even though she knew Stevie had retained a hired gun for such purposes, she did not refer Gordy—who was after all still her boss—to the lawyer. Instead, actually breaching her husband's client-attorney confidentiality, she insisted that Stevie would not have agreed to sending a letter like that.

Hearing later of Gordy's call, Stevie apparently felt so guilty that he buckled, seriously undermining his own objectives and stabbing his lawyer in the back by calling Gordy, who recalled that Stevie was "very upset" about the latter being humiliated by a routine missive from a lawyer trying to act in his client's best interests. Breaching his own case, Stevie timidly explained to him that he'd wanted to renegotiate his contract—"but not that way," though what other way he had in mind to get big money from a notorious tightwad was unclear. He even, Gordy said, "apologized" for the episode and added that the lawyer "had acted without his knowledge," which must have given Big Daddy a good laugh. If Stevie was buckling under on day one of his free agency period, how far could he possibly stray from the flock, and at how low a price would he come back home?

More satisfying for Gordy, Stevie quickly canned the lawyer, and did not immediately hire another one. *That* certainly was how Gordy preferred to play it—hadn't he always? Yet if Stevie was uncomfortable with the kind of brass-knuckle tactics for which he hired the lawyer in the first place, he was no less determined to parlay his freedom into a nexus of creative autonomy—far greater than Gaye had reaped and earned, and far more than Stevie at present had. What the lawyer had told Motown still applied: Stevie wanted up to a *twenty*-cent-per-record royalty and total artistic control of all song content—meaning he would be able to spend Motown's money any way he pleased, and record whatever he wished. He also wanted his own 0publishing company, relieving Motown of its cut on any publishing royalties.

Any one of these concessions alone would have been unprecedented at Motown. Together, they were tantamount to creating a "Stevie Wonder exception," with the subsidizing of a separate and nearly independent subdivision operating under a completely different set of rules. Having wanted to bum-rush Stevie into re-signing on his terms, it was Gordy now who needed a stiff drink, and time to make a decision. What's more, Stevie was unimaginably offended when a week after his birthday Motown called him in for the disbursement of his trust fund account.

With great expectations, he sat down with Gordy and a court representative, whereupon he was handed a check—not for $3.5 million but just a little less, $3.4 million less.

The $100,000 came as a total shock. After the meeting, Stevie dropped in at Ted Hull's home, something he still did when he wanted to unburden, looking "obviously shaken," in Hull's words. However, Hull had little sympathy for him. "Frankly, I wasn't surprised in the least," he says, familiar with the "huge flow of money it took to make and maintain his career." Having gotten bupkes from Motown himself, and now struggling financially, he recalled that "I had a hard time feeling sorry for him."

Feeling sorry enough for himself, Stevie now decided he could no longer be Mr. Nice Guy. He sent a wire to Ewart Abner, now president of Motown—Gordy having promoted himself to Chairman of Motown Industries. As Ewart recalled, the gist of the letter was that "because he was twenty-one, his contract was voidable and he [was exercising] that option to void it."

Abner maintained that he was not overly surprised, that "we had expected it because he had been chafing at the bit, he had been saying to us that he didn't think we understood where he wanted to go and what he wanted to do. We knew . . . he was going to demand absolute creative control over his own product." (At other times

Abner told a different story, saying that Stevie's "void me" order had "freaked me out.")

And so Stevie Wonder was officially free of Motown, but for how long? It's likely that neither Gordy nor Stevie figured it would be very long. But a complication arose when Stevie announced that he needed to clear his head and go somewhere to make music on his own. That someplace would not be L.A. with the rest of the surviving Motown stable—including Syreeta Wright Wonder—but New York City, assimilating into a new, hip music crowd just as John Lennon was doing. To Stevie, that sounded like a pretty heavy thing to do.

Never before had Motown subsidized an artist on his own so far from its home base. But just ten days after his birthday "emancipation," he was on his way east. But was he really flipping off Gordy? According to Gordy's memoirs, no. "During the whole time," he wrote, "Stevie made it clear that he was staying at Motown." It was just that "Stevie was ready to fly," he added poetically. If this take is so, the question was not whether Stevie would be back under the Motown big tent, but when.

Perhaps so, but before that would happen, Stevie and Gordy would shadowbox with each other for so long that when the prodigal son returned, he would be all but unrecognizable.

11

The Direction
of Destiny

It was a completely different thing that was in my head. I don't think you can gradually leave a kind of music. You can't mix one concept with another. It has to be an abrupt change where you say, "Okay, this is what I want to do from now on and all the other stuff belongs to the past."

—*Stevie Wonder, to journalist Constance Elsner, 1971*

Stevie Wonder now took to the road, accompanied by Gene Kees, who had been working as his musical director on tours, Stevie's cousin John Harris, and his brother Milton. With Harris at the wheel of a new Buick station wagon Stevie bought for the journey, they blew out of Detroit a week after his birthday and into New York a day later, settling in at a Howard Johnson Motor Inn on Eighth Avenue.

His arrival in the Big Apple was not among the day's big news. Whether Stevie Wonder was on his own, whether he had a contract or not, what music he was involved with—none of that qualified as even mildly interesting to the public at large. It really only mattered to Stevie, though as for conducting negotiations with Motown or other labels that might want him, he seemed not to be in any rush. The first inkling of his status came in one of the British papers, to which he explained that he'd decided "to just not sign with anybody for a while and just cool it."

While it was clear to everyone that he was still a Motown artist, contract or no, he was wily enough to drop tantalizing hints about talking with other labels—sure that such talk would get back to Gordy and hopefully get him to cave on a new deal. Sometimes he even took mildly harsh shots at the company, such as that "it's very difficult to keep a relationship like [his with Motown] when things are moving and people are living in all different parts of the world"—an obvious slap at the move westward, which he wanted no part of. Indeed, his own move three thousand miles away was a way, he said, of "convincing" Motown he was serious about his new course, and if he had "insulted" Gordy by doing so, tough.

With a touch of finality, he concluded that "I had gone about as far as I could go. I wasn't growing. I just kept repeating 'The Stevie Wonder Sound,' and it didn't express how I felt about what was happening in the world. I wanted to see what would happen if I changed."

It didn't take him long to dive into a new musical environment. And it's revealing that his first steps taken were toward the synthesizer.

But he walked a fine line. For soul and rock purists, the Moog and its imitator, the ARP, had become symbols of a cheapened musical order, a shortcut originally envisioned by movie and record producers as a way to save money on musicians by using a machine that could be programmed to gurgle out fleecy facsimiles of horn, string, and drum noises. The last thing he wanted was to become an avatar of processed sonic cheese that would cut the heart and soul out of his music. One thing he would never do, he resolved, was to use the synthesizer in place of strings, as most producers did. In fact, he didn't want to replace anything. Rather, he would use it to widen and deepen the spatial field, *with* strings, if need be. Though the synthesizer had been used in classical and pop applications, he heard Walter Carlos's wavy riffs on *Switched-On Bach* as amenable with a supernatural kind of funk.

There were plenty of synth commodities on the market now, including *The Moog Strikes Bach* and *Chopin à la Moog* by Hans Wurman, *Switched-On Gershwin* by Gershon Kingsley and Leonid Hambro, and on the pop side, *Switched-On Bacharach* by Christopher Scott, *Switched-On Rock* by the Moog Machine, Kingsley's *Music to Moog By*, and *Moog Plays the Beatles* by Marty Gold. But it was one called *Zero Time* that really caught his ears. This was an experimental work by a pair of sound-engineers-cum-hippies named Robert Margouleff and

Malcolm Cecil under the cryptic pseudonym Tonto's Expanding Head Band, all the sounds of which came from what they called "The Original New Timbral Orchestra," or TONTO, a polyphonic, souped-up Moog III analog synthesizer that Cecil, the more tech-savvy of the two—and music-savvy, having been a highly respected bass player in several bands in his native England—had built to engulf sundry other Moog and ARP synthesizers. Looking more like a condo than an instrument, TONTO needed an entire room to house all of its modules, panels, cables, and other gizmos, and programming it required both men to constantly fiddle with knobs, dials, and sliders.

That room was located in the basement of a converted church on West 57th Street that was now Media Sound Studios. Margouleff, who ran the place, had acquired the synthesizer for the all too usual reason, to use in the recording of commercial jingles and such without having to pay musician fees he couldn't afford.

"Bob hired me," says Cecil, "because he didn't really know how to program music for the synthesizer, or how to do much of anything with it. I'd just finished a six-week stint at the Record Plant studio as the audio-video repairman. And it didn't take me long to expand the Moog for personal use. I had some serious musical things I wanted to explore, which we did on *Zero Time*, doing things like combining the seventeen musical scales of Egypt, which sounded very Middle Eastern yet very jazzy. I'll never forget this. Herbie Mann, the great jazzman, who owned the label we did *Zero Time* for, came by during the sessions, saw what was going on, and said, 'A *synthesizer!? You?* You're a purist!' And I was. But I was captured."

As was Stevie, mostly from afar, admiring the potential of a machine that could unleash, channel, and rechannel sound wave frequencies far more thoroughly across the spectrum of audible sound than any other instrument, with patterns of modulation that honed various frequencies into tonalities, timbres, and "mood." This was especially so on *Zero Time*, on which those waves pumped through amplifiers came out not coldly mechanical but subtly layered, in warm and mesmerizing aural shades that could either pound or murmur.

TONTO revealed for Stevie, as it did for Malcolm Cecil, the many dimensions of recorded music, and he would in time embrace it in nearly intimate terms, once saying, "It's like the synthesizer is a . . . friend, I could almost say, assisting me in expressing myself."

Stevie has said he first became aware of the team of music geeks—an odd couple indeed, both in their early thirties, one a burly, swarthy, gay son of a Long Island furrier who was the mayor of his town, the other a twiggy blond Brit, both with fright-wig-style hair down to their asses—when he found *Zero Time* in a record store soon after his arrival in New York and listened to some tracks through headphones. Making some inquiries, he found a link and was on his way to see them.

"It was over the Memorial Day weekend," recalls Cecil. "I had an apartment upstairs in the building where Media Sound was and I heard the bell ring downstairs. It was very hot that day and I was literally stark naked, and I stuck my head out of the window and my friend Ronnie Blanco yelled up, 'Somebody wants to see TONTO.' I threw on a pair of shorts, went down to the basement, threw on the lights to the studio, and there was Stevie, in a pistachio suit, a copy of *Zero Time* under his arm.

"I took him into the TONTO room and he said, 'So this album was made on that thing?' I said yes and put his hands on it, and when he did he realized it was all knobs and that he would never be able to operate it himself. Then we went over to a piano, he sat down and began to noo-dle on it, and by instinct I turned on the tape and we started to record. By the time we got to the second tune, he's saying, 'Okay, let's put some synthesizer on this.' Bob was away for the weekend but I called him and said, 'Get your ass over here.' He showed up two or three hours later and we were still at it. In fact, at one point we were doing a song called 'Crazy Letters' and Stevie said to me, 'You're a bass player, why don't you play bass on this.' It was just that crazy, and it was assumed we would be working together from then on."

Most every day for the next several months, Cecil and Margouleff, whom Stevie told about his free agency on leave from Motown, were engaged in some of the most unorthodox sessions imaginable—the kind that could never have been held at Hitsville, where the show was always run with timepiece precision by producers and arrangers who really were the stars and controllers of the records; even when Stevie was allowed to produce, he didn't have the final say.

"Stevie wanted to get away from all that," Cecil says. "He hated having had to go through this routine where he would bring his songs to people like Gene Kees who would then take it to someone at Motown and Stevie wouldn't hear it again until it was time for him to go in and do his vocal, and in the meantime the arrangement would be done and the track already recorded. He wanted none of that. He wanted to be with a song every step of the way.

"Bob and I short-circuited the whole process up front, to pare it all down to what Stevie was doing at any given moment and be there to record it. We lived with him and the songs and took them through all the steps. That's why when Stevie called the album that came out of it *Music of My Mind*, we supported him, because we really did live inside his mind with him and saw where the music came from."

In keeping with that leitmotif, outside musicians were not hired, though there were other reasons for that. For one thing, Stevie wanted to plumb the many layers of the synthesizer; for another, it would save on production costs. In any case, it would have been difficult for sidemen to follow Stevie's eccentric meters and tonalities.

"We only used two guys, on just one track for each. Art Baron, a trumpet player from Stevie's tour band was on one. And Howard 'Buzz' Feiten [the ex–lead guitarist for the Paul Butterfield Blues Band and the Rascals], who was a friend of ours, was in the studio tinkering on guitar during a session and Stevie said, 'Hey, man, wanna play on this?' But Stevie had to play most of the stuff himself, for example, the drums, because nobody else could have followed his time, which varied so wildly. We tried a really fine drummer, Bernard Purdy, but only Stevie could make it work because Stevie knows exactly what he wants and how to do it, the rest of the world can only try to keep up with him.

"That's why we always had tape running at all times, a two-track 'room tape.' We kept it rolling because we never knew when Stevie was gonna come up with something. In fact, we fired more than one assistant for turning it off. The room was always to be 'live.' They had to keep that tape machine fed because if Stevie was in the room, something was always happening. It would always start with him just noodling on the piano, then everything would build, with our collaboration, on the lyrics, on the arrangement, and in the end we'd take all the bits and pieces and transfer them onto a sixteen-track tape machine.

"You had to be ready, always. Sometime we'd be off the floor setting up some programming, but Stevie would be at the piano doodling something. So we set up a piano and microphones. We preserved everything—hours and hours of those tapes, with bits of hundreds of songs. We'd go over those tapes all the time, and if there was something really good we'd reference it, then later rewind it and say, 'Hey Stevie what about this thing?' He'd go, 'Oh yeah' and start singing to it and, like that, you had a song. By the end of the first week we worked with Stevie, we had seventeen songs already done."

Continuing the telemetric process begun by Clarence Paul and continued by Sylvia Moy, Cecil would relay the lyrics to Stevie when he laid down his vocals. "We had an open microphone in the control room," he says, "and I would read the words to him half a line ahead. In fact, if you listen to some of those records you can hear my voice, very faintly, because it leaked from my headphones. I was always amazed because Stevie had the ability to hear my line and take it in while he was singing the previous line, then come in with it, perfectly rendered."

Living inside Stevie's mind, too, meant having to go on the road when it did. "We began doing the sessions at Media Sound," Cecil recalls, "but within a month or so it became clear that we were going to be following him around. He was in L.A. and called and said, 'Come out, I'll put you guys up in a hotel,' and we dropped everything and went out and stayed at the Hallmark Hotel for three weeks while he was doing his live shows, and during the day we went to Crystal Sound and the Record Plant, where I had connections with both studios. We tried Wally Heider's mobile studio but Wally charged a fee for everything—'You want a microphone? That's extra.' 'You want a cable for that microphone? Extra'—so that was out.

"Then whenever Stevie went on tour in England, we went too, and recorded in some of my old stomping ground studios. In fact, we'd later go over to London just to cut strings with the BBC Radio Orchestra. I had told Stevie there was a difference in how strings sounded on the West Coast of America and in England—we never cut strings in New York, that was a horn town. The strings in Hollywood sound much scratchier. That's due to many factors: the weather, the tape machines, the studios, the players, and the instruments. The average age of the violins in those London orchestras is over a hundred years old. If you care about music like Stevie and we did, those things matter."

Because it was impractical to fly TONTO around with them, the tapes made on location by Margouleff and Cecil were all carted back to New York where they could be mated with the synthesizer. But with Stevie eager to test the acoustics of other studios around town, they sometimes loaded the contraption into a U-Haul truck and took it to Electric Lady—Jimi Hendrix's old shop—and the East Coast Record Plant.

If this seemed chaotic, it was perfectly matched to the spontaneous combustion going on inside the studio, and the ongoing framework of far-out dynamism coated, and coded, by the sound waves emitted by TONTO—which, smartly, was used sparingly. Rather than ride it with a lead foot, Margouleff and Cecil kept it around the ethereal edges; on several tracks it's a chore to distinguish where Stevie's familiar organ or Clavinet notes end and the synthesizer begins. What's more, they *did* ride Stevie hard, damping his tendency to coat his lyrics and vocals with too much sap, especially in the love psalms that were his meat and potatoes.

"There are four ways in which you can look at someone like Stevie, who's a singer and composer," says Cecil. "There's the lyrical/vocal side, and then the music/instrumental side. His order of strengths is that, first, he's a very, very fine singer. His next best is playing. His third best is composing. And the thing he does worst is lyrics; he's not a great poet. All [the lyrics] of his songs before us were written by his girlfriends or wives, or other people. On the albums we did with him, most are only credited to him. And those were the best songs he did. Why? Because we never let him slide. We wouldn't stand for crap. We pushed him hard, which was something he needed, and lacked later on.

"To put work together the way the three of us did, we had to live inside his mind, and he inside ours, too. And Stevie really did depend on us to make it right. We weren't just the guys who ran the synthesizer. We were his producers, his engineers, his sounding board, his collaborators, the arbiters of what he did. Really, what we told him to do was what he did. We really were a team. I'd be on one control of TONTO, Bob on another, and Stevie was playing. It was the three of us working on the same sound. Let's say we wanted a triple bass line. Stevie would play the keyboard bass—*ba ba ba ba ba*—and the reason it would sound the way it did was because Bob and I would be turning a filter on. It was a very complicated thing; we had to be light on our feet. We were like world-class athletes in that studio."

· · ·

No great surprise is that to them, *Music of My Mind* was as much theirs as his. And the transition to a new, synergistic amalgam of Stevie Wonder could be heard right from track one, "Love Having You Around," a funky pop tune from the Stevie-Syreeta reservoir in which TONTO's main effect was to electronically distort Stevie's voice into a tinny coil—he didn't actually sing, just mouthed the words into a tube while hitting deep organ keys. It was a technique often said to be first used by rocker Joe Walsh and his "talk box" on "Rocky Mountain Way," but which is predated here by at least two years, and longer by Margouleff-Cecil on *Tonto's Expanding Head Band.*

On the bulk of the LP the synthesizer ducked in and out in small doses, intensifying the funk and desire of Stevie's primordial romantic preening and answering just what was on his mind, as in the ballads "I Love Every Little Thing About You," "Seems So Long," and "Happier Than the Morning Sun." On the more up-tempo fare TONTO kicked in harder, especially on the twitchy Sly Stone–like funk-rock hybrid "Keep On Running," the openly raunchy "Sweet Little Girl" with its faux-porno soundtrack textures and heavy-breathing proto-rap (in which he tells his paramour he's more turned on by her than his Clavinet, surely the ultimate Stevie Wonder bouquet), the equally nervous electrified percussion of "Girl Blue," and the closing cut, "Evil," cowritten with Syreeta's sister Yvonne Wright, where he humanizes evil in order to decry it for having "taken over God's children's eyes," leaving love "an outcast of the world."

That song wasn't as crucifying, however, as the two-part, neurotically tempo-shifting "Superwoman (Where Were You When I Needed You)," a surprise public confessional (though few knew it) that his marriage was over. In an eight-minute argosy, the title becomes an ironic cudgel as he ridicules his woman—"Mary"—for cutting him out of her life while seeking stardom, taunting, "Does she really think that she will get by with a dream?" Accusingly, he noted that when summer was here "you were not around," and when winter came "you went further south." His conclusion: "Our love is at an end."

This stuff was brutal, and it stunned friends of the couple, but as Cecil says, "It was the reality. Stevie felt Syreeta had abandoned him when she didn't come to New York." Of course, Syreeta could have believed just the opposite, that Stevie could have adapted to L.A. but that she had no choice but to be there. In any event, when Syreeta heard the song, she got the message. The marriage, indeed, was over.

For a bargain-basement price tag, Stevie got an album made to order and with great care, each detail, great or small, overseen by Margouleff and Cecil, who hired designers and photographers for the jacket. The cover, designed by Daniel Blumenau, was a close-up of Stevie, his goggle-style shades reflecting a montage from the inner sleeve of "mind images," including those of himself, Eastern statues and dancers, and a charging bull. In derivation and actualization, *Music of My Mind* bore no conscious traces of Motown. Its thematic abstract as a product of one man's mind necessitated the subjugation of "outsiders"; accordingly, Margouleff and Cecil were listed, almost discreetly, as "associate producers" and "engineers," a relegation they understood. "We were trying to focus on Stevie," says Cecil. "It was about what was in his mind, not ours." Stevie, pitching the album in interviews, said, "I had to see and feel what I wanted to do, and feel what my destiny was [and find] the direction of destiny."

And yet in the end that direction seemed to lead right back from where he'd come. As if confirming he indeed was signed, sealed, and delivered to Gordy in everything but on paper, he came to a provisional agreement with Motown to release it, on the Tamla imprint, a seamless continuation of its Stevie Wonder brand. *Music of My Mind* was released on March 3, 1972, under terms that Stevie had been claiming for nearly a year were now inoperative and unacceptable: Motown owned all publishing rights and paid out at the old royalty rate. By way of explanation, Stevie cited some kind of "verbal understanding" and said rather nonsensically that "because they don't understand what I'm doing, they just let me get on with it."

However, if it was supposed to be a mutual extension of favors, Cecil suspected a different motivation on the part of Motown. "I think they were trying to make Stevie believe that he couldn't be a hit without them," he says. "Motown put the album out but they wanted it to fail. They didn't care about it—why would they? They put no money into it. We didn't bill a dime of the expenses to Motown, it came out of Stevie's pocket. They did absolutely no promotion or publicity at all.

"I remember when we were in L.A. with Stevie, I went up one day to see Ewart Abner in the Motown office on Sunset Boulevard. This was before the album came out and he was completely dismissive about it. He asked, 'So what's the single supposed to be? I don't see one here.' I said, '"Superwoman" is a single.' He said, '"*Superwoman*"?! That's shit! That's not a single.' Let's just say Ewart Abner found not a lot to be excited about."

Embraced by Motown or not, *Music of My Mind* was the first original Stevie product to see daylight since "If You Really Love Me" (and, less notably, an obscure holiday single, "What Christmas Means to Me," in late 1971). It should have garnered a lot of attention, but Motown's yawning indifference, even hostility, became a self-fulfilling prophecy, its lack of nourishing keeping it off the radar screen for the buying public. With no stampede to learn what was going on in Stevie Wonder's mind, *Music* did well to hit No. 21 pop, and a still admirable No. 6 R&B. "Superwoman," released on April 25, if not stronger than a locomotive, got to No. 33 pop, No. 13 R&B.

Of equal importance, the "heavy" rock crowd again took notice, most approvingly, moving the ball deeper down the field. Heaviest, of course, and most influential in what was a second wave of black cross-over to a white rock-and-roll mainstream, was *Rolling Stone*. There, Vince Aletti lauded it as "the best thing to come out of Motown since Marvin Gaye's *What's Going On* and perhaps even more impressive as a personal achievement"—not that there weren't slings, such as that it "bears some of the stretch marks . . . from his last album overreach, the abrasively uneven *Where I'm Coming From* [that came] under the heading Self-Indulgence [and had] a tendency toward gimmickry that often eludes his fine sense of control." However, wrote Aletti, the album "falls quite comfortably within Stevie's grasp and the effect is both satisfying and exciting." He even pronounced "Keep On Running" a "knockout" and averred that the vocal tendril on "I Love Every Little Thing About You" was a "beautiful, subtle sound [that] I associate with Brazilian music and [is] marvelously effective here."

If Stevie wasn't quite where he wanted to be yet, he was getting close. Very close.

Lost in their creative haze, and near sequestration, Margouleff and Cecil rarely looked up to wonder if perhaps they should have codified the terms of the partnership with Stevie in a written contract laying out how they would profit long-term from it, and such related arcana as how they'd be credited on albums. Instead, "It was one hundred percent verbal," says Cecil.

"For all of us, it was all about the music. Stevie was just twenty-one. And I was totally green when it came to how business was done in America.

Bob was much more into the business end of it, he ran the studio operation, but for us it was never a job. It was being in a different warp, a state of mind. Stevie wasn't a client, he was basically our whole existence. I mean, we just billed him as we would a regular client, almost as an afterthought. We charged by the hour, $25 an hour for engineering and $100 an hour for the synthesizer services. All we knew was that Stevie had a hundred grand, so that became the budget."

When asked, in amazement, if he and Margouleff actually did have to get by on a hundred thousand, he guffaws. "Damn right we did," he says. "We put out the first *two* albums for way under $100,000."

For months of near-daily sessions for *Music of My Mind*, the cost was a major bargain. As Cecil's billing records show, Stevie's tab came to around $68,000—"and that was for all work through *Talking Book*," Cecil points out. If he and Margouleff ever considered the monetary ramifications, they saw their work with Stevie as an investment in a very big and promising future.

"On the very first day, and I'll never forget this," Cecil recalls, "Stevie told us, 'I want you to be directors of my company, oh, and I also want you to get a point on my records'—because at the time he had no contract and he was set on having his own publishing and production companies when he got one.

"That was why we did everything for him and why we gave up everything else we were doing with anyone else or even our own projects. But we didn't get it in writing. Stevie just kept saying, 'When I sign my deal with Motown, that's when we'll settle up.' It was always like that was going to happen tomorrow. But there were a lot of tomorrows."

The two gurus had a lawyer who might have recommended getting these issues tied down on paper. He was an elfin character named Johanan Vigoda, who at one time ran the Vee-Jay record company and worked in some capacity for Jimi Hendrix. At the time, though, Cecil says, "We really didn't consult him about it. He was trying to get us a deal for a second album for Tonto's Expanding Head Band, which he did with Polydor Records. But that was when all the problems started between us and Johanan. Because Stevie Wonder was obviously a much bigger moneymaker than we were."

The same exact thought occurred to Vigoda, a parvenu with a wild mane of hair, a doctorate in law from Harvard, and a laid-back sangfroid, who favored hippie chic couture and was once described as "a cat laying on the floor of his office, spitting pumpkin seeds out the side of his mouth in fatigues all day long." When Stevie came into his purview through his work with Margouleff and Cecil, Vigoda was thrilled when Stevie took to hanging out in his office, even if it was primarily to hit on his secretary, an exotically dark and sexy woman of mixed blood named Yolanda Simmons.

By the end of the year, Stevie was shacking up with Simmons in a room he had taken as a semipermanent lodging at the posh and hip Fifth Avenue Hotel, having sent Gene Kees and Milton back to Detroit. By then, as well, Vigoda was his mouthpiece. Within the rabidly competitive tribe of showbiz lawyers crawling up and down Broadway, that signified Johanan Vigoda as a made man. It also meant that Stevie would monopolize his priorities.

Job one for Vigoda was to take over the negotiations with Motown for a long-term contract that would give Stevie unprecedented terms and authority for a recording artist. This sent Vigoda to L.A. for long periods, his pursuit of that end so dogged over the first half of 1973 that Gordy would write in his memoir that Vigoda was "ten times tougher" than Stevie's original lawyer who had so antagonized him. In time, Vigoda would wear down Gordy on Stevie's demand for a 50 percent royalty, though only to the industry "superstar" norm of 12 percent. But Gordy held firm on most everything else, and as Vigoda would later recall of the grueling process, "They basically surrounded me with lawyers. Every six hours, they would bring in another two lawyers with a fresh draft, around the clock. Berry hired all these outside law firms to cover me. They would have all these fancy lawyers in their suits with their yellow pads and I showed up in jeans, bandana, and cowboy boots. I would do yoga, stand on my head, to deal with it."

Sometime after *Music of My Mind* was released, Vigoda was again in L.A. for another round of negotiations. When they broke off with no resolution, he called Stevie with the bad news. With nothing better to do that night, Vigoda pored over the numbing 240-page contract that Motown had presented to him and which he had rejected. Vigoda began scribbling a few changes, leaving untouched the clause adumbrating Gordy's right to choose Stevie's single releases, which Vigoda had previously said was a deal-breaker. The next day he sent the new draft to MoWest, but, expecting Gordy to kill it, he was packing for the trip back to New York when a messenger came to the door with an envelope; inside it was the contract, signed by Gordy and Ewart Abner.

The price tag for bringing Stevie Wonder back to the Motown clan for another five years was $1 million, given as an advance on royalties. While Gordy retained the authority over single releases, Stevie had a wide swath to record whatever he chose with zero input from Motown, and won back half of the publishing royalties on all his previous work, as well as on all future work, in addition to the same twelve percent rate on royalties from sales.

Taking a bow in an April 26, 1973, *Rolling Stone* profile of Stevie, Vigoda high-mindedly proclaimed that the deal was no less than a means of emancipation. Stevie, he said, "needed the freedom. He needed the money basically, to fund the freedom," and duly noted, "He made more on the initial advance than he netted the entire previous ten years"—though of course that would not have been a chore, since Stevie had only pocketed $100,000 for that decade of hard labor. It was also, Vigoda concluded, "a very important contract for Motown . . . and for Stevie, representing the interests of Motown . . . and in breaking tradition, he opened up the future for Motown." At long last, Vigoda wanted the world to know, Motown now owned "a major, major artist"— never mind that they already owned two fairly major ones, Marvin Gaye and Diana Ross.

Stevie, though, took no bows for bringing Gordy to his knees. Curiously, he said very little about the deal—and not a word to Margouleff and Cecil, who were left similarly uninformed by Vigoda. They had been so immersed in work that they didn't know at the time—and for several *years* after—about Stevie's homecoming deal with Motown, and that as a result, his financial outlook had brightened considerably since the lean days when he promised them a piece of his empire that was sure to come.

"In fact, we never heard about him signing with Motown until, I think, after *Innervisions*," Cecil says—a flabbergasting revelation given that they existed within an industry always buzzing with leaked details or gossip about people's money and record deals. Yet their oblivious-ness is plausible, since there has always been a good bit of ignorance and confusion about Stevie's business covenants—one example being that almost nowhere in the repositories of Stevie Wonder literature, other than the recollections of Ted Hull, is it noted that he received that meager $100,000 from Motown from his liquidated trust fund. Instead, it somehow became accepted fact that the million-dollar prize that came to him two years later was the original payout.

To be sure, Stevie has never been a beacon of clarity on these sorts of fiduciary matters. And if it might seem to Malcolm Cecil that this was not coincidental to the fact they were kept in limbo waiting for that one-point equity in the Stevie Wonder business even as Stevie's bottom line grew by leaps and bounds, for Cecil—who grew tremendously fond of Stevie on a personal level—the very premise that Stevie could have betrayed him and Margouleff that way is almost too painful to consider, though the sadness in his voice and his eyes in reliving that part of the story is a telltale marker of latent bitterness that Stevie at the very least either forgot or reneged on his word, which to Malcolm and Margouleff had been more potent than a signature on paper.

Was Stevie aware that they were being ripped off? The question makes Cecil choose his words with great care. "I don't think that he was necessarily in any position to do anything else," he says. "He had lawyers to deal with that. We were just trying to keep Stevie in the studio and on a trajectory ever moving upward. And Stevie wouldn't think of being in there without us. It was immensely gratifying what we were doing together. We just short-circuited the whole legal thing of it. We thought we'd make music and work out all the rest afterwards."

He pauses. "I was stupid to believe that. But in the perspective of those times, the way the record business worked . . . basically, it was all a scam. Everything in the industry was set up to attract young bands and young artists and bleed them dry. Stevie had been a victim of that at Motown, but then he became a big part of the power structure, even though he himself might not have consciously known what was being done in his name."

Neither is Cecil wont to rip Vigoda for such decisions. "I can't really take him or Stevie to task," he says. "That's not where my heart is. Johanan was the one who introduced me to my tai chi master who changed my life. But, yeah, I won't say we didn't have problems as the result of his actions. The whole thing was just totally fucked up. Things were kept secret from us because had they been revealed, we would have wanted to solve the issue. It's quite clear now that Bob and I were kept in the dark because it occurred to someone that we should be kept in the dark."

If that determination wasn't made by Stevie or Vigoda, then who? Cecil isn't reluctant to name other names. "To be honest, I lay it squarely at Yolanda's feet. Because you can't beat pillow talk and I think that's where it started, and it sort of festered from there. And then Stevie was bringing in people like Ira Tucker, who sort of became Stevie's right-hand man. That was really the beginning of the end, when Ira got involved, because they [Stevie's posse] were all very, very black-oriented and just disliked Bob and I because we weren't black. There was nothing else to it. That's not a hunch; it was something Ira made no secret of. One time he said to us, 'You motherfuckers ain't gonna get shit from us.' Oh, wait, that's not quite correct. He said, 'You *honky* motherfuckers ain't gonna get shit from us.'"

Cecil's reference is to Tucker Jr., son of the widely admired frontman of the veteran gospel group the Dixie Hummingbirds, Ira Tucker Sr. Unlike his brothers who sang with the Hummingbirds, Tucker fils couldn't carry a tune, but he knew how to carry water; he knew most everyone in the industry and wasn't shy about aggrandizing himself as an invaluable promotions man. Stevie liked his jive-talkin' and promises to get him into the big national magazines, and hired him in that role early in 1972. The move came after a disastrous tour of England, when Stevie put together a travel band and another edition of Wonderlove but chose to perform only his newer work and was actually booed by some audiences, who, despite the Brit music papers' enthusiastic reviews of *Music of My Mind*, had come to hear oldies.

That bummer of a trip convinced him that he needed more than an album and good intentions; he needed to be marketed as a contemporary act among the mainstream rock-and-roll culture. Stevie was certainly ready to cash in on his higher ground. By now Vigoda had set up a publishing company to parlay the rights he now owned on his songs, which was called Black Bull Music, after Stevie's astrological sign of Taurus. A production company also was created, Taurus Productions, to house artists Stevie might sign and produce independently, as well as to funnel movie soundtrack projects. All of this, of course, was contingent on Stevie keeping on delivering hit songs, albeit those different kinds of hit songs—and, as critically, hit albums—a surety that was presaged as a sure thing when in April he gained his first real exposure in a *Rolling Stone* cover story, a long profile by Ben Fong-Torres entitled "The Formerly Little Stevie Wonder," which sounded more appropriate to

1965 but was a trenchant reminder that he needed to be rediscovered by the rock multitudes.

Before he could dally with his next album, however, he had to deal with the breakup of his marriage prophesied by "Superwoman." Neither he nor Syreeta made much of an effort to salvage it. Once she had openly wished to have at least twelve of his children, but now, even when they found time to be together, the things on Stevie's mind did not include romance. As she would describe those moments, "He wakes up with the tape recorder, and he goes to bed with the tape recorder. If you were able to get in between, that was great."

Of course, it was obvious by now to Syreeta and most everyone else that she was one of the few females who *wasn't* getting "in between." "A black man is not complete without a woman [who] should be warm, black-oriented and cookin' at both ends," Stevie told a black New York newspaper around that time, and this was something to which Yolanda Simmons and a coterie of other females could attest. Neither was Stevie shy about showing off how complete he was, boasting a whole lot of "cookin'" women at his side in public and in the papers.

No longer making love, he and Syreeta decided not to make war over divorce. Not generally known was that they had been surrogate parents to a young girl from Detroit named Tina, for whom Syreeta had become legal guardian in the late 1960s. Stevie had no desire to subject his first "daughter," nor Syreeta, to the pain of a legal battle. And so while they retained lawyers for the eventuality, and as malevolent as "Superwoman" was, Stevie, who by rote oozed so much love "for all the people in the world," aggrandized her with statements like "We have a very beautiful relationship that's still a beautiful love for each other . . . that will forever exist." What he wasn't, he decided, was "so possessive . . . that it becomes a drag," and that "a dude needs a certain kind of freedom." The only real problem between them, he averred, was that "she's a Leo and I'm a Taurus . . . that's like putting two sticks of dynamite together." Syreeta, for her part, concurred that "we both haven't lost anything but gained a friendship for life."

If all that joy and love seemed like perfect Hollywood bullshit, the fact was that after the anvil was lifted they once again began collaborating with a renewed closeness. The divorce went ahead, to become final in the autumn of 1973, with no claims of monetary settlement or property claims—they'd already sold the house in Inkster—other than what was already in place through songwriting co-credits. Although Cecil believes that one of the conditions of the divorce was that Stevie had to produce an album for her, it seems more likely he wanted to do that anyway, because it happened quickly. They began cutting tracks and vocals in L.A. And when Stevie went to London on the ill-fated tour, Margouleff and Cecil recorded string arrangements for her album. In June, the debut album *Syreeta* was issued as a now familiar blend of soft and mellow jazz, funk, and transcendental posturing, leavened subtly by TONTO and embellished by Stevie adding vocals on several tracks. It was nothing but pleasant—with a real kick in the socially piquant "Black Maybe"—but came up empty, failing to chart and fading away in short order, another casualty, as Stevie believed, of Motown neglect. In fact, he would not be content until he could try again to break Syreeta out big.

As for his own work, he, Margouleff, and Cecil again became enmeshed in seamless sessions throughout the summer, nary a one with any sense of order. "Stevie didn't make albums, he made songs," Cecil says with subtle distinction. "There was never any long-term concept. Every session started the same, with the question being asked, 'Okay, what do you want to do today?' We'd begin something, then Stevie would play something else on the piano and say, 'Let's record this one.' It was organized chaos. We'd just keep track of them all, and when it came time to put out an album we'd go through them and ask over and over, 'This one, Stevie?' He'd never commit, so Bob and I would play a game, we'd take opposite sides. I'd go, 'We gotta do this,' and Bob would say, 'No way.' Stevie would have to make the call.

"And on this album, we got to thirty-two songs he wanted, which was crazy. I told him, 'Stevie, this isn't an album, it's a talking book,' referring to the spoken-word albums of the day that ran at a speed of sixteen and two-thirds rpm and lasted forty-five minutes a side. We needed it to be eighteen minutes a side. Then he said, 'Let's just put out an album of singles.' Well, I could just imagine what Motown would say about an album of thirty-two singles. Finally, we talked Stevie down, which wasn't an easy thing to do, and as sort of an inside joke we called the album *Talking Book*, which actually worked on a number of levels, including the spiritual thing that he always wanted."

•   •   •

Talking Book **emerged** as a different animal than *Music of My Mind*. For one thing, Stevie was more comfy with and inured to the boundaries of the synthesizer. For another, he trashed the quaint one-man-band shtick, which was doable now given his expanding fortunes—which Margouleff and Cecil assumed was mainly from his frequent live concerts, at which they were often on the mixing board. Now he could populate the studio with musicians he dug. These included, in addition to holdover Buzz Feiten, seventeen-year-old Detroit native Ray Parker Jr. on guitar, sax men David Sanborn and Trevor Lawrence, bassist Scott Edwards, drummer Greg Copeland, trumpeter Steve Madaio, and percussionist Daniel Ben Zebulon.

Also sitting in on a few sessions was the famous British blues guitarist Jeff Beck, whom Margouleff and Cecil had signed on to produce an album concurrently with *Talking Book*. Beck, says Cecil, "loved hanging out with Stevie," who took such a liking to the volatile but ultra-cool gitarzan that when the latter wanted to record one of Stevie's new songs, a sinewy funk-rocker called "Maybe Your Baby," Stevie, who wanted to keep it for himself, gave him a consolation prize, writing for him a jazz-funk groove that was then titled "Very Superstitious."

Stevie constructed that song to carry an oblique social message requiring some thought—that in the year of Richard Nixon's impending landslide reelection, when the portents of the Watergate scandal were ignored by the public, there was mass superstition in the willingness of people to choose conditioned belief and demagoguery over principle. "When you believe in things that you don't understand / Then you suffer," the hook went, before the stern warning: "Superstition ain't the way."

Margouleff and Cecil recorded the rhythm track of the song—its title truncated to "Superstition"—with Stevie at Electric Lady in the spring. They struck lightning with an effervescent and savory ball of fire that rolled out of the speakers, its drum-thumping intro beat ushering in Stevie's itchy, twanging Clavinet that for three minutes was basted by TONTO. In spots the Clavinet was multitracked for a stereo effect, the tracks bouncing off each other, as twittery horns, Hammond B3 organ, and Fender Rhodes piano runs built to a sizzling stroganoff of electronic funk—an instant milestone in the no longer experimental art of electro-funk. Clearly, this wasn't merely hit material but something singular, a dead solid perfect melding of message, melody, and musical idiom—or, as P-Funk bassist Bootsy Collins refers to the song, "funk heaven."

"I'll tell you what the secret of that song was, and that of many after it," says Cecil. "It was something called a 'slap echo.' What that means is, while he was playing the keyboard we would run back an echo on each note, which created an extra sound between the notes, even very quickly played notes. That's what gave an edgier, more urgent feel to what was being played. It's a very powerful tool, and I'm proud to say that nobody could ever really figure out what it was."

Still, before anyone really knew the import of all this creativity and technology, the song hung in limbo when Stevie dithered on completing the lyrics. As Cecil recalls, "He couldn't find a line after 'writing's on the wall' and 'ladders 'bout to fall.' I was trying to get something out of him for a week, and Jeff had to go back to England and was waiting for the song. So when Stevie came in to Electric Lady, I didn't lead him into the control room. I took him into an office, locked the door, and told him, 'You're not coming out until I have the words to "Superstition."'

"I was joking, of course, but Stevie sat in there for an hour making up lines transcribed by my secretary Kate. And about an hour later, under the door came a note with the line about the 'thirteenth-month-old baby' who 'broke the looking glass' and the 'seven years of bad luck' and 'good things in your past.'

"I don't have any idea where it came from, or even if it made total sense, but it was *it*, man. We all knew he'd nailed it."

That night, a Friday, Stevie did his vocal, then split for a Fire Island weekend. Beck went back home, anticipating cutting it himself—it being implicit, albeit never put in writing, that he would release it as a single first. Then on Monday, an excited Stevie bounded in.

"Great news!" he told Cecil. "Motown loves 'Superstition,' man, they wanna release it as a single!"

"Uh, okay," Cecil said, a bit nonplussed, "but Jeff's gonna have it out first, right?"

"No, no, no. Jeff can't have it."

"What do you mean? You wrote it for him."

Cecil recalls, "He was sheepish about it. He was screwing Jeff, and he knew it. But Motown absolutely adored the song and that changed everything, so principle flew out the window. And Jeff was really pissed, as he should have been."

As was CBS Records president Clive Davis, who when *he* heard the song loved it too, and weeks later spent $40,000 for Beck to record it. At which point Cecil had the task of telling the bullying Davis he couldn't release it. Incredulous, Davis asked—oddly, since Cecil had no part in the Beck recording—"Do you know what a producer does? I'll tell you in five words: a producer gets it done." He then asked Cecil if he had gotten a release for the song. Only a verbal one, Cecil said.

"Then you didn't get it done! You're not a producer!" a red-faced Davis sputtered, then threw a stack of papers on the floor at Cecil's feet, screeching, "You pay these bills!"

Says Cecil, "And I did. I felt so bad about it, I ended up paying that $40,000."

Beck's rather drab cover of "Superstition" eventually was heard on the 1973 album *Beck, Bogert & Appice*, a major bust panned by rock critics—including Stevie, who said he was "disappointed" in the version. But then neither did his own version stack up. By his reckoning, Quincy Jones's orchestral cover on the latter's 1973 LP *You've Got It Bad Girl*—on which Stevie played the harp—was the best one he ever heard. Still, he felt contrite about the double-cross, telling Fong-Torres that "I did promise him the song, and I'm sorry it happened," though he did note Beck's "arrogant statements" about the episode, and promised to "get another tune to him that I think is as exciting, and if he wants to do it, cool." That one turned out to be the Stevie–Syreeta Wright composition "'Cause We've Ended as Lovers," which Beck put on his first solo album, *Blow by Blow*, in 1975. Released as a single, it would become a hit seemingly everywhere but the United States. (The historical connection was closed, felicitously, when Stevie and Beck did a duet of "Superstition" during a Rock and Roll Hall of Fame benefit concert at Madison Square Garden on October 29, 2009.)

It would take until the fall before Motown would exercise its right to issue "Superstition," but Stevie, cognizant of its sonic power, had already begun to play it at his concerts, establishing a public familiarity with it well before it was on vinyl. At the same time, he, Margouleff, and Cecil continued working on *Talking Book* into the summer. Another song with hit potential arose quickly, a very light and mellow jazz-funk love testament, "You Are the Sunshine of My Life."

When he cut it, he had a nifty idea. He had written as the first lines, "I feel like this is the beginning / Though I've loved you for a million years," but realized he needed a preamble to set it up, so he wrote a prologue using the title line to address "the apple of my eye" who would forever "stay in my heart." Wanting to sing the "beginning" line himself, as his poetic entree, he gave the intro vignette to Wonderlove vocalists Jim Gilstrap and Lani Groves, who split the verse, Gilstrap first, then Groves, in smooth succession. (By some accounts, the female part is attributed—incorrectly—to another Wonderlove singer named Gloria Barley, with whom Stevie was having a fling at the time. Cecil's memory and his session logs say otherwise.)

With an excess of tunes in the can by early spring, Stevie began putting together a touring schedule for the summer. However, Johanan Vigoda had something bigger in mind. Something really outta sight.

12

Apocalypse Now

I wrote "Higher Ground" before the accident, but something must
have been telling me that something was going to happen to make
me aware of a lot of things, and to get myself together.

—*Stevie Wonder*

Riffling through a copy of *Variety* one day while hanging out in the studio, Vigoda was fixated by a major rock
event soon to kick off. "We gotta get Stevie out on a big tour," he rasped
to Malcolm Cecil. "The Stones' tour is coming up. We need to get him
on that!"

He might just as well have said that he needed to reverse gravita-
tional pull, for all the likelihood of it ever happening. But the little
man was thinking big. At the time, *Music of My Mind* had just hit store
shelves and, by rote, would have been slotted into the R&B market.
Vigoda believed that would be its death, and that of Stevie's entree as
a post-sixties progressive rock act. Not that anything on that album, or
the ones to follow, had much on it in a pure rock groove beyond the
obligatory guitar clanging. To Stevie, though, these were distinctions
without a difference in the amalgam of rock in 1972. If you sang serious
music, you were rockin' on the same collective stage. As Sly Stone had
sung, only the squares had to go home.

Stevie had been scared off from having management by horror
stories about how Jimi Hendrix was royally ripped off by his manager

Michael Jeffrey, who had recently died in a plane crash (which Stevie attributed to karma). So it fell to Vigoda to make the stage a literal melting pot if Stevie was to continue the white crossover he'd enjoyed in the 1960s, attracting the attention of older white audiences who now flocked to already legendary Rolling Stones tours. Just how much the world had been turned on its head in a decade was evident in the fact that in 1965 the budding Stones had opened for Stevie on one of *his* tours. That was before the age of million-dollar, corporate-sponsored caravans through sold-out stadiums, the latest and biggest of which would be the Stones' jaunt in support of *Exile on Main Street.*

But how would it be possible, or even tenable, to get a young soul man on a stage and into a maw where all the faces were white and British? Certainly, Berry Gordy seemed little inclined to use his declining clout to bring about such a thing. As it was, Motown had put almost no resources behind *Music of My Mind.* Fortunately, doing it all in-house, Stevie reaped one more benefit from Malcolm Cecil, who was still a much-respected figure in the British rock brotherhood from his days as the premier bass player in the country. Cecil, taking the cue from Vigoda, called in favors back home and soon heard from an old crony who was now working in the Stones' management. The fellow, he says, "was very excited because he said the Stones *loved* Stevie. He said they'd been thinking about having Bob Marley open for them but that if Stevie wanted the gig, he could have it."

Knowing the stakes and the new realities, Stevie was hardly offended by the caste, and he would need to keep swallowing his pride after he joined the tour on June 6 in Vancouver and it worked its way east across Canada and then down and back up through the States. For one thing—more than a tad ironically in retrospect to Margouleff and Cecil—Stevie was not cut in on the massive profits. He was paid a flat, nominal fee, usually no more than around a thousand dollars per show, or around $50,000 for the tour. Since he came aboard not just with his musicians and singers but Yolanda, Ira Tucker Jr., and other hangers-on, as well as Margouleff and Cecil to work the mixing board, he had to pay for their work and/or lodging out of his pocket, and would end up poorer than when he began.

"It wasn't a money-making thing, that wasn't the idea—exposure was the idea," Stevie would later say. "I want to reach the people. I feel there is so much through music that can be said, and there's so many people you can reach by [having them listen] to another kind of music besides what is considered your only kind of music. . . . I say as long as it's change to widen your horizons, it's cool."

How long it stayed cool and not a serious pain in the arse is debatable. Within weeks of the two-month journey, the now post-Motown Martha Reeves and the Vandellas, given a pittance as the warm-up to the warm-up act, had dropped out. Meanwhile, the Stones' open condescension for Stevie and his troupe became outrageous in ways large and small. They may have loved his music, but they hated the overheated reaction he got each show during his strictly limited fifteen-minute set. Finding it tough to follow him, much as the big Motown acts had early in his career, they took steps to undercut him—or even make him disappear. Although Vigoda had hired the New York PR firm of Wartoke Concern, which did publicity for the Woodstock Festival, the tour's promoters froze them out. One of the executives handling Stevie, Jane Friedman, recalled that "on most of the dates Stevie's name never appeared on the marquee."

Suddenly, too, Malcolm Cecil encountered hurdles, such as that "the spotlights were being saved for the Stones, Stevie couldn't be illuminated. Then I found taped on the board a note telling me I couldn't turn the volume up over a certain level because only the Stones could be that loud [laugh]. I just ripped up that note and mixed it all the way up. So there was a running feud between me and the Stones' sound guy the whole time."

It was hard enough for Stevie to even get himself noticed. A Wartoke publicist, Jeff Powell, tried to drum up interest in him along the route, but newspapers, he said, "simply refused to cover a black act. Same with the radio." As a result, some audiences were genuinely surprised he was on the bill. The unkindest cut of all was that the Stones stood by meekly for all this, as if they'd done enough for him by letting him step onto firmly white territory.

To all appearances, the comity between them was real. Stevie never ceased smiling and grooving. Most nights, Mick Jagger would lead him by the hand onstage for a shared encore jam, usually "Uptight" followed by either "Satisfaction" or "Jumpin' Jack Flash." At those interludes, Stevie's tight and talented band—Feiten, Parker, Scott Edwards, Copeland, Madaio, saxophonist Trevor Lawrence, keyboardist Greg

Phillinganes, and saxophonist Denver Ross—would put the diffident Stones to shame. In fact, the latter were more often than not in poor form onstage and an absolute mess off it.

The *Exile* tour would stand as both the high and low point of the Stones' fabled career, their recorded material never more resonant but as a touring unit a self-indulgent caricature of excess and avarice. Under-rehearsed, beyond stoned, and wasting time with pseudo-celebrities like Truman Capote, Princess Lee Radziwill, Andy Warhol, and, inexplicably, Zsa Zsa Gabor, they left in their wake a trail of mayhem, fights, arrests, injuries, gate-crashing, and white powder. A film made of the tour called *Cocksucker Blues* was kept from release by the Stones for reasons made obvious in bootleg copies available today—its scenes of Keith Richards snorting lines and throwing a TV from a hotel window, Jagger jerking off, the band engaged in group sex, and tour personnel developing heroin addictions might have gotten them barred from performing in any number of countries.

Early on, Stevie, beckoned to join in such demented doings, begged off, not willing to make a mockery of his antidrug posturing, even if it offended his hosts. At one point he sniffed to a reporter about "people blowing money on cocaine when they could be giving it to those who need it. We artists owe more than our music to, like, black people. We should give them some time, and, maybe, some money too." During a swing through Texas, Greg Copeland, whom Stevie later said was having a "nervous breakdown," played sloppily, drawing Stevie's ire. "Tell you what," Copeland snapped at him, "*you* play the goddamn drums!" Copeland then quit. Left in the lurch, Stevie told the tour manager he wouldn't be able to perform until a new drummer was found. One was, and Stevie didn't miss a show, but Richards and Jagger were livid that he'd even contemplate it, with the former telling a British magazine Stevie was a "stupid cunt," which only someone with the zonked-out (non)sensibilities of a Keith Richards could have understood.

Even more bizarre would be Mick's indictment that Stevie's troupe not only couldn't "keep up" with the ragged Stones onstage but that, at the hotels, "they spend the night fucking and sucking." That he didn't say that with admiration and envy was to take absurdity and hypocrisy to world-class levels—or worse, if he meant he believed black people getting down and dirty made them seem like animals, as opposed to the sophisticated Caligulas the bawdy white degenerates fancied themselves. Whatever he meant, it was too hilarious to take seriously but hurtful to Stevie nonetheless. Asked about both Stones' remarks by Ben Fong-Torres in *Rolling Stone* a year later, he delivered some choice shots of his own.

"If Keith did say that," he said, "he's just childish because I love people too much to just want to fuck up and miss a show. And it's crazy, the things he said, if they were said—and if he did not say them he should clarify them, because I will always hold this against him; I can't really face him. I'd feel funny in his presence."

As for the "fucking and sucking" business, he avoided it—his and his group's jungle-fever descents were, by his determination, nobody's business. He preferred to cast the Stones as not merely two-faced but actual liars, claiming that it had been cool with them that he might have to miss a show because there'd be no drummer, but "the next thing was I read all this shit." In another interview, he branded the Stones' brigand of sycophants as "parasites"—a word he couldn't, or wouldn't, use for his own growing crew of courtiers.

Somehow, they all got through the two months, alive if not well, and in later years he would smooth things over with Keith. Indeed, at some point the bitterness was submerged and what had been tepid jams between the Stones and Stevie became far more congenial, and uproarious. Apparently this could be credited to Mick. "That's what I heard," recalls Michael Sembello, who would later join Stevie's band in 1974 as lead guitarist. "Buzz Feiten told me, 'Man, Mick Jagger really stood up for Stevie.' Because what happened was that the promoters wanted to let Stevie go. They said to the Stones, 'Look, you got this guy opening up and he's wearin' the fucking audience out. You need someone to come in and just warm the audience up and that's it. And Mick stood up and said, 'Stevie stays, I don't give a shit what anybody says.' That was the most egoless thing I've ever heard anybody do."

That late-blooming accord peaked just as the tour played its final dates with three shows at Madison Square Garden—the last, on July 27, doubling as Jagger's birthday party, an occasion that had the stage accoutered with balloons and several mile-high birthday cakes on rolling carts. Of course, in no time the show descended into a Three Stooges movie with cake everywhere and food fights between and during songs. Stevie, his hair braided into tight cornrows, was led out for the encore by Mick, stepping through slabs of mashed cake. Dropping onto his piano stool, he and both bands jammed with abandon to endless choruses of Chuck Berry's "Bye Bye Johnny." At that point, knowing he'd survived this sometimes *Titanic*-like cruise—and no doubt relieved it was over—he had every reason to feel like letting the good times roll.

The rock press noticed, too. A *New York Times* review read, "Spectacular as the Stones were, [the] most vivid musical memories are of the charged-up playing and singing of the blind soul singer/musician Stevie Wonder and his crisp band, Wonderlove." The *New York Post* chimed in, "Stevie Wonder is second fiddle to no one."

It was only months later that his role on the tour—which was of inestimable help to him—would be the subject of the two big Stones' loopy talk, which caused some talk inside the industry that perhaps he wasn't the easiest person to deal with. This had already become something of an issue because of the growing influence of his "friends" along for the ride. But if that sort of thing was the toll he had to pay to be in this fast lane, he sure as hell wasn't about to slow down.

The "Superstition" single, beefed up with a more muscular horn arrangement than on the album track and backed with the Stevie–Yvonne Wright "You've Got It Bad Girl," was released on October 24. It barely took a breath in tearing up to No. 1 on the pop chart—returning Stevie to the top of the pop after ten years—and to No. 1 R&B early in 1973, en route to thirteen weeks in the Top 40. This was no small feat. Of the dozen loosely defined "soul" records to go all the way in the previous two years, only a pair by Sly Stone, "Thank You (Falettinme Be Mice Elf Agin)" in 1970 and "Family Affair" in 1971, could be defined by the evolving funk genre. These were undeniably pivotal moments in mainstream music, and "Superstition" didn't merely spread the gospel of funk, it remodeled it, in a way plainly different from the Sly/Parliament-Funkadelic/Confunkshun template of popular R&B salted with guitar feedback licks.

That Stevie would branch off into his own leading edge of sinewy, melodic funk could have been seen coming, in his always fresh-sounding experimentations (though a case can be made that even Stevie's TONTO-synthesized rubatos were influenced by Billy Preston's early-'70s electrified Clavinet grooves such as on "Outa-Space"). "Superstition" was a counterpoint to Sly Stone and a continuation of his own funk schema begun so intriguingly albeit unobtrusively with "Shoo-Be-Doo-Be-Doo-Da-Day" and "You Met Your Match" (which may well have influenced Preston).

It worked so well that Sly was suddenly an anachronism by 1973, as all along the music watchtower rockers and soul men began to hook up synthesizers to amplifiers, birthing the newly synth-driven "spaceship" funk of the veteran R&B band Earth, Wind & Fire, the Commodores (Motown's only new '70s act of real import, whose first hit, the 1974 "Machine Gun," was a sibilant instrumental of proto-disco funk), and a newly rebred P-Funk, wavy synthesizers firing on "Give Up the Funk (Tear the Roof off the Sucker)." Many looking for clues could only study the drum-and-synth intro of "Superstition," a kind of Rosetta Stone of the new funk mainstream; only Stevie and TONTO could really make funk amenable across the rock spectrum

Stevie hardly stopped evolving there; funk was only one signpost to follow. The mercurial music critic Robert Christgau pointed out in a February 1973 *Newsday* dispatch that "his music is more than modernized blues/soul/jazz/gospel, borrowing from disparate white sources as well. Unlike Jimi Hendrix, he doesn't have to win over the black audience, and unlike Hendrix and Sly Stone, he doesn't seem likely to destroy himself. He is blessed with an unpretentious natural optimism that proceeds from his experience, for after all, he had all the odds against him and never lost a round. Potentially, Stevie Wonder could be the center of a whole new kind of rock and roll."

Talking Book unveiled one satiating chunk of pop music after another, with a cohesion that fused his usual mix of mushy love songs and pounding funk-rock in a way he couldn't on *Music of My Mind.* There was, for example, "Big Brother," which Stevie had wanted to be the first single but he was late in completing it. The timing was lucky; the obvious Orwellian monition—the first of his several bristles aimed at Richard Nixon's pelt—could never have seeded the music landscape as did "Superstition," and might have caused a backlash with seething vows that, unlike the obliquely barbed "Superstition," seemed threatening. The toll for "children dying every day" was "I can't wait to see your face inside my door," while others mocked, "I don't even have to do nothin' to you," inferring that karma would. Though the edges were blunted by a bouncy, swirling synthesizer jam that sounded at times like concertos of bagpipes or harpsichords, it was way too barefaced to not be dangerous.

"Big Brother" was the only overtly political piece on the album, but hardly the only piece of bloodletting. "Maybe Your Baby," the song Jeff Beck originally wanted, was an unnerving, seven-minute dolor of betrayal by and vengeance to a woman "steppin' out with my best friend," with the creepy admission that his inner boiling "is scarin' me to death." The blissfully titled "I Believe (When I Fall in Love It Will Be Forever")" wallowed in "Shattered dreams, worthless years," staring "into a cold and empty well." "Tuesday Heartbreak" also scorched a cheating lover, with a punch-out final line: "Oh baby, get away, alright." In "You've Got It Bad Girl," he memorably, if not with the most credibility, dissed women who were after him to starfuck, being open only to those who can "let my love live in your mind."

God knows from what pit in his soul this stuff came from. Yet without skipping a beat he veered from psychodrama to the Hallmark-card poesy of "Sunshine of My Life" and "You and I," a delicate, deeply echoed, and affecting ballad that shimmered as he exuded, "God has made us fall in love" Resolving the failure of his marriage, there was a two-song epilogue to it, both cowritten with Syreeta. In one, "Looking for Another Pure Love" (featuring a Jeff Beck guitar solo), he revisited his anger ("All my days before today were happy and secure until your phone call") and then purged it on "Blame It on the Sun"—in which he wondered whether the truest love he found "may not be here forever to see me through." That premonition would, sadly, prove prophetic.

Not only was the order of the cuts on *Talking Book* cannily interstitial, but they all said something, trenchantly. So too, unlike *Music of My Mind*, could the flavor and melody of each track remain strong in the ears and the consciousness, even months, years on, easily reactivated by title alone. TONTO made its own statement; on not a single other cut was the tripping hip-hop vibe of "Superstition" reprised. While all the tracks shimmered, some with quiescently delicate beauty, others with a funky burnish, they seemed discrete, each with a rhyme, reason, and groove all its own. Ready to go in October, the album was pressed with a jacket cover of Stevie, hair braided, chin and upper lip hirsute, wrapped in a burgundy kaftan, African tribal bracelets on his wrists, legs curled under him on an arid clearing, hands sifting through the macadam—and, most noticeably, his eyes not shielded by sunglasses.

"That was the first time Stevie was ever seen without his shades," says Malcolm Cecil. "Bob [Margouleff] took the picture himself, and it was important for Stevie; he wanted everyone to see him as he really was, see his face, his eyes. I'm sure at Motown they thought it was too shocking an image. But Stevie could not have cared less. Stevie wanted that image to be very very Jesus-like, with the robe, the biblical script, the earth, and he thought it would be ludicrous to be Jesus in designer shades!"

However Motown felt about the image, they clearly were unhappy about Stevie's insistence that there be an inlaid Braille inscription on the cover, which read, "Here is my music. It is all that I have to tell you how I feel. Know that your love keeps my love strong—Stevie." Says Cecil, "Bob and I thought that was a great idea. But Motown hated it, because it required extra-thick cardstock which of course cost more, and with the added size you could only put twenty albums on a shelf, not twenty-five. That's when Motown took making the cover away from Bob and me."

Ewart Abner *still* could hear no viable singles among the tracks—incredibly, not even "Superstition"—and Motown was no more eager to promote this album than they had *Music of My Mind.* This time, though, it didn't matter. "Superstition" did the work for them. The album, released just days after the single, rode the same cresting wave, catapulting to No. 3 pop and No. 1 R&B—the first time Stevie had gotten there with an album. In midwinter it rode a second wave when in February its second single, "You Are the Sunshine of My Life," backed with "Tuesday Heartbreak," retraced the same path, rising to No. 1 pop the week of May 13—only the second Motown act after the Supremes to chalk up back-to-back No. 1 hits—and No. 3 R&B.

A cash cow, *Talking Book* sold in the hundreds of thousands in real time and over one million to this day, eventually to be certified gold, then platinum. It also landed on the British Top 20 album chart, the first time Stevie had done so since *My Cherie Amour* in the late 1960s. "Superstition" went to No. 11 and "Sunshine" No. 7.

Critics now seemed to have no quibbles left. *Rolling Stone's* progression from grudging to glowing was complete with Vince Aletti's January 4 posting, which judged the album "more relaxed, dreamy at times, the laid-back funk of the vocals resting on a deliciously liquid instrumental track like a body on a waterbed. . . . Even at its dreamiest, the music has a glowing vibrancy" and was "an extension and refinement of the work begun in *Music of My Mind*. . . . Making it all seem quite effortless, Wonder has produced another of the very best albums this year. . . . Altogether, an exceptional, exciting album, the work of a now quite matured genius and, with Marvin Gaye's *What's Going On*, Sly's *There's a Riot Goin' On* . . . and Wonder's own *Music of My Mind*, one of the most impressive recent records from a black popular performer. Also, it might be noted, one of Motown's handsomest covers, braille and all."

Indeed, *Talking Book*'s only real flaw was that it would be overshadowed by Stevie's next three works, which no doubt explains why on the 2003 *Rolling Stone* Top 500 albums list, it came in ninetieth—though if one operates on the thesis of the real-time review, there plainly cannot be eighty-nine albums of greater significance, nor the wide gulf that separated *What's Going On* at No. 6 from *Talking Book* and *Riot Goin' On*, at No. 99.

The spoils also included some hardware. "Superstition," Grammy-nominated for Best R&B Song and Best Male R&B Vocal Performance, took home both.

He could now sit back and sip on his success like it was a mai tai, while reading his clippings. In the spring of 1973 came the *Rolling Stone* cover story, in which Ben Fong-Torres noted a couple of intriguing things, one being that a woman named "Coco" was Stevie's "most constant companion since his divorce"—which must have made for interesting table talk with Yolanda Simmons. Another was that Ira Tucker Jr., who was quoted extensively, was "an assistant to Stevie for five years now," though as could best be determined it was more like five months. It did not occur to Fong-Torres, nor was there any reason it should have, that an annexation of his turf by such folks may not have shored up the article's conclusion that "now in his eleventh year in show business, formerly Little Stevie Wonder is finally in absolute control."

Stevie's conceits included the seemingly mandatory Garboesque boredom and weariness with the upward spiral and the hoi polloi. For one, he was restless about all that freaky technology that had sent him into the stratosphere. "I'd like to get into doing just acoustic things, drums, bass, no electronic things at all," he said, clarifying that these things were "earthy and in the direction where my head is slanting—like going to Africa. Maybe I'll just take a tape recorder over there and just sit out and write some stuff."

In fact, the mandatory Back to Africa subtext had begun to include the style of his garb and the opening of concerts with a rivulet of undulating tribal rhythms and exhortations he called "The Monkey Chant," accompanied by tom-tom-like drumming. In what would become a recurring theme, he spoke of picking up and going to Africa. "I'd love to go to Ghana," he mentioned, "go to the different countries and see how I'd like to live there." These all seemed to be manifestations of the conscious "blackening" of Stevie Wonder, another of which was the blackening cordon of people around him.

One consequence, perhaps not incidental, was that Margouleff and Cecil were seemingly being marginalized within the Stevie clique, even as they continued working with Stevie nearly 24/7.

"I remember when Stevie wrote an open thank-you letter to the Grammy people," Cecil says, "and he bought space for it in *Billboard* and *Cashbox*, which is customary. It was like, I want to thank my mother, my grandmother, this guy, that guy, and it just went on and on. And at the very end, it was, 'and to Bob and Malcolm and all the staff at the Fifth Avenue Hotel.' So it was like the maître d', the men's room attendant, and us. That's how it was, and that was Ira Tucker's doing."

Tucker would gain tons of attention in the press as "Stevie's main man," and his loyalty to him was seemingly vowed in blood. Asked to participate in this book, he declined on grounds that he didn't have Stevie's "permission to talk." As long as Margouleff and Cecil could keep Tucker and the new cadre of unfamiliar faces at bay and out of the studio, the recording process still thrived, but those sacred walls were giving way.

Another album was kneaded from existing and new material, with a dispatch that was now rare in the industry. These were mostly stripped-down tracks on which Stevie returned to playing most of the instruments and sang almost all the vocal parts. This was partly due to Wonderland's diffusion, with Ray Parker Jr. and David Sanborn finding projects of their own. With Buzz Feiten moving on, too, there was no electric guitar part on the entire album, only an acoustic part by Parker on one cut and Ralph Hammer on another. Malcolm Cecil played bass on one track. Still, not a minute of it would suffer for quality. Rather, it was as if Stevie, having laid out where he was at on *Talking Book*, could say many of the same things in a more direct, natural way with, as he would later say, an "acoustic feel" that proved less could be more.

Not that this meant "soft." In fact, after the stream of dreamy ballads on *Book*, he wanted to turn up the pitch and the intensity, and turn down the weepiness to proportionate levels. The irony was that, at its most powerful, the stuff he came up with could make one cry at the points when it cut deeply from ear to soul. It would have more of his biting political/social agenda, hitting as hard but more adeptly than "Big Brother," blended once more with an unabashedly spiritual uplift. In his head, in his visions, the colors of songs like these were complementary. He would now splash those colors so that everyone could see them as he did—by hearing them. The title was simple but amazingly profound—*Innervisions*, one word, coining a wholly new sensory perception.

Many of the harder edges of the work were instigated by Cecil. "We had some interesting songs on that album," he says with a grin, "and they came about really because I used to have conversations with Stevie, long ones, on deep subjects. I mean, we spent so much time together and sometimes there wasn't anything else to do. Sometimes I'd read books to him. I had a bulging library of political and historical volumes. Obviously, *1984* was one he became fascinated with. And I'd encourage him to write more songs that had bite. Whenever Stevie came in with a song, I'd twit him, 'Oh, another bloody love song, huh Stevie?' Well, then he began coming in with songs like 'Big Brother,' to shut me up.

"You'd never know what would spark something in him. In 1972, Nixon took the U.S. off the gold standard, which nobody paid any attention to, but I pointed out to Stevie that technically this meant the entire American currency was now counterfeit, for many good and boring reasons. Stevie thought it was absolute treason. Next thing I knew he came up with 'He's Misstra Know-It-All,' which began, 'He's a man with a plan / Got a counterfeit dollar in his hand'"

Not that he needed any additional reasons to skewer his favorite bogeyman; not with body bags still coming back from Vietnam every day, escalating cuts in federal aid to inner-city schools and housing projects, and the slimy scab of Watergate beginning to break open. Richard Nixon was always reptilian to Stevie, but now he had no hedge about getting extra personal—and nasty, not by name, but with no clarification necessary. "He's Misstra Know-It-All," which was saved for the album's final cut, was a five-and-a-half-minute drip of sarcasm about the man who "Makes a deal with a smile / Knowin' all the time that his lie's a mile."

Yet there was no ham hand behind it. The song, with its smooth, piano-driven, gospel-filtered funk and Stevie's tempered vocal, rounded those sharp edges into a restrained intensity that pervaded the work. Track one leaped right into Stevie's other prime peeve, no doubt more so having survived the Stones' tour, with the antidrug parable "Too High," which also steered away from what could have been harrowing—its theme chipped from Curtis Mayfield's "Freddy's Dead"—to maintain a laid-back, bass-stirred synth-funk that made a knowing point: that the drug bane had become infused into a kind of mainstream ennui, hopeless it all was. "I'm too high / I'm too high / I hope I never ever come down," was the hook.

There were the requisite palliatives for such dark cultural mirrors. Seemingly in response to the alarms he himself had sounded, at least in the title and texture, was the salsa-flavored "Don't You Worry 'Bout a Thing," though beneath the maracas and choruses of "Chevere, chevere" (Spanish for, roughly, "groovy") it was wryly sarcastic, "Positively 4th Street" raillery of social climbing, scorning the same kind of self-pitying target for whom he had only a middle finger—"I'll be standing on the side when you check it out."

The simply gorgeous Antonio Carlos Jobim–style acoustic guitar concerto "Visions" was actually a vision of vulnerability and self-doubt, worrying if the "milk and honey land" around him is "a vision in my mind?" Providing his own panacea for such angst was an open recruiting pitch for transcendental meditation, "Jesus Children of America," which might have been unbearable had he not set it up by calling out traditional religious huckstering—"Tell me, holy roller / Are you standing for everything you talk about?" The only real schmaltz was in the itchily paced, densely layered love ballad "Golden Lady," and "All in Love Is Fair," in which he revisited yet again his broken marriage, ruing within another unadorned piano-arpeggio-streaked ballad, with near-operatic fervor, "I should have never left your side."

As the work developed, two songs were putatively its centerpieces. The first was one Stevie would spare no expense to get on vinyl, and reflected an anger only basted by the sins of Richard Nixon (with whom he nevertheless clasped hands again at the White House in early 1973 after being invited to a luncheon at the two-year-old Kennedy Center's National Cultural Center). Recently Stevie had been becoming more and more unsettled about the casuistry of American justice. In May that year, the fatal shooting of a ten-year-old black boy named Cloephus Glover by a New York City cop who was let off the hook sent him into a rage, and he contacted the family offering to sing the eulogy at the funeral. Later he told reporters ominously, "I hope black people realize how serious things are and do something serious about it." He went on, "Black people have a serious problem because we are not united. Everybody else is together. We must learn to appreciate ourselves."

His sense of outrage was not color-blind. Two years earlier, he'd taken up the cause of White Panther Party founder John Sinclair, whom he had known in the mid- and late 1960s when Sinclair managed the Detroit proto-garage-punk band the MC5, which performed in the street at the 1968 Democratic convention. In late 1969 Sinclair was busted for selling a joint to a cop and sentenced to ten years, turning him into a radical-chic martyr and earning a song about his plight by John Lennon. When Lennon headlined a "Free John" concert held at the University of Michigan's Crisler Arena in December 1971, Stevie offered his presence, sharing the stage with unlikely confreres such as folksinger Phil Ochs, Yippie/SDS rabble-rousers Abbie Hoffman, Jerry Rubin, Rennie Davis, and Bobby Seale, and Beat Generation poet Allen Ginsberg. Three days later, Sinclair was let out on bond; his conviction was later overturned when the Michigan Supreme Court ruled that the state marijuana laws were illegal.

However, it was the Cloephus Glover case that was on his mind when he penned what would turn into a six-verse, seven-minute-and-twenty-two-second apocalyptic doom chord about the squalid ironies of the boy born in "Hardtime, Mississippi, surrounded by four walls that ain't so pretty," his father cursed to working "for fourteen hours / And you can bet he barely makes a dollar." Arriving wide-eyed in New York City, he soon finds out that "This place is cruel / Nowhere could be much colder" as the victim of a frame job, with neither defense nor mercy.

Titled "Living for the City," reflecting the line in the song about downtrodden blacks who are "living just enough for the city," its fever gradually built into an emotional distress level, rising from a hushed but simmering organ-synth mesh and a bass pounding like a heartbeat to the entry of a hard snare—and sneer—when his even vocal turned briny and agitated. At the four-minute mark everything recedes again, a sole organ sounds, funereally, while an aural/visual screenplay begins with bustling street noise, then a voice calling, "Last stop, New York City." A bus door swings open, another voice says, "Wow, New York, just like I pictured it, skyscrapers and everything"—an apple-pie scene that sours within moments when a street hustle erupts, a scaly voice cooing, "Hey brother, come here, slick, wanna make yourself five bucks, man?" followed by confusion, sirens blaring, doors slamming, a brusque "Turn around, put your hands behind your back!" then a plea of "What'd I do? I was just crossing the street." Slicing through time, a "judge" drones, "A jury of your peers, having found you guilty—ten years."

The surreal "movie" ends with a putative cop bullying, "Come on, get in the cell, nigger. God!" The jail door slams hard, cueing the music to reappear, and Stevie, now sounding very different—harsh, pissed, even rabid, sings, "If we don't change the world will soon be over." With a gospel choir, one of whom is Syreeta Wright, Stevie wails, "No, no, no!" over synthesized pandemonium, until everything stops dead, a last "noooo" echoing into nothingness.

It was enough to leave a listener breathless, limp, burning, irate, even teary—at least then, when such stark truths could have only been heard as daring, though even now it occupies the same zenith with the Stones' "Gimme Shelter" as rock's ultimate apocalyptic visions. This was in no small part because he refused to compromise on real truth—the victimization of the song the fault of black and white predators—and certainly not on his art. While the song kicked to the solar plexus, it came out an ample but delicately layered soufflé of funk ingredients, stately and mesmerizing yet never dictating the need to feel pity or anger. Hell, you could even dance to it.

That Stevie was obsessed about this track was seen in his desire to get the proper aesthetic in the fleeting "characters" in his movie. "He wanted genuineness," says Cecil, "so we had to get real cops, which only happened because Bob's father was the mayor of Great Neck and he got some cops to meet us in a parking lot. We told them, 'Just say what you'd say if you were arresting a guy for drugs,' and they did the rest—*they* came up with the 'nigger' line, which pleased Stevie immensely. If he'd said that in the guise of a cop, that would have been offensive instead of real as real can get."

It was easier for the other voices. His brother Calvin uttered the "Wow, New York City" part, and Johanan Vigoda handed down the sentence as the "judge"—"We only needed one line, but he went on for an hour and a half." As for his own vocal, that too needed a certain world-weariness. "It had to be in no way mellow, so what Bob and I did was, we got him riled up. Stevie hates to stop him during his vocals, so we did it, and did it again, until he was totally pissed off and he was tired and his voice hoarse. Bob and I looked at each other, like, 'By God, I think he's got it.'

"It was a great and trying record to make. Everyone needed to recover from it."

It didn't seem necessary, or possible, to tack anything else onto what had been deemed a completed album, but very late in the game, on May 11, Stevie had a revelation—or so it seemed to him. He was messing around in the studio when, he recalled to rock writer John Swenson, "I did the whole thing—the words, the music and recorded the track—in three hours. That's the first time I ever finished a song so fast, and that's very heavy. It was almost as if I had to get it done. I felt something was going to happen. I didn't know what or when, but I felt something."

This was a dread he had been feeling for some time now, that he was walking on the rim of a personal apocalypse. It was unfocused, nothing that could be an effect of any specific cause, less so given the spectacular fruition of his ambitious musical archetypes, and perhaps another symptom of his chronic bouts of depression. Indeed, recently he had been told by a young female fan that she had decided to kill herself but was talked back by Stevie's music. It is also plausible that, this being Stevie Wonder, he *was* picking up widgets of the future in his antennae. Or maybe he was full of shit and playing Hamlet out of boredom—or to begin marketing a potential hit song he knew he had. Whatever the case, he openly dropped dark hints, telling Fong-Torres he had premonitions of an early death, with the cryptic addendum, "I'll be here until I die."

Such darkness was evident in the studio, too. "He had this thing about death," Cecil noted. "It scared him—and us."

Accordingly, he had a need to address the issue in song. The first example may have been "Golden Lady," with its inscrutable line "I'd like to go there / Take me right away." But the revelation was "Higher Ground," an amazing record that could have been heard as something like a suicide note with a melody—that is, if one had *heard* the song beyond its bubbly litany of how the world was going down the tubes—soldiers that kept on warring, powers that kept on lyin', and people that kept on dyin'. In this mordant context, even true lovers and true believers were more pitied than admired.

His solution, as ever, was God, only now there was a strange ring to that: that all the apocalypse unfolding around him would engulf him, because good intentions and pretty songs could not spare a sinner who had used up his chits from God. The famous lines about the sinning of "my last time on earth" and how "It won't be too long" before he reached his highest ground almost seem like the stuff of a Martin Luther King "I may not get there with you" moment.

But even more than deep thought the record would provoke involuntary body movement. This is likely his best and most effortless-sounding funk-rock groove, prompting the assumption that the "higher ground" was a neat inspirational bauble, Stevie's version of the U.S. Army slogan—he was just striving to be the best he could be. The three minutes and forty-two seconds of the song blasted off with prickly, overheated synthesized Clavinets guided by Stevie's frenzied drumming and carried by his comfortably gritty double-tracked vocal. It never snagged, never flagged, only took off for higher musical ground with every note.

Stevie had to have it on *Innervisions*; holding it back for the next album was out of the question. The problem for Margouleff and Cecil was how to master the recording at the highest audio quality—something that with all the songs Stevie was demanding to be put on the record was seemingly not possible given that a long-play, 33 ⅓ rpm album could not be longer than eighteen minutes per twelve-inch side lest the quality suffer from compression, not unlike today's digital mp3 files downloaded at lower bit rates. As Cecil recalls, "It had gotten completely out of hand. We had twenty-three and a half minutes on one side and twenty-four on the other, and in mixing it down with George Marino, our engineer, for every extra minute we lost one decibel and you couldn't compensate without it sounding terrible. I was literally in tears with Stevie on the phone, begging him to let us take a song off each side. He said, 'No, no, no. You gotta do it, you gotta find a way.' He made me promise I wouldn't take anything off."

Stevie had gone off on a tour and was in the Carolinas at the time, while Margouleff and Cecil in L.A., where most of the album was recorded. When they were unable to deliver the work to Motown, Berry Gordy called Cecil to his office. "Where's my album?" he growled. Cecil explained the snafu. Gordy had never heard of such a thing. Gruffly he told Cecil, "Then it's your problem. You gotta get it done."

It was easier said. But Cecil, who at one point said he might have to take the master to a studio in Germany where the editing equipment was more advanced, hunkered down in a studio in Burbank with brand new record-cutting lathes. He spent sixty straight hours cutting and mixing and remixing, calibrating sections of the tape that lost volume with pumped-up EQ levels. Some things that he did he cannot remember. But, finally, he says, "I don't know how it happened, but it all worked."

The overstuffed album, with no loss in fidelity, was ready to roll out by late summer. On July 31, its first single, "Higher Ground," went out on the market backed with "Too High." On August 3, *Innervisions*—its cover a color pencil illustration by L.A. pop artist Efram Wolff depicting Stevie's face within a coffin-like portmanteau, gazing skyward, a widening funnel emanating from his eye and angled above a hilly grotto intercut between spaces of plain white (a variation of this would be used on the sleeve for "Living for the City")—hit the market.

Three days later, as the refrain "It won't be too long" was just beginning to pour from radios and stereo systems, news came out of North Carolina that for a most nervous few days suggested Stevie Wonder was right; it hadn't been long at all.

* * *

What happened that day has always been veiled in gradations of murk and mystery, which accounts for why Malcolm Cecil speaks of it with open skepticism, saying things such as he "heard that Stevie had his 'quote' accident."

The details that first seeped out had it that early in the evening of August 6, 1973, Stevie was being driven by John Harris down Interstate 85. Harris tried to pass a truck loaded with logs but made contact with it, loosening one of them. The log flew off the truck and crashed through the windshield, hitting Stevie, who was sitting in the front passenger seat even though he almost never did. As shards of broken glass billowed, the log plowed into his forehead, shattering his glasses and knocking him unconscious.

As Stevie would tell *Billboard* a year later, the drama unfolded like this: "We had done a show that Sunday and stopped at this Radio Shack to get a cord to plug my tape recorder into the car, a reel-to-reel that I carried around with me, and I had two-track mixes of *Innervisions*. I had my headphones on. We were on our way to North Carolina to do a performance to raise money for a black radio station when the accident happened.

"I remember we left, and you're never supposed to leave the scene of an accident. What happened was my brother picked me up, put me in a car and drove the back roads to the highway to get to the hospital. At the hospital, the doctors said that if they hadn't moved me, I would have died, because help was taking too long to get there."

He was first taken to Rowan Memorial Hospital in Salibsury, where it was determined that he had a broken skull and brain contusion. More unusually, Stevie's band was in South Carolina with him but were traveling separately. "He'd rented three cars," says Mike Sembello, the new lead guitarist, "and the funny thing is, we came down the same road and passed a wreck and believe me, it looked ugly. We thought somebody really got fucked up. We didn't know it was Stevie. We got to the hotel and that's when we heard."

Some early reports passed wild, baseless speculation that he was dead, or close to it. Berry Gordy, woken by a phone call, was told Stevie was not expected to live. When the band found out where Stevie was, they sped to Rowan. "When we got there," Sembello says, "they wouldn't let us see Stevie. We thought the only reason why they'd do that was because he'd already died."

Such alarming rumors were refuted by hospital spokespeople, who said he was in intensive care "making satisfactory progress" and "slowly regaining consciousness." The second day, he was transferred to North Carolina Baptist Hospital in Winston-Salem, where there was a neurosurgery department; however, while he remained there for a week, no surgery was performed. Adding to the air of incertitude was that, as Sembello says, few people were permitted to see Stevie other than Harris, who was unhurt, Calvin, and of course, Ira Tucker Jr.

"I knew they wouldn't allow Bob and I to go to see him," says Cecil. "We would have flown cross-country in a heartbeat. In fact, I told Ira, who was handling everything and making all the decisions who could see him, that we would take tapes of the songs from the album there and play it for Stevie, because he was unconscious for four or five days. But Ira said no. He wouldn't even tell us where Stevie was. I could never understand why he did that. It just seemed idiotic."

As it happened, Tucker would begin to tell the story of Stevie's accident to the outside world, with some inspirational turns that to Cecil and Margouleff had a familiar ring. He would relate how he was unable to recognize Stevie, whose "head was swollen about five times normal size," and that "nobody could get through to him"—until he had sung "Higher Ground" into Stevie's ear, continuing, "His hand was resting on my arm and his fingers started going in time with the song. I said, 'Yeeeah! This dude is gonna make it!'" Later, after Stevie had had "a near-miraculous physical recovery," Tucker said he brought a Clavinet into the room. "You could tell he was afraid to touch it," he related. "He didn't know if he'd lost his musical gift. You could see the relief and happiness all over his face when he finally started playing it."

After two weeks, Stevie was well enough to be flown to L.A., to continue treatment at UCLA Medical Center. In time, some of his friends did get to see him. He surely looked a tad woozy and generally out of it, loaded as he was with Darvon and Valium. However, other than suffering a loss of his senses of taste and smell, for how long doctors didn't know, the only real physical damage seemed to be a big bump on his forehead. As he said to a reporter, "What's a few scars here and there? I've got my life."

Later, he said, "I thought about doing the plastic surgery thing, so I went to this doctor. He was looking at this side of my head, then he went to the other side. And I said, 'What are you looking at the other side for?' And he said, 'Well, I thought we could do some work here.' I said, 'Oh no. Forget it. Leave it alone.' I just let it be one of the scars of life I went through. I came out at the end of it with the blessing of life."

He had every reason to wax philosophical about cheating death, and his own premonitions. His morose Hamlet period now over, he would aver, "Anyone who has had such an event never looks at life quite the same way. I felt it was a second chance at life . . . I was unconscious and for a few days I was definitely in a much better spiritual place that made me aware of a lot of things that concern my life and my future and what I have to do to reach another higher ground."

It was, to be sure, a remarkable episode in many ways—including the timing, which cast his words and lyrics about death into a decidedly relevant and immediate light, illuminating his own powers of palmistry and those of God to reclaim lost souls such as his. Only a cad or cruel cynic would have digressed to make note that under the circumstances, the illumination also bathed "Higher Ground" and *Innervisions.* Nowhere, and by no one, was it claimed the whole thing was some kind of elaborate publicity stunt—logically, did a man coming off a number one album and two straight number one singles need to stoop so low? But neither was the incidental publicity unwelcome. And if Tucker had done a bit of stage-managing and novelizing—the specifics of which would have the very plausible-sounding nugget that Tucker knew Stevie was okay when he began hitting on his nurses—he would have only been doing his job.

Still, Malcolm Cecil has never been quite sanguine about the "quote" accident. "I really don't know what to make of it," he says. "I know when Ira started taking that story all over—that he sang 'Higher Ground' and Stevie opened his eyes and looked straight at Ira and said, 'I'm back, baby,' that was bullshit. When I saw Stevie, he did have a big scar on his forehead, and seemed quite proud of it. In fact, some years after he called me out of the blue, after we hadn't seen or spoken to each other for years, and said, 'Hey, man, let's go to the movies, let's

go to Grauman's [Theater] and see *One Flew Over the Cuckoo's Nest.*'
Because we used to go to the movies a lot. He'd poke me and ask,
'What's going on?' and I'd narrate. But this time he'd seen it. Because
when the scene comes on after Jack Nicholson has a lobotomy, Stevie
goes, 'See the scars on his head?' And he ran my hand across his forehead.
He took me there just to show me he has the same scar Jack Nicholson
had in *Cuckoo's Nest.*

"No, I don't know what it means, if anything. I'm just saying that
[the accident] possibly wasn't all that it seemed. I've spoken to John
Harris since and he's very cagey about it. It was strange. But there were
a lot of strange things happening around Stevie at that point."

13

Stevie in Wonderland

Stevie was never the same after the accident. I'm not talking about physical. He was just a different guy. He pulled away into his own world, controlled by people who had no connection to his art. It was harder to get through to him. That was when he began to slide. It affected the entire process that had worked so well. But he couldn't comprehend that. That's what was sad, seeing his genius start to slip away and not being able to stop it, shake him and say, "Stevie, get real again."

—*Malcolm Cecil*

I n September 1973, six weeks after being peeled off the highway in North Carolina, Stevie returned to New York. He was still a bit queasy and frequently on painkillers, but his sense of taste had been restored—though he had a partial but irreparable loss of smell—and he was straining to get back to work. Interviewed by *Esquire* for a feature that ran in April 1974, he drove writer Burr Snider to exhaustion trying to keep up with him. In fact, he barely dropped off his bags at the Fifth Avenue Hotel before he was off, Ira Tucker Jr. in tow, to a Grambling–Morgan State football game at Yankee Stadium, at which a young lady fan, teary-eyed, told him, "Stevie, we prayed for you, honey. Everybody prayed for you. Tell me the truth, are you all right?"

"I'm doing okay," he assured her. "I just get tired a lot easier than before"—a proposition belied by his schedule, which had him rehearsing with his band for new recordings and composing new songs, which he was now literally writing in his sleep at times, telling Snider, "Some of the heaviest tunes I ever wrote will never be heard because they came in a dream. Do you know how horrible that is? . . . In my dream . . . it sounds so good, I'm seeing it and everything, and then when I wake up it's all forgotten."

There was also the matter of his "comeback" performance, which came when he was invited him to make a surprise pop-in at an Elton John concert in the Boston Garden on September 25. He was flown to Boston in Elton's private jet and plied with champagne and Courvoisier, though Elton was in a foul mood and barely interacted with him, then was brought onstage after the encore—"A friend of mine is here," Elton teased—to a genuinely warm ovation from the sold-out house. The two piano-jammed and sang, for some reason, "Honky Tonk Women" before Stevie launched into "Superstition," to a tumultuous reaction.

By then, "Higher Ground" had taken off on its run up the charts to No. 4 pop, No. 1 R&B, and *Innervisions* to identical rankings on the album lists by Halloween, resting on a bed of rhapsodic reviews—the always central one coming in *Rolling Stone*, in which Lenny Kaye exalted Stevie for "never los[ing] that basic optimism, the ability to once again rise and return to the fray. . . . [His] depth and range of technical judgment is flawless." A second *Stone* review, by Jon Landau nine months later, said that Stevie "has replaced Sly Stone as the most significant individual black innovator in the twin fields of R&B and rock. He has also replaced him as the most popular black music personality. [His] appeal now crosses every boundary. . . . At his best, he does things no one else can." *Playboy* touted "a beautiful fusion of the lyric and the didactic, telling us about the blind world that Stevie inhabits with a depth of musical insight that is awesome."

Any dissent, rare as it was—such as Jon Tiven's verdict in *Circus* that "just when Stevie had some momentum going, he went and put together a concept album of homogeneous music and rather typical lyrics"—seemed peevish. (By any objective measure, *Rolling Stone* was on more stable ground, slotting *Innervisions* twenty-third on its 2003 Top 500 album list.)

By now, it had become a matter not of whether but how many Grammys he'd cop; in January, he was nominated in seven categories. At the televised show in March, he won five—two for "Superstition" (Best Male R&B Vocal Performance; Best R&B Songwriting), one for "Sunshine of My Life" (Best Male Pop Vocal Performance), and for *Innervisions* Best Engineered Recording and the big taco, Album of the Year. He arrived by limo at L.A.'s Shrine Auditorium, accompanied by Lula Mae, Calvin and Milton, and Ira Tucker. Each time he arose the first four times he won, he pleaded with Lula Mae to come up with him, in vain. Finally, when he went up for the album prize, "You Are the Sunshine of My Life" piped through the loudspeakers, he grabbed his mother by the arm, much like she had grabbed his at those tent-show rallies, and she hung on for dear life as Calvin guided Stevie onto the stage. When the applause died down, he raised the shiny statuette over his head, then handed it to Lula Mae. Identifying her to the house, and the millions at home, he said, "Her strength has led us to this place." After he whispered into her ear to say a few words, she stood transfixed, tears streaming down her cheeks; all she could manage was a completely extemporaneous, "Thank you all, for making the sunshine of my life."

As an afterthought, the engineering award meant that Margouleff and Cecil finally got some kudos. This would be the only time they would be nominated for their work with him, and only in this limited category because Stevie was listing them on the record sleeves as engineers, associate producers, and, on *Innervisions*, for "Programming of ARP and Moog Synthesizers"—even though any rationale for such public undervaluation had expired after *Music of My Mind.* Inside the hall that night, they were quite nearly invisible. When Stevie won for best album, he could have found a few moments as well to give them a shout-out. He did not.

That was not the only time they felt like small change. Says Cecil, "We had to buy our own table, and it was way in the back. And we got our awards in the afternoon, the nontelevised part of the show. Otherwise our names were totally suppressed out of everything. This was as Stevie wanted it, or how his handlers did. He was to be the genius who did everything all by himself. And that's how it went down."

•   •   •

During his sabbatical, Stevie had had to cancel a number of concert dates. By mid-November, though, he was onstage again, for a benefit at Shaw University, which had made him a trustee. Although a trip to Africa was also shelved, after the new year he made appearances in Cannes, France, and at sellout performances at London's Rainbow Theatre. And while he'd also postponed a five-week, twenty-city tour in March and April of 1974, he kept the Madison Square Garden date in late March. That night, before twenty-one thousand people, he jocularly pointed to his scarred forehead and said, "Thanks to God that I'm alive." Joining him onstage to pay him homage were Sly Stone, Roberta Flack, and Eddie Kendricks, who in 1971 had split from the Temptations to go solo. He also had reaped his first exposure in a national newsmagazine; the April 8, 1974, issue of *Time* ran a short spread with the title "Black, Blind and on Top of Pop," telling without much meat the familiar saga of his rise, fall, and resurrection.

But if Stevie's touring was truncated for a while, otherwise he seemed to be all over the place, dipping his hands into projects besides his own. On his periodic trips to L.A., he dropped anchor at the Record Plant and with Margouleff, Cecil, and his backup band produced *Stevie Wonder Presents Syreeta*, her second album, the title slyly implying that he'd earned a do-over by dint of Motown's indifference to her little-heard 1972 debut LP. Indeed, it was in every sense a Stevie Wonder record, its synthesized funk turning out some splendid Stevie-Syreeta love songs—including several more true confessions about their marriage such as "'Cause We've Ended as Lovers" (the song covered by Jeff Beck), "Just a Little Piece of You," and "When Your Daddy's Not Around," as well as heavier, hard-rocking fodder like the unashamed political admission "I'm Goin' Left." Yet Motown again left the record to fend for itself. Released in June, with the Stevie cachet or not, it died a quick death, neither it nor its two singles denting the charts.

He also coproduced an album by former Wonderlove singer Minnie Riperton, whose voice was a fey and delicate instrument that could accommodate five and a half octaves—at the top of its range it became an indelible trill that Stevie thought could only come from a songbird. Riperton's manager, writer, and producer was her husband, Dick Rudolph, who with Minnie cowrote most of the songs on the LP, *Perfect Angel*, with Stevie writing two including the title track as well as playing drums and keyboards. Not that the public knew this; under his Motown contract,

Stevie was permitted to do work outside of the company—*Perfect Angel* was on the Epic Records label—only under anonymity. He did, however, earn what was believed to be a 5 percent cut on its royalties.

While in L.A., he attended music theory classes at the University of Southern California, at least minutely fulfilling his vow to be a college man. Laying down future roots, he moved Lula and the family from Detroit and into an airy five-bedroom home in the San Fernando Valley, money now not being an issue. He still held off on hiring a personal manager—Ira Tucker Jr. having become accustomed to making the big decisions for him—but he did realize he needed someone to invest and stand guard over his considerable assets and hired an industry account-ant named Charlie Collins. As well, he could keep Wonderlove on call, at a salary of around $30,000 for each a year, their checks written monthly whether or not they had actually worked. That was not small change in those days. "Are you kidding? I'd never seen that much money in my life," says Sembello. "And it went up to $50,000, plus royalties for songs I wrote with him. *I* had to hire an accountant. Without that money, there wouldn't have ever been a career for me later as a rock-and-roll star. So thank Stevie for 'Maniac'"—Sembello's massive No. 1 hit from the *Flashdance* soundtrack in 1983.

Stevie foresaw building his own studio in L.A., but was hesitant to mess with the perfect alchemy he'd made at Media Sound and Electric Lady in New York, and the Record Plant, Crystal Industries, and Westlake Studios in L.A. However, if he was on tour, he would habitually test studios on a whim.

"Oh God," a grimacing Sembello says, "one time, this was later on during *The Secret Life of Plants*, we were in Louisiana looking for some studio in the middle of nowhere, and we were going across the Pontchartrain Bridge and there was a KKK sign on some building. Little did we know that we happened to be in a town where the KKK had its headquarters! That was so Stevie, that his people picked a studio in the middle of fuckin' Klan country! One of 'em said, 'Well, you know, it's in the woods, it's nature, it's the plant thing.' They're thinkin' about plants and I'm seein' headlines in my head saying 'Stevie Wonder and Band—the White Guy, Too—Lynched in Louisiana.'

"Nothing happened, but do you really need to go through that? But that was life with Stevie. You can't predict it. It just sort of goes here and there, running on crazy biorhythms."

. . .

The studio forays didn't lack for material, nor ideas, given the huge backlog of song fragments he had cut with Margouleff and Cecil, more of which would find their way onto his next work. The title was a mouthful—*Fulfillingness' First Finale*, which evoked some rather labored explanation from Stevie such as that it "was just me working the word: the idea of fulfilling and fulfilling is like a female. The other part . . . the 'first finale,' was sort of referencing an ending of the period after *Music of My Mind* and these three [previous] albums."

The temptation in 1974 would have been for Stevie to ease the way onto a lower musical road—the sharpening genre that was disco. After all, the electronic musical motif he had sired was particularly fitted to the ethereal blasts of syncopated rhythm now bouncing off dance club walls, though in a crude, soulless incarnation that would find its apogee with 1980s techno-pop, a musical incarnation so distant and alienated that it seemed shorn of all human emotion, and thus hard to associate on any level with Stevie Wonder.

Indeed, to an emotional junkie like Stevie, such bastardization of soul was a sin and very nearly a crime. Thus did he keep a safe distance from disco, per se—as opposed to the overall mission of all funk and R&B, to get the feet and body moving. Never was there a more intrinsic metaphor for him—he wanted to stay there. So whether or not anyone understood what Stevie meant by that windy title, the new work was neither crude nor anywhere near as tangled as his explication. Straightforward and foursquare, running the usual thematic gamut, it sprung from the same creative sorcery.

"With Stevie," Sembello says, getting a little wavy, "the song is out there in the universe, you just have to find it. It was an entirely new way of making music. It was all instinctual. It sure wasn't Motown where it was A goes into B goes into C. *Nothing* fit when we went in to record, none of it made sense to anyone but Stevie. To us, it was all cosmic dust in the wind. And there was Stevie in the middle of it all.

"Stevie never needed an arranger. Mozart doesn't need an arranger. He only needed Bob and Malcolm to turn the knobs and switches and start boiling toad's eggs. It was all madness. But it's what happens when a genius is in the room. Picasso could say, 'I see the picture,' when no one else did. And Stevie could see his pictures. We saw it, too, but in parts. Some people can see something as a whole, some people can see it in ten thousand parts. But it still comes out genius in the end if you're working on the same wavelength.

"What it is, is experimentation to the extreme under extreme violation of certainty. You had this . . . *thing* called TONTO from an alien station; it's extraterrestrial. And Bob and Malcolm, who come from another planet, would hand this thing, this weird sound, to a black guy from Detroit, and with it he creates some timeless shit. I'm lucky to have been a part of it, 'cause that's the shit, man. And if you ask me, those two guys up there on the bridge of the mothership were really the ones who made it possible for him to go the ends of the universe."

Seeing Margouleff and Cecil elbowed aside at the Grammys, Sembello was sickened, if not overly surprised. "That was typical bullshit for what was going on at the time," he says. "All these black guys were around Stevie and it was like, 'Hey, don't give these two Jews any credit.' And these guys had made Stevie Wonder. They did things with his genius that mortal humans can't even grasp. And then the Jewish guys can't get the credit? That, my friend, is seriously fucked up."

Sembello himself would run into some of the same chilliness after he came aboard on a whim by Stevie that, as he easily admits, defied all logic. "I was a twenty-year-old, snot-nosed kid in Philadelphia and all I wanted to do was play jazz. I was a Chick Corea prodigy, listened to Coltrane and Miles. Then one day I found myself at some Stevie Wonder audition at the Heritage House. I had no idea I was there to see the pope. To me Stevie Wonder is the little kid who sings, '*Everybody say yeah*.' And I'm the only white dude there. I'm like Jethro. I got long braids, overalls, work boots, and they're lookin' at me, saying, 'Let's put a robe on this white boy and give him sandals.'

"These are some of the greatest musicians in the world; they're all ten years older. They don't know *what* to do with me. Then too, I don't know any Stevie Wonder songs. Everybody else has Stevie Wonder books, sheet music, they know every note of every song. I just played jazz over everything, but Stevie heard something. Because now he sits at his piano and someone asks, 'Whatcha gonna play, Stevie?' He says, 'Just follow me, man,' and he starts playin'—*jazz*, 'Giant Steps,' I think, and his head is swaying back and forth. Everybody's standing around. They were waiting to play some funk thing; they don't know what to do.

"So after six hours of that, they have a big huddle, and I hear people yelling at each other, and the next thing they call me over and Stevie goes, 'Hey man, what's your sign?' I didn't know what he meant. I had no idea about that astrology shit. I thought he meant my nationality. So I say, 'I'm Italian.' And Stevie breaks up and he turns to his guys and says, 'See? He's Italian. He's *not* white'—evidently that's what the yelling had been about. Then he tells me, 'You're in the band.'"

Sembello believes his inclusion breached some sort of unwritten racial quota, not that he hangs this on Stevie. "At that time," he says, "he could only have one white guy in a Motown band, that was the rule. And they already had [trumpet player] Steve Madaio, so they were bending the rule for me! I didn't know it then, but that's what they were arguing about."

Running in a band with what he calls "these funky-looking black guys," his scraggly dreadlocks leading the others to mock him as a "Pasta-farian," he felt like the proverbial square peg. "No one knew why I was there—*I* didn't know why I was there, a white Italian vegetarian. And the people in the audience, you don't even want to know. . . . At the Apollo, they'd throw shit at me. One time, Stevie was doing a real soft song and from the audience a guy screams, '*Motherfucker, what are you doing up there?*' And Stevie stopped and he looked at the guy and said, 'Hey, motherfucker, get up here and stand toe to toe with my boy and say that to his face. Otherwise, shut the fuck up.'

"I was just so lucky, thrown into it like I was. And we became so close. Stevie is such a beautiful human being, man, when his people weren't giving him orders. All Stevie really wanted to do, and this is what I love about him, was to find the answer in music. We both had that in common. Neither of us did drugs—I'd be in my room juicing carrots while the rest of the band was out whoring around and Stevie would come in and we'd hang.

"What else did he have to do? He wasn't gonna go home with a hooker, he was past that. It was a lonely life for him. Like, we'd go to France or somewhere and people would think, wow, that's exciting. Well, no. We'd get on a bus, get on a plane, stay in a Holiday Inn. You don't see anything. So we'd hang out. We had this really special thing. We had interests, like we were into chanting mantras, then we'd write songs, play music. I had this little two-track recorder, and believe me, we put some far-out shit on *that* thing.

"The thing with Stevie was, he wasn't an R&B guy; he wasn't funk. He was about *music*. He wanted to do jazz, he wanted to do an album of songs by *my* heroes. But here's what they did to him, all those Perrier-drinking motherfuckers who were controlling the guy's budget. They'd say, 'We need more songs like "Superstition."' He'd say, 'Fuck that,' but you know, you can't fight the power of a song like that, so you keep trying to top it."

Fulfillingness congealed as a less constrained and more free-flowing work than *Innervisions*. The edges of each track were also more clearly defined—and a degree less funky, though hardly, as *Rolling Stone*'s Ken Emerson posited in his review, "less specifically black than its predecessors." Stevie, full of lightness and optimism after the accident, submerged his usual snark to burble without complication throughout the work the theme stated in the title of track one—"Smile Please"—in which he sang over a lilting electric piano line and tripping bongos.

The suicide watch over, there was only a crème brûlée of hope, sanctimony, and sex. On track two, "Heaven Is 10 Zillion Light Years Away," with a lightly gospel background chorale that included Syreeta and the teen idol turned Muzak pop icon Paul Anka, he cut God a break, agilely matching a galloping backbeat with a dreamy vocal that went: "And I say it's taken Him so long / 'Cause we've got so far to come." Track three, "Too Shy to Say," a classic torch song, ingeniously united the Motown godhead James Jamerson on acoustic bass and the brilliant pedal steel guitarist "Sneaky" Pete Kleinow in a smooth mesh of soul and country behind feel-good lyrical fodder like "You bring me up / When I've been down / This only happens when you're around."

As always, his greatest knack was being able to navigate above and around pretension—notably on "Bird of Beauty," in which he urged nonchemical flights of fancy: "There is so much in life for you to feel / Unfound in white, red, or yellow pills / A mind excursion can be such a thrill." Guided by his belief, as he said later, that "God was telling me to take a vacation," the song was über-precious, with one verse sung in Portuguese as translated by Brazilian jazzman Sergio Mendes. But it was just too damn engaging a slice of lip-smacking pop.

When he did get down and get funky, he unleashed the kind of power he had in "Superstition" with "Boogie On Reggae Woman," the lone dance (and *not* reggae) groove of the LP and a raw horny bomb of fuzzy synth and boogie-woogie piano, with Stevie leering and baying, "I'd like to make love to you / So you can make me scream." Neither could he resist his third Nixon poison dart, "You Haven't Done Nothin'," his ticklish jeers ("It's not too cool to be ridiculed / But you brought this upon yourself") cushioned by the coolest intro ever, a dizzying swirl of keyboard runs punctuated by the kick of a bass drum.

As the song coursed on, a white-hot brass section stabbed his delirious vocals and backup by the second hottest Motown act of the era— "Jackson 5, join along with me!" he beckons—who pumped out choruses of "doo-doo-wop" as Stevie moved in for more ragging. By the end, hoarse and nearly postcoital, he must have known he had never made, nor would ever make, a better record. Or a more ironic one, considering that within three weeks of the album's release, his foil would be waving bye-bye on the White House lawn where he had once glad-handed Stevie, it having been proven that he had indeed done somethin', most of it illegal.

Still, the overall chromatic mien was as Stevie, shaman of love, capable of drawing romantic blood out of a stone, such as with "Creepin'," the cast of which was, well, creepy in its dark echoes but becomes custard when he sings, "I can hear you sighin' / Sayin' you'll stay beside me," with Minnie Riperton's sugary backup as an added salve. Another, "It Ain't No Use," throbs with the ache of a romance being ended, but is overruled on the final track, and thus the work's coda, the yearning, forgiving "Please Don't Go," on which the Persuasions sang backup.

During the last round of sessions, Stevie, Margouleff, and Cecil in July flitted back to L.A. to mix the album at the Record Plant. While they were there, John Lennon, during what came to be called his "lost weekend" misadventure in L.A., was in another studio cutting an album with Phil Spector. If not a witness, Stevie was on the premises as a now famous rock burlesque erupted when the burnt-out Beatle and the whacked-out producer argued, the latter pulling out (not for the first or the last time in his life) a gun and shooting a hole in the ceiling of either the studio or the bathroom, depending on who's telling the story.

According to a parenthetical tale, Spector at one point actually pointed his piece at *Stevie*. Why has never been explained, nor why this would not be more hysterical than harrowing, since unless Spector announced that he was holding a gun on him, how would Stevie have even known it? Mike Sembello, who was there, remembers seeing a crazed Spector chasing Lennon down a corridor, "shooting a gun over his head and screaming, 'You motherfucker!' I said, as I was ducking for cover, 'What the fuck did I sign up for?'" But he saw nothing that involved Stevie. Nor did Malcolm Cecil, who was in the studio with him when the fireworks started. But then, Cecil had other, bigger convulsions to deal with on that trip.

During one tense overdubbing session at Crystal Sound, the years of mounting frustration and decreasing appreciation for him and Margouleff boiled over. "We used to do our work in a small group, with Stevie and an assistant engineer," Cecil says. "But then Stevie began having all the leeches come into the studio. That day, there must have been thirty people in the control room, and they were making this huge din." Cecil, trying to feed Stevie his lines at the time, stopped.

"Excuse me," he yelled out, "can we have a little bit of quiet in here? We're trying to work."

In years past, Stevie would never have tolerated outsiders disturbing a session. But now he directed his ire not at the mob but at Cecil. "Hey man," he said through the headset, "don't talk to my friends like that!"

His neck burning, Cecil retorted, "Well, maybe your friends would like to do the overdub." Rising from his chair, he took off his headphones and walked out of the room, with not as much as a glance at Stevie, who was speechless. "That was the last time I ever recorded Stevie," he says. "That was the breaking point, and it was a long time in coming."

Margouleff was absent from the studio for this paroxysm, and being more forbearing, stayed on, teaming up with L.A. producer/engineer John Fischbach, who had a fraction of Cecil's technical expertise. Meanwhile, Stevie tried to smooth things over with Cecil. During the last of their conversations, Cecil no longer avoided addressing the thorny issue he had for so long.

"Are you going to tie my work to the royalties?" he asked.

Says Cecil, "The answer was no, so I said, 'Then that's it. I can't go back. I won't work for you.'"

With a pending deal to record another Tonto's Expanding Head Band album, and the awkwardness of juggling allegiances with Cecil and Stevie, Margouleff would eventually decide the same thing; by the end of the year he had left, marking the end of Stevie Wonder's glorious history with TONTO. But because Cecil and Margouleff left Stevie with, as Cecil makes it, 250 songs on tape, their work would grace two more Stevie albums.

Stevie believed the loss was manageable, that he had learned enough about synthesizer technique and modalities to handle it on his own, with help from Fischbach as his West Coast engineer, and in New York, Cecil's adjutants Austin Godsey, Joan DeCola, and Gary Olazabal—who, seeing their own pots of gold, split from Cecil. As Stevie would be assuming more control, the time seemed right now to go ahead and build that studio of his own, which he did in the Koreatown section of downtown L.A. He called it Wonderland and began lining its rooms with expensive synthesizers and all manner of sophisticated recording and mixing equipment.

To Cecil, the name of the new digs was apt. "It *was* Wonderland," he says, "because he thought he knew how to do what we did. And that was sheer fantasy."

The *Fulfillingness* cover, designed by none other than Ira Tucker Jr., was a front-back montage by movie poster artist Bob Gleason, dream-weaving depictions of things like past album covers, Grammys, wild elephants, Stevie's boyhood, JFK, Martin Luther King, a Motortown Revue bus, and a keyboard rising like a stairway to heaven. The album was released on July 22, 1974, its route to the penthouse assured, shipping gold, meaning it cleared half a million in advance orders before it even got to a record store. (Again, gold, then platinum, certification for the album would come post-1977.)

But Stevie was leading such a charmed life now that an added bonus came when the Minnie Riperton album he had produced, *Perfect Angel*, released eighteen days later, rode the huge success of the Riperton-Rudolph song "Lovin' You" right to the top of the pop and R&B charts in early 1975. For Stevie—just as when Aretha Franklin's 1973 cover of "Until You Come Back to Me (That's What I'm Gonna Do)" went to No. 3 pop, No. 1 R&B—it was a windfall, since both the single and album sold over a million copies, each going gold. That summer, too, the funk band Rufus took a song Stevie had written for them, "Tell Me

Something Good," to No. 3 on both the pop and R&B lists. Johanan Vigoda, as president of Black Bull Music, seemed to suddenly have a full-time job simply tabulating Stevie's songwriting/publishing royalties.

The main trough was *Fulfillingness*, which didn't stop climbing that keyboard stairway, rising hand in hand with "You Haven't Done Nothin'," which, backed with "Blame It on the Sun," had been released July 19 as the first single and sprinted to the top of the pop chart (for four weeks) and the R&B chart in early autumn. By then, the LP, slavishly praised by the critics—for Emerson, it was "a new plateau [that] makes Stevie Wonder's dreams seem attractive and real" and "a culmination of what has come before, but by no means a final destination"—eased onto the top rung of both the pop and R&B album charts, presenting Stevie Wonder with his first No. 1 pop LP since *Recorded Live: The 12 Year Old Genius* in 1963, and his third straight No. 1 R&B LP (the quirk was that *Innervisions*, having gotten onto the charts earlier in the year, would sell more copies, as the year's fourth-top-selling LP behind *Goodbye Yellow Brick Road*, *John Denver's Greatest Hits*, and Wings's *Band on the Run*.) Then, when "Nothin'" began to fade, "Boogie On Reggae Woman" was issued on October 23, with "Seems So Long" on the flip, and retraced the same giant steps, to No. 3 pop, No. 1 R&B.

The spoils were predictable; *Fulfillingness* nabbed Grammys for Best Male Pop Vocal Performance, Best Male R&B Vocal Performance (for "Boogie On Reggae Woman"), and of course Album of the Year. (There simply is no rational justification for *Rolling Stone* not finding a place for this album anywhere on its Top 500 album compilation.) As well, carrying over from the previous year, "Living for the City" won Best R&B Song, and "Tell Me Something Good" Best R&B Vocal Performance by a Duo, Group or Chorus.

The last months of 1974 were Wonderland indeed. There was a thirty-city Fall Festival Tour, ending with a Christmas show in Madison Square Garden. In November, Los Angeles mayor Tom Bradley proclaimed a Stevie Wonder Day. Early that month, a cover story about him ran in *Newsweek* titled "Stevie, The Wonder Man." It was crammed with breathless babble by writer Maureen Orth, who gushed that he was "recognized as the most creative—and popular—pop musician of his generation," and reported that with "40 million records [sold]

Stevie is the favorite of young, old black, white, the hip and the square. . . . [As] an innovator admired by musicians from Paul McCartney to Henry Mancini [he] symbolizes the vaulting new prestige and popularity of black musicians in America."

As difficult as it would seem to be unhappy with such puffery like that, it left Stevie with his nose out of joint. For one thing, Margouleff and Cecil, whom Orth had interviewed prior to their exit, chose this moment to go public with their enmity for the circle fronted by Yolanda Simmons and Ira Tucker Jr.—"the drones," Margouleff called the cabal, who he said "[were] going to drag [Stevie] down and isolate him from the very things that made him good." Cecil's shot went like this: "I wouldn't put up with the crap his organization puts me through if I didn't believe Stevie has the power to be a very, very important figure, and not just musically." Of course, the "crap" had gotten so bad after that that they *didn't* put up with it.

Stevie, though, was more somehow peeved that his exposure in a national newsmagazine was little more than a "starfucking," as satisfying a starfuck as it was. In fact, it was not materially different than in tone than the *Time* blurb, which did not seem to irk him. Yet, still out of joint months later when he sat for a June 1975 *Rolling Stone* cover story called "Stevie Wonder, Growing Up," he explicitly referred to the *Newsweek* write-up, saying, "They have it all fucked up. I mean there I am on the cover for America to see, which is cool, but it seems to me that they missed the whole point. [They say] I'm a superstar. Well, I say supershit! . . . It was as if they *decided* that black music was the thing that was going on *now* [and] they had to go find some black cat who . . . they're looking for a *symbol* of all this that they think is going on."

The protestation seemed a bit ungrateful and caviling; it was not altogether clear just *why* he was so upset. Despite his post–"Higher Ground" mellowness, he seemed to have developed a thin skin and peevish grievances for the slightest of reasons. One of them had to do with Motown's quite understandable desire for him to make hits as good as "Superstition" when he wanted to indulge his wider musical interests— as if stepping as far from funk as he could, he wrote a song for Barbra Streisand, "All in Love Is Fair," which was a dud in late 1974—and thus seethed about "record companies who naturally assume that they know everything there is to know."

He also lumped into that crowd "people who write about performers and artists"—never mind the rave notices he always enjoyed for his albums, because the Madison Square Garden Christmas show had drawn a sourpuss critique in, of all places, the haughty pages of the *New Yorker.* In a piece titled "The Importance of Stevie Wonder," Ellen Willis sniffed at the "bathos" and "fatuous aspects" of his "message of universal love" and his "overly self-conscious medley of oldies," and mused that even the "defiance" of "You Haven't Done Nothin'" was diluted by bleeding-heart stage patter that she wished "had some political content and that he didn't sound quite so much like a 1963 brotherhood speech," though she did allow, "Still, I had a pretty good time."

With a bit of hyperbole, Stevie said, "People were saying, that boy's all washed out [and] I was *lowering* myself, that I was never going to do anything worthwhile again. Which is stupid, naturally." The vicissitudes, pressures, and betrayals of superstardom being what they were—at least as he now regarded them—he had a very un-Stevie-like conclusion: "I tell you, I love to perform. [But] all this superstar shit can go out the window."

With another five-year Motown contract due to expire in May 1976, Johanan Vigoda in early 1975 once again began commuting to L.A. for negotiations with Ewart Abner. If Stevie had been content with a mere million dollars the last time around, now he was hell-bent on breaking the bank. He had little sympathy for the deteriorating state of Motown; he figured Gordy had brought it on himself with his arrogance, expecting undying loyalty from his flock even as his interest in moviemaking became inversely proportionate to his lack of interest in music. Stevie intended to milk every drop out of the fact that he was virtually propping up the company by himself now—that year, *Rolling Stone* noted, "Motown's roster has steadily eroded [having] lost the Four Tops, Gladys Knight and the Pips and, most recently, the Jackson 5." As well, it was about to lose two of its hallmark acts, Marvin Gaye and Diana Ross.

Vigoda, like a basilisk, was ready to pounce on that vulnerability. And Stevie, on his end, adeptly played with Gordy's head further. Suddenly he began making it known that he might be inclined to quit the business—just coincidentally, at the end of 1975—and go live in Africa. The story was planted in the Brit music papers, always a good conduit for gossip, with Stevie convincingly telling *New Musical Express*, "People ask me why I am going to Africa when there's so much to be done here. Well, America doesn't make a lot of people aware of what's happening in other parts of the world. I hope to bring back an alternative way from Africa. . . . I want to do something for blind people over there. Like 40 percent of the blindness in Ethiopia, for example, is caused by a fly that carries a fungus to the cornea. . . . I want to set up a foundation to combat this illness."

His next work, he mentioned, was going to take a while in development, implicitly, beyond May 1976. It would be a continuation of *Fulfillingness*, which had originally been planned as a double LP but was truncated to get it out promptly, but would be, he said, "released in two parts." The second, with the working title *FFF Part 2*, would be a double album, after which he mused, the title could be taken literally, as his ultimate apocalyptic vision. After that, he just might be burnt on the whole Stevie Wonder thing. "I might wait a long time, maybe more than a year, before I release another album," he said, which would be a transformation. "This is the last of this kind of stuff that I'll be doing—different songs and essentially the same instrumentation. I think my next thing might be a large orchestral thing." Why, he might even "drop the name Stevie Wonder and become part of Wonderlove."

Gordy had to be terrified that Stevie was serious about any or all of this; and that even if he re-signed him at an enormous price and brooked the Africa scenario, he'd be seeing a transformed, less commercial Stevie Wonder. Yet what choice did he have? Riding on four monster Stevie albums in as many years, he'd been able to increase his profit margin by $50 million, staving off bankruptcy and financing his mostly flop movies. Motown, for all its travails and loss in pop culture prestige, was a capitalist machine, the biggest black-owned corporate entity in the world. If it lost Stevie, then what? Gordy and Abner knew what Stevie and Vigoda did, and had to walk on eggshells during the negotiations. Thus, Abner could only gingerly pull rank. Addressing the African scare, for instance, he said, "We shall try to point out to Stevie that he can do more good for the cause by raising money in concert than by going out there to work."

While the honchos hashed it out in private, Stevie kept his public profile high. In May, he traveled back to the Kennedy Center in Washington, D.C., as honoree at "Human Kindness Day," a noble-minded event sponsored by local arts and educational groups and the National Park Service. Later, at the foot of the Washington Monument, where "Fingertips" had poured out of radios throughout the Mall twelve years earlier, he and Wonderlove played a free one-hour concert for 125,000 people. In June, he performed in San Francisco at a benefit for the National Newspaper Publishers Scholarship Fund. In August there was the "One to One" concert at Madison Square Garden to benefit mentally handicapped children, a cause to which he donated $10,000. (The encore, a reprise of "Give Peace a Chance," with Stevie, John Lennon, and Roberta Flack, would appear on Lennon's *Shaved Fish* LP.) He also played at the financially strapped, mostly black Shaw University in Raleigh, North Carolina, and established a fund to keep the school from closing, and in Jamaica gave $40,000 to help build what would be called the Stevie Wonder Home for Blind and Retarded Children.

Clearly, Stevie's swagger, and no doubt his biorhythms, were at peak levels. His always frazzled and unsettled personal life had solidified after Yolanda accepted the elemental requirement that, despite his much-stated desire otherwise, he would not marry her. Whether he arrived at this desideratum after the realization that he had Motown over a barrel and would soon be swimming in dough that could be at issue in a future divorce, or simply because he realized he did not love Yolanda enough to tie the knot, only he knew. Within his crowd, he and Yolanda were as good as married anyway—Malcolm Cecil for three decades believed that they *were* married—so it hardly mattered. However, it did to him.

"I don't even think the money made him hold off," says Mike Sembello. "Money was never really tangible to Stevie. He didn't see it or carry it—shit, everybody else was spending it. Stevie loved Yolanda, but Stevie loved many women. And at some point, I imagine he woke up one day and it came to him that there's love and there's *one* love in your life that's meant to be forever—and his was Syreeta. That was the thorn in his side. We always wondered what the fuck happened between them because he loved her so much. But she was the one that got away.

"Stevie is more emotional than us. He suffers over big philosophical issues like love and peace and war and death. He also is petrified by loneliness, being without someone to be his eyes. So he just decided he'd be happy being happy, and he couldn't bear to be without Yolanda and that meant something to him, it was something important in his life."

He was indeed on a high when she became pregnant late in 1974—another of his grand designs for life that he felt the time and stars demanded—and on April 7, 1975, gave birth to his first child, a daughter they named Aisha Zakiya, Swahili for "strength" and "intelligence." During that interregnum, his thoughts turned to domestic tranquillity. He bought a home on a sprawling lot on ten acres in the Hollywood Hills not far from where he'd put up Lula Mae and the family, though he would be there only rarely between touring and his continued New York activities—which didn't stop him from springing for a Mercedes 450 SEL, and later a Rolls-Royce Silver Cloud, so that when he was in L.A. he could get around in style. In New York, where Yolanda and Aisha would live for now, he moved out of the Fifth Avenue Hotel and bought a four-story, hundred-year-old town house on the Upper East Side. He hired a nanny, paid Yolanda a salary as his bookkeeper, and paid for her to attend fashion design classes.

These new digs, toys, and other expenses cost him millions, but it seemed like a pittance when that August, word came from Vigoda that could have knocked over a horse: Motown had put on the table on offer beyond belief. For Stevie's services over the next seven years, the company would pay him a guaranteed income of $13 million up front, and he would also get a bump in the royalty rate to 20 percent and control over single releases. The numbers were Babe Ruthian, the filthy lucre shattering all industry records, surpassing by miles the $8 million tab for Paul McCartney and Elton John paid by MCI and Capitol respectively, and the royalty cut slaying what was thought to be the "superstar rate" of 12 to 15 percent.

There were other concessions as well. He would now be able to produce—openly—albums for other labels' acts. Perhaps just as important to Stevie was the immediate fate of a *Stevie Wonder Anthology* that Motown wanted to put out. This, a triple album of forty songs, all culled from 1963 to 1970 save for six from *Where I'm Coming From* tacked onto the reverse side of record three, was yet another example of the classic Motown marketing strategy of endlessly repackaging the same product—an almost comical tactic that has always been reliably profitable. Stevie, however, was aghast that an album pitched as an anthology would extirpate the last four meteoric years of work that defined who and what he was and redefined the reach and meaning of soul music.

Gordy may have believed he could get away with this, and circumvent Stevie's sovereignty over album content, because the material came before his 1971 contract renewal. When Stevie found out about it, two hundred thousand copies had already been pressed, leading Vigoda to demand that the presses stop. Out of courtesy to Stevie, Gordy did, and agreed as part of the new contract to keep the album on hold for two years. Vigoda, knowing that was the best he could do given the date-sensitive issue, grabbed at it, both he and Stevie hoping that by 1977 the album would be seen as more of a curio—which, because they insisted that it be renamed by adding the phrase *Looking Back*, it was, only rising to No. 34 pop, No. 15 R&B, not to any great disappointment to Stevie.

Abner, who must have been speechless when Gordy agreed to these provisions, could not help but admit, as he had a year before in *Newsweek*, that "I'm unashamed to say Stevie and Marvin changed our approach. They loosened us up. We make a lot of money and we didn't have to change. They taught us how to have a little fun." By any strict rationale, Gordy surely overpaid Stevie to keep him in the studio and not, say, Ghana or Ethiopia—he needn't have worried, as those fancies were quickly forgotten once the deal was made—but at any price it seemed well worth it. As *Rolling Stone* observed, along industry corridors, the verdict was that re-signing Stevie had "saved Motown's ass."

In return, all Stevie had to do was make an album bigger and better and more profitable than the ones that had already broken the bank creatively and commercially. Yet if Stevie believed this was possible, and was pumped on giving life to his self-stated magnum opus, he just couldn't wrap his mind around the daily grind of sifting through songs and hammering out the best ones on vinyl. Playing father and homebody was one reason, but perhaps not the biggest. It may have been that the king's ransom he'd earned, rather than driving him to hard labor, gave him license to take his bows—and hefty appearance fees—out on the road, living in a cartoon salmagundi of dashikis, denim, and *Jetsons*-style bubble wrap (the mandatory uniform of funk bands), his beaded braids bouncing with every swivel of his head, joyously banging out what was now a long docket of pop culture favorites. Right after the turn of the new year, he was off to Japan, then Africa, then Jamaica, where he jammed for the first time with Bob Marley and the Wailers. And, as always, there were the humanitarian/political engagements, including a rendezvous with Reverend Jesse Jackson at a Push for Equality concert in Memphis, and a luncheon with the Black Congressional Caucus.

In the interim, recording sessions kept being put off until tomorrow, then the next tomorrow. The new album, which was being hyped by Motown before a single song was cut, became an enigma. As months came and went, a question was being heard all around the industry: Where's the Stevie Wonder album? Malcolm Cecil, who certainly had an interest in the work, having turned over to Stevie all the tapes he and Margouleff had made with him, wondered just who the hell was allowing him to be so dilatory.

"We never would have let him get away with that," he insists. "We always pushed Stevie—we had to, because he had so many songs in his head at once that he needed to be sat down and be told, 'Stevie, we're doing this one. Let's get to work.' There were times I literally locked him in the studio. He wouldn't be able to get out until we'd gotten a song done. We didn't care if he had a tour or a show to get to. Stevie loved to perform, which is a wonderful thing, and he's the best there is, but if you're going to make records you have to decide you're going to make records."

Deciding such things, however, was seldom a matter of urgency, or priority. As *Time* had observed a year before, "Life with Stevie . . . is a circus of indecision, chaotic scheduling and the totally unexpected. 'It is not that he is a prima donna or purposely rude,' says a friend, but 'he just doesn't have days or nights, and he's seldom thinking more than ten minutes ahead.'" He had also become extraordinarily insular. In a February 1975 *New York Times Magazine* profile, writer Jack Slater described him as "a rather wary person [who] trusts few people," quoting him this way: "I distance myself. . . . I remove myself from people but I don't feel alienated from them." The distinction apparently lay in the fact that, as he added, "If people want to take the time to listen to my music, they can hear me, my way of thinking."

If the Stevie caravan was a "circus," for his lead guitarist it was more like a burlesque show. "We called what was happening running up a wall," says Mike Sembello, "because we'd start to go and wind up back where we started. It was so fucked up. He'd hire people—basically, he hired his whole family. There was his brother, who's been studying to be an accountant for like thirty years, Calvin. He's the Rain Man of the family. [laughs] I love Calvin. But, oh my God. He'd give jobs to all his relatives. A cousin or a nephew, or a cousin of a nephew, guys with no experience, and they'd piss everybody off. His brother, Larry, had his own office. I'd walk in and he'd be wearing a headband and trying to play instruments. And I'm thinkin', 'You can't explain genetics.'

"Stevie, he's such a child, such a beautiful human being. Calvin is, too. But it was so sad. You couldn't get anything done. You'd go weeks, months, and you wouldn't hear from him. Then, out of the blue, he'd call at 4 a.m., because Stevie never sleeps, and he'd want to record something. Or he'd tell you to get to the airport in an hour for a trip to wherever it had been decided he was going. It was crazy.

"This is what I love about Stevie. He's so helpless, unspoiled. It's all about the music and the rest is like, it'll all work out because it just has to. [laughs] God love him. If he didn't have so many hit records, he'd be living in the street."

14

"We're Almost Finished"

I've known some of the people [at Motown] a very long time.
They've let me get away with things that other companies may not
have allowed.

—*Stevie Wonder, 1975*

s things stood in the fall of 1976, it was anything but
clear when and *if* he would get around to his masterwork.
By then, no Stevie Wonder product had been released since "Boogie
On Reggae Woman" in late 1974. Slowly, though, a concept and structure
began to take on life, and a title chosen as a canon and guidepost—
Songs in the Key of Life.

As Stevie dissected the mission behind this simple baptism, "It
was like the beginning of another kind of place. Its title came from a
dream I had where I was asking, 'How many songs are there in the key
of life?' Then it became the challenge of starting again and doing it
a different way." Actualizing it was something like sensory overdrive, on a
mass scale. With TONTO gone, Stevie lined his studios on both coasts
with the most expensive cutting-edge synthesizers, the main weapon
a $40,000 Yamaha GX-1, the company's first polyphonic synth, which
could bend, shape, and multiply the melodies played on its three keyboards. To Stevie, it was a "dream machine," his own TONTO, and he
toted it from studio to studio, he and his new engineers acclimating to

it for months trying to recreate what TONTO, through its two keepers, had done.

The studio on any given day was usually clogged not just with the hangers-on but scores of musicians and singers—though not Margouleff and Cecil to nudge Stevie along, something no one else dared to do. The chamber would buzz with chatter and suggestions that alternated between whimsical, nonsensical, and practical; when the last happened, Stevie's ears would take it to fruition. For example, he had written a brassy song called "Sir Duke," a breezy, exhilarating homage not just to Duke Ellington but a coterie of legendary jazz masters whose names whizzed by in the lyrics as if riding a passing train.

Recording the track at Crystal Industries in L.A., he rehearsed the band and cut it live. But the bass line he'd written was impossible for Nate Watts, a recent addition to the band, to play. "When I worked it out on the fingerboard," Watts recalls, "I had to bend up the last fret to reach the highest note." Normally, that would mean a weakened bass note, but Watts's long fingers held the power, creating by sheer accident a unique "two-feel" line that throbbed as it held the bottom together, allowing a wiry horn arrangement to top off a bracing blast of old-time jazz rhythm. "Stevie let me loose, and I hammered it. I was the new guy, but he had me feeling like I was James Jamerson."

Nate Watts would need to adapt to the fitful schedule of the "Stevie experience." Once, after recording all day, he says, "I had just gotten home and into bed exhausted when Stevie called and said, 'I need you to come back—I've got this bad song.' He had written an eighth-note keyboard bass line and when I did it on the bass Stevie liked it because he said it sounded angry. Well, yeah. You bet it sounded angry—because it was 3 a.m. and I had to come all the way back to the studio!"

That track was "I Wish," Stevie's irresistible flashback of life as a "nappy-headed little boy" hanging out with "those hoodlum friends of mine" and the "wooping" he took. As in "Sir Duke," Watts took his bass on a joyride up and down the scale, with a growling burr, and on the indelible intro his sinewy plucking (with the audible squeaks of his fingers manipulating the chords on the neck of his bass left intact) merged with synthesized guitar picking, before the horns came in to punctuate Stevie's gritty vocal. Arguably, "I Wish" was the last great opus of the "classic" Stevie Wonder phase.

Another new cohort on board was Gary Byrd, a poet and DJ at New York's WLIB, who Stevie charged with writing lyrics for some new songs. One was called "Village Ghetto Land," which was intended as a parboil of 'hood reality. "We wrote the song in New York," Byrd recalled, "then he went to L.A. and I didn't speak to him for three months. Then, suddenly, he calls at 2 a.m.—Stevie has no idea of the time or time zones and he never sleeps—and he says, 'Hey, I gotta add a new verse. I'm in the studio. Call you back in ten minutes.' Ten minutes!" Byrd came up with a seething verse about "families buying dog food" and babies dying before they're born, "infected by the grief." Stevie laid down the vocal, and the song—on which every sound was made by the "dream machine," it being indiscernible to most that not one note was played by any instruments it replaced—was in the bank. "Now *that*," Byrd attests, "was pressure."

Mike Sembello, of course, was used to that sort of thing. He too had cowritten one of the songs that wound up on the album—"Saturn," a funk slow jam that, given the title, was taken as a spaced-out galactic excursion but was actually a metaphoric cousin of "I Wish." Says Sembello, "Originally, it was 'Saginaw,' but Stevie heard it as 'Saturn' on the demo and it was perfect because to Stevie, Saginaw is another planet, a state of mind lost in time and space, and far, *far* away."

Each song on the album would be one germ of larger conceptual threads. For instance, "Ghetto Land" was soul-mated with the eight-minute "Black Man," carrying another Byrd lyric in tribute to little-known African American history-makers, done as a classroom exercise, its hook vowing that "with justice not for all men, history will repeat again." And "Saturn" was a down-tempo change of funk pace between "Sir Duke" and wild, Sly Stone–like onslaughts like "Contusion" and "All Day Sucker," which returned Stevie to his old clattering Clavinets.

The tides moved from lighthearted to heavy, from middle-of-the-road to harder lanes of jazz and funk. The profound ones were kept to a few, but, like "Ghetto Land," they kicked to the gut, none harder than "Pastime Paradise," a swelling, Kafkaesque elegy of "the evils of the world"—in which he ticked off, slowly and mournfully as a tolling bell, ills such as "Dissipation . . . Consolation . . . Segregation . . . Dispensation"—with bleak strings and finger cymbals growing in intensity, joined by Hare Krishna chanting and a massive chorale anchored by the wailing of the West Angeles Church of God Choir, imploring, "Let's start living our lives / Living for the future paradise," before a grim gong pealed and echoed into nothingness.

Neither, being Stevie Wonder, could he resist stretching preachiness to stupefying levels, stretching the self-explanatory "Love's in Need of Love Today," to over seven minutes—and stretching conventional industry wisdom that such a song, by content and duration, could never be the first track of an album, by doing just that. Just as aureate, if half as long, was "Ngiculela—Es Una Historia—I Am Singing," a snappy love paean times three—its verses in Zulu, Spanish, and English—with the epitaphic coda that as long as there was a happy song to sing, "It never seems so bad."

With any of these tracks, the subject matter was secondary for Stevie to carving out an aural multiformity, as was technical perfection. At the session for "As," by example, Nate Watts, improvising with jazz great Herbie Hancock, got so carried away that, he recalled, "I made two mistakes—right before the first chorus and right before the last chorus. I asked Stevie if I could fix them. He said no, he liked the way they felt." Each cut, then, developed as unique variation. "Knocks Me Off My Feet" was an airy commix of piano and gospel chorus; "As" memorable for its synth-contrived harpsichord sound; "Summer Soft" for its dewy harp—a *real* one, not a synthesized ersatz; "If It's Magic" for its bluesy, torch-song emotion; "Joy in My Tears" for its stringed sentimentalism; "Another Star"—featuring Wes Montgomery disciple George Benson on guitar—for its salsa undertow.

Another sermon, "Have a Talk with God," even weighed down by torpid lyrics (cowritten by his brother Calvin) embodying God as a "free psychiatrist that's known throughout the world," was affecting as a pop, funk, and rock mix, fixed to a beat very close to that of the Band's "The Weight." On "Ebony Eyes," an obvious hosanna to Diana Ross ("She's a miss beautiful supreme / A girl that others wish that they could be"), his rough, staccato cadences recalled Otis Redding far more than Ross herself.

Stevie intended that *Songs* be a family affair. Injecting traces of his bloodline, he inscrutably dropped a tincture of Lula Mae in the title of an instrumental jazz jam with some old-times'-sake harmonica woofing, "Easy Goin' Evening (My Mama's Call)." And, most enduringly, there was "Isn't She Lovely," a straightforward three-chord sonata for his new daughter—"Life is Aisha / The meaning of her name"—who having been "made from love" led him to rejoice, "We have been heaven-blessed."

It was offered without guile or pretense, from the intro of an infant's bawling—*not* Aisha, contrary to urban myth—and on through a parfait of layered synth, frisky Benny Benjamin–style drum fills, improvised harmonica riffs, and some taped bits of at-home family reverie. It was clearly a winner, as sprightly as "Don't You Worry 'Bout a Thing," but it would never go out as a single, so averse was he to snipping it for time or tainting it with crass commercialism.

Not that it mattered. Though Malcolm Cecil was not alone among critics who found it torture to bear its endless recycling—*"Isn't she lovely?"* he croons in a fey, mocking voice. "It's just so smarmy. It's tripe. I would have forced him to do something better. In my opinion, that's not a high point. It's not 'Living for the City.' It's living for the easy song, which I suspect he believed himself"—it was quickly extracted from the album by DJs and played to death, more than any other Stevie Wonder song. Neither did Stevie refuse any of the filthy lucre it made for him.

To be certain, *Songs* contained some clunkers, pretensions, and aggravations, yet undeniably it grabbed the ears like an opiate cocktail. Because he placed songs in no particular order, he knew buyers would need to listen hard to try and figure out its riddles and meanings—a game still played three decades later. But *was* there an overall meaning? Stevie would write in the liner notes that while the work "was a challenge, an album relating to life. . . . It's impossible to cover all of what life is about." If that was a cop-out, a drawing back from past works in which he *did* seem to claim all the answers, he might have added that life was just too damn short to stress about it.

More central to his id right now was for him to relocate himself underneath the craziness going on all about him, which more than anything may have led him to the anxieties he enumerated in *Rolling Stone*—another of them being that he had become too isolated from his audiences, no doubt explaining why in that same article he added, almost as an afterthought, "When I look out at an audience, all I see are beautiful people." Now, as if pushing out at the walls of isolation that had been built around him, he would soon say, "I feel that the people who listen to my music, or the fans that I have, are closer to me than some of the people who are my close acquaintances or friends."

In this prism, a trenchant line in "Talk with God" ruing about "Never communicating with the One who lives within" seemed to have little to do with God and everything to do with Stevie Wonder.

• • •

As the album had dragged on, and on, it became a running joke. As early as mid-1975, Stevie had assured Motown the album would be in the can within weeks. It was no idle promise given that he then paid $50,000 for a block-long, 60-by-270-foot billboard in Times Square reading "Stevie Wonder/Songs in the Key of Life," his trademark grinning face to the right of clouds, stars, and a rainbow. At the time, advance orders were pouring in totaling around a million and a half copies—meaning it would ship platinum. Motown began sending out invitations to the media for a lavish unveiling of the work. But Stevie kept pushing back the release date. Motown became so tired of answering questions about the delay that its executives would wear T-shirts with the inscription "We're Almost Finished." Stevie's posse, at the suggestion of Calvin, wore their own T-shirts with the titles of various songs from the album. But after a year the gag, like the shirts, wore thin, and for Gordy there was nothing but embarrassment. Having had to constantly fend off distributors who had paid long ago for large orders of the record, he had to give them deeper discounts on their services.

Stevie was surely costing Motown money. Expecting an album and several hit singles a year, there had been none of the latter in over a year and none of the former in over *two* years. Finally, in early October 1976, it *was* finished: twenty-one tracks, seventeen on the double LP and four on a "bonus" EP (on the new audiotape market, a two-cassette package), with a running time of 106 minutes. Far distant now were the days of bringing in three albums for $65,000; this one reportedly cost around a million dollars—"Sure, because it took him five years to do it," says a sardonic Malcolm Cecil. "We used to do an album in a few months. And I'm sure he was happy to pay all that, just to be able to finish it."

Sparing no expense, he included a twenty-four-page booklet of lyrics, barely scrutable Stevie aphorisms (for example, that he was on a "mission to spread love mentalism") and a long honor roll of music and non-music people including James Taylor, Stephen Stills, Harry Nilsson, the Doobie Brothers, Frank Zappa, Jesse Jackson, Louis Farrakhan, Abdul-Jabbar (presumably the Lakers center), and Bob Margouleff and Malcolm Cecil. The dedication was to Yolanda: "You have given me more than I ever knew existed"—but with the proviso "My mind must be polygamous and my spirit is married to many and my love belongs to all. . . . Je t'aime," followed by names like Francine, Lory, Veronica, Angie, Syreeta, Yvonne, Coco, Pam, and Yolanda Z., and a blank line under which was written, "There's an empty space for you." He signed the jacket, in a shaky scrawl, "STEVLAND," the curious cognomen later to be discarded by Lula.

The media unveiling of the album was at a place called Longview Farm, a 145-acre grange in Worcester, Massachusetts, owned by Gil Markle, a music industry executive and buddy of Johanan Vigoda, who had built a recording studio used by many rock acts seeking a bucolic environment—Don McLean, to name one, had recorded "American Pie" there. Despite this history, it was a "bizarre" choice, wrote Maureen Orth, for "a black and blind urban artist." Stevie, who chose the place to play the album for the media, had, she reported, "made his entrance [in] a cream-colored Tom Mix cowboy outfit with a gunbelt that said 'Number One With a Bullet' on the back and two of his albums hanging as holsters."

Bullet, indeed. The LP debuted at No. 1 days later, it mattering not a whit that some of the critics grumbled about various things, Vince Aletti even complaining about the *album cover*—"Wonder's image sinking into a vortex of what resembles orange crepe paper looks not only offhand but like a last-minute amateur effort; the effect is hideous and offensively cheap, considering the album's $13.98 list price." He also fussed that, while the album "offers something fresh at each listening, something right for every mood . . . it has no focus or coherence . . . turning what might have been a stunning, exotic feast into a hastily organized potluck supper." Yet its allegedly "heavy-handed" content and "preposterous lyrics" could not keep Aletti from dishing out a five-star verdict, in that "his spirit dominates here and seems to fill up the room. His voice snatches you up. And won't let go."

He got that right. Thirty-three years on, *Songs* still holds its élan—notwithstanding the mezzo-mezzo fifty-sixth-place ranking on the *Rolling Stone* all-time album list. Another such compilation, by the Yahoo! Music Playlist Blog in 2008, which weighed albums' staying power, sales value, critical ratings, and awards, made *Songs* the top dog. In its time, *Songs* seemed for a time to be a permanent fixture; it held the No. 1 spot thirteen weeks in a row, then was moved out by *Hotel California*, but after dropping to No. 4 leaped back up to No. 1 for a fourteenth week, and refused to leave the chart for *eighty* weeks. Early on, in mid-November, *Time* foretold that "with sales already totaling a phenomenal 1.7 million, the album could well earn Motown most of its $13 million back before year's end." It was an understatement; in 1977, *Songs* (after being on the market for two months) would sell more copies than any other album except Fleetwood Mac's *Rumours.* To date, it has sold ten million in the United States alone (it also went Top 10 in Britain, Norway, Sweden, and the Netherlands), making it one of only nine original-content albums (not greatest hits packages) to be certified diamond.

The first single, "I Wish," backed with a non-album track, "You and I," was released in late November and cruised to No. 1 pop and R&B early in 1977; the second, "Sir Duke," went out in March with, oddly, "He's Misstra Know-It-All" on the flip, and did the same for three weeks on the pop chart. It took until August, when "Another Star" was issued, for the magic to fade, that song rising only to No. 32 pop, No. 18 R&B, and a final single, "As," to No. 36 pop and R&B. Of course, "Isn't She Lovely" had been played from the start, so much that for some it became the aural equivalent of a root canal, but it kept the album out of the bargain bins for months.

In a Madison Square Garden charity concert in December, Robert Christgau even sensed in Stevie some "Sly-calibre hubris. . . . At his Garden appearance in June, Sly couldn't fill the seats for his own wedding. . . . Stevie's show of agape, on the other hand, sold out. Sometimes the man's success is enough to make you believe in faith." This review was the one in which the critic called Stevie a "fool," yet like Aletti, he too top-graded *Songs,* as he had done and would do with all but two of Stevie's albums from *Talking Book* on. So if Stevie Wonder was a fool, Christgau admitted, it worked, for him, for us. "Stevie," he wrote, "may sometimes be sanctimonious as well as sanctified . . . his dream of brotherhood for our grandchildren may cloud over the ironies of our condition more than he can ever understand. But . . . he creates an aural universe so rich that it makes us believe. . . . And it is not foolish to believe that the transcendence of philosophy is the reason we want music in our lives." The short version: yes, we *needed* Stevie Wonder.

The post-*Songs* lacuna was a long victory lap. Nominated for seven Grammys, Stevie would win four—Album of the Year, Best

Male Pop Vocal Performance, Best Male R&B Vocal Performance, and Best Producer. Though he couldn't make the February ceremonies in L.A., being on tour in Africa, he agreed to do a satellite feed from Lagos, Nigeria, smiling and thanking people each time he won on a big screen in the hall. The final time, the signal went dead. The only thing on the screen was static, prompting the bewildered host, singer Andy Williams, to unthinkingly ask, "Stevie, can you see us?" It was a classic blooper, but a classic existential question, too. The classic existential answer being, yes, he *could* see, in more ways than can be imagined.

Two months later, Yolanda gave birth to an eight-pound, seven-ounce baby boy named Keita Sawandi Morris, the given names South and West African words for "worshiper" and "founder." Again paternity occupied Stevie, and he recorded no new product well into 1979. A Motown impatient for a hot follow-up began to stew again, their frustration magnified by the fact that Stevie was constantly in the public eye. He made a trip to London. He jammed with Bob Marley at the Black Music Association convention in Philadelphia. He made drop-in appearances at concerts by the Commodores; Earth, Wind & Fire; Billy Preston; and Ella Fitzgerald; and at the Grand Ole Opry in Nashville, warbling the country tune "Behind Closed Doors." He played a Duke Ellington memorial in L.A., another in Atlanta on what would have been Dr. Martin Luther King's fiftieth birthday at the invitation of Coretta Scott King, and at a surprise birthday party for Marvin Gaye. He also made the news when after his friend Lee Garrett, who'd cowritten "Signed, Sealed, Delivered," and more recently, "Let's Get Serious," became suicidal and locked himself in the bathroom of his house in L.A., a gun to his head, Stevie was brought over and talked Garrett out of killing himself.

The long line of artists recording songs written by Stevie grew to include George Benson ("We All Remember Wes"), the Pointer Sisters ("Bring Your Sweet Stuff Home to Me"), Minnie Riperton ("Stick Together"), Michael Jackson ("I Can't Help It") and Jermaine Jackson ("Let's Get Serious," which Stevie produced as well). But it wasn't that Stevie was avoiding his own projects; in fact, he was in the studio nearly every day. However, as with *Songs*, he was taking forever with it. Worse, the project mortified Gordy.

It was the soundtrack for a movie adaptation of the 1973 book *The Secret Life of Plants* by Peter Tompkins and Christopher Bird, an academic hypothesis that had plants and humans sharing physical, emotional, and spiritual feelings. When film producer Michael Braun optioned the book as a visual documentary and made a deal with Paramount Pictures to distribute it, he sent word to Stevie about composing the score. It was wild and weird stuff, and Stevie agreed to take it on, as a way of daring himself to "get serious" and make "all the superstar shit go out the window" by mastering a different medium.

This was no simple task, even for Stevie—*especially* for Stevie. He would be expected to commit music to images he could not see, only "feel," just as the plants theoretically did. Of course, nearly everyone who heard of this undertaking believed it was some kind of joke. Which to Stevie made it more of a turn-on, knowing how atypical it was. As he said in a January 1977 *Ebony* interview, "I think the images of me arise out of people's own insecurities, their own needs," meaning what they *wanted* him to be. But he had his own needs, too, and if this fulfilled them, he was down for it. What's more, he had even prepared for it, without knowing; as *Rolling Stone*'s review would later point out, the final track of *Songs*, the instrumental "Easy Goin' Evening (My Mama's Call)" was much like the first track of *Plants*, in that it "commences with a quick, slapstick keyboard fill and then expands into an undulating instrumental whose billowing bass and synthesizers evoke a quivering field of flowers in bloom . . . a sly parody of the kind of sweet bombast associated with silent-film melodramas."

Enter *Stevie Wonder's Journey Through the Secret Life of Plants*, which basically did the same, the "dream machine" and his other synthesizers creating a new, indefinable sonic "language," cosmic, botanical, or otherwise. Indeed, Cecil believes there was a subliminal prod behind the album. *Plants*, he says, "[*Plants*] was Stevie showing Bob and me he could produce a total immersive synthesizer experience without us, so he could say, 'Eat your hearts out, boys.'"

Whatever the motivations, in the historical lens these sessions are an important milestone as Stevie was now recording in a digital format. The industry at the time was on the cusp of the digital revolution, just learning about converting analog signals into the noiseless, crystal-clear binary code, and in September 1979 the first major digitally recorded album was released, Ry Cooder's self-produced *Bop Till You Drop*. Stevie was right behind him on the cutting edge. Recently he'd purchased a Sony

PCM-1600 digital recorder for his Hollywood studio, and for *Plants* had no fewer than *six* engineers in the booth.

Feeling his way through as he did, he again paid no heed to the clock or the calendar. Technology and the usual studio tarrying aside, he was getting on-the-job movie score training from Braun, who had to explain each scene in excruciating detail through one side of Stevie's earphones while at the same time Gary Olazabal would count down the frames remaining in the scene; each of these would be put on one track of a four-track tape, with the sound of the movie on a third. The fourth track would be left open, for Stevie to do his thing. It was an arduous process, but Braun was floored. "A lot of veteran composers wouldn't know what to do, except in the most mundane literalistic way," he said. That Stevie did it at all was "uncanny."

By nature, literally, it was eclectic. By design, it was biblical, sometimes canonical. The entire first side, a critic would note, "coheres as a musical-botanical Talking Book of Genesis," and the opening cut was called "Earth's Creation." The instrumental flux, guided by each scene, rose and then dissolved, flowing from mellow to manic, melodramatic to dainty, mystical to funky to symphonic. Synthesized effects popped into the spatial field, differently each time—as a kazoo on a track called "Race Babbling" or a funereal organ on "Ecclesiastes" and "Ai No, Sono" (on which a chorus of Asian children sings the verses), a fluttering trumpet in the marching-band beat of "Earth's Creation," a buzzing (ill-fated) fly on "Venus' Flytrap and the Bug"—which also featured garrulous cawing and a verbal exchange between Stevie and his son—a birdlike trill on "Outside My Window."

Every track came with a novel element: "Power Flower" a smooth falsetto backing; "Send One Your Love" a din of verbal background clattering. Tribal chanting and tom-toms pealed on "Kesse Ye Lolo de Ye." "Come Back as a Flower"—cowritten and with a lilting vocal by Syreeta Wright—used as its rhythm track recorded rainforest noise. On "Tree," jungle squawks united with their synthesized versions. On "Voyage to India," the gentle swoosh of the sea seems to buoy a bed of sitars. On "Seasons," Syreeta reads a fairy story as if to a child, the wind howling outside an imaginary window. The album's last cut, "Finale," recast in subtly different shades excerpts of previous tracks, with great flourishes of full orchestral impact, timpani booming and cymbals crashing on the big screen. Everything was molded to free-flowing visuals shot with microscopic lenses and time-lapse photography by director Walon Green, a former Oscar-winning screenwriter, stitching a rhythmic pulse meant to add "human," animate qualities to the fauna and flora. The music was in ultra-clean Dolby Sound. The effect was riveting, even startling. But that was the rub. It was one thing for the music to distend and dramatize natural phenomena as part of a multisensual experience. But how would the music come off disembodied, stripped of its essential visual context? True, Stevie had "seen" the images in *his* mind, but would they materialize in anyone else's? It was something that worried him. In fact, he admitted that the project "might throw some people," and that "I think my fans will accept it, but I'm not totally sure."

Stevie would not agree to boil the work of a two-hour movie into a forty-five-minute album, insisting that he heard it only as a complete work. This meant he would be following one double album with another. At Motown, this was a touchy matter—it would have been tough enough to promote it as a regular album. Gordy was also aware that Stevie wanted to count the album, as he had with *Songs in the Key of Life*, as *two* albums, which would let him get closer to meeting the requirement in his contract that he deliver an album per year. If Gordy could swallow that dodge with *Songs*, to do so with a mostly instrumental album about *plants* gave him agita. Still there was nothing he could do. Stevie had all but been crowned king of Motown—after *Songs* Gordy had greened him even more, advancing $37 million on future royalties, as an inducement to keep him busy. And Stevie seemed to be eager to please him, waxing effusive about Motown being "the only viable black-owned company in the record industry," and that "it is vital that people in our business . . . make sure that Motown stays emotionally stable, spiritually strong, and economically healthy."

But beneath the florid talk, he had no intention of allowing Gordy to crimp him, or his own needs or terms. Finally, he had hired a manager to help him do that. A manager who had just a little pull at Motown. This was none other than Ewart Abner, whose job was to do now for Stevie what he once earned his keep by denying him. (Though by now there was a certain incestuousness between the Motown and Stevie camps, with Vigoda having taken to calling himself "a lawyer for Motown.") With Abner gone, Gordy had no choice but to step back in as Motown president, though he much preferred making movies and hanging at the Polo Lounge with other Hollywood fat cats. Gordy was really over a barrel when it came to Stevie. For one thing, he had lost touch with the record business. For another, Motown was again spitting up losses, with little else beside Stevie as a profit leader. For yet another, he couldn't say no to Stevie Wonder.

In every way, Stevie had him checkmated.

Plants, however, seemed to be doomed before it ever saw light. The movie and soundtrack were due for a late October release, but Paramount postponed the film for two months. Motown, though, was in no position to wait any longer, and so Stevie went back into the studio to make revisions in the album that would render it commercially viable on its own. A half dozen songs were given lead vocals. As a result, the title track and "Same Old Story" morphed into sanguine pop. "Send One Your Love" was surgically transformed into a laid-back light R&B fodder, "Race Babbling" into convincing disco, "Seed's a Star" into hip-hop funk, "Black Orchid" into a yearning ballad, the added lyrics stunning—"A touch of love in fear of hate. . . . A pearl of wisdom entrapped by poverty."

But "commercial" was the last word many would have used for the finished work, and no one fretted about it more than Gordy. In *To Be Loved* he recalled, euphemistically, "I got a sinking feeling it might not be the smash we so desperately needed from Stevie. But because he was such an innovator . . . I was hopeful. I wanted to be wrong real bad." It was a hope that got more faint. In an almost comically pathetic turn, Motown, at Stevie's urging, tried sending the album out with a scented cover—until the perfume seeped through and ate away the vinyl record inside; thousands of copies had to be discarded. The jacket cover was kept simple and clean—green bedrock with a line drawing set inside a small quadrangle (the fifty-third best ever album cover, according to *Rolling Stone* in a 1991 survey), but even this was an issue, such was the cost of its special embossing, die-cutting, and a Braille inscription ("Inside this embossed square is the outline of a flower with veined leaves"). Trying to recoup what already were losses on it, Gordy cut by half the intended pressing run of two million copies, then braced for the worst.

As with *Songs in the Key of Life*, but far more so, Malcolm Cecil was not impressed. "I have one short description of Stevie's work since

Innervisions—self-indulgent," he says. "I also believe this is partly my fault. The way that I like to produce is, I like to make people think it's their idea. That's how you get the most out of them. The downside of this is, if you're really successful at it, they really *do* think it's their idea, and therefore they don't owe you anything, any allegiance, any future considerations.

"That is I think what happened to Stevie. He began to believe it was all him. He began to believe his own publicity. He was hell-bent on proving it. He got himself all the right equipment, and then Yamaha was giving him stuff for free. He had tremendous success with *Songs in the Key of Life*. He couldn't make a mistake. The only problem was, he couldn't program all those synthesizers. He didn't know how to make the sounds, something he covered up quite nicely on *Songs*, but that was it, as far as grand achievements."

Similarly unsold was a confused critical cognoscenti. *Rolling Stone*'s Ken Tucker could find little good to say, calling the album "uneven" and "full of tiny pleasures and bloated tedium . . . plucking the exhilarating moments from [it] is a harrowing, highly subjective task. One person's nectar is another's Karo syrup, and the stamens of Wonder's *Plants* are bursting with both." He likened it to "Walt Disney nature documentaries," though the old Stevie naiveté was still winsome: "Like the radicalized Rousseau he is, Stevie Wonder presumes nature to exist in a state of pure innocence. Thus, the presexual condition of children is equated with green, tender sprouts, a neat, bold leap."

Later, much later, in the long view and broad context of Stevie's overall oeuvre, this dog would have its day, too. It would be vested a legacy, as a glint of sunlight through the branches of primordial New Age. A number of latter-day singers would cite it as a "secret pleasure." But in its maiden journey, about the best that was said about it in reviews was that it was "brave" and "courageous"; among the other opinions was that it was "laughable," "soporific," "pointless," and "an uneventful one-way ticket to Dullsville."

By the numbers, the album did remarkably well, surely because it carried the Stevie brand. *Plants* rose to No. 4 early in the new decade on both the pop and soul chart, and was certified gold. As well, the alluring "Send One Your Love," released as a single, went to No. 4 pop, No. 5 R&B. Still, with a million units out on the street, it needed to move more than half to make money. The remaindering of the other half million cost

Motown dearly, as Gordy remembered in his memoir—"That [million copies] turned out to be around nine hundred thousand too many," he wrote, understating sales by four hundred thousand—it probably just *seemed* to be that big of a bath. Its epitaph was coined by a Motown wag, who punned that the album "went out gold and came back *plant*-inum."

Before the tanking became clear, a hopeful Stevie had big promotion plans. He threw gala unveiling parties on both coasts, in Malibu and at the Bronx Botanical Garden, then debuted selections from the album during a three-hour concert in Lincoln Center's Metropolitan Opera House, accompanied by the National Afro-American Philharmonic Orchestra as scenes from the shelved movie were shown on a big screen. The tepid response was the first clue of what was to come, and others arrived when during a nationwide tour with a full orchestra, many of the venues were half-filled. In Detroit, he couldn't keep from scolding, "I would have liked to see Cobo Hall *full*."

Overall, the *Plants* episode was a temporary flub, but a telling one. Even the yes-men in his ring of leeches agreed that it would be for the best if he cut the tour short and end any more experimentation. He did both. Fearing that the interlude had bored or turned off enough fans to disrupt the furious momentum he had built up through the decade, he decided it was imperative to quickly record another album, one that could supplant and make everyone forget the last few months.

The fiasco would not affect his Midas touch; for Stevie, the bottom line would always be golden. However, in the epigrammatic sense, Malcolm Cecil was right. The end of the seventies was also the end of Stevie Wonder as the daemon of a black Mozart. His days of being bankable, popular, even beloved were still in midlife. But as for being singularly triumphant and important in the purely artistic sense, those days were over.

15

The Clock of Now

Since he is young and gifted—and open—his music will probably continue to grow, to expand in new directions. One can easily imagine a Stevie Wonder, at fifty or sixty, becoming what would then be a kind of latter-day Duke Ellington.

—*Jack Slater*, Ebony, *January 1977*

I want people to think of me like I do Stevie. I want to be an artist who is appreciated.

—*Diana Ross, during her Central Park concert, 1983*

Further driving *Plants* into the ground was that the movie itself drew flies when it went into theaters, making Paramount a loser in a project that aided no one. By the time it became a memory, and the second single, "Outside My Window," died aborning, reaching only No. 52 pop, No. 56 R&B, the album was on its last legs before being remaindered to the back bins of the record stores—something that Stevie believed was related to Motown's lack of belief in or promotion of the work. But Stevie, setting land speed records for recording, had completed *Hotter Than July*, and Motown was able to rush it out not in July but September, relieved that it made no sweeping mission statements other than palatable pop-soul—and that, thank the Lord, it was all on one forty-five-minute record.

July touched all the usual Stevie bases but with no pretense or hype. It was also a homecoming of sorts to the old comforts of

R&B—literally, with one track, "All I Do," a sugarplum of blooming love ("You made my soul a burning fire / You're getting to be my one desire") he'd written in 1966 with Clarence Paul and Morris Broadnax. The song was geared for the 1980s disco mien with backing vocals added by Michael Jackson (who had recorded Stevie's "I Can't Help It" on his recent solo debut album *Off the Wall*), Betty Wright, and the O'Jays' Eddie Levert and Walter Williams.

He did sample Nashville with "I Ain't Gonna Stand for It," a cheatin'-heart tale with twangy steel guitars and mimicked redneck vocal, and Jamaica with the convincing if "Stevie-ized" reggae nod to Bob Marley, which was not just an homage to Marley and his notion of "Third World Oneness" but an unintended eulogy. Marley was diagnosed with lung and brain cancer just after the album came out, and died in May 1981. Yet the blues-funk beat of Nate Watts's pounding bass and the bluesy synthesized jive kept Stevie rooted to his musical gravity center, which was realized fully with the blithe funk of "Did I Hear You Say You Love Me" and "Do Like You"—a romp about his kids learning to dance, with their voices spliced in—and buttery love ballads, the Brazilian-flavored "Rocket Love," and "Lately."

Uncluttered and uncomplicated, the album limited its moral indignation to two tracks, the indignant "Cash in Your Face"—from the one-liner real estate brokers would give black home seekers, "You might have the cash but not cash in your face"—and the song he wanted to be the thematic cause célèbre of the album, "Happy Birthday," to highlight the proposed national Martin Luther King birthday holiday rejected by the U.S. House of Representatives in 1979. The idea had come to Stevie years before when on January 15 Malcolm Cecil mentioned it was King's birthday.

"I suggested to him that we should record him singing 'Happy Birthday' to Dr. King," Cecil recalls. "And Stevie said, 'But I don't know how to play that song. So he wrote the hook for a different 'Happy Birthday.' He held on to it until that album, when the movement for the holiday was gaining steam."

Sagely, the song was the bubbliest one on the album, with Stevie adding relevant lyrics—"There ought to be a law against anyone who takes offense," he said of the holiday—to a merry synth-percussion jam that wittingly or otherwise got the song noticed and played. But it was probably why most would hear the album as a nondemanding, pleasant way to spend forty-five minutes. No one, not even the critics who returned to the laudatory fold, believed it would alter musical currents the way those 1970s works did. And they were right; *July* breezed to No. 3 pop, No. 1 R&B on the album chart, while "Master Blaster," unveiled by Stevie while on tour in London, went to No. 5 pop, No. 1 R&B and "I Ain't Gonna Stand for It" to No. 11 and No. 4 early in 1981.

The album's success restored him, ensuring his presence as a headliner onstage and on the platform. Only months later, he was in Washington, D.C., in a parade for the King holiday bill. When Congress dallied, he contacted Coretta Scott King, the powerful congressman John Conyers who had introduced the bill in 1979, and the D.C. congressman Walter Fauntroy, and helped coordinate a march on Washington and a Rally for Peace concert on the Mall on January 15, 1982. He made the announcement of these activities at a press conference with Coretta King at the Los Angeles Press Club.

At the rally he was all over the place, including superseding Jesse Jackson in giving the keynote speech for fifty thousand multiracial, shivering people. Standing at the foot of the Lincoln Memorial for the second time, after a rousing rendition of "Happy Birthday," he intoned, off the cuff, that "Dr. King let an unfinished symphony which we must finish. . . . We need a day to celebrate our work . . . a day for a dress rehearsal for our solidarity."

Getting it done was no easy task. While he no longer had Nixon to kick around, Ronald Reagan was, if anything, even less supportive of causes of this sort; he had actually campaigned to repeal the Voting Rights Act and his base was, let's say, hostile to men like King. But once more, music had filled the air over the Mall, alloying pop culture and a social correction. Something about that, as well as him standing up there making the case and not Jesse Jackson, was trenchant. In the *Washington Post*, columnist Herbert Denton astutely wrote, "It was Wonder, with his lyrical talk and song," who "seemed to better understand the yearnings" of the now younger socially involved set.

Having just turned thirty, and a fixture in the culture for two decades, Stevie had more than earned those props. Still, Reagan never offered an encouraging word for the holiday, and Stevie killed a Motown release of "Happy Birthday" (it did go out in Britain, where it hit No. 2 on the chart), saying it would only be appropriate when the holiday was a reality. The rally led to a petition drive that netted six million signatures, the largest such petition in U.S. history, and that turned the tide. In November 1983, the bill passed—Stevie was in the Senate gallery with Coretta King the day of the vote there—and was signed into law by Reagan days later. Stevie called the victory "not a cure-all but a healing aid," but his war wasn't over, in that South Carolina and Arizona refused to abide by the law, on states' rights grounds. Stevie called for an economic boycott of the two states, which actually did happen and had a small but helpful effect on latter-day governors there coming around a decade and a half later. That November, "Happy Birthday" was finally released, in limited quantities at Stevie's behest, as an historical stamp, remixed as a twelve-inch single with excerpts from some of King's speeches.

Time, however, could not bring him any closer to real love. While Yolanda had given him more than a decade of love and two children, she grew more convinced that he was returning little to her in the way of respect. For many of those years, she had lived under the double standard of "Stevie law," putting up with tales of his "polygamous" escapades with the other women whom, according to his liner-note confession on *Songs in the Key of Life*, he considered himself "married" to. But when he couldn't seem to get all that out of his system by his thirtieth birthday, she'd had it. When she became more distant, he knew the union was cracking, and as he did with "Superwoman," gave voice to his ambivalence (or hypocrisy, as the case may be) in song, the vehicle being "Lately," which contained not a word of contrition about his cheating but angst about having "the strangest feeling . . . of losing you" and her increasing distance—"Far more frequently you're wearing perfume / With you say no special place to go / But when I ask will you be coming back soon / You don't know, never know." Another line was that his eyes "always start to cry 'cause this time could mean goodbye." This habit of using songs for his side of the story, incidentally, struck some as inherently unfair, a prerogative exercised only because he *could*. Robert Christgau, for one, would retro-slam "Superwoman" in the mid-1980s as "calm, condescending cruelty" and "male chauvinism."

In 1982, the couple, facing the same crossroads as had Stevie and Syreeta, took the same path, agreeing to part as more than friends but less than eternal lovers. At least that's the noble, cosmopolitan spin he put on it.

Yolanda, who had been living with Aisha and Keita in a house Stevie owned in Alpine, New Jersey, remained there with them, sending them through school in relative anonymity. He would visit with the kids when she brought them periodically to the New York brownstone. By then, he had pulled from his harem of "polygamous" playmates a new main squeeze, Melody McCully, for whom he had an instant affinity since she, like Syreeta, was a songwriter. Seamlessly, she was now on his arm for select road trips and sojourns to L.A., where he now owned a studio, two homes, and, beginning in 1985, the soul music radio station KJLH, which he purchased from the owner of a funeral home and has since remained under his corporate purview, Taxi Productions. In 1984, Melody—who some in his circle would soon believe, as they had with Yolanda, was married to Stevie, and who began to identify herself as Melody McCully Morris—made him a father again, giving birth to a son, Mumtaz. And he was nowhere near done yet.

Through it all, and before he'd turned thirty, he eased deeper into the role of pop and soul elder statesman: a man capable of wicked ingenuity, but also coasting more and more on a commercial woolsack. As ever, it seemed to do his head good to retrench, shut his own work down for a while, and spread his artistic wealth by playing on sessions for the likes of B. B. King, James Taylor, Buddy Miles, and Smokey Robinson. The endless litany of artists recording his songs continued apace. Roberta Flack and Donny Hathaway cut two, "You Are My Heaven" and "You Are My Heart," on their joint album, and Dionne Warwick put his "With a Touch" on her *Friends in Love* album. Quincy Jones's *The Dude* album, on which Stevie also played, included Stevie's "Betcha Wouldn't Hurt Me," sung by Patti Austin, and Smokey's album *Warm Thoughts* carried Stevie's "Melody Man." Ironically, *without* Stevie's aid, Syreeta Wright scored her biggest hit. Having cut the cord in the late 1970s, she self-produced two previous albums, and finally her duet with Billy Preston, "With You I'm Born Again," from the mediocre 1979 movie *Fast Break* and also a track on the 1980 Wright-Preston album *Syreeta*, raced to No. 4 and went gold.

Stevie was more than keeping pace with the technological boom in music. In 1981 he spoke glowingly of the prototype of a contraption called the Emulator. With this floppy disk–based keyboard workstation he could sample all manner of sounds, each of which could be stored on a five-inch disk and played back as a musical note on the keyboard, or he could collect prerecorded libraries of sounds on disk. Hearing his testimonial, the Emulator's inventor sent him the first unit made for general use, with the serial number 001.

It was still rudimentary compared with the thicket of computerized processors, generators, disk memory, compression equipment, and other madness on the horizon, which would be a tech playground for him, but no one could say he wouldn't be ready each step of the way. He had also established a close relationship with Raymond Kurzweil, who in 1976 invented the first text-to-speech synthesizer, the Reading Machine, an invaluable tool for the blind, and to Stevie in particular as a composer. Kurzweil had since built the first electronic synthesizers that emulated orchestral instruments with amazing accuracy. A prototype, the Kurzweil K250, was manufactured for Stevie in the early 1980s with Braille buttons and sliders. Over time, he acquired five more.

Not that many music fans knew much of this technological nebula, which was a tribute to Stevie, in that nothing in his music seemed processed. And it could still move tons of vinyl tape, and compact discs. The latest proof of this—and the power he held over Gordy—was the second anthology released by Motown, the 1982 *Stevie Wonder's Original Musiquarium I*. This was the sequel to the 1977 *Looking Back* anthology, inflated into a double LP, the better to keep his contractual obligation to give Motown an album a year, but also because, having blown millions on his homes, studio, radio station, record label, and recording expenses, his accountants told him he was nearing bankruptcy. Thus when Gordy offered a bounty of $2 million, Stevie held out for $3 million, with the promise that he would add four new songs. Gordy went for it.

The album release, fulfilling the expiring contract, coincided with a new seven-year agreement, the monetary details of which were kept under wraps at Stevie's request, not eager to repeat the crush of attention paid to the last price tag and the outstretching of hands that came with it. "People thought I was walking around with $13 million in my pocket!" he complained. But neither did he care to have it known that he was taking less, around $10 million less, a number reflective of his slight ebb but sold to him more as a consequence of hard times during the Reagan Recession.

To his credit, Stevie did not cheat Gordy on the four new songs, which in fact made the album feel like a new work—a ploy further exploited by Stevie and Motown with the peculiar title, with no subtitled "anthology" or "greatest hits" anywhere on the sleeve—and enabled the release of new singles. One, "Do I Do," a ten-and-a-half-minute disco-ready wassail with a Dizzy Gillespie trumpet solo, found Stevie, as if in heat, half singing, half rapping prickly gabble about having "candy kisses for your lips" and " honeysuckle chocolate dripping kisses full of love for you"—and engaging in impromptu byplay with the band ("Nate! I know the record is about to end, but we're just going to play and play until it goes away!"). The track could wake the dead, and Motown readied it as the second single, cropped to three minutes. The first single, though, had been finished months before, "That Girl," a slow-dance funk turn that Motown was able to get out late in 1981, netting a No. 4 placing on the pop chart, No. 1 R&B.

The others were also winners. "Ribbon in the Sky" was a gorgeous piano-driven ballad. For the last, Stevie even squeezed in a message song, "Front Line," a melancholy plaint of an on-the-skids Vietnam vet (prefiguring by two years Springsteen's "Born in the U.S.A."), which cadged Stevie's line "They put a gun in my hand and said, 'Shoot until he's dead.'"

Motown was surely blessed—even through no effort of its own. It received a huge break when in late March, a month before the release of *Musiquarium*, Stevie's duet with Paul McCartney, "Ebony and Ivory," hit the market. One of two duets on the latter's *Tug of War* album recorded during a Stevie trip to the UK and billed as "Paul McCartney with Stevie Wonder," it killed, going number one on both sides of the pond, seven weeks in the States—by far the longest span Stevie had spent there, and for Paul second only to "Hey Jude's" nine-week run. It hurt little that the song, an excruciatingly lame melody and lamer metaphor of racial unity, was immediately heard as either one of the best or worst songs ever.

Musiquarium—the abstruse title itself a kind of sequel to the allegorical clinch of man and nature—took a fast track up the chart to No. 4 pop, No. 1 R&B, in midsummer. That, and the branch-off of "That Girl" and "Do I Do" (No. 13 pop, No. 2 R&B), gave Stevie a nice cushion. What's more, recording the new songs was not a chore but a breeze. Nate Watts recalled that at the "Do I Do" session at Wonderland, "Stevie was real comfortable with the whole band at that point, so we just went in and jammed and played what we wanted. He gave me more freedom on that song than on just about any other."

Four years later, when *Rolling Stone* again ran a profile of him, titled "The Timeless World of Wonder," he would say, with rare understatement, "I haven't gone to sleep yet."

Of Stevie Wonder, it could be said, simply but amply, that he was *there*, indelibly, even saintedly for some, just not with quite the same seismic effect. Something about him was more settled, and admirable for coming through battle as he had. With his 1970s conquests, he had fought—and won—the good fight for the inclusion of soul in mainstream pop, and was not required to make the same sort of mark in its aftermath, meaning the pressure was off and he could do that, if he chose. The complication was that these victories provoked music to splinter again, not out of mutual exclusion but a desire in the soul bastion to get "real" again; '70s romantic soul was repatented into retro R&B by boy bands who weren't born when Stevie Wonder was singing it at Motown. The funk-pop blacktop built largely by Stevie resurfaced in Quincy Jones's pumiced funk with Michael Jackson, and the funk-rock of Sly Stone was "taken higher" on grittier, more raw and open sexual turf by Prince.

Meanwhile, the synthesis revolution he led had become the new thing in white rock, most piquantly by the Brit techno-pop bands, but also now in the guitar-driven rock of bands like the Eagles and Van Halen—the synth of the latter's "Jump" perhaps the signal rock moment of the 1980s. In this shakeout, just as whites at first found no place in hip-hop and rap—white *artists*, that is, the rise of hip-hop and rap being almost entirely due to their enormous popularity among white suburban kids—blacks were turned off by punk and heavy metal evolutions of '70s rock, though there could be blissful convergence such as Run-DMC and Aerosmith.

For his part, Stevie would have no stomach to build another bridge between the two orbits; nor did he believe it was necessary. Rather, with so much going on in so many different and seemingly exclusive directions, he chose to keep his finger on the general pulse of music. Toward that end, in 1982 he opened his own label, independently, in no way associated with Motown, calling it Wondirection and signing for small amounts of money acts that moved him.

These included his own backup unit Wonderlove, blues legend Willie John's sons Kevin and Keith John, the obscure bands Grease and Boots Rising, and his old collaborator Gary Byrd's stab at being a rapper with a group called the G.B. Experience. One of the very few records he gave any time to was Byrd's "(You Wear) the Crown," a seminal rap song that demanded blacks register to vote for president, a year ahead of Reverend Jesse Jackson's quixotic White House quest. Stevie set it to a springy, cyclical melody, and put Syreeta and gospel legend Andrae Crouch in the chorus, and while it went nowhere—he released it as a twelve-inch disc, meant mainly for disco play—it was for him a memorable, if not abiding, dip in the rap pool.

He also teamed up, short-term, with the Bob Marley disciples Third World, whose 1979 cover of the O'Jays' "Now That We Found Love" was, he believed, a real stride in reggae's pop crossover, though some island purists found the band overly slick and commercialized—a critique Stevie himself would be hearing more and more. After he performed with them that year at the Sunsplash Festival in Jamaica, he wrote and produced two songs, "Try Jah Love" and "You're Playing Us Too Close" for their *You've Got the Power* album, which made the lower region of the R&B chart, a first for reggae.

His own work was done capriciously, in his own good time. *July* proved he hadn't lost his fastball, and he would not be cajoled or shamed into making more starts. The *Los Angeles Times* music writer Robert Hilburn reported that Stevie was "maintain[ing] something of a low profile"; to *Rolling Stone's* Jon Pareles, he was "laying low"—although it couldn't have been *that* low, since over this interlude he had played harmonica on Elton John's "I Guess That's Why They Call It the Blues," was a headliner on the *Motown 25* anniversary TV special, was inducted into the Songwriters Hall of Fame, attended the Grammy Awards, and guest-hosted the May 7, 1983, *Saturday Night Live*. On the last, he did an hilarious turn, channeling his hoary peeves into wicked barbs, aimed squarely at British rock critics (playing one, he sniffed, accent and all, "I hate R&B—it's just a noise!"), racist movie stereotypes, showbiz managers, TV commercials, and even himself, mocking his blindness by walking into walls and things, and playing "Little" Stevie Wonder clad in a little-boy suit, his voice altered as if by helium into an annoying screak.

Then there was a run of concerts at New York's Radio City Music Hall, at which he even made "Ebony and Ivory" palatable, singing it with a chorus of children. This was a new, mellow Stevie, the defensiveness of the disastrous *Plants* tour a memory. On this, the "You and Me" tour, he joshed and minced, self-mockingly announcing, "I've got some bad news for you—yesterday I quit the business." At some dates, he recruited the early hip-hop luminary Grandmaster Flash to play "DJ" and even rapped with him, as best he could. Most everywhere, he'd conduct a sing-along of "Happy Birthday." He made a triumphal return to Detroit, receiving the key to the city from the mayor and doing a sold-out, four-concert engagement for which promoters paid him a $1 million fee. One show was filmed for a special on the then nascent HBO, titled *Stevie Wonder Comes Home*.

He would contribute two songs to Eddie Murphy's debut album as an R&B singer, and played harmonica on Chaka Khan's hit cover of Prince's "I Feel for You." Even so, his lack of studio product did raise the thought that he may have run dry. A memo went around that Stevie was having a "crisis of confidence." At the Grammys, Quincy Jones, who with Michael Jackson swept the awards that night, Stevie-style, for *Thriller*, ran into him in the men's room and began to upbraid him for slacking off, even offering to produce Stevie's next album if that's what it would take to get him off the stick. Stevie was not moved. It took him four years to complete *In Square Circle*, which Motown, again to its embarrassment, promoted early, way too early, having to wait for it because Stevie got waylaid by Dionne Warwick. Warwick, who was coordinating the music for a new movie from MGM, *The Lady in Red*, a remake of the 1976 French romantic farce *Pardon Mon Affaire*, took Stevie to meet co-writer and director Gene Wilder, who asked him if he could perhaps contribute two songs for the flick. Stevie did, then another, and another, until he had eight. He would share vocals on two of them with Warwick, Warwick would sing one alone, and one more was an instrumental.

He took this work to Motown and a skeptical Gordy, who was adamant that he wanted *In Square Circle* and not a soundtrack, the very thought of which made him shudder—until Stevie played him "I Just Called to Say I Love You," a song for which he had written the melody seven years earlier, and only now quickly tacked on lyrics that paralleled the movie's plot of sexual fantasy gone awry in mistaken identity. Gordy's trained ears heard it as an instant hit, and as barter to foot the soundtrack, he had the new Motown president, Jay Lasker, get a commitment from Stevie that "I Just Called" would go out as a single. Backed with an instrumental version of the song, it was released on August 1, 1984, a full three weeks ahead of the soundtrack with a picture of him under the woman in red and a cover line reading "Music Produced by Stevie Wonder."

He had produced it as a sheer pop fluff ballad, within a sad but catchy soundscape etched by an understated synthesizer and Nate Watts's buoyant bass at the bottom and a tinkling piano at the top, with a somnolent Stevie reciting his orison of lost markers—"from New Year's Day to chocolate-covered candy hearts to the first of spring to a song to sing"—that could only be broken by that phone-call confession. It was certainly the kind of commercial contrivance Stevie had pardoned with "Ebony and Ivory," and upon initial listening, just as bad.

But Gordy was right. Racing up the charts and displacing Prince's "Let's Go Crazy" at the top of the pop and R&B lists in mid-October, "I Just Called" lingered there for three weeks and in the Top 40 for fifteen weeks, a phenomenal hit equaling the tenure of "Ebony." It went platinum several times in the United States, lugging the soundtrack to No. 4 pop, No. 1 R&B on the album charts, and to a platinum certification. It also begat early in 1985 one more Top 20 hit, "Love Light in Flight," and a twelve-inch disco-aimed single, "Don't Drive Drunk." In England, "I Just Called" *did* go crazy, selling more than any single there in 1984 except for "Do They Know It's Christmas," the one-off consciousness-raising about Ethiopian famine relief by Bob Geldof's potpourri of Brit rockers under the name of Band Aid, and to this day more than all but twelve records there. (It was also number one in Norway, Sweden, Australia, Switzerland, and France.) This amounted to a small fortune for Stevie, Motown, and MGM (even with the flick doing only moderate business), with "I Just Called" earning him an Academy Award for Best Original Song from a Motion Picture, as well as a Golden Globe, a BAFTA (the British Academy Award), and a Grammy nomination. He was also Grammy-nominated for Record of the Year, which went to the composers of Tina Turner's "What's Love Got to Do with It."

Blessed by this fortuitous and lucrative detour, *In Square Circle*, when finally ready to go in mid-September 1985, had a charmed life. And so did Stevie. For years he had scorned rock and rollers for "selling out" their most intimate possessions—their best songs—for outside commercial profit, but his principles, well, *bent*, when met by a surge of corporate demand post–"I Just Called." The first use of a Stevie Wonder tune in an ad campaign came in, of all places, Spain, where Chrysler licensed "Don't Drive Drunk" for a commercial (though in the song being "drunk" was a metaphor for addictive love). That seal broken, the corporate honoraria would become a deluge, one that he would not stanch.

Circle, which was presold gold, was not kept under wraps; over months of teasing, Stevie had previewed "Overjoyed" and "It's Wrong (Apartheid")," and dropped the titles of most of the others. The first single, "Part Time Lover," was put out in August. Chipped off from "I Just Called" (the first line went, "Call up, ring once, hang up the phone / To let me know you made it home"), it too was about an illicit romance, but a far better song with a harder, meaner, funkier beat and an enthusiastic vocal and scatting. By Halloween it would be sitting at No. 1 pop and R&B, and would became the first single to simultaneously top the pop, R&B, adult contemporary, and dance/disco charts (the last a twelve-inch disco version with a Luther Vandross vocal intro). The other nine tracks were trim, tightly formatted sectors of Stevie-hood, making far more sense than Stevie did in the liner notes explaining the work, writing that hearts recall "cycles of love"—thus the circle—whereas minds explore "the square root of the universe," with the songs being "the cosmic carrier."

Somehow, the songs survived, with no real explanation needed. There were the usual love confessionals, either frothy ("I Love You Too Much," "Whereabouts"), melancholy ("Stranger on the Shore of Love," "Never in Your Sun"), or belatedly revelatory (in "Overjoyed" he sings, "Over hearts I have painfully turned every stone / Just to find, I had found what I've searched to discover"). There was the mandatory, and by now ad nauseam, cloaked homage to Syreeta, "Go Home," wherein he muses, "She only wanted to give me the love she knew someday I'd need / But I kept saying girl you're wrong, go home." Another song, "Spiritual Walkers," was a dreamy paean either to Michael Jackson or the Jehovah's Witnesses, the door-to-door millenarian proselytizers with whom Jackson had cast his lot.

His two detours into de rigueur social commentary were "Apartheid"—a seven-minute jag of African tribal hammering with a warning to his nemeses in Cape Town—"The clock of now says it's time / For you to make up your mind" or else lose redemption—and "Land of La La," a bustling electronic music tableau with a derivative theme stripping away the facade of "Movie stars and great big cars and Perrier and fun all day" to its underbelly of "lost angels," which if it was intended as a West Coast "Living for the City" only suffered in comparison, with one critic strafing it as "soulless" and "minor."

In fact, there were ingredients absent from the bulk of the album that couldn't be defined, only that they weren't there. "Compare this to [previous works] in your head and you'll be hard-pressed to specify what's missing," wrote Robert Christgau, "but slap on *Talking Book* or *Hotter Than July* and you'll hear how cushy it is—polyrhythmic pop rather than polyrhythmic rock. Stevie's effervescence is so indomitable that it's a pleasure even so, but nothing rises far enough out of the stew." Jon Pareles concurred: "If you're the kind of person who likes to slap a good album into the cassette deck and forget it, stop reading here. Because much as I admire Wonder's skill, spirit and inexhaustible hooks, when I hum along with *In Square Circle* I feel a little like I've been had."

Assuredly, more than enough went into cassette decks for it to thrive, going to No. 4 pop and to the top of the R&B chart. It also won Stevie yet another Grammy, for Best Male R&B Vocal Performance. "Part Time Lover" was also nominated for Best Male Pop Vocal Performance, which went to Phil Collins for *No Jacket Required*. But such anointment was by now seemingly less about quality than, well, anointment. And no one was about to register any complaints about that.

Such was the world of Stevie, a steady admixture of music and causes, with no dearth of the latter—a typical example being his jam with Bob Dylan and Jackson Browne at a "Peace Sunday" antinuclear rally at the Rose Bowl in 1982. A more famous one came three years later, when he was a most conspicuous presence when the obligatory American edition of Band Aid and "Do They Know It's Christmas" came to fruition for the same cause of famine relief in Africa.

The groundwork for this storied fold of rock altruism was laid by Harry Belafonte, who lined up Lionel Richie and Michael Jackson to cowrite and Quincy Jones and Michael Omartian to coproduce the

anthemic, even narcotizing "We Are the World." Belafonte had queried
Stevie about writing and producing the project, but he was mired in
sessions for *In Square Circle*. Still, there was no way he'd miss the session
attended by everyone who was anyone (though Madonna and Prince
would beg off), and he helped nail down the participation of old
Motown cohorts like Smokey Robinson. After the project snowballed
into an enterprise that would be paid for by CBS Records and involve
forty-five artists, the song was cut at L.A.'s A&M Studios on January 28,
1985, under the name of USA for Africa (meaning United Support of
Artists for Africa). Stevie left his mark all over it and the ensuing video,
the grab of which were vocals that bled from one star to another, some
paired in a duet for the first and last time—Billy Joel and Tina Turner,
Willie Nelson and Dionne Warwick, Kenny Rogers and Paul Simon,
and Michael Jackson and Diana Ross. Stevie was given the second line,
following Richie's lead-in, Jackson the first solo rendition of the title
hook, Bruce the second, Stevie the third, in an extended, gritty duet with
Springsteen. Ray Charles, a giant chorus behind him, brought it home.

It was a hellacious undertaking. Over the seven and a half minutes
of the song, Jones had to find a key in a happy medium, but in early takes
it was too high for Springsteen, Nelson, and Bob Dylan, who stood silent
until a new take could be done. Waylon Jennings stormed out because
he hated the lyrics. A nervous Dylan, unused to singing in a collective
of peers, could barely hold the tune, until calmed by Stevie—who, as
he would recall, kept saying, "I have a lot of respect for you, man," both
kissing up to and challenging him to get it right. He also kept the mob
loose, joshing that if they didn't shape up, "Either me or Ray is gonna
drive everybody home." None of this was evident on the recording or the
video, in which Stevie, in the front row with Jackson, held hands with
Diana Ross while bouncing up and down. But Stevie was also rebuffed
when he wanted to add a line in Swahili, until Geldof, the only Brit
on the record, said that Ethiopians don't speak Swahili; even Michael
Jackson's support for keeping the line didn't save it. Stevie would participate in live performances of the song, at the Apollo Theater and,
in July, the Live Aid concert in Philadelphia. By then it was a runaway
freight train, going number one for four weeks and in most of the world,
winning four Grammys, selling seven and a half million copies in the
United States (an album with it sold another three million), and raising
$63 million.

With no moss growing under his high dudgeon, Stevie then tackled the AIDS epidemic in much the same way, in a kind of old-fart "We Are the World" lite. For this he was recruited again by Dionne Warwick, who also had nabbed Elton John and Gladys Knight to record a cover of the sentimental Burt Bacharach–Carole Bayer Sager pop cruller "That's What Friends Are For," originally recorded by Rod Stewart for the movie *Night Shift*. Cut in L.A., the single, credited to "Dionne & Friends," came out just as "Part Time Lover" was peaking, and itself went No. 1 pop and R&B early in 1986, spending four weeks at the top and becoming the top-selling song of that year and raising $3 million. It was charitable for Stevie, too; just as "We Are the World" stoked *In Square Circle*, "Friends" helped lift the middling song "Go Home" to No. 10 pop, No. 1 R&B. It also won him more hardware—for all of which he would have needed a warehouse to hold—a Grammy in 1987 for Best Pop Performance by a Duo or Group. (It also was nominated for Record of the Year, losing to Steve Winwood's "Higher Love.")

That, however, would be the last time a Stevie Wonder single made the pop Top 10.

Victory in the King holiday war notwithstanding, Stevie grew sensitive to criticism in activist circles that, blind or not, he was just not militant enough in his statements in and out of the studio, a rap no doubt influenced by how often he would fall back into a safe, comfortable, middle-of-the-road pop sensibility in his music. Stevie himself had touched on this, telling *Ebony* with remarkable candidness that he'd pondered whether his blindness had become a crutch of sorts, sparing him from what real pain and real activism looked like and redirecting his energies in a "safe" direction.

"I perhaps spend more time with music than I would if I had sight," he said. "If I did see, I'd maybe be more militant. Seeing so much which goes down, I'm sure I would be more affected; affected in ways which might not find expression in song."

Such guilt may have led him to the freeze frame on Valentine's Day 1985, when he joined a sit-in demonstration on the freezing asphalt outside the South African embassy in D.C., whereupon he was swept up in a police raid and arrested—though he would insist, "I wasn't disturbing the peace; I was singing." A memorable photo ran in the papers of a cop herding a grim-looking Stevie into a police car, hands cuffed in front of an enormous white fur coat. The picture was worth its symbolic weight. Though he never spent a minute in a jail cell, released with a warning from a clement judge, he had gained some serious altitude and gravitas. A month later, clutching his Oscar at the Dorothy Chandler Pavilion, he basked in a swell of hero worship and accepted the trophy "in the name of Nelson Mandela," with whom he claimed he could now better relate. Then in May he was honored at the UN's Special Committee Against Apartheid, saying in his speech that "the resettlement camps are wrong. If they're so great, why don't the whites live there?" before giving a performance of "It's Wrong (Apartheid)." He could be pleased that soon afterward he was banned from South Africa, a place he had no intention of going until apartheid collapsed under its grotesque weight, which is just what he did.

If Stevie had made a cottage industry out of grieving for the world and its evils, on a more personal level he also would find himself shuffling in a sad and endless procession to the funerals of his old Motown cohorts. He had already seen the passing of Benny Benjamin in 1969, Tammi Terrell in 1970, the Temptations' Paul Williams in 1973, Florence Ballard in 1976, and James Jamerson in 1983. In the 1990s they would be joined by David Ruffin, Eddie Kendricks, and Melvin Franklin. Minnie Riperton died in 1979 and John Lennon in 1980. And of course there was the one that hit Stevie the hardest.

Through the years he and Marvin Gaye had leaned on each other, sharing the wild, manic ride to success and innovation neither could have dreamed of, but also parallel depression and suicidal demons. If there was a virtue, and saving grace, to Stevie's dark moments, it was that he never succumbed to confusion and hopelessness and drugs as Gaye did. Because while he could be as helpless as Gaye, he could be salvaged by his music. Gaye, on the other hand was by the 1980s a lost soul, buried in cocaine-fueled paranoia and isolation and stalked by the IRS. He seemed to get his head together after he split from Motown and prospered with "Sexual Healing" and the *Midnight Love* album. He and Stevie spoke of recording a duet, and Stevie was composing a yearning love song, "Lighting Up the Candles" for the purpose—which contained the fatalistic verse "Destiny and fate decided / They would get in our way."

On April 1, 1984, a day before his forty-fifth birthday, Gaye picked the fight that his deranged, abusive father ended with a fatal shot to his son's chest. Informed by phone of the tragedy, Stevie thought it was an April Fools' prank. Assured otherwise, he cursed Gaye for letting his life get out of control. "I felt something was about to go wrong," he said later, "I just didn't know that it was going to be . . . a possible losing of someone." Four days later, Stevie delivered the eulogy at L.A.'s Forest Lawn Cemetery, saying Gaye had "encouraged me that the music I had in me I must feel free to let out." He then sang "Lighting Up the Candles," which he had completed only hours before. He also dedicated *In Square Circle* to Gaye, printing that ominous stanza from the song on the jacket.

Not long before, Stevie, falling into another depression, had convinced himself that *he* would be one of those in a casket being mourned. In 1980, he had sat for a Barbara Walters TV interview in which she read him a recent quote of his that went, "I used to feel that by 1980 . . . my life would no longer be." Stevie, not punting, responded that "I will not get completely into it, but I will say that there is a belief that I have . . . a feeling that I accept." Walters asked if he had thoughts of suicide.

"Never gonna take my life," he said.

"Then why do you think your life is going to be short?" she persisted.

"It's a feeling, okay?" he replied, a bit snippy. "And if feelings don't lie, then it's so."

Half a decade later, he was relieved that he'd been wrong; as far as he was concerned, his feelings of premature death *did* lie. He would not end up like Marvin Gaye after all.

16

Epilogue . . . Prologue

I'm not trying to compete with what's out there now. I'm really trying to compete with *Innervisions* and *Songs in the Key of Life*.

—Kanye West, 2005

Another victim of dissipation he witnessed heading for doom was Motown itself, at least the Motown he and the world knew.

Although the company turned its biggest ever profit in the early 1980s, Gordy knew this was an illusory spike with no lasting value. Without a stable of contemporary artists, its bottom line was precarious at best, even with the always reliable Stevie Wonder product. The next one would be a work Stevie delivered in 1987, with almost lightning rapidity for him, *Characters*, a clearly less profound work that folded Stevie into the heavy-footed, bass-driven techno-funk-pop of the 1980s and yielded a Top 20 hit in the dance-club favorite "Skeletons," as well as a blistering duet about unattainable love with Michael Jackson, "Get It."

In going for the "urban" market, Stevie—a bit sadly, in retrospect—narrowed his musical scope, permanently, as it turned out. However, its No. 17 pop charting early in 1988 (his worst showing in fifteen years) was an acceptable trade-off for a strong No. 1 R&B rank, paving its way to gold and, today, platinum status, and leaving him with a place in the evolving music shakeout. Still, a No. 4 R&B placing for "Get It" was hardly worth its No. 80 pop showing, which presaged that Jackson was not bulletproof and may have begun to lose altitude post-*Thriller.*

Characters' dependable profits, however, did little to stem Motown's economic slide, which could have been gleaned back in 1983 when the majesty of Motown drew a last breath with the *Motown 25* anniversary TV special. In 1986, wanting to stanch the bleeding, Gordy agreed to sell his Jobete Music publishing fortune. The only hitch was that because Stevie co-owned the publishing of his songs, Black Bull would need to sign off on any such deal. With fingers crossed, Gordy flew all the way to France, where Stevie was on tour, to ask his consent.

"Stevie," he told him, "I am in serious trouble and I'm thinking of selling Jobete."

Though Stevie's half interest in his songs wouldn't have been affected, he was incredulous. "Sell the publishing company!?" he said, looking highly offended. "How can you sell the publishing company?"

As Gordy recalled, the discussion "moved from banter to bickering" and then so bitter that he actually had the gall to stupidly say the company might be healthier "if I could have depended on you to deliver me albums when you were supposed to."

"Yeah," Stevie countered, not needing to draw a distinction with other Motown product, "but when I do give you albums, you know they're gonna be good!"

Not getting what he wanted, Gordy tried to make the sale without Stevie's songs as part of the package. The buyers demanded Gordy cut his price in half, which queered the deal. *"Thank God for Stevie,"* he wrote as a final note to the story in his memoirs. Indeed, by waiting he made out like, well, a bandit. In late 1988, he sold all of Motown to the entertainment conglomerate MCA and Boston Ventures for $61 million (he retained the movie production operation under a new name), explaining that had he not, the company would have been shuttered, leaving him to endure the slings and arrows of being, as he put it, "just another nigger who made it to the top and died broke." Instead, though industry insiders believed he'd sold short, he could brag that he'd gone from "eight hundred dollars to sixty-one million. I had done it. I had won the poker hand." Then, in 1993, he sold Jobete to EMI for $132 million.

Stevie did not begrudge him either time, the full extent of Motown's collapse having become known to him, to his horror. He knew the company could only survive with an infusion of fresh blood, from the top down. As for himself, having taken a liking to the late-1980s Motown figurehead presidents Jay Lasker and Jheryl Busby, and a decade later Sylvia Rhone,

Stevie would have no desire to jump ship, a decision presumably aided by his knowledge that he could not have gotten anything like the $3 million or so Motown was still prepared to shoot his way when his contracts came up every seven years.

Accordingly, the business of Stevie Wonder was kept booming.

His coterie had grown beyond a hundred people, still headed by Ira Tucker Jr., Calvin, Milton, his cousin Damien Smith, Ewart Abner, and Johanan Vigoda—who made out quite nicely, first owning a home and 198 acres in the Catskill Mountains before migrating to Palm Springs and focusing on running Black Bull Publishing (when he wasn't dealing with a "serious scrape with the IRS," according to Gil Markle, his friend and owner of Longview Farms). But there was a swarm of others, too, on the payroll in some function or other, including the shifting personnel of Wonderlove; Gary Olazabal; personal assistant Birdis Coleman; chief technician and keeper of his $3 million synthesizer collection Mick Parish; sound technician Aquil Fudge; secretary Chrysanthemum James; and business assistants Brian LaRoda and Chris Jonz. At a rock awards show hosted by TV rock concert impresario Don Kirshner, Stevie came in with so many people that Kirshner says he had to take some very important industry people out of their seats to accommodate Stevie and his crew. (Ewart Abner, who had returned to Motown until it was sold, would then run the Motown Historical Museum until he died in 1997.)

However, being Stevie, and being *seen* as Stevie, seemed to leave scant room for actual recording. The 1980s ran out with no new product. Starting with his 1989 contract, he was no longer held to the album a year requirement that he'd never met, a barometer of his ebbing impact and the slackening thirst for Stevie albums, but also a recognition of his patriarchal status that rendered his past work at least as emblematic—and marketable—as anything current. Indeed, by now the veneration of Stevie Wonder was in full gear. In 1989 came his compulsory induction into the Rock and Roll Hall of Fame (he had been, insanely, passed over the year before in his first year of eligibility) along with the Temptations, the Rolling Stones, Otis Redding, Phil Spector, Dion, Bessie Smith, and the Soul Stirrers, and at thirty-eight he was the youngest ever to go in (Michael Jackson would also be thirty-eight when he was inducted). Presented by Paul Simon, he mounted the stage in a molto cool black leather suit, two gold necklaces swinging from his neck, his eyes uncovered by sunglasses, accompanied by his son Keita and daughter Aisha. Seven years later, he would be given a Lifetime Grammy Achievement Award.

For a while, comically to everyone but Stevie, stories periodically appeared in the papers that he was seriously considering running for mayor of Detroit, which would have required a move even more note-worthy than going to Africa—moving back to Detroit. "I feel that God has an even bigger plan for me," he said. "I would like to think of myself as a unity mayor." But, typically, he never followed through, the idea lost among many others in a shuffle of here-today, gone-tomorrow thoughts. There was, however, little talk of impending music projects. Though he had begun, at his usual halting tempo, laboring on his next album, a run-on "statement" given the working title *Conversation Pieces*, he detoured from it when early in 1991 another soundtrack project came along. It was for the latest Afrocentric movie by director Spike Lee, *Jungle Fever*, star-ring the on-the-rise black actors Wesley Snipes and Samuel L. Jackson.

Because the plot—exposing the raw nerve of interracial love—was compatible with what Stevie wanted to be his return to more pointed content, he took the job, with the surprising twist that the eleven songs he put on the soundtrack were ironically less overtly "urban" than *Characters*. The aural lingua of deep-seated funk was embedded on track one, "Fun Day," by hip-hop "African" percussion, and there was a tentative Stevie rap on another called "Each Other's Throat." But in the main it was cool, retro pop-soul, with some dewy love songs like "These Three Words" and "Make Sure You're Sure" keenly tracing the movie's blurring of hard ethnic outlines. The title track and "Gotta Have You" were pure good-time Stevie chanties, with Nate Watts's super-amped bass all but chewing up the scenery. And it was, he decided, an apt venue for "Lighting Up the Candles," the song intended for Marvin Gaye.

Jungle Fever **also** returned Stevie to Malcolm Cecil, whom he called in on a one-shot basis to help recreate the '70s synthesizer textures he had not been able to get quite right since Cecil split, such as the synth "talk box" effect he now reprised with "Chemical Love." For the engi-neer, there was no misapprehension. "It wasn't a 'reunion,' it was a job," he says. "Oh, it was pleasant. We have a great deal of love and respect for each other. But nothing had really changed with Stevie. I was the only white guy in the entire place with the exception of Mick Parish, who was like his roadie. And it took three weeks just to sort through the equipment that was all junked up in his studio. Stuff was on shelves untouched, too high for anyone to reach. It was comical, pathetic. Stevie wanted me to continue on some projects after that, but it never worked, it wasn't real. Stevie wasn't going to put anything behind it, so I drifted away again."

For Motown, which was eager to hop on the Spike Lee bandwagon, *Jungle Fever* was largely a disaster, as it was for pretty much everyone except Samuel Jackson, who won best supporting actor awards in Cannes and from the New York Film Critics Circle. The movie, released in early June, tanked at the box office, dragging the soundtrack down with it, with many never aware that Stevie had composed its music. While the three singles released from it (a fourth was canceled) made Top 10 R&B, only one, "Gotta Have You" got as *high* as No. 92—though that did not keep it from being Grammy-nominated for Best R&B Vocal and Best Song Written for a Motion Picture, which went respectively to Luther Vandross and Bryan Adams.

Now the wait began again for the album he had put aside. Again, weeks turned into months into years, with no new work but plenty of appearances, such as the Bob Dylan 30th Anniversary Concert Celebration, at which Stevie sang "Blowin' in the Wind"; a Top 20 R&B duet with Whitney Houston, "We Didn't Know"; and joining in Quincy Jones's album *Handel's Messiah: A Soulful Celebration.* He made a trip to Ghana to perform at Accra's National Theater.

Finally, early in 1995, after a *four-year* wait, his impending album— now retitled *Conversation Peace* (the original title was co-opted by jazz guitarist John Pisano in 1994)—was good to go. Motown had to hold its breath, worrying if Stevie still had it. The answer was: yes and no. As Stevie's twenty-seventh studio album, excluding anthologies and movie scores, it worthily lengthened the chain of his life's work. Indeed, to Stevie it was nearly canonical, and the acknowledgments in the liner notes, some three hundred strong, made the mob on *Key of Life* seem like a tea party, naming not just everyone in his employ (but not Ira Tucker Jr., who may have finally fallen out of his favor) but seemingly everyone in the business (but not Berry Gordy), the nation of Ghana, Senegalese president Abdou Diouf, and not Melody McCully but "the

Loves of My Life." There was, too, a typical Stevie epigram with both fatalistic or beatific leanings: "Standing on the Edge of Eternity can be good or bad, either of which is determined by the road that we choose in our love-taking or love-making. There needn't be a Taboo to Love, if you truly take the time out with your heart, to Love."

The content was more intimate. He chucked the big band and played all the instruments on most tracks himself, save for Nate Watts, to heighten what were intensely personal feelings. It was, in fact, a kind of *What's Going On* redux, at times nearly as aggrieved and hopeless as the Marvin Gaye exemplar. The title track cursed man's atavistic habits—"Staring right at 2000 AD / As if mankind's atrocities to man has no history," and for good measure had Holocaust and slavery references. In "Rain Your Love Down," synthesized thunder seems to answer his demands for divine intervention to "rid this world of drugs, disease, crime, and pain." The harrowing "My Love Is With You" is a gang obloquy, recreating in excruciatingly painful aural and lyrical imagery the street murder of a young couple he knew, though in truth, lines about "my life they've taken" and a call to "Spread the love I've given / I'll be there" seemed to reflect his fixations with his own death.

Stevie being Stevie, of course, the universal anecdote to life woebegone was love endless and divine—the *real* thematic glue of the album—and the pandemic salve of his music. He had earned his chits with some major contemporary acts, and here he called them in. "Tomorrow Robins Will Sing," an island turn, features a reggae "rap" by Edley Shine; "Take the Time Out" unleashes African rhythms with a chant by Ladysmith Black Mambazo; "Sensuous Whisper" is pure, if synthesized, jazz with a backing vocal by Anita Baker. Of course, there was the Stevie calling card of feel-good pop, such as on "Edge of Eternity," "I'm New," "Treat Myself," and "For Your Love." Nothing felt as good, however, or reeked less of self-importance than "Cold Chill," the ultimate rejection song—and dance groove—in which, feeling "hot to trot and about to pop tryin' to find some girl to get into," he gets only a drink in his face—a "cold chill on a summer night," leaving him to mutter like a schlemiel, "Baby, that ain't so nice."

With the failure of his *Jungle Fever* retro soft-soul, he went back in through the "urban" door, multiple-tracking sparse hip-hop rhythms preprogrammed on digital synthesizers and on his newest toy, the digital drum machine, which was originally as reviled as the original synthesizer but intrinsic to the new order of electronic pop. The only "real deal" was Watts's thick bass and some guitar leads. For all this, he went with a different studio alchemy, using two new associate producers, Derrick Perkins and Vaughn Halyard—Watts was also listed as such—and enlisted Bob Margouleff to mix two tracks. This being the first Stevie album released primarily on CD, he refused to crop a single one of the thirteen tracks, which ran seventy-eight minutes; none were under four minutes, and the title track and "Cold Chill" nearly seven.

For all that, *Conversation Peace* mustered the usual twinkly notices, Top 20 status—No. 16 pop, No. 2 R&B in early summer—and Grammy. At the least it further cemented him into a contemporary niche almost independent of his own legacy; indeed, for a younger audience it made him a still relevant artist. On balance, that was plenty good enough. He could still bring down—and even sell out—a house, and play new stuff for a niche or even esoteric crowd, which was more than the creaky Stones or even Springsteen could do.

For Stevie, this outreach, and sharpening a niche idiom, was a wise move. He knew better than anyone that the once reliable Stevie Wonder formula was not quite reliable now. Proof came in a double-CD live album, *Natural Wonder*, recorded on tour in Japan and Israel and released in November 1995 with fanfare, as it was the only live set to see light, post the 1970 *Stevie Wonder Live*. Yet it was shut out on the pop chart and paid only a brief visit to the R&B, at No. 88. A year later, a two-CD anthology, *Song Review: Greatest Hits*, the third such argosy of his oeuvre, was released and bombed worse, its lone charting at No. 100 R&B.

Nonetheless, he could still nab Grammys without really trying. Even a semi-flop of a single, "For Your Love," won Best R&B Vocal and Best R&B Song—on the same night he got his Lifetime Achievement Award.

Of course, his classic work could always be heard in the grooves of those who *could* dominate. His music had already been sampled to death when Coolio darkened and charred "Pastime Paradise" to synch it to the ghettoscape Stevie had painted in "Village Ghetto Land" (which itself was sampled by rapper Warren G as "Ghetto Village"), making the resulting song, "Gangsta's Paradise," the top song of 1995 and the *Dangerous Minds* soundtrack number one for four weeks, and winning the Best Rap Grammy. He hadn't taken a pass on controversy, either. Three years later, he cowrote with and did backing vocals for Babyface's "How Come, How Long," again having at spousal abuse in the aftermath of the O. J. Simpson murder case, blasting "the way he proves himself a man by beatin' his woman with his hands." Judged "too hot" for radio play, it still copped a Grammy nomination for Best Pop Collaboration and its video an MTV Video Music Award.

He did indeed seem to be everywhere, and everything. In 1999, Will Smith sampled "I Wish" for his number one single "Wild Wild West," and George Michael and Mary J. Blige covered "As." And Stevie's contribution to Herbie Hancock's *Gershwin's World* album—a sassy jazz take on W. C. Handy's "St. Louis Blues," with the slickest harmonica licks he'd ever laid down and a vocal nuanced between happy and sad as he sounded the old refrain about that evenin' sun goin' down—earned him another Grammy, for Best R&B Vocal. By decade's end, the mother of all Stevie Wonder anthologies, the four-CD, seventy-two-track *At the Close of a Century* box set, had been released. Though it only climbed to No. 100 on the R&B album chart, it was still certified gold, no mean feat for an expensive piece of goods. One could have literally looked up on any given day and noticed Stevie. He might have been delivering the presentation speech for the induction of the late Little Willie John into the Rock and Roll Hall of Fame, or an invited guest of President Bill Clinton at a White House reception for British prime minister Tony Blair, or a VIP applauding Al Gore in the gallery of the Democratic convention, or at an award show accepting yet one more honor for himself.

By contrast, he still seemed not to be able to manage his personal life with any degree of consistency. In 1990, Melody delivered his second daughter, Sophia Morris. But it wasn't enough to save the relationship, and a year later they were done. As with Yolanda and his first two children, he gave Melody the house they'd shared in the L.A. suburb of Palmdale. There, his son Mumtaz progressed through school with no one knowing who his father was. Then in June 2001, Stevie came to Highland High School on graduation day, where he sang "Stay Gold," a song he wrote for Francis Ford Coppola's 1983 movie *The Outsiders*. Later, during a speech to the graduating class, he recited a line from the song that assured, "One breath away and there you will be / So young and carefree again you will see."

Those were words he might well have applied to himself. He was in a new millennium now, in his fifties, already having come through vinyl, eight-track, cassettes, Walkmans, CDs, rock videos, and mp3s— yet deliberating on beginning anew, within the broad context of past glories but in new, sharp tints. He said to *Billboard* in 2004, "The '70s was my first chance at total expression; being able to do things the way I felt. But I am as excited now as I was at the beginning. . . . For me to say I've reached my peak is to say that God is through using me for what he has given me the opportunity to do. And I just don't believe that."

Such rebirth entailed a rethinking of his "polygamous" comfort zone. Following the split with Melody—whom he used as a background singer on *Conversation Peace*—he had seemingly reveled in no-guilt shagging, practicing (not that he needed any) the same empty routine he had followed forever. "I just can't figure it out," Maureen Orth had quoted an incredulous aide back in 1974. "There'll be ten women in his dressing room and he picks out the foxiest one every time." Explaining how *that* technology worked, Stevie said, "I can usually tell about a woman by her conversation, her voice and the way she carries herself. Some women can have a very beautiful outer face and a very ugly inner face."

For a good decade, he seemed not to care about capping that horn of plenty; he even found reason to make clear in the *Characters* liner notes that "there's nothing I won't share with my children or their mothers. But I am not engaged and have no plans to marry." That dictum didn't change when in 1996 he had moved in with another makeshift "wife," his wardrobe assistant Angela McAfee. Four years later he moved out, after he fell madly for a younger, higher-cheekboned replacement, fashion designer Karen Millard, who went under the professional name of Kai Milla and had a young son named Miles from a previous marriage.

Now he decided the time was right to take the giant step—or so it was for him—of committing himself again to marriage; they tied the knot early in 2001. Stevie adopted Miles, and in September, just days before the terrorist attacks on the World Trade Center, Kai gave birth to a daughter, Kailand Morris. Not long after, he bankrolled her designer fashion line, which they pitched during a visit to *The Oprah Winfrey Show*.

Such tranquillity would be a well-needed bulwark, and often. Because now people were coming out of the woodwork to make him crazy. Miraculously, given his success, he'd been sued only once, in 1985, when of all people Lee Garrett—whom he had only talked out of pulling the trigger of the gun he held in his mouth—filed suit alleging that he had actually cowritten "I Just Called to Say I Love You" and deserved a piece of its royalties. As Stevie related, "It was said that I'd stolen the song. That wasn't the case at all. I used to play the beginning of [the song] at different birthday parties. The reality was we had that history, plus proof through tapes and other things." Still he said, "That experience was a deep one. It was my first time going to court. And it was an amazing pain to go through. . . . But God got me up and out of that."

Now, in October 2001, just weeks after 9/11—Stevie was part of the massive celebrity memorial at Madison Square Garden, leading an emotionally charged rendition of "America the Beautiful" as the finale—and days after the birth of Kailand Morris, Angela McAfee lodged a palimony lawsuit in Los Angeles Superior Court, which led to the inevitable headline "Stevie Sued by Part Time Lover."

McAfee insisted she was more than that, explaining that, as Stevie had sweet-talked her, "God had told him Angela was his wife." She claimed they had an oral agreement that he would be the sole source of income and that she would be a homemaker, and that if they broke up he would pay for her clothing, household needs, medical, twenty-four-hour security service, and any other expenses. She also said she helped him deal with "medical, personal and family problems," that she redesigned his home with Braille inscriptions, and put him on a strict diet and exercise regiment to help him control high cholesterol, high blood pressure, and mounting weight problems. The haymaker was that he had infected her with herpes, knowingly, without ever telling her he had the disease.

Wonder's attorney, Laura Wasser, saying there was no contract, oral or written, countersued, alleging McAfee had stolen $160,000 worth of his property, though she seemed most concerned with rebutting the headline-stealing claim. "Since he does not have herpes, one can only wonder where she contracted the disease," she said, hitting below the belt. When neither side impressed the judge, who ordered them to settle out of court, Stevie paid an undisclosed amount.

Things could have gotten even ickier when he soon got word that a former Wonderlove singer who apparently had shared a few intimate times was going to write a "tell-all" book about the "real" Stevie, which would be replete with salacious revelations. It's not clear whether

Stevie moved in, perhaps with pleas, sweet talk, or an offer that could not be refused, but according to a media insider the singer had "second thoughts." The book never happened, and nothing would disturb the tranquility of his swelling family life. On May 13—his fifty-fifth birthday—Kai gave birth to Mandla Kadjaly Carl Steveland Morris, "Mandla" being Zulu for "powerful" and "defiant," "Kadjay" Swahili for "born from God," the names coming at the suggestion of Nelson Mandela.

Mourning, however, had become all too common. That same difficult year of 2004, both Syreeta Wright and his brother Larry Hardaway were diagnosed with terminal cancer, prompting him to write a song called "Shelter in the Rain," in which he vowed, "When the final candle's flickered out . . . I'll be your comfort through your pain." By the time it was done, Larry was gone, and Stevie could only sing it to a comatose Syreeta as she lay dying in a hospital bed, heaving and with tears streaming down his face. Only days later, on July 6, she too was gone. Her death was beyond painful; it was the loss of a part of him that had never been salvaged—the part of him that loved a woman, *really* loved, in his soul as well as his loins.

That scar had not healed when, two years later, on May 31, 2006, the *other* woman he loved unconditionally, the one who gave him life and the soul of Hurtsboro, breathed her last. Beset with respiratory ailments and hypertension in recent years, Lula Mae Judkins Hardaway—who had lived to see twenty grand- and great-grandchildren—began to complain of pain in her leg, which became so bad she was taken to the hospital. There they diagnosed her with a blood clot and within a day she went under the knife. As hardy a woman as she always was, however, her heart gave out during the operation and the doctors were unable to resuscitate her. She died on the table, unconscious, without being able to see her Stevie one last time. By the time he got there, she was gone. That, as much as her death itself, devastated him. Not long before, when she took sick, Stevie, during a *Tonight Show* appearance, said to Jay Leno, "Mama, I'm not ready to lose you yet!"

Now he had. He could cope with the loss by reaching for the balm of banality, saying things like, "Sorrow is a reality of being alive," and "I want to take all the pain that I feel and celebrate and turn it around." Yet for all of his children and his legion of friends and fans, and all of his loyal adjutants, as he sat sobbing during the funeral at the West Angeles Church of God, he knew that without Lula Mae he was all alone now.

If there was anything that could brook such deep wounds, if only for a while, it was being able to reprise the role of Stevie Wonder, genius and national treasure. No invitation seemed out of the question.

For Nate Watts, who still is on the payroll after three decades, each gig was a hurdle for the band. "When he did a Super Bowl pregame show [in 2006], Steve tried a tune we hadn't done in over twenty years," Watts recalled. "He said, 'Nate, remember this?'—and it was an unreleased song! We in the band went, 'Huh?' 'Cause Stevie never prepares a set list for gigs like that, he just wants to fly it. He'll pull out an Ellington or Coltrane cover, whatever he feels like doing.

"I figure I know around eighty to one hundred songs, but Stevie has in his head *thousands* of songs. He doesn't know how tough it is for us to come right in, but he expects us to, so we do. I can do that because I know him so well; I know his musical patterns, so I know where he's going before he goes there. But sometimes, I'll be totally out of it. I do the best I can to keep up, but it's like, Stevie, bro, you're on your own!"

As for his procession making the rounds of cheesy but high-rated TV shows such as *American Idol* or *Dancing with the Stars*, he wasn't the only legend taking a few dollars for a few minutes in the public spotlight; Smokey and the Tempts were doing it, too. None of them needed the bread. But all of them, even Stevie Wonder, needed the attention.

It was no longer a major event when he came out with an album. By 2005, it had been a decade since the last one, and none was breathlessly being awaited, such was his ongoing role buttressing other artists—and simply standing at the podium at the Grammys, which he had done so much he could have built a condo there. In 2003, his performance on the post-9/11 *America: Tribute to the Heroes* album, "Love's in Need of Love Today," with Take 6, won for Best R&B Vocal, and he was nominated for Best Pop Collaboration for "The Christmas Song," a duet with India.Arie. That year, Motown, in lieu of new product, cranked out *another* anthology, the twenty-one-track *Stevie Wonder: The Definitive*

Collection, which rose to No. 35 pop, No. 28 R&B, and went platinum. And, in lieu of Stevie, Motown did the next best thing, releasing a volume of Stevie songs sung by others, *Conception: An Interpretation of Stevie Wonder's Songs*, among the selections of which were "Higher Ground" by Eric Clapton, "Overjoyed" by Mary J. Blige, "All In Love Is Fair" by Marc Anthony, "Send One Your Love" by Brian McKnight, and "I Don't Know Why I Love You" by John Mellencamp. In these grooves was the proof that his music was pandemic, capable of being molded and interpreted to any musical idiom, without a stretch—six years later, at his Gershwin Prize ceremony at the White House, it would be even more so, easily adapted to classical, opera, and country forms.

Dropped into the middle of this Stevie casserole was his latest album to date, *A Time to Love*, which rolled out, first with hip gimmickry on September 27, 2005, exclusively on Apple's iTunes music store, and in general on October 18, though it seemed not necessarily final, only that he decided it was time. Only a few months before, he had listed on his Web site fourteen tracks from the work, of which a mere six he stuck with. Many of those that made it on were collaborations—Paul McCartney and India.Arie on the title track (cowritten with the latter); Prince on guitar and En Vogue on backing vocals on "So What's the Fuss"; flutist Hubert Laws on "My Love Is on Fire"; Kim Burrell on lead vocal on "If Your Love Cannot Be Moved." Two were reserved for his daughter Aisha to sing lead, as an aid to her singing career, "How Will I Know" and "Positivity."

Thematically, it was love songs, nothing but love songs—welcomely and intentionally so, a small blow for the noble cause of restoring man's vulnerability that had been weeded out of soul music by the macho snark of hip-hop and rap. Save for the raucously funky "Fuss," sonically it was uniformly lush, middle-of-the-road pop-soul peppered with light synth-funk, with the second half, the last five cuts, lovesick ballads. As on *Conversation Peace*, nifty, tautly melodic orchestral effects were concocted from his now common digital sampling equipment, reluctantly but necessarily in an era when large-scale recording sessions were passé and far too expensive. Naturally, he had helped usher in this new digital revolution, back when it was daring. Now he was merely going with the flow, content to be a part of it as long as he could maintain a modicum of independence, which he could exercise through his gift of melody.

A *Time to Love* was one of the year's pleasant surprises, rising to No. 5 on the pop chart, No. 2 on the R&B, in becoming his twelfth album to at least go gold, though its four singles didn't do much. And in its wake he was, of course, overflowing with prospective projects, most of which he would likely never get around to. He had told *Billboard* after winning the trade paper's 2004 Century Award that he wanted to do a harmonica-based jazz album with Herbie Hancock and Toots Thielemans, a gospel album, a musical, a book, and a film. "Maybe I wouldn't limit it to one film. There are some things that could be talked about in the first part of my life. It would be very inspirational in the things that I went through growing up as a little boy being blind and the things my mother had to contend with plus my brothers and sister in the days before Little Stevie Wonder and Stevie Wonder. Then maybe there would be another film about the second half of my life. We're still telling that story now."

John Glover laughs, having heard it all before. "He's been saying stuff like that and he's always dead serious about it—when he says it. But he usually gets distracted and goes on to something completely different and forgets about them. With Stevie, it's not about the plan, it's about the challenge. When he needs to prove he can do something, that's when it gets done. For a long time he won't feel that, and he'll be out of the loop. People will push him, but that won't get him moving. Then suddenly he gets it in his head that he had to, you know, build the better mousetrap and, bang, there it is."

A *Time to Love* yielded five more Grammy nominations, for Best Pop Vocal ("From the Bottom of My Heart"), Pop Collaboration ("A Time to Love" with India.Arie), R&B Vocal ("So What's the Fuss"), R&B Vocal by a Duo or Group ("How Will I Know" with Aisha), and Album of the Year, winning the first two. He also was nominated for a duet he had done with Beyoncé Knowles, "So Amazing." The following year, he reeled in Grammy number twenty-one, Best Pop Collaboration, for a duet with Tony Bennett on a slowed-down, violin-coated version of "For Once in My Life," from the latter's *Duets: An American Classic* album.

Stevie was in Milwaukee for a concert at the Summerfest 2009 when he answered another of those dastardly calls. This time it was that

Michael Jackson had died at age fifty of cardiac arrest under mysterious circumstances in L.A.

His relationship with Jackson was in many ways similar to the one he had with Marvin Gaye. He had been in the middle of those two in age, and felt he understood both of them as well as anyone possibly could. While he didn't need to communicate with them on a daily basis, there was a kinship because of their self-torturing impulses, and that created complicated emotional ties that ran between love and scolding. Stevie had always regarded the troubled Michael as a kind of analog of himself, both of course having been annexed by Motown and made into very similar creations of and their childhood lives defined by—and limited in many ways—Berry Gordy and his queer "family" expositions.

Still, Stevie worried terribly about Jackson, at once trying to deny his "madness" and the anecdotal evidence of pederasty and defend his behavior as part of the same search for identity as his music.

As Quincy Jones had done with him, on the scattered occasions Stevie spoke with Jackson about *his* periodic ennui in the 1990s, he repeatedly attempted to kick his ass into gear by junking the leeches all around him, ceasing putting in his body all the shit he was clearly taking, and getting into the studio—ironic advice, to be sure, coming from him. As Jones supposedly had too, he airily spoke of the projects they should be doing together. They'd done songs and videos that had not been released to the public; now they agreed that they would put them out. But Stevie had about Michael the same unfocused but foreboding premonitions of death that he'd felt about Marvin Gaye.

When he agreed to write a short requiem about Jackson's death for *Time*, he chose his words carefully, shading the madness into heroic individuality. "At the end of the day," he said, "we're all human beings, and for those who can't see that it is possible for a man who's an adult to have a childlike spirit, it doesn't mean that they're weird, it doesn't mean they're a freak, or whatever ridiculous things that people say. We have all kinds of people in the world. The most important thing is that your heart is in a good place."

His performance at the memorial service at the Staples Center on July 7 was unforgettably heartfelt and unforgettably sad. Clad in black from neck to toe, seated at his piano stool only feet from the casket, he said quietly, tersely, affectingly for anyone who knew of his own neuroses about early death, "This is a moment I wish I didn't live to see come.

I do know God is good, and as much as we would want him, God must have wanted him far more. I'm at peace with that." With that, he began to play and sing the heartbreakingly congruous "Never Dreamed You'd Leave in Summer" and "They Won't Go When I Go," both, says Malcolm Cecil, "in perfect voice, a beautiful performance. I thought he'd lost it, but he hasn't. Stevie can still make you cry at moments like that."

Motown blood surely ran thick. But even he knew that Michael had been too tortured to ever be redeemed, and that when Stevie sang in "Spiritual Walkers," "They have no defense / Except inner sense," he was wrong. Stevie had a good bit of that. But Michael did not.

He could be relieved he was not as troubled as Michael, that something pulled him back from the brink. Referring to the messy revelations that emerged from Marvin Gaye's confidants after Marvin's death, he joked, "When I die, I'm gonna have my people gagged!" Of course, he need not go that far given the extreme loyalty of his own inner crowd, most whom have been with him for two or three decades. Nathan Watts, for example, not only still is on call at a hefty salary to lay down a bass line when Stevie needs it, but by default has found himself acting as a kind of shield for him. But for Watts the job was something like being a night watchman at the funhouse.

"Stevie lives in Oz now," says Mike Sembello. "He's like the boy in the bubble. Nate's the only one around him with clarity, but even Nate doesn't know how to get him. He'll say, 'Uh, Stevie's not available right now.' Then a month later Stevie will call at 4 a.m. And I'll be pissed at him. I'll tell him, 'Hey, man, you don't love me anymore.' He'll go, 'No, no. I just found out you called.' It's fucking ridiculous. He's in some kind of other dimension. He definitely needs some air."

Malcolm Cecil, the last time he tried a year ago, had better luck getting through. "I had the magic number," he grins, "the old 'inside' number from when we did *Jungle Fever.* It was also the same message from then, which when you hear it you know Stevie's screening the call. I started saying, 'Stevie Hardaway Judkins . . .' and he knew my voice and picked up.

"The reason I called was that somebody told me they heard that Stevie's production Grammy for *Innervisions* was up for auction in L.A. I thought, 'Wow, Stevie must be real short of money to put his Grammy up. That's not like Stevie.' So I had to call and tell him about it, and he said, 'Ah, man, it was stolen.' He went through this tale of there being a fire at the Bekins facility where he stored all his memorabilia, and after the fire was out everything was strewn all over and somebody pilfered the Grammy and a bunch of paper, tapes, whatever. I asked if he wanted me to call the auction house and tell them it was stolen, and he did. I then made all these calls and got the cops involved, but the auction house produced a sheaf of papers that it was legal. Long story short: the Grammy sold for $40,000. You know who bought it? Stevie did."

The deeper meaning of that story to Cecil was not that it could have happened to anyone, but that it could have only happened to Stevie, given the state of disarray all around him.

"His business is pretty much run by a lady called Stephanie," he says, meaning Stephanie Andrews, who has cowritten a number of songs with Stevie, including "If Ever" and "Treat Myself." "Her office is basically the control room [at Wonderland], with the business done out of an old Record Plant truck parked in the back. This is how crazy the organization is—a multimillion-dollar recording act being run like a tattoo parlor on Sunset Boulevard."

Times had changed, and he had helped change them. Once, the Motortown Revue bus was fired upon in the Deep South. Once, he sang songs of great moral indignation about Richard Nixon, stood on the White House lawn with him in frozen loathing; he'd pulled an end run around Reagan; he was busted by cops at the South African embassy, then lived to see apartheid crumble and Nelson Mandela become president. Now, 150 million record sales later, Steveland Judkins Morris was a confidant of a president named Obama and an overnight guest in the Lincoln Bedroom. He'd earned his way there, of course. But he was still *Stevie*, not Mr. Wonder. A superstar who you can imagine being in your living room. A man in whom can always be found a vein. His helplessness, the lack of semblance and rich man's adornment around him, it all fits. Fits *him*.

He was, surely, a survivor, and the sole caretaker of the black Camelot that was Motown, which in its latter generation was just a brick in a corporate wall, and Stevie about the only one there with a modicum of loyalty and a long sense of its history. MCA was said to treat Motown "like a Third World country," and it would be handed off like a corporate football over the coming decades, from MCA to PolyGram to Seagrams to its current berth in the Universal Music Group.

Hitting sixty, he was in many ways still the twelve-year-old "Fingertips" kid, but much more patient. Motown, having long ago learned the consequences of prepublicizing albums he swore were "almost ready," let them drip out, the last to date being the March 2009 release of his first ever live DVD, *Live at Last*, including twenty-seven songs as performed over several concerts at London's O$_2$ Arena. Stevie, dropping more hints—or blowing hot air—about other would-be projects, mentioned, oh, another Tony Bennett duet and an album with Quincy Jones spotlighting Marvin Gaye tunes. And, keeping his Grammy bona fides in order, he took home his twenty-second in 2009, "Never Give You Up," a collaboration with veteran soul singer Raphael Saadiq and CJ Hilton from Saadiq's thrice-nominated album *The Way I See It*.

His oldest friend, John Glover, could only guess into what direction he would rotate. "Stevie has been in the studio all these years," he says, "not just for the albums he's put out. He must have miles and miles of tape, songs that would blow your head off. It's just a matter of when he wants to do something with it. Who knows, maybe he's been saving it for when he's sixty, because nobody's ever made important albums at that age, not the Stones, Dylan, McCartney, anyone. They accept that. But Stevie doesn't. With Stevie, it's always, 'Hey man, wait till you hear what I'm doin'.' So I believe he's got something up his sleeve. Something that he really believes is the best he's ever done."

Now *that* would be a tall order to fill. But Stevie Wonder *was* everywhere and Stevie Wonder *was* everything, after all, and in the run-up to that inconceivable milestone of May 13, 2010, the luminous life of a beautiful mind *did* seem something that felt quite like a prelude, yet another rebirth.

Not that there would not be still more convulsions. On June 4, 2009, his now twenty-year-old son Keita Morris was arrested by Los Angeles police on charges of felony domestic violence. It happened after a woman called 911 saying an argument she was having with him had gotten violent. When cops arrived they noticed bruises on her and took Keita into custody; he posted $50,000 bond and was due to stand trial in 2010. Yet it was precisely *because* of body blows like this that it really didn't matter what he had in store, only that he had *something* left in him, and a desire to revisit what *did* matter. Indeed, when you're Stevie Wonder, pain portends probation; redemption is always possible if he has anything to say about it. Not to mention everlasting favors to old paramours. In 2009, when sold one of his many homes, a forty-five-hundred-square-foot mansion in the Hollywood Hills, the listing agent was none other than Melody McCully.

It was the little glimpses like this of what he was, and is, that mattered. Things like the surprise appearance on the *Extreme Makeover* TV show in April fulfilling a request from the family of a dying man with six adopted special-needs children to come and sing "I Just Called to Say I Love You" to him. Or when he closed out the 2009 Grammy show with no fanfare, just his piano and his harmonica—the essential pose of all that mattered.

Once, he was sure he would never make it this far. And if he can still be a bit maudlin about his longevity, and apt to concede with a crotchety whine, "It's harder being young these days. Free love now will get you free death. Or a palimony suit," he was now willing to admit something in a 2005 *USA Today* interview that for him was higher ground in excelsis.

"I regret," Stevie Wonder said, "that I can't live forever."

Discography: Stevie Wonder's Chart Hits

Singles

Catalog Number (1961–1981 Tamla; 1982 on, Motown)	Title (Writing Credits)	Release Date	Peak Position (R&B)
54061	"I Call It Pretty Music (But the Old People Call It the Blues" (Cosby/Paul)	6/62	101
54080	"Fingertips (Part 2)" (Live version) (Cosby/Paul)	5/63	1 (1)
54086	"Workout, Stevie, Workout" (Cosby/Paul)	9/63	33
54090	"Castles in the Sand" (Wilson/Davis/Gordon/O'Brien)	1/64	52
54096	"Hey Harmonica Man" (Cooper/Josie)	5/64	29
54119	"High Heel Sneakers" (Higgenbotham)	7/65	59
54124	"Uptight (Everything's Alright)" (Moy-Wonder-Cosby)	12/65	3 (1)

Catalog Number (1961–1981 Tamla; 1982 on, Motown)	Title (Writing Credits)	Release Date	Peak Position (R&B)
54130	"Nothing's Too Good for My Baby" (Moy-Cosby-Stevenson)	4/66	20 (4)
54130 (B-side)	"With a Child's Heart" (Basemore-Moy-Cosby)	4/66	131 (8)
54136	"Blowin' in the Wind" (Dylan)	6/66	9 (1)
54149	"A Place in the Sun" (Miller/Wells)	10/66	9 (3)
54147	"Travelin' Man" (Miller/Wells)	2/67	32 (31)
54147 (B-side)	"Hey Love" (Paul/Broadnax/Wonder)	2/67	90 (9)
54151	"I Was Made to Love Her" (Cosby/Hardaway/Wonder/Moy)	5/67	2 (1)
54157	"I'm Wondering" (Moy/Wonder/Cosby)	9/67	12 (4)
54165	"Shoo-Be-Doo-Be-Doo-Day" (Moy/Wonder/Cosby)	3/68	9 (1)
54168	"You Met Your Match" (Hunter/Wonder/Hardaway)	7/68	35 (2)
(Gordy 7076)	"Alfie" (Instrumental) (As Eivets Rednow)	8/68	66
54174	"For Once in My Life" (Miller/Murden)	10/68	2 (2)

Catalog Number (1961–1981 Tamla; 1982 on, Motown)	Title (Writing Credits)	Release Date	Peak Position (R&B)
54180	"I Don't Know Why (I Love You)" (Riser/Hunter/Wonder/Hardaway)	2/69	39 (16)
54180 (B-side)	"My Cherie Amour" (Moy/Wonder/Cosby)	2/69	4 (4)
54188	"Yester-Me, Yester-You, Yesterday" (Miller/Wells)	10/69	7 (5)
54191	"Never Had a Dream Come True" (Wonder/Cosby)	1/70	26 (11)
54196	"Signed, Sealed, Delivered (I'm Yours)" (Hardaway/Wright/Wonder/Garrett)	6/70	3 (1)
54200	"Heaven Help Us All" (Miller)	10/70	9 (2)
54202	"Never Dreamed You'd Leave in Summer" (Wonder/Wright)	3/71	78
54202 (B-side)	"We Can Work It Out" (Lennon/McCartney)	3/71	13 (3)
54208	"If You Really Love Me" (Wonder/Wright)	8/71	8 (4)
54216	"Superwoman (Where Were You When I Needed You)" (Wonder)	5/72	33 (13)
54223	"Keep On Running" (Wonder)	8/72	90 (36)
54226	"Superstition" (Wonder)	11/72	1 (1)

Catalog Number (1961–1981 Tamla; 1982 on, Motown)	Title (Writing Credits)	Release Date	Peak Position (R&B)
54232	"You Are the Sunshine of My Life" (Wonder)	3/73	1 (3)
54235	"Higher Ground" (Wonder)	8/73	4 (1)
54242	"Living for the City" (Wonder)	11/73	8 (1)
54245	"Don't You Worry 'Bout a Thing" (Wonder)	3/74	16 (2)
54252	"You Haven't Done Nothin'" (Wonder)	7/74	1 (1)
54254	"Boogie On Reggae Woman" (Wonder)	11/74	3 (1)
54274	"I Wish" (Wonder)	11/76	1 (1)
54281	"Sir Duke" (Wonder)	3/77	1 (1)
54286	"Another Star" (Wonder)	8/77	32 (18)
54291	"As" (Wonder)	11/77	36 (36)
54303	"Send One Your Love" (Wonder)	10/79	4 (5)
54308	"Outside My Window" (Wonder)	3/80	52 (56)
54317	"Master Blaster (Jammin')" (Wonder)	9/80	5 (1)
54320	"I Ain't Gonna Stand for It" (Wonder)	12/80	11 (4)
54323	"Lately" (Wonder)	4/81	64 (29)
54331	"Happy Birthday" (Wonder)	7/81	94 (17)
54328	"Did I Hear You Say You Love Me" (Wonder)	7/81	(72)

Catalog Number (1961–1981 Tamla; 1982 on, Motown)	Title (Writing Credits)	Release Date	Peak Position (R&B)
1602T	"That Girl" (Wonder)	1/82	4 (1)
(Columbia 18-02860)	"Ebony and Ivory" (As Paul McCartney with Stevie Wonder) (McCartney)	3/82	1 (8)
1612T	"Do I Do" (Wonder)	5/82	13 (2)
1639T	"Ribbon in the Sky" (Wonder)	9/82	54 (10)
1745M	"I Just Called to Say I Love You" (Wonder)	9/84	1 (1)
1769M	"Love Light in Flight" (Wonder)	11/84	17 (4)
1808T	"Part-Time Lover" (Wonder)	8/85	1 (1)
(Arista 602119)	"That's What Friends Are For" (As Dionne & Friends Featuring Elton John, Gladys Knight and Stevie Wonder) (Bacharach-Seger)	10/85	1 (1)
40502ZT	"Go Home" (12-inch) (Wonder)	10/85	10 (2)
1832T	"Overjoyed" (Wonder)	1/86	24 (8)
1846T	"Land of La La" (Wonder)	3/86	86 (19)
41440ZT	"Skeletons" (12-inch) (Wonder)	1/87	19 (1)
1919MF	"You Will Know" (Wonder)	4/87	77 (1)
1930MF	"Get It" (As Stevie Wonder and Michael Jackson) (Wonder)	8/87	80 (4)

Catalog Number (1961–1981 Tamla; 1982 on, Motown)	Title (Writing Credits)	Release Date	Peak Position (R&B)
4616MT	"My Eyes Don't Cry" (12-inch) (Wonder)	5/88	(6)
42810ZT	"With Each Beat of My Heart" (12-inch) (Wonder)	2/89	(28)
44013ZB	"Keep Our Love Alive" (Wonder)	9/99	(24)
44269ZB	"Gotta Have You" (Wonder)	1/90	92 (3)
44909ZB	"Fun Day" (Wonder)	4/91	(6)
8600447	"These Three Words" (Wonder)	7/91	(7)
1437TMGCD	"For Your Love" (Wonder)	6/95	50 (11)
422860416-7	"Tomorrow Robins Will Sing" (Wonder)	8/95	(60)
1510TMG	"So What's the Fuss" (Wonder)	10/05	96 (34)
1513TMG	"From the Bottom of My Heart" (Wonder)	12/05	(25)
(Columbia 88697)	"Never Give You Up" (As Raphael Saadiq Featuring Stevie Wonder & CJ Hilton) (Saadiq)	1/09	(31)

Albums

Catalog No. (1961–1981 Tamla; 1982–1986 Tamla/Motown; 1987 on, Motown)	Title	Release Date	Peak Position (R&B)
240	Recorded Live: The 12 Year Old Genius	6/63	1 (1)
250	With a Song in My Heart	12/63	(74)
255	Stevie at the Beach	8/64	(68)
268	Up-Tight	5/66	33 (2)
272	Down to Earth	11/66	72 (8)
279	I Was Made to Love Her	8/67	45 (7)
(Gordy 932)	Eivets Rednow	11/68	64 (37)
282	Greatest Hits	12/68	37 (6)
291	For Once in My Life	12/68	50 (4)
296	My Cherie Amour	8/69	34 (3)
298	Stevie Wonder Live	3/70	81 (16)
304	Signed, Sealed, and Delivered	8/70	25 (7)
308	Where I'm Coming From	4/71	62 (7)
313	Greatest Hits Volume 2	10/71	69 (10)
314	Music of My Mind	3/72	21 (6)
319	Talking Book	10/72	3 (1)
326	Innervisions	8/73	4 (1)
332	Fulfillingness' First Finale	7/74	1 (1)
340	Songs in the Key of Life	9/76	1 (1)
(Motown 804)	Looking Back (Anthology)	12/77	34 (15)

Catalog No. (1961–1981 Tamla; 1982–1986 Tamla/Motown; 1987 on, Motown)	Title	Release Date	Peak Position (R&B)
371	Journey through the Secret Life of Plants	10/79	4 (4)
373	Hotter than July	10/80	3 (1)
6002	Stevie Wonder's Original Musiquarium	5/82	4 (1)
6108	The Woman in Red (Movie Soundtrack)	8/84	4 (1)
6134	In Square Circle	9/85	5 (1)
6248	Characters	9/85	17 (1)
72750	Jungle Fever (Movie Soundtrack)	5/91	24 (1)
530 238-2	Conversation Peace	3/95	16 (2)
530 546-2	Natural Wonder (Live)	11/95	(88)
530 757-2	Song Review—A Greatest Hits Collection	9/96	(100)
012 153 992-2	At the Close of a Century (Box Set)	11/99	(100)
440 066 164-2	The Definitive Collection	6/02	35 (28)
000240202	A Time to Love	10/05	4 (2)
000947902	Number Ones	10/07	171

Index

NOTE: Page numbers in *italics* refer to photos.